Introduction to Byzantium, 602–1453

Introduction to Byzantium, 602–1453 provides students with an accessible guide to medieval Byzantium.

Beginning with the near collapse of Byzantium in the seventh century, the book traces its survival and development through to its absorption by the Ottoman empire. As well as having an overall political narrative, the chapters cover a wide range of topics including society and economy, art and architecture, literature and education, military tactics and diplomacy, gender and education. They also explore themes that remain prominent and highly debated today, including relations between Islam and the West, the impact of the Crusades, the development of Russia and the emergence of Orthodox Christianity. Comprehensively written, each chapter provides an overview of the particular period or topic, a summary of the ongoing historiographical debates, primary source material textboxes, further reading recommendations and a 'points to remember' section.

Introduction to Byzantium, 602–1453 provides students with a thorough introduction to the history of Byzantium and equips them with the tools to write successful analytical essays. It is essential reading for any student of the history of the Byzantine empire.

Jonathan Harris is Professor of the History of Byzantium at Royal Holloway, University of London, UK. His recent publications include: *Byzantium and the Crusades* (2nd ed., 2014); *The Lost World of Byzantium* (2015) and *Constantinople: Capital of Byzantium* (2nd ed., 2017).

Introduction to Byzantium, 602–1453

Jonathan Harris

Routledge
Taylor & Francis Group

LONDON AND NEW YORK

First published 2020
by Routledge
2 Park Square, Milton Park, Abingdon, Oxon OX14 4RN

and by Routledge
52 Vanderbilt Avenue, New York, NY 10017

Routledge is an imprint of the Taylor & Francis Group, an informa business

British Library Cataloguing-in-Publication Data
A catalogue record for this book is available from the British Library

Library of Congress Cataloging-in-Publication Data
Names: Harris, Jonathan, author.
Title: Introduction to Byzantium, 602-1453 / Jonathan Harris.
Description: Abingdon, Oxon ; New York, NY : Routledge, 2020. | Includes bibliographical references and index.
Identifiers: LCCN 2019058832 (print) | LCCN 2019058833 (ebook) | Subjects: LCSH:
Byzantine Empire– History–527-1081. | Byzantine
Empire–History–1081-1453. | Byzantine Empire–Historiography.
Classification: LCC DF571 .H37 2020 (print) | LCC DF571 (ebook) | DDC
949.5/02–dc23
LC record available at https://lccn.loc.gov/2019058832
LC ebook record available at https://lccn.loc.gov/2019058833

ISBN: 978-1-138-55642-3 (hbk)
ISBN: 978-1-138-55643-0 (pbk)
ISBN: 978-1-315-15002-4 (ebk)

Typeset in Perpetua
by Swales & Willis, Exeter, Devon, UK

In Memory of Ruth Macrides (1949–2019)

Contents

Figures

Boxes

Maps

Preface

This book is an introduction to what might be termed 'middle' and 'late' Byzantium. It is designed to provide a gateway for those who are coming to the topic for the first time but also to give teachers points of discussion on which they can expand. The three centuries of Late Antiquity (c.300–c.600 CE) have been deliberately omitted. There are a number of reasons behind that decision, of which the most important is the author's want of the expertise needed to cover the earlier period. The world of Late Antiquity was, in any case, very different from that of post-650 CE, so that the upheavals of the seventh century constitute as tangible a break as, say, 1776 or 1914. I have made various other arbitrary decisions in the way I have presented Byzantine history. The long and unfamiliar names of the protagonists can sometimes present a barrier and it does not help when different books use discrete spellings for the same person. So while I have tried to transliterate surnames as closely as possible to the original Greek, Nikephoros rather than Nicephorus, Phokas rather than Phocas, when it comes to first names I have taken a different course. Where there is a recognised English equivalent, I have used it: Isaac rather than Isaakios, and John rather than Ioannes. I have done this not because I wish to anglicise the Byzantines but because I want their history to be accessible to an international audience who will be more familiar with these versions. To avoid confusion, I have adapted the spellings in quoted extracts to conform to this model.

During the gestation and writing, I received a great deal of help from all quarters. My home institution, Royal Holloway, allowed me to take two terms of sabbatical leave in which to complete the book. The Dumbarton Oaks Center for Byzantine Studies in Washington, DC generously provided photographs of items in its collection. Oxford University Press kindly gave me permission to reproduce the text in Box 15.1. I am indebted to Brian McLaughlin for his help with Byzantine Greek and for letting me to use his Kantakouzenos translation, to John Haldon and Michael Hesemann for allowing me to use their photographs, to Joni Joseph and Ashley Schwartz of Dumbarton Oaks for their advice on images, to Maria Mavroudi and Shaun Tougher who provided invaluable feedback on the proposal and draft text, and to Catherine Aitken, Laura Pilsworth and Morwenna Scott of Taylor & Francis who all helped to firm up my ideas into something tangible and, I hope, publishable. The copy editor Katharine Bartlett and the production manager Colin Morgan did a superb job of tidying up the text. At the end of the day though the greatest influence on the book has come from relays of students who have taken my undergraduate and postgraduate courses and have helped me to appreciate the wide gaps in my own understanding of this sometimes rather perplexing world. I think that it was Albert Einstein who said that if you cannot explain something simply, then you do not understand it yourself.

Royal Holloway, University of London
November 2019

Introduction

0.1 What's in a name?

'Byzantium' and 'the Byzantine empire' are terms used by historians to describe the eastern half of the Roman empire which survived after the western provinces were lost in the invasions of the fifth century CE. The terms were coined in the sixteenth century by the German Protestant scholar Hieronymus Wolf to distinguish this state from the classical Roman empire which was perceived to have ended in 476 CE, when the last emperor of its western half was deposed. Other terms have been tried over the years. Those writing in French for a time preferred *l'empire romain d'orient* and some British historians likewise adhered doggedly to 'the Eastern Roman empire' or 'the Later Roman empire'. In the end, 'Byzantium' and the 'Byzantine empire' stuck, although neither term is satisfactory. Throughout the period covered by this book, the inhabitants of this large and powerful state did not use the word 'Byzantine', unless they were referring specifically to residents of the city of Byzantion or Constantinople. Instead they considered themselves to be Romans and their state as the Roman empire. They had good reason to do so, in that the emperors who ruled them were the direct successors of the first Roman emperor, Augustus (27 BCE–14 CE). Moreover, the word 'Byzantine' is not only anachronistic but decidedly unhelpful since it has entered the English language in a negative sense as either 'excessively complicated' or 'devious and crafty'. Applying it to this medieval state is to denigrate it and to imply it was somehow rather less impressive than its Roman predecessor, the unworthy product of the latter's decline and fall. Even the use of the word 'empire' is unhelpful in this context. It invites comparison with the European colonial empires of the nineteenth and twentieth centuries, yet Byzantium seldom conquered or acquired territory: for most of its history it was fighting merely to hold on to what it had.

Consequently there are those who feel that these accepted terms should be abandoned but no one can decide on what to replace them with. To call Byzantium the 'Roman empire' would be to invite confusion with a very different kind of society. The term 'Romania', that was sometimes used for it during the Middle Ages, has been proposed, but that would likewise lead to complication because that is the official name of a modern European republic. So it is that, for the time being, Byzantium is here to stay.

0.2 The study of Byzantium

It goes without saying that historians have arrived at very different understandings of Byzantium over the past five centuries, usually conditioned by the nature of the times in which they lived. For Hieronymus Wolf and the German protestants who initiated Byzantine studies in the sixteenth century, the impetus was provided by the search for another society and Church that had rejected the authority of the pope. In the seventeenth century, the centre of interest moved to France and to the circle of the Abbé du Cange who published his *Historia Byzantina* in 1680. Again, there was a contemporary agenda behind the study of a vanished empire. Du Cange made it clear in his laudatory preface that the Byzantine ideal of the Christian emperor placed on Earth to protect the Faith and the Church was perfectly suited to the ambitious king of France, Louis XIV.

During the eighteenth century, however, the political climate changed in a way which, while it was to foster the ideals of human rights and constitutional liberty, also created a very negative image of the Byzantine empire in Western European and American thought. The intellectual movement known as the Enlightenment championed human reason as the primary source of authority and legitimacy, arguing for personal liberty, government that was answerable to the governed and toleration of religious diversity. Autocratic Byzantium with its identification of orthodox religious belief with loyalty to the emperor was apparently the antithesis of everything that Enlightenment intellectuals believed in. Consequently the historiography of the day presented it as a degenerate shadow of vanished Roman greatness. A typical example is Baron Montesquieu, a French political philosopher whose emphasis on the separation of powers was to influence the constitution of the United States. In his *Considerations of the Causes of the Greatness of the Romans and their Decline* (1734), he identified a balanced constitution as an ingredient in Roman success. Thus, the transformation of the well-regulated Roman into the autocratic and unconstitutional Byzantine empire was a retrograde step. The sternest Enlightenment critic of Byzantium was the English historian Edward Gibbon, for whom the empire's thousand-year history was merely a long, drawn-out decline.

It was only with the rise of a more detached and scientific approach to history in Germany during the nineteenth century that historians began to try to assess Byzantium on its own terms rather than judging it by the standards of their own day, the pioneering figure being Karl Krumbacher. Nevertheless, the old perceptions still lingered, which accounts for some over-enthusiastic twentieth-century historians such as George Ostrogorsky (see Box 3.3) and Steven Runciman (see Box 12.2) attempting to redress the balance by occasionally making rather exaggerated claims for Byzantine greatness. Even today, books about Byzantine history often begin with a protest against the negative portrayals found in Gibbon and his contemporaries. Moreover, try as they might to arrive at an objective understanding of Byzantium, historians of the late twentieth and early twenty-first century reflect contemporary concerns in their work just as much as their predecessors did. There is now a greater interest in social issues, on the role and experience of women and on issues of gender and identity.

It should be remembered, though, that while these debates and interpretations have come and gone, some of the greatest advances in the discipline have come as a result of the efforts of those who had made original texts more widely available. Byzantium produced a vast corpus of literature over its thousand-year existence but most of it survives only in the original manuscripts that are locked away in libraries and archives. The patient work of collating, editing, publishing and translating these works goes on steadily and will continue for many years to come.

0.3 Byzantium in 602 CE

This book begins at the very end of a period known as Late Antiquity that is regarded as having begun in around the year 300 CE. During those three centuries, the Roman empire had been radically transformed in numerous ways, so that it is understandable that later historians felt that it needed a new name. A glance at the map reveals the most obvious change: the borders of the empire of 602 were rather shorter than the old Roman ones. While in the east, the frontier was more or less where it had been in 100 CE, enclosing Asia Minor, Syria, Palestine and Egypt, between 400 and 480 the western provinces from Italy to Britain had been lost to invasions by migrating peoples from the north. Under Emperor Justinian I (527–565) (see Figure 0.2), a serious attempt had been made to reconquer the lost lands of the west. As a result, in 602 the empire now once again held part of North Africa, Sicily, some areas of Italy and a foothold in southern Spain around the city of Cartagena (see Map 0.1). Other areas were never recovered. Much of Italy was occupied by the Lombards and most of Spain was in the hands of the Visigoths. Gaul (modern France) had become the kingdom of the Franks and the old province of Britain had been divided between the Angles, Saxons and Jutes.

Within the territories that remained, there had been further changes over the centuries of Late Antiquity. Perhaps the most striking was that Rome, which had given the state its name, was no longer the capital and the emperors no longer resided there. Stuck awkwardly on the edge of imperial territory, it was largely in ruins after being bitterly fought over during Justinian's reconquest of Italy. Ever since the crisis of the third century, when the emperors had found that Rome was too far from the threatened frontiers, they had been basing themselves in other cities. In 324, Emperor Constantine I (306–337) (see Figure 0.2) had selected the city of Byzantion as his place of residence, because it was in a perfect strategic position, halfway between the Danube and Mesopotamian frontiers, at the crossing point between Europe and Asia (see Figure 0.1). After expanding and rebuilding it, in 330 he renamed it Constantinople or the city of Constantine. Over the next three centuries, the city grew apace so that by 602 it probably had a population of about 700,000 and was the unquestioned capital.

Geographic contraction and the eastward move of the capital city were driving a third major change, that of language. In 602, the inhabitants of Byzantine Italy and North Africa would have spoken some form of vernacular Latin as they always had. But with much of the west now lost and with the centre of administration moved east from Rome to Constantinople, Latin was rapidly ceasing to be an official language. Most Byzantines would have spoken Greek on an everyday basis, a version of the language known as *Koine* or Common Greek. In Egypt and Syria, it is true, Coptic and Syriac were widely spoken but Greek prevailed in the major towns and cities. For that reason, Greek was fast becoming the only language of the court, the administration and of intellectual life.

Figure 0.1 Constantinople as depicted in a sixteenth-century map. Note the city's harbour, the Golden Horn, to the right and the town of Pera (Galata) on the other side of it

To anyone travelling through the eastern provinces of the empire in 602, the changes in borders, capital and language might not have been immediately apparent. After all, Greek had always been widely used in Asia Minor, Syria, Palestine and Egypt and the loss of the western territories and the moving of the capital to Constantinople probably made little difference on the ground in those areas. There was a continuity in urban life there too with large and prosperous cities functioning much as they had always done. Alexandria in Egypt was the second-largest after Constantinople with a population of about 200,000. Antioch in Syria had about 100,000 inhabitants. Athens and Beirut were important intellectual centres. Asia Minor, the landmass that is now Turkey, was peppered with flourishing urban centres such as Ephesus, Sardis and Pergamon. Cities were fewer and smaller in the western provinces, the most important being Ravenna, which was now the administrative capital of Byzantine Italy, and Carthage, the main town of North Africa.

There was a fourth change that had taken place between 300 and 602 which could not be concealed or ignored. It had had a huge impact on the life of every inhabitant and had come to dictate many aspects of their everyday existence. The old Olympian gods of ancient Rome had been abandoned and replaced by Christianity. The process had begun in 312 CE when Emperor Constantine, convinced that he had emerged triumphant from a civil war because of the intervention of the God of the Christians, had begun to favour the Church and he ultimately accepted baptism. Over the next century, all of Constantine's imperial successors, with one exception, were also Christians, so inevitably

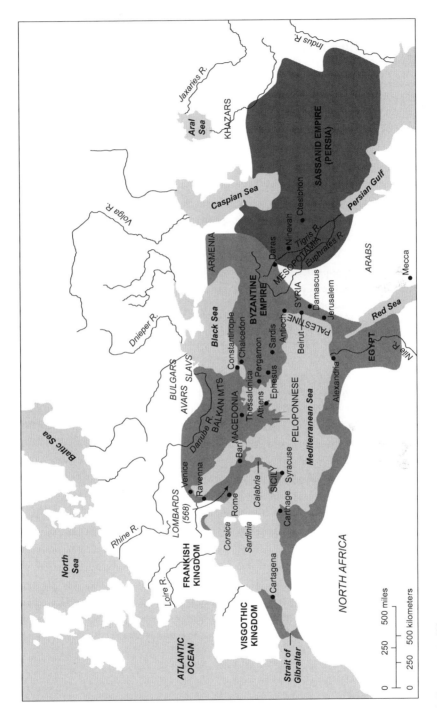

Map 0.1 Byzantium in 602

their co-religionists prospered. To start with, no attempt was made to prevent pagan worship but by the reign of Emperor Theodosius I (379–395), the Christian Church was in a strong enough position to move against the opposition. Laws were passed banning pagan sacrifice and the temples were razed to the ground by Christian mobs with the tacit encouragement of the authorities. By 602, the empire was almost completely Christian, apart from its Jewish inhabitants and perhaps a few diehard pagans who had to live very quiet lives to avoid the notice of the authorities.

The advent of Christianity had brought with it a change in the way the people perceived the world around them. Jerusalem had been an obscure and unimportant town under the pagan Roman emperors. Now it became a place of immense religious significance with pilgrims flocking to the Holy Sepulchre, the tomb where the body of Jesus Christ was placed after his crucifixion and where it lay for three days before his resurrection. The change in religion also brought Rome to prominence once more, albeit in a different way from its former political role. It too was a place of pilgrimage as the two foremost Apostles of Christ, Saints Peter and Paul, were buried there. Its bishop, known as the pope, was the most important churchman in the Christian world. He was seen as having greater authority and prestige than other bishops because he was the direct successor of St Peter to whom Christ had allegedly entrusted the keys of the kingdom of Heaven.

Christianity also changed the way that the Byzantines perceived their ruler. The image of the emperor had always been highly visible with statues, busts, painted portraits or mosaics of the present incumbent on public display in the main squares of cities and towns. Some Roman emperors were even revered as gods after their death in temples specially dedicated to them. Now that the emperor was a Christian that option was closed as it would be outright blasphemy to suggest that he was divine, alive or dead. Instead the theory developed that the emperor, or *basileus* as the Byzantines called him in Greek, was the next best thing to a god: a kind of delegate and earthly reflection of God. It was no coincidence, the Byzantines believed, that the birth of Christ had taken place during the reign of the first Roman emperor, Augustus. Clearly God's plan for the salvation of mankind included a provision for the government of Christians on earth and the of protection their faith and their Church, until the second coming of Christ. Indeed, Jesus himself had told his followers that they should 'Render unto Caesar what was Caesar's' (Matthew 22:21), that is to say that they should obey the Roman emperor. Only the Byzantine emperor, the successor of the Caesar of Christ's day, was regarded as holding this position. No other ruler, even if he was a Christian, had been entrusted with this commission of universal rulership. The theory was reflected in the way the emperors were physically portrayed. Their portraits were to be found as often inside churches as out on the streets and whereas in the past the emperor had been portrayed as an ordinary man, now he was often given a halo or nimbus around his head. So, in some cases, was the empress. The halo did not necessarily denote personal holiness on the part of the emperor but rather it was an indication of the sanctity of the office that he held.

The theory was also reflected in the layout and architecture of Byzantium's capital city of Constantinople. Although Constantine I had probably not intended it to replace Rome, he certainly modelled it on the old capital. He provided it with a forum, a senate, statues and columns looted from other cities and a stadium for chariot races, known as the

Figure 0.2 Emperors Constantine (right) and Justinian portrayed in a tenth-century mosaic in the cathedral of Hagia Sophia

Hippodrome, the equivalent of the Circus Maximus. Just as Rome had a grandiose imperial residence on its Palatine Hill, so Constantinople was given the Great Palace, a sprawling complex of buildings, churches and gardens on the city's eastern tip. As well as buildings that harked back to Roman past, Constantine erected others that reflected the Christian future, notably the first cathedral of Hagia Sophia and the great church of the Holy Apostles. This merging of the Roman and the Christian in the city continued under Constantine's successors, especially Justinian I. He provided Constantinople with its most famous Christian monument by rebuilding the cathedral of Hagia Sophia in 537, along with most of the other churches in the city (see Figure 0.3). By then, Byzantium's capital had the monumental appearance it required as befitted the capital of God's appointed representative: both a seat of worldly power and a religious centre. In view of its importance, the clergyman who presided over its Church could not be just a bishop and was given the title of patriarch, like the patriarch of Jerusalem. He came to be regarded as second only to the pope of Rome in the religious hierarchy.

So Byzantium in 602 was very different from the empire of 300 and yet some aspects were much as they had always been. What people could not have known at the time was that it was on the edge of a precipice. Over the next century, a series of tumultuous upheavals were to sweep away much of the Roman inheritance and leave it as a completely different kind of society.

Figure 0.3 The cathedral of Hagia Sophia or Holy Wisdom

0.4 The tragic end of Emperor Maurice

In spite of the ambitious political theory and the showcase capital, by the end of the sixth century Byzantium was in trouble. Huge resources had been expended on Justinian's reconquest of North Africa and Italy and, even before the emperor's death in 565, the expanded frontiers had started to come under serious pressure. In 568, recently reconquered Italy had been invaded by the Lombards who had occupied most of the interior and confined the Byzantines to certain key cities such as Rome and Ravenna and to the far south of the peninsula. On the eastern frontier, war broke out in 573 with Sassanid Persia whose king was eager for an opportunity to repeat his success of 540 when he had crossed into Byzantine Syria and captured and sacked the major city of Antioch. The Danube frontier was particularly prone to attack as it lay directly in the path of peoples migrating westwards from the Steppes of Central Asia so that, by the later sixth century, the Balkan provinces south of the river were coming under attack from the Slavs. They were a relatively backward and unsophisticated people who might not have posed too great a threat in themselves, had they not come to be dominated by the nomadic, aggressive and militarily very efficient Avars. The latter were a Turkic people, superb horsemen who were also very advanced in siege technology. They had subjugated most of the Slav tribes along the Danube and incorporated them into their own army, thus creating a major threat. In 584, this Avar–Slav coalition invaded the Balkans in huge numbers, penetrating as far as Thessalonica and settling on the land round about.

As well as facing threats on its borders, Byzantium was divided internally. For the past century and a half, many of the inhabitants of the eastern provinces of Syria, Palestine and Egypt had become increasingly alienated from the government in Constantinople by a long-running theological dispute over the nature of Jesus Christ. All Christians agreed that Jesus was God born in a man's body but there was sharp disagreement over the extent to which he was human and the extent to which he was divine. In 451 the Fourth Ecumenical Council, held at Chalcedon opposite Constantinople, had attempted to put an end to the debate. It declared that Jesus had two natures (i.e. divine and human) without separation. That is to say that Christ was simultaneously human and divine: the Catholic definition. It was an attempt to please everyone but it did not work. Many theologians, known as Monophysites or Miaphysites, objected that this formula lessened Christ's Godhead and they argued instead that he had only one, divine nature. While the clergy and people of Constantinople, Palestine, Asia Minor and the western provinces accepted Chalcedon, many of the inhabitants of the eastern provinces were strongly opposed to it. Inevitably the theological split mingled with other matters and adherence to Monophysitism became a sort of rallying point for all those dissatisfied with government from Constantinople and resentful of the heavy taxes imposed by the Greek-speaking elites on the Syriac and Coptic-speaking majority.

The separatist danger that the dispute opened up meant that the emperors could not just leave it to the theologians to resolve the issue but they vacillated in their response. Sometimes they tried to find some kind of theological compromise, sometimes they tried to force the Monophysites to accept Chalcedon. Under Justinian I, Monophysite bishops were deposed and replaced with candidates whose theological views were more acceptable. Monophysite monks were driven out of their monasteries. As a result, two rival hierarchies emerged. There was an official, Catholic patriarch of Alexandria, recognised by the government in Constantinople, and there was a rival Monophysite one, who had the loyalty of the vast majority of the population. Most other cities in the eastern provinces also had two bishops, one Catholic and one Monophysite.

While this was happening, Byzantium was ruled by Emperor Maurice (582–602). He had become emperor not by birth but by marrying the daughter of his predecessor and he may well at times have regretted doing so, given the rather poisoned legacy that he inherited. That said, Maurice was an able military leader, who came quite close to finding a military solution to the multiple threats. The emperor had no troops to spare for Italy but he managed to hold the line by reorganising Byzantine forces there into the so-called Exarchate of Ravenna. A similar reform was carried out in North Africa around the same time with the creation of the Exarchate of Carthage. The main change seems to have been that civil and military power were merged in the hands of the Exarch, who governed these areas, so giving him wider powers to act independently without needing to call on the emperor for aid. In the east, Maurice countered the Persian threat by astutely intervening in a Persian civil war and aiding King Khusro II (591–628) to regain his throne. A grateful Khusro made peace with the Byzantines and even ceded them part of Armenia in gratitude for their help. That peace held firm for the rest of Maurice's reign. He even attempted to grasp the nettle of the Catholic–Monophysite split since the acquisition of part of Armenia in 591 had brought another Monophysite population under Byzantine rule. It would appear that Maurice did manage to get some kind of union agreed with the Armenian church, which was a major achievement, even though not all Armenians accepted it.

Unfortunately, in dealing with the Avars and Slavs, Maurice was not so successful. Although, after concluding peace with Persia in 591, he was able to commit more troops to the struggle, they made no headway. They frequently defeated the Avar–Slav armies yet they proved unable to deal a knockout blow. In his desire to bring the war to a conclusion, Maurice made a fatal mistake which was to cost him his empire and his life. He decided that, to deal with the Slavs and Avars once and for all, he would send an army to follow them north of the Danube and attack them in winter when they least expected it. The winter of 601–602 was a particularly harsh one and the Byzantine troops soon became extremely disgruntled at the harsh conditions they were being forced to endure. So they mutinied and proclaimed a junior army officer called Phokas as emperor. The army then marched on Constantinople, entered the city and murdered Maurice along with his five sons. That is the point where this book begins in earnest.

Box 0.1 Byzantium in film

The ancient Roman empire is familiar to global audiences from a number of memorable Hollywood epic films, from William Wyler's *Ben Hur* (1959) to Ridley Scott's *Gladiator* (2000). Byzantium, on the other hand, has never tempted international film-makers to produce anything on that scale. The closest to date is probably Alejandro Amenábar's *Agora* (2009), although that deals with Late Antiquity rather than the period covered by this book. Those films that do feature aspects of middle and late Byzantine history tend not to circulate internationally. They are usually made in countries that incorporate areas that were once part of the empire or whose culture, religion and language reflect its influence. In spite of those links, the Byzantines are often given the role of the villains of the piece, the evil empire against which the protagonists have to struggle for freedom.

One example is the Bulgarian production *681 AD: The Glory of Khan* (1981), directed by Ludmil Staikov, which follows the creation of the Bulgarian khanate under its ruler Asparukh (c.640–701). It features a dramatic recreation of the crossing of the Danube, the building of Pliska and the defeat of the Byzantine army at the battle of Ongala (see Section 3.5), all seen through the eyes of a fictitious Byzantine envoy called Belisarius. Emperor Constantine IV (668–685) is among the historical characters, presiding over an oppressive and declining empire. In line with the Communist ideology prevailing at the time, the Bulgar invasion is presented as a proletarian liberation of a subject people, the local Slav peasants rushing to Pliska to join the Bulgars against their imperialist overlords.

The Byzantines play a similar role in Faruk Aksoy's Turkish-language *The Conquest 1453* (2012), which chronicles the fall of Constantinople to the Ottoman Turks (see Section 15.5). At an alleged cost of $17 million, it was the most expensive movie ever made in Turkey and most of the budget was spent on the computer-generated imagery of Ottoman cannon battering the walls of Constantinople. Less was spent on the actors, few of whom were well known, even inside Turkey. The film is, of course, sympathetic to the Ottomans and Sultan Mehmed II's attack is presented as an entirely justified response to aggression. To enhance the drama, Emperor Constantine XI and the Byzantines appear as formidable, if rather self-indulgent, adversaries, and Constantinople is depicted as a rich and powerful city. The reality was that by 1453 much of Constantinople was in ruins and that the defenders were outnumbered by the attackers by something like a hundred to one.

A more positive portrayal of the Byzantines appears in the Russian film *Viking*, which was directed by Andrei Kravchuk and released in 2016. It follows the fortunes of Vladimir, prince of Kiev (980–1015), who wages a blood feud against his half-brother Yaropolk. Interspersed among the violent battle scenes are evocative recreations of tenth-century Kiev and Cherson (see Section 7.4). Two-thirds of the way through the film, some Byzantine envoys arrive by ship in the Crimea, like a kind of divine intervention. They offer gold for Vladimir's military services but also bring the redemptive message of Christianity. By adopting the Orthodox faith, Vladimir is at last able to break the cycle of violence and revenge that has dictated his life to date and open a new chapter in Russian history. The film reflects the return of Orthodox Christianity to the centre of Russian life since 1989, a further illustration that attitudes to Byzantium are always coloured by current events and by cultural background and assumptions.

Further reading: Przemysław Marciniak, 'And the Oscar goes to … the Emperor! Byzantium in the cinema', in *Wanted: Byzantium: The Desire for a Lost Empire*, ed. Ingela Nilsson and Paul Stephenson (Uppsala: Uppsala Universitet, 2014), pp. 247–55.

Points to remember

- The terms 'Byzantium' and 'Byzantine empire' are inadequate modern constructs but no one can agree on a better alternative.
- Western European and American historiography of Byzantium has inherited a negative stereotype which still persists today.
- Approaches to Byzantium from eastern European countries often reflect a different set of contemporary agendas and concerns.
- Byzantium considered itself to be a continuation of the Roman empire and its inhabitants believed their ruler to have a unique status in the Christian world.
- By 602, Byzantium was having difficulty maintaining both internal unity and the integrity of its frontiers, which were to give way completely during the seventh century.

Suggestions for further reading

Ben-Tov, Asaph. (2009), *Lutheran Humanists and Greek Antiquity: Melanchthonian Scholarship between Universal History and Pedagogy* (Leiden and Boston MA: Brill). Chapter 2 of this book is extremely informative about the first steps in the study of Byzantium taken in sixteenth-century Germany.

Cameron, Averil. (2014), *Byzantine Matters* (Princeton NJ: Princeton UP). A historian of Late Antiquity, Cameron explores the cultural preconceptions that have impeded and distorted previous understandings of Byzantium and continue to do so.

Harris, Jonathan. (2017, 2nd revised edition), *Constantinople: Capital of Byzantium* (London and New York: Bloomsbury). Taking Constantinople in the year 1200 as its starting point, the book discusses the link between the city and Byzantine political ideology.

Kaldellis, Anthony. (2015), *The Byzantine Republic: People and Power in New Rome* (Cambridge MA and London: Harvard UP). Kaldellis argues that as the basis of authority in Byzantium was derived directly from ancient Rome, it should be regarded as a continuation of the same empire. He also makes a good case for Byzantine emperors being more answerable to their subjects than has generally been assumed.

Kaldellis, Anthony. (2019), *Romanland: Ethnicity and Empire in Byzantium* (Cambridge MA and London: Harvard UP). Attacks the labels 'Byzantine' and 'Byzantium' and considers why they developed in the first place.

McKitterick, Rosamond and Quinault, Roland. (1997), *Edward Gibbon and Empire* (Cambridge: Cambridge University Press). A collection of essays that explore aspects of Gibbon's attitude towards the Byzantine empire and to the Middle Ages generally.

PART I

Crisis and survival 602–820

1 Major literary sources for the period 602–820

Our knowledge of Byzantium comes from a wide variety of sources: inscriptions, archival documents, saints' lives, speeches, manuals and legal codes, to name but a few. Much of this material is written in Greek, the literary language of the Byzantine empire, but sources in Arabic, Armenian, Latin, Slavonic and other languages are important too. Here, and in subsequent source chapters, the focus will primarily be on one particular type of information source: major literary histories, written in Greek, many of which are now available in English translation. Other types of source will be considered as well, as they often provide all kinds of insights to supplement the major histories.

Figure 1.1 Mosaic of a Gospel book from the Neonian Baptistry, Ravenna

1.1 Byzantine literature and education

To understand the historical writing of the Byzantine period, it is important first to consider the kind of educational and cultural environment in which it was produced. In 602, most Byzantines living outside Syria and Egypt spoke *Koine* or Common Greek on an everyday basis (see Introduction 0.3), the language of the New Testament and of the Greek version of the Hebrew Bible, known as the Septuagint. Literacy would have been relatively widespread because church schools that taught children to read the Gospels and the Psalms were often to be found in urban areas. For a privileged few, there was higher education which began at age 14 but that involved a much more challenging curriculum. No longer did students read texts that were written in something very close to their mother tongue. Instead they grappled with much richer and more complex forms of Greek that had been written many centuries before. They were introduced to the great epic poems of Homer, the *Iliad* and the *Odyssey*, that preserved the idiom of around 900 BCE. Most of the set texts, however, were written in the language of the fifth and fourth centuries BCE, known as Attic Greek. They included numerous historical works such as those of Herodotus (c.484–c.425 BCE), Thucydides (460–395 BCE), Polybius (c.200–c.116 BCE) and Arrian (c.86–160 CE), but the Byzantines were interested in other forms of literature as well. They read the comedies of Aristophanes (c.455–c.386 BCE), tragedies such as those of Aeschylus (525–456 BCE), the speeches of Demosthenes (d.413 BCE) and Lysias (c.458–c.380 BCE), and the philosophy of Plato (d.348/7 BCE) and Aristotle (384–322 BCE). Their interest extended to what would now be called 'scientific' writing: the medical works of Dioscorides (c.40–90 CE) and Galen (129–c.210 CE), and the mathematical treatises of Euclid (fl.300 BCE).

It may seem odd that a militantly Christian society like Byzantium should base its higher education on pagan texts, many of which featured or discussed the myths of the old Olympian gods. The curriculum had, of course, been inherited from pre-Christian times and as the Church became stronger, there were some voices raised to demand that the pagan writers be discarded in favour of theologians and Fathers of the Church. That never happened because everyone agreed that the pagan writers offered the most perfect examples of 'correct' Attic Greek prose style. It was important to study them because in Byzantine educated circles it was simply not acceptable to write in Common Greek. So students were trained not just to read the ancients but to write in the same way. The most common exercise for students was to write dialogues in the style of Plato, recreating what might have been said, for example, by Alexander the Great to the king of Persia. It was a gruelling course but one which was worth enduring because it provided the qualification for entry to the civil administration. In fact, in 360 a law had been passed barring anyone who had not been schooled in this way from holding one of these lucrative posts. In 602, this higher curriculum was offered at schools all over Byzantium, in Antioch, Alexandria, Athens, Beirut and, of course, Constantinople where in 425 a university of 31 faculties had been established with a view to producing literate administrators.

Most of the history that was produced during the period 602 to 1453 was written by people who had completed this course of higher education and who often held posts in the administration or in the Church. They wrote not in Common Greek but in the archaic Attic

Figure 1.2 Byzantine marble relief, now on the façade of St Mark's church in Venice. It depicts a scene in Greek mythology where the hero Hercules has completed his fourth labour and has captured the savage Erymanthian boar. He brings it back alive to show King Eurytheus, who is terrified and hides in a bronze jar. The sculpture reflects the way in which educated Byzantines prized their classical heritage

language in which they had been schooled. The reign of Justinian I was chronicled in detail by his contemporaries Procopius and Agathias, both highly educated laymen. In the first decades of the seventh century, an official called Theophylact Simocatta wrote an account of the reign of the ill-fated Maurice though his Attic style was a great deal clumsier than that of Procopius. A deacon called George of Pisidia, who was a member of the clergy of Hagia Sophia, wrote two narrative poems describing the campaigns against the Persians and Avars waged by Emperor Herakleios (610–641) (see Section 2.2). Alongside these highly polished literary productions stands the rather simpler *Chronicon Paschale* or Easter Chronicle, compiled by an anonymous individual in around 630. It records events from the beginning of the world until 628 and it would appear from the title to have continued up to 630, but the last page is missing from the sole surviving manuscript. It is one of the most important sources of information for the reign of Phokas and the early years of Herakleios since the author was clearly describing events that he was living through. He also gives the full text of the despatch sent to Constantinople by Herakleios to announce his Persian victory which was read out publicly in Hagia Sophia on 15 May 628.

Then suddenly everything went silent. The tradition of writing literary histories in Attic Greek came to an abrupt end. It is not difficult to see why. The Persian and Arab invasions saw the loss of Antioch, Alexandria, Beirut and other cities with their schools and libraries. Constantinople and Athens held out against the invaders, but for much of the seventh and eighth centuries they were beleaguered fortresses where the needs of defence took priority over everything else. Higher education seems to have been drastically scaled down, although it probably did not disappear altogether. Moreover, the string of defeats was perhaps so disheartening that few felt inspired to take up their pen to record events at the time. There was some history written such as the chronicle compiled by an individual called Trajan the Patrikios in the early eighth century. Sadly it has not survived and is only known from allusion made to it by later authors. As a result, the period 630–750 is one of the worst documented and it has to be pieced together from sources that emanated from outside Byzantium or were written much later.

1.2 Patriarch Nikephoros

Only in the late eighth century was a history written in Greek that has survived until today. The work of a clergyman called Nikephoros, the *Short History* covers the years from Maurice's murder in 602 to the marriage of Irene to the future Emperor Leo IV (775–780) in 769 and is written in Attic Greek. Given that he must have been born in around 758, Nikephoros cannot have been an eyewitness to any of the events he describes apart possibly from those at the very end of his account. His work must therefore be a synthesis of earlier sources that are now lost, such as Trajan the Patrikios and a shadowy individual called John of Antioch. It would seem that he was not always able to find the information that he needed: there is a gap of 27 years in the *Short History* from shortly after the death of Herakleios in 641 up to the assassination of Constans II in 668. Lack of available source material probably also explains why the work as a whole is so short. While Nikephoros was remote and unconnected with the events he describes, he was by no means a detached and dispassionate observer. The later pages of the *Short History* cover the first phase of the period of Iconoclasm (see Section 4.2) and Nikephoros was a convinced iconophile who supported the veneration of holy images. He was appointed patriarch of Constantinople in 806 by the iconophile emperor Nikephoros I (802–811) and he stood down in 815 in protest at the policies of the iconoclast Leo V (813–820). His iconophile sympathies were bound to be reflected, especially in his account of the reign of the arch-iconoclast Emperor Constantine V (741–775), although he is relatively restrained in comparison with some later writers.

1.3 Theophanes Confessor

In around 808, a clergyman called George the Synkellos set himself the task of compiling a chronicle of events from the creation of the world to his own time but when he died in about 811, he had only reached as far as 284 CE. The work was inherited and continued

Figure 1.3 Marble relief of the Apostles as sheep on either side of the throne of Christ. Like Figure 1.2, this sculpture was probably taken from Constantinople to Venice in the aftermath of the Fourth Crusade (see Section 12.5)

by a monk called Theophanes, who was the abbot of a monastery in the western Asia Minor. Two short biographies of him survive and they portray him as an affable character, always ready to wine and dine guests at his monastery. That might explain why he become rather overweight and he allegedly suffered from kidney stones so that he was bedridden the last years of his life. He nevertheless managed to continue the chronicle and to take it up to 813 CE.

The Chronicle of Theophanes shares some of the weaknesses of Nikephoros' work. It largely covers events that took place long before Theophanes was born and so it is essentially a file of extracts borrowed from earlier sources, many of which are now lost. Like Nikephoros again, Theophanes had an axe to grind. Although his father had held office under the iconoclast Emperor Constantine V, Theophanes himself was an ardent iconophile. Indeed, he was to suffer for his beliefs and so earn his epithet of 'Confessor'. In 815, soon after the accession of Emperor Leo V, Theophanes was summoned from his monastery to Constantinople and urged to abandon his support for icon veneration. When he refused, he was imprisoned for two years, then exiled to the island of Samothrace where he died less than a month after his arrival. Although this persecution probably took place after Theophanes had stopped working on the chronicle, he is vitriolic in his accounts of Leo III (717–741) and Constantine V and clearly very unfair to them, his genial personality notwithstanding. Apart from the obvious bias, there are plenty of other things wrong with Theophanes' chronicle. It is a rather unsophisticated work. While Nikephoros attempted to write in 'correct' Greek, imitating the classical language, Theophanes used a decidedly haphazard idiom, that is sometimes ambiguous and misleading. He had a rather simplistic outlook, interpreting any disaster or setback as God's punishment for sin and attributing any victory to direct divine intervention.

In spite of all its faults, for a number of reasons Theophanes' chronicle is the most important work of historiography produced in Byzantium in this period. Unlike Nikephoros who broke off in 769, Theophanes included the period when he himself was an eyewitness and participant. He had held office in the imperial administration before he became a monk and so had a personal knowledge of politics and government. He later attended the Seventh Ecumenical Council at Nicaea in 787 and he was well acquainted with some of the major figures of the day. Moreover, for the period before his own time, Theophanes consulted a much wider range of sources than Nikephoros did, not just ones compiled inside Byzantium in Greek but those from outside too. He seems to have used a chronicle or chronicles written in Syriac and so was able to fill in the gaps left by Nikephoros and to provide a much fuller narrative for the seventh and eighth centuries.

The most helpful aspect of Theophanes' work is his careful system of chronology, which he inherited from George the Synkellos. The narrative is divided into year-long sections, commencing on 1 September, which in the Byzantine calendar was when the year began. Each section is prefaced with chronological tables, which give the year since the creation of the world and the birth of Christ, which Theophanes, following the Alexandrian tradition, believed to have occurred 5492 years after the creation. The year of the reign of the Byzantine emperor was given next, then that of Persian king (later the Arab caliph) and the patriarch of Constantinople. Finally, the years of some other important ecclesiastical figures, such as the pope or the patriarchs of Antioch, Jerusalem or Alexandria, were listed too. In this way, Theophanes was able to reconcile the various different dating systems used by his sources. Although painstaking, Theophanes' chronology is not always completely accurate. He seems to be a year out between 609 and 659 and again from 727 until 774. Luckily, in his chronological lists, Theophanes also gave the indiction, a recurring cycle of 15 years and from this it is possible to correct the inaccuracy. In spite of the errors and the bad Greek, the Chronicle of Theophanes enjoyed a high reputation in Byzantium and it became known in the West through a Latin translation made by the papal librarian Anastasius in the 870s. Without it, the period 602 to 780 in particular would be a great deal more obscure and we would have no chronological framework in which to place it, for writers such as Sebeos (see Section 1.5) were extremely vague when it came to dates.

Box 1.1 Theophanes' chronological method

This is a typical year from Theophanes' work: 6104 from the creation which corresponds to the 12 months from 1 September 610 CE to 31 August 611 CE, shortly after Herakleios' succession. Note the care that he takes to get the date right:

> Herakleios, emperor of the Romans (31 years), 2nd year
> Khusro [II], emperor of the Persians (39 years), 23rd year
> Sergios [I], bishop of Constantinople (29 years), 3rd year
> Zacharias, bishop of Jerusalem (22 years), 3rd year
> John, bishop of Alexandria (10 years), 3rd year

> *In this year, the Persians captured Caesarea in Cappadocia and took therein many thousands of captives.* The emperor Herakleios found the affairs of the Roman state undone, for the Avars had devastated Europe, while the Persians had destroyed all of Asia and had captured the cities and annihilated in battle the Roman army. On seeing these things he was at a loss what to do. He made a census of the army to find out if there were any survivors from among those who had revolted with Phokas against Maurice and found only two … On 3 May of the same year, indiction 15, a son was born to the emperor by Eudokia, namely the younger Herakleios, also called the new Constantine [III].

This is from the section of the chronicle where the dates are inaccurate by one year. The indiction given near the end of the passage enables us to date the birth of Constantine III to May 612, rather than 611. The sentence in italics at the beginning of the passage is significant as it would seem that Theophanes derived that information from a source written in Syriac outside the Byzantine empire.

Source: Theophanes Confessor (1997), *The Chronicle of Theophanes Confessor: Byzantine and Near Eastern History, AD 284–813*, trans. Cyril Mango and Roger Scott (Oxford: Oxford University Press), p. 429 (spelling adapted).

1.4 Other types of source: hagiography and military manuals

Works of hagiography or biographies of saints were produced in very large numbers during the Byzantine period, but they are not always helpful sources of historical information. Many of them are about legendary saints who may never even have existed and they contain all kinds of miracle stories that are clearly fictional. Even when a hagiographical text has a historical person for its subject, it often makes use of the *topos* – a standard and unvarying literary description. If the saint's childhood is described, for instance, it will invariably emerge that they never played with other children and spent long hours in prayer. That said, some saints' lives can be remarkably informative.

One example is the biography of Theodore of Sykeon, a monk and later bishop who lived in Asia Minor during the reigns of Maurice, Phokas and Herakleios. His biography was written by a younger disciple called George who described the saint's childhood in conventional terms but he also tells us a great deal about everyday life in the village of Sykeon where Theodore lived. He received frequent visits at his monastery from the headmen of other villages seeking his advice and he would entertain them to dinner. He was credited with numerous miracles on behalf of the local farmers, such as preventing locusts, dormice and other pests from devouring their crops, halting floods, ending droughts and curing both people and animals, but Theodore's biographer makes it clear that not everything that he did for the local community was necessarily miraculous. He would prescribe remedies for illnesses, recommend which doctor to employ or sometimes advise against medical treatment altogether and suggest a visit to the hot springs instead.

Similarly, if anyone was oppressed by an imperial tax collector, he would go to Theodore for advice and the saint often took the side of the villagers when they were subjected to unjust exactions. Theodore's biography also contains information about political events of the day, including the reign of Emperor Phokas (602–610) (see Section 2.1). Theodore visited Constantinople in 609–10 and was summoned into the emperor's presence. Phokas was bedridden with gout and asked Theodore to pray for his recovery. The saint did so but at the same time told him off him for murdering so many of his political opponents. Many other works of hagiography contain similar details, such as the biography of St Luke of Steiris (see Box 7.2).

Another important literary genre in Byzantium was that of military manuals, a form of writing which stretches back to antiquity, the earliest extant example being from the fourth century BCE. The manuals described strategy and tactics in time of war, the different kinds of enemy, their tactics and the best way to deal with them. As with hagiography, there are certain drawbacks to using the manuals as a source of historical information. They are particularly marked by the Byzantine tendency to imitate the authors of classical antiquity so that a considerable proportion of the information in them is simply reproduced from earlier manuals and does not necessarily provide any authentic insight into Byzantine military tactics.

One such manual is the *Strategikon*, which was compiled during the reign of Emperor Maurice or shortly afterwards. As with all the manuals, some of the information that it provides is taken directly from the work of classical authors such as Polybius but much of it clearly reflects the situation in the later sixth century when Byzantium's main enemies were the Persians and the Avars, along with the Slavs and Lombards. The author of the *Strategikon* gives advice on the tactics used by each group and the best way to counter them. In discussing tactics, he used particular examples from actions fought in the recent past. For example, in the section on night attacks, he recalls how the Avars launched one against the Byzantine cavalry that was stationed outside a fortified camp in 592. Similar military manuals are *On Skirmishing* and the *Sylloge Tacticorum* which will be discussed later (see Boxes 3.2 and 8.1).

1.5 Sources from outside Byzantium

For all their long and proud literary tradition, the Byzantines had no monopoly on historiography. Their neighbours wrote it too, in their own languages and with their own concerns and emphasis. There survives, for example, a *History of Khusro*, written in Armenian by a bishop who may or may not have been called Sebeos. It covers events from 594 to 661 with an understandable focus on Armenia. It supplements the *Chronicon Paschale* for Herakleios' Persian campaign but it is indispensable for the period of the early Arab invasions as it provides important details that are found nowhere else. Above all, it was compiled in the 660s, relatively close to the events that it describes.

There are sources in Coptic emanating from Byzantine Egypt, such as Isaac the presbyter's biography of the Monophysite monk Samuel of Kalamun who fled persecution by patriarch Kyros in the 630s. The work of John of Nikiu is essential in understanding the Arab conquest of Egypt in 640–642 (see Section 2.4). There are numerous short chronicles written in Syriac, such as the *Melkite Chronicle* and the *Chronicle of Zuqnīn* which both provide extra information about the cross-border warfare between Byzantium and the Umayyad caliphate. The most important source written in Arabic is the *History of the Patriarchs of Alexandria* which was probably started by an Egyptian Monophysite bishop called Sawirus ibn al-Muqaffa (d. 987) and then continued by other clergymen after his death. It provides important information about the Arab invasion of Egypt and the response of the population, but Sawirus and his continuators were writing a long time after these events. There are also histories in Arabic written from the Islamic point of view, such as that of the Persian scholar al-Tabari (839–923). He was active in Baghdad under the Abbasid caliphate where he produced his universal history, a monumental work that ran from creation to the year 915 CE. Again, though, he was writing in the late ninth and early tenth century, long after the period in question here. He had to rely on remote and often garbled sources and incorporated much anecdotal and improbable material. He was also primarily concerned to create a narrative of the glorious and unstoppable march of Islam.

Box 1.2 An Arabic source on the Muslim conquest of Syria: al-Baladhuri's *Book of the Conquests of Lands*

Like al-Tabari, Ahmad ibn Yahya al-Baladhuri (d.892) wrote in Baghdad under the Abbasid caliphate. When it came to writing the history of the early expansion of Islam, he found himself confronted with conflicting information which he conscientiously tried to weigh up. Here he discusses the capture of the Byzantine city of Damascus by the Arab commanders Khalid ibn al-Walid and abu-Ubaidah during the 630s and attempts to reconcile the different dates in his sources:

> According to al-Wakidi, the conquest of Damascus was effected in Rajab, year 14 [i.e. August or September 635] but the date which Khalid's statement of capitulation bears was Rabi II, year 15 [i.e. May or June of 636]. The explanation is that Khalid wrote the statement with no date, but when the Muslims were preparing to set out against those gathered for their fight in al-Yarmuk, the bishop came to Khalid asking him to renew the statement and add as witnesses abu-Ubaidah and the Muslims. Khalid granted the request and inserted the names of abu-Ubaidah, Yazid ibn-abi-Sufyan, Shurahbil ibn-Hasanah and others as witnesses. The date he put was the one in which the statement was renewed.

Damascus may have fallen in the later summer of 635 but other sources place its surrender after the battle of Yarmuk, in around September 636. Al-Baladhuri also gives two versions of how the city was captured. In one an enterprising band of Arabs clambered over the walls at night and then opened the gates to the main army. In the other, the Arabs took advantage of the opening of a gate for a funeral procession to rush in themselves. In both cases the bishop of Damascus then negotiated the surrender. The fact was that by the time that al-Baladhuri was writing everyone knew that Damascus had been taken but no one could be sure how or exactly when.

Source: Ahmad ibn Yahya al-Baladhuri, *Origins of the Islamic State*, trans. Philip K. Hitti (New York: Columbia University Press, 1916), p. 189.

Lastly there are sources in Latin emanating from the western provinces of the empire and beyond. Some of them, such as the work of Paul the Deacon (see Box 4.3), are especially informative about events in Byzantine Italy. The *Liber Pontificalis*, or Book of the Popes, is a series of biographies of popes starting with St Peter which chronicles the sometimes rather strained relations between Rome and Constantinople over matters such as Monotheletism and Iconoclasm. Often, Latin sources written outside the empire can include small but important details that are completely absent in the records produced in and around Constantinople.

Box 1.3 A Latin source for seventh-century Byzantine history: the *Gesta Dagoberti*

This short biography of Dagobert, king of the Franks (629–634), describes a Frankish embassy to Constantinople in around 630 and the making of a treaty, which is not mentioned in Byzantine sources:

> In that year, the envoys of King Dagobert, whose names were Servatus and Paternus and whom he had sent to the Emperor Herakleios, returned to him to announce that a treaty had been concluded with Herakleios. Now since Emperor Herakleios was extremely well-read, eventually he had become a most skilled astronomer. He recognised from signs among the stars that a circumcised people would by divine command devastate his empire. So he sent to Dagobert, king of the Franks, requesting that all Jews in his kingdom should be baptised according to the Catholic rite. King Dagobert, possessed and led at that time by his zeal for God, with the advice of priests and the wisdom of men, ordered that all Jews who did not wish to undertake rebirth through holy baptism, should immediately take themselves beyond the borders of the kingdom. This was something that the king enforced with the utmost thoroughness. However, it was not the Jews who had been pointed out to Herakleios but the Agarenes, otherwise known as the Saracens [i.e. the Arabs], since it was by them that his empire would afterwards be violently attacked, invaded and devastated.

It goes without saying that this anti-Semitic tale needs to be treated with some scepticism. The *Gesta Dagoberti* was written in around 830, at the abbey of St Denis where Dagobert was buried. The story of his responding to Herakleios' request by expelling the Jews was doubtless, like many of the stories in the *Gesta*, concocted to enhance his reputation for sanctity and boost the pilgrimage traffic to St Denis. That does not mean that this source should be dismissed as a complete fabrication, though. There is every reason to believe the Herakleios was in contact with Dagobert in around 630. With the Persians defeated, the emperor may well have been planning to move against the Avars and Slavs in the Balkans but he had few resources to mobilise against the Lombards in Italy. The Franks were therefore an ideal ally who might be induced to cross the Alps and attack the Lombards, so taking the pressure off the Byzantine strongholds of Ravenna and Rome. Maurice had used this tactic with good effect in 584 and the chances are that Herakleios arranged something similar with the envoys sent by Dagobert.

Source: 'Gesta Dagoberti I. Regis Francorum', in *Monumenta Germaniae Historica: Scriptorum Rerum Merovingicarum*, vol. 2 (Hannover, 1888), pp. 396–425, at 409 (author's translation).

Points to remember

- Literary culture in Byzantium was based on the study of the literature of ancient Greece and the imitation of its language.
- The later seventh to mid-eighth centuries form one of the most poorly documented periods of Byzantine history.
- The works of Patriarch Nikephoros and Theophanes Confessor are our major Greek sources of information, but they are flawed in many ways.
- Other literary works such as hagiography and military manuals are important, although they have their drawbacks too.
- Material written in Arabic, Armenian, Coptic, Latin and Syriac provides important insights to supplement Nikephoros and Theophanes.

Some primary sources in English translation

Al-Tabari, Abu Jafar Muhammad ibn Jarir. (1985–2007), *The History of al-Tabari*, trans. Franz Rosenthal and others, 40 vols (Albany NY: State University of New York Press).

Anonymous. (1989), *Chronicon Paschale 284–628 AD*, trans. Michael Whitby and Mary Whitby (Liverpool: Liverpool University Press).

Anonymous. (2010, 3rd revised edition), *The Book of the Pontiffs (Liber Pontificalis)*, trans. Raymond Davis (Liverpool: Liverpool University Press).

Anonymous. (1992), *The Lives of the Eighth-Century Popes (Liber Pontificalis)*, trans. Raymond Davis (Liverpool: Liverpool University Press).

Eleusios, George. (1977), 'The Life of St. Theodore of Sykeon', in *Three Byzantine Saints*, trans. Elizabeth Dawes and Norman H. Baynes, 2nd ed. (Crestwood NY: St Vladimir's Seminary Press), pp. 85–192. Only selections from the text are translated here.

Isaac the Presbyter (1983), *The Life of Samuel of Kalamun*, trans. A. Alcock (Warminster: Aris and Phillips).

Maurice. (1984), *Maurice's Strategikon: Handbook of Byzantine Military Strategy*, trans. George T. Dennis (Philadelphia PA: University of Pennsylvania Press).

Nikephoros. (1990), *Short History*, trans. Cyril Mango (Washington, DC: Dumbarton Oaks). There is another translation by Norman Tobias and Anthony R. Santoro, *Eyewitness to History: The Short History of Nikephoros, Our Holy Father the Patriarch of Constantinople* (Brookline MA: Hellenic College Press, 1989).

Palmer, Andrew. (1993), *The Seventh Century in the West-Syrian Chronicles*, ed. and trans. Andrew Palmer (Liverpool: Liverpool University Press).

Sawirus ibn al-Muqaffa. (2017), *History of the Patriarchs of Alexandria: The Copts of Egypt before and after the Islamic Conquests*, trans. Hugh Kennedy, 3 vols (London: I.B. Tauris).

Sebeos. (1999), *The Armenian History Attributed to Sebeos*, trans. R.W. Thomson, Tim Greenwood and James Howard-Johnston, 2 vols (Liverpool: Liverpool University Press).

Theophanes Confessor. (1997), *The Chronicle of Theophanes Confessor: Byzantine and Near Eastern History, AD 284–813*, trans. Cyril Mango and Roger Scott (Oxford: Oxford University Press). There is another translation by Harry J. Turtledove, *The Chronicle of Theophanes: Anni Mundi 6095–6305 (AD 602–813)* (Philadelphia PA: University of Pennsylvania Press, 1982), although, as the title makes clear, it presents a smaller section of the chronicle.

Suggestions for further reading

Howard-Johnston, James. (2010), *Witnesses to a World Crisis: Historians and Histories of the Middle East in the Seventh Century* (Oxford and New York: Oxford University Press). A survey of the surviving literary sources for the seventh-century Middle East, in Arabic, Armenian, Greek and Syriac, with some very useful analysis and discussion of the sometimes rather confusing sequence of events that they describe.

Kaldellis, Anthony. (2011), *Hellenism in Byzantium: The Transformations of Greek Identity and the Reception of the Classical Tradition* (Cambridge: Cambridge University Press). Kaldellis' central theme is how the Byzantines viewed their inheritance of ancient Greek literature and thought. He includes a section that covers the seventh century, a period of crisis when there was little leisure to read and appreciate the works of the ancients.

Neville, Leonora. (2018), *Guide to Byzantine Historical Writing* (Cambridge: Cambridge University Press). A reference guide to histories written in Greek between 600 and 1480, that covers both those in the Attic Greek tradition and other less standardised texts, providing details about the time of composition, content, authorship and subsequent scholarly debates.

2 Herakleios and the wars of survival (602–642)

The seventh century CE was a momentous period in the history of the Middle East. Perhaps only the twentieth century can match it for the intensity with which war was waged and the rapidity with which empires fell and rose. Byzantium lost vast swathes of its territory yet at the same time somehow managed to survive against all the odds. In view of the paucity of sources discussed in the previous chapter, there is inevitably much that we will never know, but we can piece together what happened and make some educated guesses as to why events turned out the way they did.

2.1 The spiralling crisis (602–622)

With the accession of Phokas in 602, the pressure on Byzantium's frontiers intensified. Now that the Byzantine army had been withdrawn across the Danube, there was nothing to stop the Slavs and Avars from resuming their attacks into the Balkans. In Italy, the Lombards picked off the Byzantine-held towns of Cremona and Mantua. In the east, the Sassanid ruler, Khusro II, saw his chance. Feigning outrage for the murder of his friend and protector, Maurice, he abrogated the peace treaty, invaded the eastern provinces and, in 604, seized the strategically important frontier town of Daras. To lend his invasion the cloak of legitimacy, he brought with him a young man who claimed to be the son of the late emperor and so Khusro could say that he was only doing for Maurice's family what Maurice had done for him.

In view of Phokas' violent seizure of the throne and his apparent ineffectiveness once he had it, it was not long before there were further revolts to which Phokas responded with a round of executions. His opponents in Constantinople then made contact with the Exarch of Carthage, who was governing one of the few areas which was not being invaded and so had armed forces at his disposal. The exarch joined the rebels and in 610 sent his son Herakleios to Constantinople with a fleet. By the time he arrived, Phokas was so thoroughly unpopular with the people of the city that his own officials arrested him and handed him over to the rebel fleet. Herakleios had him executed on the deck of his flagship and was crowned emperor in Phokas' place in Hagia Sophia later the same day.

In the short term, the change of rulers made not the slightest difference. In fact, things went from bad to worse. The Persians invaded Syria and Palestine and they encountered little effective resistance, capturing Damascus in 613. The greatest disaster occurred in

May 614 when the Persians stormed, captured and pillaged the holy city of Jerusalem, seizing one of the most precious relics in the Christian world, the True Cross on which it was believed Christ had been crucified. From Jerusalem, the Persians moved on to invade Egypt, capturing Alexandria in 619. It now looked as if the Persian empire would be recreated as it had been in the great days of Darius and Xerxes in the sixth and fifth centuries BCE. By the same token, it looked as if Byzantium was finished.

2.2 Defeat into victory (622–629)

It was 12 years after his accession before Emperor Herakleios was ready to strike back and even then he had to make a tough decision on whether to take on the Persians first or the Avars and Slavs. He certainly did not have the resources to fight both simultaneously. In the end, the choice was made for him. Khusro II turned down his peace overtures so he made a treaty with the Avars instead, promising to pay them an annual tribute if they would not attack Constantinople. With his flank secure, in the summer of 622, Herakleios marched east and inflicted a minor reverse on a Persian force that had invaded Asia Minor. The victory was heartening but not on a scale to swing the tide of the war in Byzantium's favour. So two years later, the emperor made a radical decision. He must have surmised that the Persians would be expecting him to attack them in the vicinity of Antioch with a view to ejecting them from Syria and ultimately from Egypt. Instead, he made a bold plan to strike into the very heart of Persia itself, marching north into Armenia and then turning south into Sassanid territory. When the Byzantine army appeared on Persia's northern border in the spring of 624, the Persians were taken completely by surprise, leaving Herakleios free to destroy their cities one after another. Moreover, the emperor did not withdraw to his own territory at the end of the campaigning season. Instead, he wintered in Armenia and renewed his attack on Persia the following spring.

In a desperate bid to make Herakleios stop his attacks on Persian territory, Khusro II adopted the same tactics. In 626, he sent an army across Asia Minor to besiege Constantinople. It would seem that he was in diplomatic contact with the khan of the Avars, for the latter decided to break his treaty with Herakleios and to lead an Avar–Slav army to invest Constantinople from the European side of the Bosporus while the Persians occupied the eastern bank. The Persian king doubtless calculated that the emperor would have no choice but to hurry back west to defend his capital. Again, Herakleios defied expectations. He decided to let Constantinople defend itself, despatching only a small contingent of his army to assist. With the bulk of his force, he continued his campaign in Persia. Unable to take the Byzantine capital, both the Avars and Persians withdrew in August 626, while the Byzantines continued to pile on the pressure by invading Persia once more in September 627. The following December, a major battle was fought at Ninevah, deep inside Persian territory, lasting from dawn until dusk. By the end of the day, the Byzantines were in possession of the field and had captured 28 enemy standards. So complete and utter had been the defeat that the Persians did not attempt to engage the emperor's army again but merely withdrew before it as it marched towards the capital city of Ctesiphon, having lost all confidence in the leadership of Khusro II. In

February 628, Khusro was overthrown and murdered by his son, Kavad, who immediately sued for peace, agreeing to evacuate all his troops from Syria, Palestine and Egypt. Thereafter, Persia descended into civil war as its military leaders vied with each other to seize the throne: there was no likelihood of hostilities against Byzantium being resumed for the foreseeable future. After six years on campaign, Herakleios was finally able to return to Constantinople in triumph in the spring of 629. The following year found him in the eastern provinces, visiting Jerusalem to restore the True Cross to its rightful place and overseeing the return of Byzantine rule after more than 15 years of Persian occupation. Few political leaders have ever been able to savour a victory so complete after coming so close to annihilation.

Figure 2.1 Gold nomisma of Herakleios with his son, the future Constantine III

2.3 Why the war was won

The sharp contrast between the desperate straits of 619 and the victory celebrations of 629–630 raise the question of exactly what had happened to shift the pendulum so radically in Byzantium's favour. An easy option would be simply to credit Herakleios himself as a general and strategist of genius. Theophanes certainly portrays him as a dynamic and inspiring leader. Before launching his eastern campaign in 622, he subjected his soldiers to intensive training and drills to prepare them for the struggles ahead. He seems also to have led the army from the front. At Ninevah in December 627, he is alleged to have killed the Persian commander and two other opponents in single combat. His bold stroke against the Persian heartland through Armenia was an inspired one which took the enemy completely by surprise. Yet personal military prowess does not seem to be enough in itself to explain the victory. After all, Herakleios' military record was by no means unchequered. He did almost nothing for the first 12 years of his reign while the Persians overran the eastern provinces and he was later to preside over another series of disastrous reverses.

That is why historians have searched for some other factor, grappling with the difficult and uninformative records of the time. One scholar who came up with a striking and influential answer was the Russian Byzantinist George Ostrogorsky. For him, the years 620–624 were a vital moment when changes were made that brought about not only Byzantium's survival but also its strength and greatness in the centuries to come. Ostrogorsky argued that, as part of the preparations that he was making for his counter-attack against the Persians, Herakleios pushed through an inspired administrative reform. He divided the remaining area of Asia Minor into military zones known as Themes, within which the distinction between civil and military administration was abolished. The governor of the Theme, known as the strategos, was responsible for administration and justice but he was also the commander of the army of that Theme, a similar arrangement to that in the Exarchates established under Maurice. It was the armies of these new administrative units, Ostrogorsky argued, that enabled Herakleios to take on the Persians once more and reverse the string of defeats.

The theory was an important and influential one and will be discussed in more detail in the next chapter (see Section 3.4 and Box 3.3). Suffice it to say at this stage that very few historians now accept Ostrogorsky's view that the establishment of the Themes was the key to Herakleios' success. The stumbling block is the matter of evidence. There is almost no mention of the Themes in contemporary seventh-century sources. The earliest allusion is in a letter written by Emperor Justinian II in about 685 but that was long after Herakleios' death. The earliest complete description of the system is that of the Arab geographer Ibn Khurdadhbah who was writing in around 850. It was not that Ostrogorsky had no foundation for his theory. He cited Theophanes who says that, in 622, the emperor went 'to the country of the Themes', thus implying that they existed at that point. But this is hardly convincing evidence. Theophanes was writing almost two hundred years later and he was probably assuming that the conditions of his own day applied under Herakleios too. He certainly does not specifically say that Herakleios set up the system. A later writer, Emperor Constantine VII (945–959), in his work *On the Themes*, specifically credits Herakleios' successors with this reform.

So if inspired leadership and the Themes do not explain the victory, what does? There are other factors which can be substantiated by credible literary and physical evidence. One huge advantage that Herakleios did have was his capital city of Constantinople which, given the technology of the time, was to all intents and purposes impregnable. The city was situated on a narrow promontory surrounded by water, the Sea of Marmara to the south and the Bosporus to the west, and to the north the Golden Horn, one of the finest natural harbours in the world (see Figure 0.1). That meant that when the Persians arrived at Chalcedon opposite Constantinople in 626, they could progress no further as they had no ships and could not link up with their Avar and Slav allies (see Figure 2.5). An attempt was made by the Avars to send a fleet of canoes to ferry the Persians across, but Byzantine warships easily intercepted and sank these frail vessels. It was left to the Slavs and Avars to mount an assault on the city from their position on the European side of the Straits, but they were confronted by the colossal Theodosian or Land Walls that stretched more than seven kilometres from the top of the Golden Horn to the Sea of Marmara (see Figure 2.2). Constructed of limestone blocks, they stood about nine metres high, were four-and-a-half metres thick and presented a three-tier defence: a moat, an outer wall and an inner wall. Adept though they were at siege warfare, the Avars had little chance of breaking through these fortifications. Herakleios knew that and that was why he had been able to remain with most of his army in Armenia and continue his attacks on Persia, even when his capital was threatened. That said, in themselves the fortifications of Constantinople do not necessarily constitute the sole key to Herakleios' success. After all, if the city had fallen, other strongholds remained, such as Ravenna, Carthage and Syracuse in Sicily. So other factors need to be taken into account as well.

Figure 2.2 The Land Walls of Constantinople, showing their three-tier construction. The site of the moat is now filled with vegetable gardens

One of them was Herakleios' careful cultivation among his subjects of a belief in the rightness of their cause and a will to win. Both George of Pisidia and Theophanes recount how, while he was training his new army in Asia Minor, he treated it to rousing, morale-boosting speeches. The main theme of these harangues was to remind the troops that the enemies they were fighting were not Christians. The Slavs and Avars were pagans and the Persians were Zoroastrians. The Byzantines were therefore fighting for the True God against infidels and if they died in the struggle they would be martyrs and would receive their reward in heaven. He also tried hard to instil a sense of outrage into his troops and the Persians had played into his hands here. When they had captured Jerusalem in 614, they had burned down churches and massacred hundreds of Christians. In stressing these points, Herakleios was in line with wartime propaganda across the centuries before and since. There was, however, one very distinctive element. He deliberately linked the struggle to painted images (or icons) of Jesus Christ, the Virgin Mary and other saints. When he set out on campaign in 622, he took with him an icon of Christ and he held it in his arms while making an impassioned speech to the troops (see Box 2.1). The Church backed him up on this. When the Avars and Slavs arrived before the Land Walls of Constantinople in 626, the Patriarch Sergios had images of the Virgin Mary and the baby Jesus painted onto the Land Walls. In using icons in this way, the emperor and the patriarch were taking advantage of the deep reverence for icons that had been developing over the previous hundred years. They were seen as symbolising the presence of the holy persons that they depicted and were accordingly cherished, reverenced and prayed to. It was not only icons that gave the defenders a connection with the divine. At this time of crisis relics, objects associated with or even the body parts of some holy person, were brought out to bolster morale. It is around now that we find the first mentions of the robe or veil of the Virgin Mary being preserved in one of Constantinople's churches. During the siege of 626, it was paraded along the city walls and was largely given the credit for the city's survival. Thus the icons and the relics were vital in keeping the Byzantines fighting when all may have seemed lost for they symbolised the divine presence with and support for the army. A belief in the rightness of their cause is undoubtedly a key element in motivating people to risk their lives.

Box 2.1 George of Pisidia on Herakleios' Persian campaign (622–628)

A literary figure of some standing at Herakleios' court, George of Pisidia composed a series of poems in Attic Greek, probably between 629 and 634, extolling the emperor's victories against the Persians and Avars. They were designed to be read out loud in the court on special occasions such as, perhaps, Herakleios' victorious return from the east. Here, addressing the emperor, the poet describes how Herakleios made a rousing speech to his troops on the eve of battle:

Taking the awe-inspiring image, depicted by God, you spoke for a short time: 'The nature and basis of my authority binds me to you, as to brothers. For we declare that this authority is based not so much on fear as on love. Against the inhuman force which the tyrant [i.e. Khusro II] has armed against legitimacy, our law is on the contrary the force of the love of mankind, and that alone counters such violence... This [i.e. Christ as depicted on the icon which Herakleios was holding] is the ruler and lord of all and the leader of our campaigns. With Him the command is more secure and through Him the victory is sacred. Trusting in Him and having arrived at this moment as one of you, I arm myself for toils. For we, as His creations, must take the field against enemies who bow down to created things.'

The passage encapsulates the main points of Herakleios' wartime propaganda: that the war was just because the enemy was not Christian, that victory was certain as God was leading the army and that his presence was symbolised by the icon of Christ that Herakleios had brought with him. Note too that George describes Christ as 'depicted by God'. He is referring to the incarnation, when Jesus was 'depicted' in flesh by being born as a human being.

Source: George of Pisidia, *Poemi: I. Panegirici epici*, ed. Agostino Pertusi (Ettal: Buch-Kunstverlag, 1959), pp. 101–2 (author's translation).

As with all the possible explanations for Herakleios' success, the role of propaganda and icons should be treated with caution. After all, these accounts may represent what writers felt should have happened rather than what did, especially as many of the authors, such as Theophanes, were clergymen. On the other hand, George of Pisidia was not a cleric and, unlike Nikephoros and Theophanes, he was a contemporary of Herakleios so his evidence needs to be taken very seriously.

There is another kind of factor that needs to be taken into consideration. While George of Pisidia and Theophanes were always happy to write about religious matters, they were much less forthcoming about economic issues which may well have made a significant contribution to Byzantium's survival. When they are mentioned, it is often in a religious context but that can still be very informative. For example, the *Chronicon Paschale* tells us that in around 615, Herakleios minted a new silver coin called the Hexagram, examples of which still exist. The author mentioned it because the bullion from which it was made probably came from melting down church treasures such as communion plates and chalices. In theory this would have been robbing the Church but the Patriarch Sergios happily gave his consent, given the gravity of the crisis. The new coin may have been part of a general financial shake-up which provided Herakleios with the means to equip and maintain a new army in the 620s. At the end of the day, though, no one will ever know for certain why Herakleios triumphed in 628 and, in any case, any neat explanation is to some extent undermined by what happened next. Byzantium was to experience a second round of heavy defeats and losses of territory to a new enemy and this time there was no coming back.

2.4 Victory into defeat (629–642)

In the early weeks of 634, news arrived that a raiding party of Arabs had crossed the border into newly recovered Syria. That was nothing new: they had been doing it for centuries. Doubtless the emperor assumed that the local forces could deal with it. When the Arabs routed a Byzantine contingent near Gaza and killed its commander, Herakleios did send a larger force to the region but he still did not consider the threat severe enough to warrant his personal presence. He remained in Antioch and entrusted the command to his brother, Theodore. When Theodore's army was similarly mauled the following year, it began to grow apparent that Byzantine Syria was experiencing not the usual raids but a full-scale Arab invasion. So another, much more formidable, army was sent against the Arabs in 636, although once more it was not led by the emperor himself. A major battle was joined on 20 July 636 near the Yarmuk River. It went on for several days but the Byzantines allegedly had the disadvantage that the south wind was constantly blowing dust into their eyes. Eventually, after heavy fighting, the Arabs emerged victorious and the entire Byzantine army had been destroyed. Shortly afterwards, the Arabs marched into Damascus, giving them their first permanent stronghold in Syria (see Box 1.2).

It is at this point that a stark contrast with Herakleios' valiant and energetic conduct during the Persian war emerges. Rather than moving at once to stem the breach, he seems to have given up. He left Antioch, probably in the spring of 637, and headed back across Asia Minor to Constantinople, taking the True Cross from Jerusalem with him. His withdrawal gave the Arabs a free hand and from Damascus they made for Jerusalem. The city held out for some time in the hope that a relieving force would come and lift the siege, but no one came. Finally, in February 638, the Patriarch Sophronios agreed to open the city gates. Antioch surrendered to the Arabs without a fight shortly afterwards. In the summer of 640, led by Amr, the Arabs invaded Egypt and marched on Alexandria. The patriarch of Alexandria, Kyros, like his counterpart in Jerusalem, was doubtless hoping that a Byzantine army would come to the rescue. When none came, he entered into negotiations with the Arabs, making a one-year truce and promising to hand over Alexandria at the end of that time if no relieving force appeared. Since none did, in September 642 Alexandria surrendered. That was not quite the end of the Byzantine presence in the region. In 646, a Byzantine fleet was despatched to reverse the situation and it briefly recaptured Alexandria. The Arabs soon counter-attacked, however, and they drove the Byzantines out the following year. In this way, the entire territory that had been recovered at such cost from the Persians in 628 was now lost once more, this time permanently. Henceforth the heartland of the Byzantine empire was to be in Asia Minor and the Balkans.

2.5 What went wrong?

If Herakleios' leadership was a reason for his victory against the Persians, then his lack of it must have been a factor in his defeat by the Arabs. The difference can be accounted for by the state of the emperor's health. By 640, he was clearly not a well man. He was suffering from some kind of cancer and he also seems to have had a nervous breakdown, probably brought on by the bad news from Syria. After leaving Antioch, he journeyed to Chalcedon but he refused outright to cross the Bosporus because he had become morbidly terrified of water. His attendants only got him across by making a bridge of boats across the strait, covering their decks with tall plants that screened out the sight of the sea. Once in his capital, Herakleios played little further part in the direction of affairs and he died on 11 February 641.

To make matters worse, a succession crisis ensued. Herakleios had married twice. By his first wife, Fabia-Eudokia, he had had a son called Constantine who was now 28 (see Box 1.1). But he had another son by his second wife, Martina, named Heraklonas, who was now 15. In a misguided effort to be fair, Herakleios left the throne to both sons jointly and commanded that they both regard Martina as mother and empress. This was an uneasy situation as the court was soon divided between the supporters of Martina and those of Constantine III. Then Constantine III died after only three months as emperor, apparently of consumption, and Martina became the de facto ruler with Heraklonas as nominal emperor. She did not enjoy this position for long. She was extremely unpopular in Constantinople and in September 641 a Byzantine army marched on the capital to back a popular demand that Herakleios' grandson Constans be made co-emperor with Heraklonas. Martina had no choice but to agree. Early the following year, there was a coup in Constantinople and Martina and Heraklonas were sent into exile. Constans now became sole emperor as Constans II (641–668) but the distraction generated by these events probably prevented help being sent to Alexandria, forcing its patriarch to surrender the city to the Arabs.

Herakleios' illness and the succession crisis certainly go a long way towards explaining the lacklustre Byzantine response to the Arab invasions but not their rapidity, completeness and permanence. One factor that undoubtedly made a difference was the change that had occurred in Arab society in the previous two decades. The Arabs had always lived by war as they had been divided into tribes which spent most of their time fighting each other. Indeed, rival tribes would sign up as allies with either the Byzantines or the Persians and continue their feud under the banners of the two great powers. During the first decades of the seventh century, the Arabs had become unified and put aside their old tribal differences, apparently as the result of the preaching of the Prophet Muhammad. After facing initial opposition, Muhammad induced the tribal leaders to accept the revelations that he claimed had been made to him by an angel of God and which he wrote down in the 114 chapters of the Quran. The unity given to the Arabs by Islam ensured that they crossed the Byzantine border as a major force rather than as the usual tribal raiders and gave them the manpower that they needed to destroy the Byzantine army at Yarmuk and to occupy the land.

Some would go further and argue that Islam not only gave the Arabs unity but the ideological will to win, just as religious belief had played a role in Herakleios' success against the Persians. In the ninth chapter of the Quran, Muhammad urged Muslims to strive against unbelievers and promised that those who did so would enter paradise: the same promise that Herakleios is alleged to have made to his own troops. The Arabs may thus have had the advantage of fighting for an exulted cause but specific, contemporary evidence that they believed in a spiritual reward for their efforts is lacking. While Islam, like Christianity, did later develop an ideology of Holy War, no one can be sure that it existed from the very earliest days of its history. The Quran's insistence that believers should strive for the faith does not make it clear that this was meant in a violent or militaristic way. The Arabs had always been enthusiastic warriors and they probably did not need Islam to incite them to battle. The unity that the new religion gave them was probably of greater significance.

Another factor that might have played a role was the alienation of a large part of the population of the eastern provinces on religious and other grounds that has already been discussed (see Introduction 0.4). Once the Persians had withdrawn from Syria and Egypt in 630, Herakleios became the latest emperor to attempt to heal the schism with the Monophysite Christians. Like others before him he decided to try a compromise, organising synods of clergy to come up with a formula acceptable to both sides. Various forms of words were tried and rejected until in 638 the emperor threw his weight behind the doctrine of Monotheletism, the idea that Christ had a single will. The idea was that it would reconcile the gulf between the two sides over Christ's divine and human natures, but it pleased nobody. Monotheletism was unacceptable to the Monophysites and very few Catholics liked it either, so that Herakleios found himself widely condemned as a heretic in his own capital. By now, the emperor's patience was starting to wear thin. He announced that it was now illegal even to discuss the question of Christ's nature and that everyone must accept his compromise. To enforce his will, he appointed a thuggish individual called Kyros to be both Catholic patriarch of Alexandria and the governor of Egypt. Kyros soon became legendary for his cruelty in hunting down the Monophysite clergy. The Monophysite patriarch of Alexandria, Benjamin, succeeded in escaping but Kyros captured Benjamin's brother, whom he is alleged to have tortured by holding lighted torches to his body before having him drowned.

It is tempting to identify this deep disunity in the Christian ranks as the main reason why the eastern provinces fell so quickly. Certainly, it is very noticeable that while the people of Constantinople were united in resisting the Persian–Avar siege of 626, the vast majority of the inhabitants of Syria and Egypt seem to have had little interest in resisting the Arabs, or the Persians before them for that matter. There was an added incentive to passivity in that the Arab invaders announced early on that they had no intention of attempting to convert their new subjects to Islam. Both Christians and Jews were to be allowed to continue their traditional worship unhindered, provided they paid a special tax to the Muslim authorities. The Arabs moreover had no interest whatsoever in the difference between Monophysite and Catholic and treated both groups exactly the same. So for the Monophysites the surrender of Alexandria in 642 was a moment of rejoicing as the exiled patriarch Benjamin I was able to return from exile. For the majority population, the change of rulers looked less like a conquest and more like a liberation.

On the other hand, Monophysite disaffection cannot in itself explain the rapid Byzantine collapse either. After all, Catholics seem to have been equally passive in the face of the invasion. It was the Catholic patriarchs of Jerusalem and Alexandria, Sophronios and Kyros, who opened the gates of their cities to the Arabs, not their Monophysite counterparts. Moreover, sorely tried though the Monophysite clergy and people were by the government in Constantinople, there is little evidence that they actively aided the Arabs during the invasion. In fact, the contemporary chronicle of John of Nikiu suggests that at least some Monophysites were dismayed by the turn of events (see Box 2.2).

Box 2.2 John of Nikiu on the fall of Byzantine Egypt (640–642)

Very little is known about this chronicler, other than that he was bishop of the town of Nikiu (now Zawyat Razin) in the Nile Delta in the late seventh century. Unfortunately, the original text of his work, which was probably written in a mixture of Greek and Coptic, does not survive. All that remains is a translation into Ethiopic which was made in 1602 and which may not be entirely faithful to the original. Nevertheless, John's chronicle is the only eyewitness account of these momentous events and as such is a vital source of information. As a Monophysite, John had no sympathy for the Byzantine authorities and hated their attempts to impose what he regarded as heretical doctrines. He provides important evidence of the ambivalent attitude of the Coptic population during the Arab invasion:

> And [the Arab general] Amr left lower Egypt and proceeded to war against Rif. He sent a few Muslims against the city of Antinoe. And when the Muslims saw the weakness of the Romans and the hostility of the people to the emperor Herakleios because of the persecution wherewith he had visited all the land of Egypt in regard to the orthodox faith, at the instigation of Kyros the Chalcedonian patriarch, they became bolder and stronger in the war. And the inhabitants of the city [Antinoe] sought to concert measures with John their prefect with a view to attacking the Muslims; but he refused, and arose with haste with his troops, and, having collected all the imposts of the city, betook himself to Alexandria; for he knew that he could not resist the Muslims … Indeed, all the inhabitants of the province submitted to the Muslims and paid them tribute.

A note of caution needs to be sounded here though. John of Nikiu and other Monophysites may well have loathed Patriarch Kyros and the Catholics but that does not mean that they regarded the arrival of the Arabs with unmixed joy. While it is true that the new rulers did not impose Islam on their new subjects and generally left towns that surrendered unharmed, their conquest of Egypt was by no means bloodless. Here John describes the Arab capture of his own town of Nikiu:

> And thereupon the Muslims made their entry into Nikiu, and took possession, and finding no soldiers [to offer resistance], they proceeded to put to the sword all whom they found in the streets and in the churches, men, women, and infants, and they showed mercy to none. And after they had captured

[this] city, they marched against other localities and sacked them and put all they found to the sword … Let us now cease, for it is impossible to recount the iniquities perpetrated by the Muslims after their capture of the island of Nikiu.

The end of Byzantine rule in the east was a catastrophe so far reaching that it could hardly have occurred without some suffering being visited on the people of the area, and John's chronicle is an important reminder of that.

Source: *The Chronicle of John, bishop of Nikiu, translated from Zotenberg's Ethiopic text*, trans. R.H. Charles (London: Text and Translation Society, 1916), p. 184, 188 (spelling adapted).

While Herakleios' infirmity, the succession crisis in Constantinople and the alienation of the Monophysites might have played a part, the most significant factor was probably something much more mundane. After its 30-year conflict with Sassanid Persia, Byzantium was utterly exhausted and too weak to embark on a new war. It was all too easy for the Arabs to take advantage, to move in and to fill the power vacuum.

Figure 2.3 Section of the defensive walls of Thessalonica

2.6 The Balkans and the western provinces

While the titanic struggle, first with the Persians and then with the Arabs, unfolded in the east, Herakleios was compelled to leave the western areas much to themselves. In the Balkans, when Phokas had withdrawn the Byzantine army from the Danube to march on Constantinople and overthrow Maurice, he had effectively left the whole region open to the Avars and Slavs. No further forces were sent to the region and, once he had taken power, Herakleios sought to make peace with the Avar khan so that he could concentrate his efforts on defeating the Persians. This he succeeded in doing in 618, though the khan was to break the treaty in 626 and the Avars and Slavs resumed their advance southwards. Encountering no resistance, they were able to overrun the whole of the Balkans, right down to the tip of Southern Greece. That did not mean that the Byzantine presence was eradicated completely. On the coasts, cities that could be supplied by sea held out against the invaders, for the Avars had no fleet of their own. One of those cities was Thessalonica (see Figure 2.3). Like Constantinople, it had very strong fortifications and, like the capital again, was believed to have a supernatural defender in St Demetrius, a soldier-martyr who was credited with beating off successive Avar attempts to storm the city. Another stronghold lay to the south in Attica, where the acropolis of the old intellectual centre of Athens had been fortified and could be supplied through its port of Piraeus. There were two important Byzantine strongholds in the peninsula known as the Peloponnese or Morea. One was the port of Patras on the north-western coast, the other was Monemvasia, a virtually impregnable island linked to the mainland by a narrow causeway (see Figure 2.4). In these isolated toeholds, the Byzantines held out in a region that was now entirely dominated by their enemies.

Figure 2.4 Monemvasia as seen from mainland Greece with the city itself invisible behind the rock

Further to the west lay two Byzantine territories that were completely untroubled during Herakleios' tumultuous reign. One was the emperor's homeland of North Africa, where the Byzantine exarchate roughly corresponded with modern Tunisia and the coast of Libya. The main town was the port of Carthage, whose defensive wall and moat had been rebuilt in the previous century. Sicily had also been left untouched by the upheavals and serious consideration was given at times to moving the capital from Constantinople to the island's main town of Syracuse. Both North Africa and Sicily were fertile and productive, exporting a surplus of corn and oil, so they generated a useful tax income to help pay for the defence of other areas.

Unfortunately not all Byzantine territories in the west enjoyed North Africa and Sicily's immunity from attack. The precarious foothold established in Spain during the 550s was slowly being whittled away by a resurgent kingdom of the Visigoths and when Cartagena was captured in 624 the Byzantine presence in the area came to an end. Similarly, the Byzantine holdings in Italy were under constant attack from the Lombards who occupied most of the peninsula while the Byzantines held Apulia and Calabria, that is to say the heel and toe, and the areas around Ravenna and Rome. At least here the Byzantines were not facing as formidable an enemy as the Avars or Arabs. The Lombards might chip away at Byzantine territory but they were not strong enough to expel them from Italy altogether. Besides, the Lombards were as much threatened by the Avars as the Byzantines were. In 611, the Avars invaded northern Italy and wiped out a Lombard army. During moments of crisis like that, the Lombards were only too happy to remain at peace with the emperor. From a strategic viewpoint, the Byzantines also held a great advantage in the possession of Ravenna. Like Constantinople and Thessalonica, it was easily defensible, in this case because the marshes which surrounded it made it inapproachable by land. It could hold out indefinitely, even when the surrounding countryside had been lost, provided it could be resupplied by sea. The city acted as the seat of the Byzantine government for the region and its exarch managed as best he could to keep the Lombards at bay with the forces he could raise locally and occasionally by attempting to incite the king of the Franks to intervene (see Box 1.3).

There was, however, a distinct danger that the Byzantine position in Italy might be undermined by the same kind of alienation of the population as had occurred in Syria and Egypt. To the emperor's Latin-speaking subjects there, he was an increasingly remote figure. He and his servants were often referred to as 'Greeks' and their main impact on everyday life was their insistent demands for the payment of taxes. It was not only laypeople who suffered but the Church too. In 640, an exarch of Ravenna replenished his coffers by marching into Rome and breaking into the pope's treasury in the Lateran Palace. It is true that, on the face of it, there was no religious divide. Unlike the eastern provinces, Italy was solidly Catholic, apart from the Lombards who subscribed to another variant of Christianity: Arianism. Unfortunately, the rift between Catholics and Monophysites had serious ramifications in Italy. When Herakleios introduced his compromise formula of Monotheletism in 638, many Italians saw the new doctrine as a betrayal of the definition agreed at the Council of Chalcedon and the pope agreed with them. In 641, Pope John IV gathered a synod in Rome which condemned the new doctrine as heretical, creating yet another split in the Church.

The situation was exacerbated by the failure of the emperor to provide an effective defence for the city of Rome. Situated on the other side of the peninsula from the Byzantine headquarters at Ravenna, it was cruelly exposed to Lombard attacks. The pope often found himself in the same position as Patriarch Kyros in Alexandria, forced to combine the roles of leader of the Church with that of governor of the city. It was left to him to organise Rome's food and water supply, to maintain the defensive walls and to recruit and pay the soldiers who guarded them. Frequent pleas for aid were sent to Ravenna and Constantinople whenever the Lombards were pressing, as in the 590s, when Pope Gregory I had written impassioned letters to Emperor Maurice. Help was promised but never sent and in the end, Pope Gregory had been left with no alternative but to make his own separate peace with the Lombard King Agilulf, paying him from the papal treasury not to attack Rome.

Yet while it is tempting to conclude that the popes and the people of Italy must have been eager to break away from the overbearing influence of Constantinople, that was not in fact the case, at least not at this stage. For them, the emperor had been placed on earth by God for the protection of the Christian people. It was their duty to obey him, and to sever ties with him would be unthinkable, even when he neglected his duty and strayed into heresy. The link was illustrated on the coins issued in Rome which carried the emperor's portrait on the obverse and the pope's monograph on the back. Indeed, many of the popes came from Byzantine territory in the east and spoke Greek as their first language. Italy was as much part of the empire as Constantinople itself.

Figure 2.5 The Bosporus strait with Constantinople, modern Istanbul, in the foreground

Points to remember

- Frustrating though the lack of evidence may be, the years 602 to 642 were clearly a key period when the balance of power in the eastern Mediterranean was altered forever.
- The argument that the establishment of the Themes led to Byzantium's salvation in the 620s has now been discredited. Factors such as the defences of Constantinople, Herakleios' leadership, morale and economy seem more persuasive.
- The illness of Herakleios, the role of Islam and the disaffection of the Monophysite population have all been cited as possible reasons behind the rapid loss of the eastern provinces.
- The exhaustion of Byzantium after the long Persian war may also have been a factor.
- The Balkans and Italy were largely abandoned by Herakleios during the crisis in the east but the Byzantines retained fortified outposts in both regions.

Suggestions for further reading

Brown, Thomas S. (1984), *Gentlemen and Officers: Imperial Administration and Aristocratic Power in Byzantine Italy AD 554–800* (London: British School at Rome). A study of Byzantine rule in Italy which lays stress on how it differed from other parts of the empire and considers the extent to which the Roman legacy lingered on there.

Kaegi, Walter E. (1992), *Byzantium and the Early Islamic Conquests* (Cambridge: Cambridge University Press). An extremely detailed study of the Arab invasions of the 630s, focusing on Syria and Palestine. It does not cover Egypt.

Kaegi, Walter E. (2003), *Heraclius: Emperor of Byzantium* (Cambridge: Cambridge University Press). A detailed and scholarly survey of Herakleios' reign that seeks to explain his success against the Persians and his failure against the Arabs.

Kennedy, Hugh N. (2008), *The Great Arab Conquests: How the Spread of Islam Changed the World We Live In* (London: Phoenix). Presents a grand sweeping narrative of the whole of Arab expansion in the seventh and eighth centuries, from the Pyrenees to Transoxania, but it includes a very effective narrative of the conquest of Syria, Palestine and Egypt.

Pentcheva, Bissera V. (2006), *Icons and Power: The Mother of God in Byzantium* (University Park PA: Pennsylvania State University Press). Uses images and translated texts to show how the Virgin Mary as revealed in her icons came to be regarded as the protector of Constantinople.

3 The dark age (642–718)

If the latter part of the reign of Herakleios is poorly documented, the second half of the seventh century is a black hole. With Byzantium teetering on the brink of destruction, no one seems to have felt inspired to record events as they happened and they are only known from later sources. Increasingly, however, archaeology is helping to fill the gap and to suggest how it was that Byzantium once more weathered the storm.

3.1 The new enemy: the Umayyad caliphate

The conquest of the Byzantine eastern provinces was only the beginning of Arab expansion. In 652, they completed the conquest of Sassanid Persia and incorporated its territories into the new caliphate of Islam. At the same time, they pushed into Byzantine Armenia, the area annexed by Maurice after his treaty with Persia in 591, and forced its governor to accept their authority. The young Emperor Constans II reacted by mounting an expedition into Armenia in 653, something we only know about from the Armenian chronicler Sebeos. He briefly restored Byzantine authority there but by 661 Armenia was once again under Arab control. This further loss of territory was not the most sinister development as far as the Byzantines were concerned. Up to now, they had retained one vital advantage in that they had command of the sea, just as they had when fighting the Persians. As a desert people, the Arabs knew nothing about maritime matters and only waged war on land. Once they had the Egyptian and Syrian coasts under their control, however, they soon began to construct ships, using local labour. By 649, the fleet was ready to sail and it mounted a completely unexpected and devastating raid on the Byzantine island of Cyprus, followed by another on Rhodes in 653. Sooner or later the Byzantines would have to respond to this danger and they had the chance to do so in 655 when their fleet, commanded by Constans II himself, intercepted the Arab one off the southern coast of Asia Minor. Given their far greater experience of seamanship, the Byzantines should have won this so-called Battle of the Masts easily. But although both sides lost heavily, the Byzantines came off worst. The emperor only escaped when he changed clothes with a young sailor who then died fighting while Constans made his getaway in a swift vessel. 'The sea', wrote Theophanes, 'was dyed with Roman blood'.

Having defeated the Byzantines by sea and with an effective fleet at their disposal, the Arabs now had a huge advantage that the Persians had not possessed and they could strike at Constantinople itself by both land and sea. They may have mounted their first naval assault on the capital as early as the 650s. Luckily for the Byzantines, as is always the case, the enemy that faced them, though formidable, was not monolithic. Islam, like Christianity, had its schisms and splits. On the death of the Prophet Muhammad in 632, a caliph or representative had been appointed to lead the Faithful in his place. When the third caliph, Uthman, was murdered at Medina in 656, he was succeeded by Ali, cousin and son-in-law of the Prophet. Muawiyah, Uthman's nephew and the governor of Syria, blamed Ali for the murder and demanded vengeance. A civil war broke out that lasted for six years until Ali was murdered in January 661. Proclaimed as caliph in Jerusalem the following July, Muawiyah then moved the capital from Medina to Damascus. Thus began the period of the Umayyad caliphate (661–750), a colossal superpower that extended from the borders of India to Egypt and which, by 730, reached as far west as Spain.

To start with the events which brought the Umayyad caliphate into being were all to the advantage of the Byzantines. During the conflict with Ali, Muawiyah needed his northern border in Syria to be secure so that he could concentrate his forces on the internal struggle. So in 659 he made a truce with Constans II, agreeing not only to cease his attacks on the emperor's territory but to pay him an annual tribute of 365,000 gold pieces. The truce provided a vital breathing space which enabled Constans to travel west to Greece, Italy and Sicily to oversee the defence of those territories and possibly to set in train an administrative reorganisation of Asia Minor. The respite could not last for long once the Arab civil war was over though. In 662, an Arab naval attack on the island of Sicily signalled that the Umayyad caliphate was intent on renewing the offensive.

3.2 Constantinople under siege

Following Constans II's murder in 668, it was his son and successor, Constantine IV who had to face the Umayyad onslaught. At some point between 668 and 674, the Arabs made their first serious attempt to capture Constantinople. A large fleet set out from Syria, sailed through the Dardanelles, ravaged the coast of Thrace and captured Cyzicus on the Sea of Marmara to use as a forward base. There it was joined by a land army which had marched across Asia Minor and together they mounted a blockade of the Byzantine capital.

In spite of the gravity of the threat, Constantinople held out. The defences that had proved so effective in frustrating the plans of the Persians and Avars were still in place and the Arab army did not even attempt to cross the Bosporus and attack the Land Walls. The presence of a fleet gave them little advantage as any attempt to make a landing on Constantinople's seaward side was ruled out by the strong currents and the sea walls. Nor did the Arabs enjoy naval supremacy in the waters around the city. A very effective challenge was mounted by the Byzantine fleet which was well equipped with dromons, swift galleys that were propelled by both sail and oar. The oarsmen sat in two or three banks and the dromons were large enough to accommodate about 50 fighting men who were stationed on the tower near the main mast. At some point, the Byzantines apparently enhanced the dromon design by adding siphons at the prows. From these they were able to shoot a highly inflammable liquid which would set enemy ships alight, the first recorded use of so-called 'Greek fire'. These vessels fought running battles with the Arab fleet in the Sea of Marmara and the Byzantines seem to have had the best of it. Frustrated at every turn,

Figure 3.1 Mosaic of Emperor Constantine IV (668–685) and his court from the church of Sant'Apollinare in Classe, Ravenna

the Arab army and fleet withdrew and shortly afterwards, the Muslim world was once more convulsed by internal strife following the death of Muawiyah. Caliph Abd al-Malik concluded another truce in 686 with Constantine IV's successor (see Figure 3.1), Justinian II, promising to pay him a slave, a horse and a thousand gold pieces a day and to share with him the revenues of the island of Cyprus. Byzantium was granted another respite from its long and grinding war with the Umayyad caliphate.

Box 3.1 Greek fire

According to Theophanes, the formula for the composition of Greek fire was brought to Constantinople in the 670s by a Christian refugee from Syria called Kallinikos. To this day, no one can be exactly sure what that formula was because it was understandably a very closely guarded secret. All Theophanes says is that the weapon 'kindled the ships of the Arabs and burned them with their crews'. It was probably a mixture of ingredients that included sulphur, pitch, quicklime and even some crude oil, specially imported from the Caucasus where easily accessible surface deposits were then to be found. Equally mysterious is the mechanism fixed to the prows of Byzantine dromons by which this substance was ignited and then projected onto an enemy vessel. In September 2002, a replica mechanism was constructed by Byzantinist John Haldon and others, based on the hints and allusions made in Byzantine texts. It consisted of a chamber in which the flammable mixture was heated, along with a pump and a siphon to ignite and project it. Although the reconstructed apparatus worked to an extent, it clearly needed very calm conditions and an enemy ship that was virtually alongside to have any hope of success. The chances of the operators accidentally setting fire to their own vessel must have been very high (see Figure 3.2).

It is therefore unlikely that Greek fire was a decisive wonder weapon. Although Theophanes credits it with seeing off the first Arab siege, Patriarch Nikephoros makes no mention of it whatsoever in his account of exactly the same events. The Arab fleet was certainly destroyed off southern Asia as it sailed home in 678 but that was the result of a storm, not of any Byzantine secret weapon. The real value of Greek fire may in fact have been purely psychological. It was often fired from gaping bronze figureheads in the shape of dragons and lions. It apparently emitted a noise like thunder as it shot out of the siphon, would burn on water and was almost impossible to put out. All that would doubtless have been enough to terrify the crews of enemy vessels without the necessity of a direct hit, especially if they had never encountered the weapon before.

Source: John Haldon, '"Greek fire" revisited: current and recent research', in *Byzantine Style, Religion and Civilization: In Honour of Sir Steven Runciman*, ed. Elizabeth Jeffreys (Cambridge: Cambridge University Press, 2006), pp. 290–325

Figure 3.2 Reconstruction of the use of Greek fire: a ship is ignited but only at very close range

Unlike that of 659, the truce of 686 was brought to an end by the Byzantines rather than by the Arabs. The young and inexperienced emperor Justinian II was eager to restore Byzantine authority in Armenia, resented having to share the revenues of Cyprus and objected to the type of gold coins in which the Arabs paid their tribute. His rash move led to a serious defeat at the hands of the Arabs at Sebastopolis in eastern Asia Minor during the summer of 692. Arab raids into Byzantine territory resumed, while in North Africa Carthage was lost in 698. In the summer of 717 the Arabs marched a powerful army across Asia Minor to link up with a fleet that had sailed up the Aegean and into the Sea of Marmara. The army was then ferried across the Dardanelles to the European side, where it constructed a series of earthworks parallel to the Land Walls. This was the most serious assault to date, with Constantinople blockaded by both land and sea.

Yet the Byzantine capital held out once more. The Byzantine fleet was as effective as it had been during the first siege. This time both Theophanes and Patriarch Nikephoros agree that Greek fire was deployed and credit it with sinking 20 Arab supply ships. The Byzantines also made use of a tactic that was to stand them in very good stead in the future: that of paying another people to attack their enemies. During the 680s, a Turkic people, the Bulgars, had moved into the northern Balkans (see Section 3.5 and Box 0.1). The Byzantines had viewed this development with alarm but after they had failed to drive the Bulgars out, they pragmatically turned the situation to their advantage. The Arabs in their long trench in front of the Land Walls suddenly found themselves under attack from behind by the Bulgars, who had almost certainly been paid to do so by the Byzantines. Theophanes claimed that 22,000 Arabs were massacred, though that is probably a gross exaggeration.

In the end though, neither the secret weapon nor the Bulgar allies decided the issue but something much more basic: the problem of supply. The Arabs were not planning to take Constantinople by storm but to starve the defenders into submission. The flaw in the plan was that the Byzantines had known for some time that an attack was being prepared and they had stockpiled food accordingly. The emperor had ordered that all citizens should provide themselves with enough food for three years and those who could not do so should leave the city. There was no shortage of water either, thanks to the huge cisterns beneath the streets. Ironically it was the Arabs who began to run short of food, especially after their supply ships had been sunk. As it happened, the winter of 717–718 was particularly severe, making it impossible to live off the land. The Arabs were reduced to eating the camels that they had brought with them as beasts of burden and when they were gone they had to make do with roots and leaves. Although reinforcements arrived the following spring, it was by then fast becoming clear that the blockade was even less likely to take Constantinople than a direct assault and the siege was lifted on 15 August 718.

3.3 The battle for Asia Minor

Constantinople and Byzantium as a whole would never have been able to survive if the state had not retained Asia Minor. Like Constantinople, this wide tract of territory possessed certain geographical advantages that made it difficult to overrun and occupy. While Syria and Palestine had no geographical barriers against invaders from the east, with the loss of Armenia the Byzantine frontier with the Umayyad caliphate ran alongside the anti-Taurus and Taurus mountain ranges (see Figure 3.3). The barrier made it much harder to move a large army further west and much more awkward to keep it supplied once it was on the central plateau of Asia Minor, with a very long march ahead of it to reach Constantinople. The terrain was slightly easier if you invaded further to the north but the winters there were more severe. In the event of a reverse, the withdrawal route would be blocked by snow for several months of the year. These physical realities explain why the hitherto unstoppable Arab advance halted at the Taurus range in the 650s.

Even if the mountain barrier prevented the Arabs from invading and occupying Asia Minor in the way they had Syria and Egypt, it did not hinder them from making smaller annual raids into Byzantine territory. They were able partly to circumvent the obstacle by acquiring two important forward bases. One was Tarsus in the area known as Cilicia just to the south of the Taurus Mountains, which they took in 673. The other was Melitene, which changed hands frequently but was usually under Arab rule during the seventh to early tenth centuries. This town was extremely important to the Arabs because it was situated on the River Euphrates and lay to the west of the Taurus range. They could retire there at the end of the campaigning season without having to withdraw over the mountains. Their armies would often spend the entire year in Asia Minor moving from place to place, looting and plundering from their base at Melitene. These raids did not result in the loss of territory. Theophanes tells us, for example, that in the year 666–667, the Arab general Fadalah ibn Ubaid marched west from Melitene, penetrating as far as

Figure 3.3 The Taurus Mountains

Chalcedon. At the end of the campaigning season, though, Fadalah withdrew back over the Taurus Mountains. He did leave a garrison of 5,000 men in the town of Amorion but that was soon retaken by the Byzantines. On the other hand, even if no territory was lost, enormous damage was inflicted, especially on the cities of Asia Minor. Most of them were captured and sacked at some point during the seventh and eighth centuries. Pergamon, for example, was taken and destroyed in about 715 and it was never resettled, just left as the poignant ruins that can still be seen today (see Figure 3.4). Sardis suffered a similar fate around the same time and it had only just been rebuilt after an earlier sack by the Persians in 616. The Arab raiders would gather up all the moveable goods that they could as booty. These included people, who would be marched back to Syria to be sold as slaves.

The Byzantines had to decide how to respond to this new challenge. Clearly the Arabs could not be allowed to devastate Byzantine territory unchallenged, but what was the best way to confront them? Meeting them head-on with a large army might seem the obvious strategy but it was risky. A complete victory, like that at Ninevah in 627, would always be a rare outcome and, though exhilarating, would not necessarily provide long-term respite. Conversely, there was always the possibility of a disastrous defeat like that at Yarmuk in 636 which had left Syria and Egypt without any effective defence. Although it is nowhere specifically documented, it would appear that this was the point when the Byzantines came to prefer alternatives to direct military confrontation. As Anna Komnene later commented, a general was expected to win but not necessarily by force of arms: other

Figure 3.4 The ruins of Pergamon today

means were equally acceptable ways of achieving the same goal. One of the favourite other means was employing others to attack Byzantium's enemies, in the way that the Bulgars were turned against the Arabs during the 717–718 siege of Constantinople (see Section 3.2). More regular use was made of another Turkic group, the Khazars, who lived in the Caucasus and what is now Georgia and who had already aided Herakleios in his struggle against the Persians. In 704, Justinian II married the sister of their khan, beginning an association that was to last throughout the century. Since their lands lay to the north of the Umayyad caliphate, the Khazars were well placed to mount raids into it, thus deflecting Arab attention away from Asia Minor.

It was not that the Byzantines had given up on doing any fighting themselves, it was merely that henceforth they did so in a different way. Rather than attempting to garrison the whole length of the frontier, they pulled their army back into the interior of Asia Minor and divided it between administrative districts known as Themes (see Section 2.3). The thinking here was presumably that in this way the defenders could not be bypassed by raiding parties and there would be a force ready to meet the Arabs wherever they went. It was important though for those commanders who were stationed well back from the frontier to know when and from where the intruders were coming. Hence the beacon that was placed on a tower of the fortress of Loulon, which stood on the border with the caliphate near Tarsus. This was lit when an Arab raiding force was observed to be gathering and the signal passed along a chain of similar hilltop beacons all the way to Constantinople itself. Once the Arabs were known to be on the move, there was the question of how to deal with them. Byzantine commanders generally adopted 'shadowing tactics'. Instead of offering a pitched battle, they would follow the Arab armies as they headed home, picking off stragglers and recovering some of the booty and captives as the opportunity allowed. The commanders could be sure that there were only certain routes that the raiders could take because there were a limited number of passes through the Taurus Mountains. They could usually guess which one the Arabs were heading for and if they moved swiftly they could have a force in place ready to mount ambushes as the enemy went through the pass, although the aim once more was to damage and harass, not to destroy. It was a cautious and unheroic strategy, a far cry from the rhetoric of holy war during the reign of Herakleios, but it could be very effective. In around 704, a Byzantine force inflicted heavy casualties on an Umayyad army that had just raided Cilicia and was heading home via one of the passes.

Box 3.2 The new tactics in a military manual

On Skirmishing is a manual of military tactics (see Section 1.4) that was compiled at some point in the later tenth century CE, apparently on the orders of Emperor Nikephoros II Phokas (963–969). The tactics described in the book were those that the Byzantines deployed against the Arab raids of the seventh and eighth centuries and which had largely been abandoned by the time that the work was compiled. This section describes what the commander of the Byzantine force was to do once he caught up with the raiders. In the first place, they were to be shadowed closely:

When [the general] is informed that the enemy have begun to move again, he should immediately set out to follow ... Let the general ride along at a distance and take every precaution to avoid being discovered following behind. He should proceed very cautiously and should order the units following the enemy more closely to keep a sharp eye out in case the enemy have left some detachments behind to ambush the men following them as well as the general himself.

When the Arabs were distracted, that was the moment to strike:

On reaching safe ground, the general should conceal his troops. With a few horsemen, let him draw more closely to the enemy. He should mount a high vantage point and hasten to get a good look at them. As they move out for attack and scatter for plunder, the general should remain at that spot until the third or fourth hour of the day. He should study the battle formation of the emir and form a careful estimate of the number of his men. When the troops going out to raid have gotten far enough from the emir's battle formation so they cannot retreat to it again or so that they will not even be aware of an attack upon the formation, since each man will be rushing to get to the villages and gather as much booty as possible, then the general should set his own battle line in proper order and launch his attack against that of the emir, now undermanned, and with the aid of God he will be victorious and bring about the complete and utter destruction of the enemy.

Source: *Three Byzantine Military Treatises*, ed. and trans. George T. Dennis (Washington, DC: Dumbarton Oaks, 1985), pp. 171–3.

3.4 The reorganisation of Asia Minor

The Byzantine response to the Umayyad threat went far beyond the adoption of new military tactics. We have already seen that George Ostrogorsky argued that Herakleios' triumph against the Persians was the result of his reorganisation of Asia Minor into military districts known as Themes. His argument seems unlikely as there is no evidence for the existence of the Themes at that time, but the reorganisation was certainly made at some point. Historians now generally agree that the most likely period was probably between the truce made by Caliph Muawiyah with Emperor Constans II in 659 and Constans' death in 668. It was then that the seven original Themes of Opsikion, Optimaton, Boukellarion, Armeniakon, Anatolikon, Thrakesion and Kibyrrhaiot were first brought into being. They certainly existed by the year 685 for they were mentioned in a letter sent by Emperor Justinian II to the pope.

But while the existence of the Themes in the second half of the seventh century is not in doubt, how they actually operated at this stage is still a matter for debate, largely because of the paucity of the source material. It would appear that each Theme had its own army and that the governor of the Theme, the strategos, was also the commander of the army. Thus their creation was probably connected with the introduction of new tactics to counter the Arab raids. The armies in the Themes would presumably ensure that there was defence in depth so that wherever the Arabs struck, there would be a force to oppose them. Ostrogorsky, however, went much further than that, claiming that the establishment of the Themes involved a radical redistribution of land. In place of salaries, the soldiers or *stratiotai* who made up the Theme armies were given smallholdings from which they were expected not only to provide maintenance for themselves and their families but also to pay for their weapons, armour and perhaps a horse. The rest of the land in the Theme was farmed by free peasants who paid taxes rather than serving in the army. For Ostrogorsky, the beauty of the system was twofold. In the first place it removed the huge burden on the treasury of feeding, equipping and paying the troops as their smallholdings now provided for that. At the same time, the free peasants contributed taxes to the treasury. Secondly, it ensured that the Byzantine armies were composed of dependable 'native' troops rather than unreliable foreign mercenaries. It was this way of providing for defence that ensured not only Byzantium's survival in this period of crisis, but its future recovery as a great power in the region.

Ostrogorsky's view was clearly and compellingly advanced and was to prove extremely influential. Not all scholars agreed with him, however, pointing out that there is almost no contemporary evidence to support the idea that the establishment of the Themes involved the simultaneous distribution of land to soldier-farmers. Ostrogorsky did cite contemporary evidence to support his thesis, such as a legal text known as *The Farmer's Law* from around 700. But while this document frequently refers to free peasants, it never mentions soldier-farmers, nor do any of the other texts. The fact was that most of Ostrogorsky's evidence was from much later, mainly the tenth century. Imperial legislation from the 940s certainly does refer to 'properties by which military services are supported', suggesting that military smallholdings did exist by that time. That, of course, does not mean that they did in the seventh century or that they were an integral and essential part of the Themes from their inception.

Box 3.3 George Ostrogorsky (1902–1976) and the Themes

Born in St Petersburg before the Russian Revolution, Ostrogorsky pursued his higher education in Germany in the 1920s and spent most of his career at the University of Belgrade, in what was then Yugoslavia. His most influential publication was his *Geschichte des byzantinischen Staates* which appeared in 1940. The central argument of the book is that the Themes, the soldier-farmers and the free peasantry were the foundation of Byzantine greatness. By the same token, Ostrogorsky argued, when during the eleventh century great landowners dismantled the Themes, absorbed the military holdings, reduced the free peasants to serfs and replaced the patriotic soldier-farmers with greedy foreign mercenaries, the state was doomed.

In presenting the history of Byzantium in this way, Ostrogorsky was by no means original. He was merely the last in a long line of Russian historians who thought along these lines, for the theory also appears in the work of Fyodor Ivanovich Uspensky (1845–1928) and others. They made much of the fact that before the tenth century, peasants in the Byzantine empire appear not to have been serfs but free men who owned and farmed their own land. An eighth-century text known as *The Farmer's Law* certainly suggests that (see Section 7.6). This perception fitted in very closely with the romantic ideals of nineteenth-century Slavophilism. August von Haxthausen-Abbenburg (1792–1866) and others argued that Russia's history had taken a more positive turn than that of Western Europe because it had avoided the corrupting evils first of feudalism that oppressed the peasantry by tying them to the land as serfs, and then industrialisation which tore them from the soil and herded them into factories. Instead, Russia had preserved unsullied the ancient institution of the village commune, where peasants held their land communally and divided it equally. This system, the Slavophiles believed, created a unity that was the source of the strength and patriotism of the Russian people under the benevolent leadership of the tsar. It was an outlook that strongly influenced Russian literature of the time, such as Leo Tolstoy's *War and Peace* (1869). There the simple peasant-soldier Platon Karatayev, 'the epitome of kind-heartedness and all things rounded and Russian', is contrasted with the disillusioned, Westernised aristocrat, Pierre Bezukhov.

Uspensky transferred this outlook to Byzantium and Ostrogorsky's great contribution was to make it widely available beyond Russia by expounding it lucidly in a Western European language. His work was later translated from German into English by Joan Hussey as *History of the Byzantine State*, and was to appear in ten other languages as well. That accounts for the enormous influence that Ostrogorsky was to have on the perception and teaching of Byzantine history throughout the world. Like all academic theories, the championing of the Themes and the soldier-farmers should not be accepted uncritically but carefully weighed up in the light of the evidence that supports it.

Source: Danuta M. Gorecki, 'The Slavic theory in Russian pre-Revolutionary historiography of the Byzantine farmer community', *Byzantion* 56 (1986), pp. 77–107.

While it is unlikely, given the lack of verifiable information, that we will ever know more about the origins of the Themes than we do now, in another area archaeology and surviving physical evidence provide important clues to the changes that were taking place in Asia Minor at this time. The Persian and Arab attacks had seen the destruction of many of the old Roman cities there, so that by 840, according to an Arab geographer, there were only five left. That remark is slightly misleading. The old Graeco-Roman cities, grouped around a forum with impressive public buildings such as theatres and libraries, had certainly gone, but they had been replaced by a new kind of settlement, better suited to the conditions of the time. They were often smaller and had been re-established on more defensible sites. Most were placed near a kastro, a castle or fortified hilltop to which the inhabitants could flee when the Arab armies approached.

One example was Sardis in the Thrakesion Theme. The ancient Roman city on the plain was largely abandoned and the new city clustered around the nearby acropolis, on

Figure 3.5 The new site of Ephesus inland from the port with the kastro above the town

which a fortress was built in the later seventh century. There was only one extremely steep approach to the castle, for the other sides are sheer cliffs. The Byzantines used the technology developed in the Land Walls of Constantinople to enhance the geographical advantage of the Sardis acropolis. A bastion was built on the approach side so that attackers could be hit by arrows from concealed slits even before they got near the walls. The same happened at Ephesus, also in the Thrakesion Theme. The old city on the coast was abandoned and the entire population moved several miles inland to be closer to the castle in time of need (see Figure 3.5).

The sites of old and new Sardis and Ephesus are still clearly visible above ground. That is not the case with Amorion in the Anatolikon Theme in the centre of Asia Minor. The city ceased to be inhabited at some point in the fourteenth century so the site disappeared for centuries. Only from 1987 has archaeology uncovered the lost Byzantine city. Amorion had less need to be moved or remodelled in the period of crisis, as it had already gone through that process relatively recently, in the fifth century CE. With the needs of defence in mind, its planners had chosen a site with abundant groundwater, thus dispensing with the need for a vulnerable aqueduct which could easily be cut in times of siege, and had erected a stout defensive wall, three kilometres long. It would appear that during the crisis of the seventh century, measures were taken to strengthen these fortifications. A second line of defence was created by building a wall around the acropolis, the hill in the centre of the city, so that the population could take refuge there if the lower wall was breached. This was something that marked Byzantium out from Western Europe where the old cities for the most part completely disappeared when Roman rule came to an end during the fifth century, rather than transforming themselves in this way.

The strangest of these defensive cities were to be found in the Cappadocia region around Caesarea in the centre of Asia Minor. There, the inhabitants used the particularly soft volcanic rock to their advantage, burrowing down and creating settlements below the surface, complete with underground chapels and granaries, that could provide a place of refuge when danger threatened. One of them, at Derinkuyu, covered some 2,500 square metres and could have accommodated up to 20,000 people. Underground settlements like this had been a feature of the region for centuries but they must have come into their own when marauding Arab armies were in the vicinity. The entrance to the settlement could be sealed with a millstone so that no one on the surface would have any idea that the city and its inhabitants were concealed beneath their feet (see Figure 3.6).

Coinage can also throw light on what was happening on the ground and on the economic changes that were taking place in this period. Copper coins, the guide to the level of basic everyday transactions, seem almost to have disappeared from circulation in Asia Minor: scarcely any have been found in a seventh century context on archaeological sites. That would suggest a severe decline in commercial activity as the old Roman cities,

Figure 3.6 The chapel of an underground city in Cappadocia, Asia Minor, present-day Turkey

once centres of trade, were destroyed one after another. On the other hand, the gold coin, known as the nomisma, continued to be minted. Introduced by Constantine the Great in 309, it maintained its fineness of 23 carats and weight of 4.55 grams throughout the period of crisis (see Figure 2.1). This was another crucial difference between Byzantium and Western Europe where the Frankish, Lombard, Anglo-Saxon and Visigothic kings lacked the bullion to issue gold coins in any number. The continuation of gold coinage meant that the Byzantine emperors had the ability to levy taxes, whether on land and produce or as customs duties payable on goods bought and sold at annual fairs. The survival of cities in a reconstituted form must have greatly assisted this economic continuity. They were not just defensive outposts or the headquarters of the strategos of a Theme, but the administrative centres from which the revenue was collected. Consequently, the Byzantine emperors could regularly refill their treasury and this gave them a surplus to spend on defence projects such as equipping the fleet with Greek fire, maintaining the walls of Constantinople and paying allies like the Bulgars and Khazars to attack the Arabs. There was undoubtedly an economic element to Byzantium's survival even though so little is known about it.

3.5 The Balkans and the western provinces

The constant threat from the Umayyad caliphate meant that most of Byzantium's resources had to be concentrated on defending Asia Minor during these years, to the comparative neglect of the Balkans and the western provinces. Fortunately, the danger in the Balkans was fading. Although much of the area had been overrun, after 626 the Avar khanate, which had been the driving force for the attack on Constantinople, had gone into decline and fragmented. The Slavs had thrown off Avar domination and they were content just to occupy and cultivate the land that they had occupied, cherishing no ambitions to expand further. The Byzantines exploited the new situation as much as they could. In the summer of 688, Justinian II led a military expedition into Thrace and marched through Slav territory to Thessalonica. It was not an attempt to reconquer the area. The emperor merely stayed for a short time in Thessalonica and then marched back, his army being mauled in ambushes as it went. However, he had made his presence felt in the region and he initiated a policy aimed at exploiting the Balkans for the benefit of Asia Minor. During the expedition he rounded up a large number of able-bodied Slavs, some of whom joined him voluntarily, some not, and had them ferried across the Dardanelles to Asia Minor. There they were settled on unoccupied land in the Opsikion Theme, which was thus brought back into cultivation and began to yield a tax revenue once more. The policy had its drawbacks. In 692, Justinian II took a large contingent of Slavs with him when he confronted the Arabs at Sebastopolis, but the unwilling recruits deserted to the enemy and helped to rout the Byzantines. Nevertheless, these were the first steps towards the integration of the invading Slavs.

What prevented that happening at this stage was the penetration into the Balkans of another aggressive Turkic people, the Bulgars. A group of them led by their khan, Asparukh, crossed the Danube in 680 and began to settle in the area between the river and the Balkan Mountains (see Section 3.5 and Box 0.1). Emperor Constantine IV understandably viewed their arrival with alarm and sent an army to drive them out. The significant Bulgar victory at the Battle of Ongala ensured that they were there to stay. They intermarried with the local Slavs and eventually adopted their language and integrated with them, establishing a khanate that was not a collection of tribes like the Slavs to the south, but a unitary state with its own heavily fortified capital city, Pliska. The Bulgars soon gave further proof of their military prowess. It was they who ambushed Justinian II's army when it returned from Thessalonica in 688. In 712, they mounted an unexpected raid on the suburbs of Constantinople, rounding up many citizens who had crossed the Golden Horn to attend weddings and festivals, taking their jewellery and silver plate with them. Accepting the inevitable, the Byzantines did their best to do what they had with the Slavs and turn the unwelcome presence of the aggressive Bulgars to their advantage. Justinian II made use of their assistance to seize back the throne in 705 and they were later drafted in to attack the Arabs during the siege of Constantinople in 717–718.

As for Italy, the Byzantine territories there were relatively free from trouble during the later seventh century. The Lombards were much less of a danger than they had been, for they had abandoned the Arian version of Christianity in 672 and so were now co-religionists, unlike the Muslim Arabs and pagan Bulgars. They ceased for the time being to attack Rome and other Byzantine cities. What did give cause for concern was the possible alienation of the people there as a result of the ongoing dispute with the pope over the doctrine of Monotheletism (see Section 2.6). The loss of Egypt in 642 might have swayed Constans II to abandon his grandfather's policy, since with scarcely any Monophysite Christians remaining under Byzantine rule, the need for the compromise formula no longer existed. He may, however, have had plans for the reconquest of the lost provinces and that would explain why in 648 he issued a decree confirming the doctrine of Monotheletism and forbidding any further discussion on the nature of Christ. The reaction in Rome was exactly the same as it had been in 641. Pope Martin I convened a synod in the Lateran palace in October 649 and condemned the doctrine as before. Constans regarded this as a simple matter of insubordination. In 653, he ordered the exarch of Ravenna to send a snatch squad to Rome to kidnap the unfortunate Pope Martin, who was bundled onto a ship bound for Constantinople. There he was brought to trial on a charge of plotting to overthrow the emperor and was sentenced to exile at Cherson on the other side of the Black Sea, where he died shortly after. Constans II also punished the papacy by being ostentatiously favourable to the archbishop of Ravenna, the first step to making him the primary bishop in Italy so as to cut down the pope's authority.

The emperor probably then regarded the matter as closed. A few years later, he made his truce with Caliph Muawiyah, which removed the Arab threat to his borders for the time being. Given that the Lombards appeared to have subsided into quiescence, it might have seemed a good time to take advantage of the respite and restore Byzantine rule to the whole of Italy. So in the summer of 663, Constans II landed at Taranto with an army and made his way northwards, capturing cities from the Lombards as he went. But when he tried to take Naples, the defences and Lombard resistance proved too strong and he was forced to give up. So instead, Constans took his army to Rome. If the pope and the people of the city were expecting deliverance from their troubles, they were disappointed, for it would seem that the emperor had come to collect not to deliver. His troops stripped the bronze tiles from the roofs of many of the churches and had them shipped off to Constantinople. Twelve days later, Constans left Rome and headed south, ultimately crossing to Sicily and taking up residence in Syracuse.

These were hardly the actions of a protector and liberator and combined with the emperor's intransigent stance over Monotheletism and his cruel treatment of Pope Martin to make him extremely unpopular in Italy. In the summer of 668, while bathing at Syracuse, he was murdered by being struck on the head with a soap dish by one of his attendants. A local army commander called Mezizios proclaimed himself emperor in Sicily, doubtless hoping to take advantage of the ill feeling against Constans to garner support. The rebellion was short-lived, as loyal troops from Africa and Italy were shipped in to crush it. Even so, Constans' successor, Constantine IV who had been administering Constantinople in his absence, seems to have realised the dangers of his father's policy in the area. He decided to break with Monotheletism for which he had neither love nor need. In 680 he convened a synod in Constantinople, known as the Sixth Ecumenical Council, which condemned the doctrine and so restored good relations with the pope and dampened down resentment against rule from Constantinople and Ravenna.

While the Byzantines had at least managed to hold the line in the Balkans and Italy, there was a marked turn for the worse in North Africa. After Egypt fell to the Arabs in 642, the province was increasingly vulnerable to invasion. As early as 647, Arab armies began their incursions into the province and by 670 the Byzantines had largely been pushed back into the hinterland of the main town of Carthage. The end came in the spring of 698 when Carthage finally fell and the old exarchate came to an end.

Points to remember

- No one will ever know precisely why Byzantium survived in the seventh century, largely because we are so poorly informed about events. All historians can do is advance plausible theories based on the limited evidence.
- It was significant that Byzantium retained Asia Minor even though the Balkans had been overrun and North Africa was permanently lost in 698.
- Archaeology and numismatics have helped to reveal an economic element in Byzantium's survival.
- In the Balkans the pastoral and unwarlike Slavs presented little threat but the replacement of the Avars with the equally aggressive Bulgars placed a barrier to a Byzantine reconquest of the area.
- In Italy, occasional stormy relations with the pope did not necessarily mean that the Byzantine position there was weak, as long as the Lombards remained quiescent.

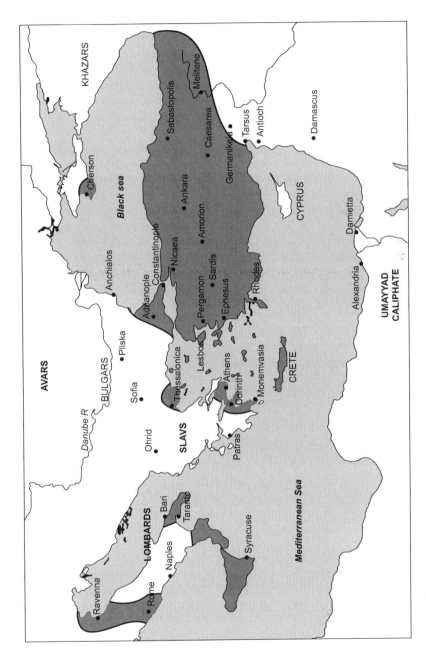

Map 3.1 Byzantium in 740

Suggestions for further reading

Cooper, J.E. and Decker, Michael J. (2012), *Life and Society in Byzantine Cappadocia* (Basingstoke and New York: Palgrave Macmillan). Discusses one particular region of Asia Minor and the kind of defensive cities to be found there.

Decker, Michael J. (2016), *The Byzantine Dark Ages* (London and New York: Bloomsbury). A useful survey of the archaeological evidence from this obscure period, focusing on Asia Minor and the Balkans.

Haldon, John F. (2016), *The Empire that Would Not Die: The Paradox of Eastern Roman Survival, 640–740* (Cambridge MA: Harvard University Press). Supplementing Haldon's earlier work below, this book explores some of the evidence that has come to light over the past 25 years and considers possible environmental factors.

Haldon, John F. (1990), *Byzantium in the Seventh Century* (Cambridge: Cambridge University Press). A landmark text in the efforts of scholars to understand this troubled century, although many of the issues it grapples with are not resolved in the book and are still not today.

Ostrogorsky, George. (1968, 2nd revised edition), *A History of the Byzantine State*, trans. Joan M. Hussey (Oxford: Blackwell). Ostrogorsky's best-known and most accessible work in which he presents his argument that the Themes were the main reason for Byzantium's survival and recovery.

Richards, Jeffrey. (1979), *The Popes and the Papacy in the Early Middle Ages, 476–752* (London: Routledge and Kegan Paul). This work traces relations between the popes and the emperor and stresses that in spite of occasional rifts, like that over Monotheletism, the papacy was not attempting to distance itself from Constantinople at this time.

4 The beginnings of the revival (718–820)

Justinian II was the last of the descendants of Herakleios to rule over Byzantium. In 695, he was overthrown by one of his generals, Leontios, who ordered that the ex-emperor's nose and tongue be split open before he was sent off into exile at Cherson. Leontios ruled for three years before he was in turn supplanted by Tiberios III Apsimar. Then in 705, the exiled Justinian II returned to Constantinople with an army of Bulgars and succeeded in entering the city by crawling in through a water pipe with a few companions. Restored to power, Justinian II took a bloody revenge on those who had ousted him. The ex-emperors Leontios and Tiberios III were both beheaded but their adherents were impaled or sewn into sacks and thrown into the sea to drown. After six years, Justinian was toppled once more and this time he was murdered, bringing the Herakleian dynasty to an end. Three more short-reigned emperors followed until in 717 Leo, the strategos of the Anatolikon Theme, seized power and the new North Syrian dynasty took over.

Periods of instability such as that between 695 and 717 were a recurring feature of Byzantine politics. The losers in the struggles were sometimes murdered, as Tiberios III, Leontios and ultimately Justinian II were, but more often they were only mutilated in some way, usually by castration and blinding by having a red-hot iron held over the eyes. Both punishments ensured that the victim could not make a political comeback since eunuchs were debarred from the imperial office and a blind man could scarcely fulfil its demands. The slitting of the nose and tongue that was inflicted on Justinian II was seldom used thereafter precisely because it had not prevented him from returning to the throne. Although mutilation was seen at the time as a merciful alternative to a violent death, it has helped to give Byzantium a bad name for cruelty, intrigue and factionalism. In fact, Byzantium was not so very unusual. In the days before elections and legislative assemblies, violent removal of a leader and their faction was the way in which the political process was worked out, not only in Byzantium but also in the Islamic world and the Christian west, where mutilation was by no means unknown. Too great a focus on the details of such upheavals and the vicious acts that accompanied them can obscure the wider picture. In the case of the century that followed the extinction of the Herakleian dynasty, a great deal of attention has been lavished on the dispute over icon veneration and the brutal persecution to which it occasionally gave rise. Behind the infighting, Byzantium was slowly progressing along the road to recovery.

4.1 The North Syrian dynasty

There was little sign of recovery when the new emperor Leo III took power, for he had been on the throne for less than six months when he had to face a crisis that could have ended not only his reign but Byzantium's very existence: the Arab siege of 717–18 (see Section 3.2). The Arabs withdrew in August 718 but that did not mean that the threat was over. The annual raids continued and in 727 an Umayyad force reached as far west as Nicaea, just 90 kilometres from Constantinople. As the years went by though, Byzantine shadowing tactics and military organisation began to pay off. In the spring of 740, news reached Constantinople that a huge Arab army had crossed the Taurus Mountains and had marched into Cappadocia where it was rounding up large numbers of men, women and children to take back to Syria as slaves. Leo III gathered his forces and headed for the area. He did not attempt to intercept the main Arab army which was, in any case, well on its way home by the time he reached Cappadocia. The Byzantines did, however, catch up with and surround the rearguard close to the town of Akroinon. When the trap was closed, most of the Arabs perished along with their commanders, although some did manage to break out and get back to Syria. It was the first time that a Byzantine army had worsted an Arab force in the field.

With the Arab defeats of 718 and 741, it is possible to discern a certain optimism during Leo III's reign. He undertook some internal reforms as if preparing his state for the future. In 720, he started reissuing silver coins after their production had tailed off in the 680s. At 1.99 grams, the new Miliaresion was lighter than previous silver coins but it circulated very widely and its design remained largely unchanged for centuries (see Figure 4.1). He began a reform of the administration and the collection of taxes and an overhaul of the legal system. At the very end of his reign, a new compendium of law, known as the Ekloga, was promulgated. That the emperor could now attend to such matters indicates that he was no longer preoccupied with mere survival.

Figure 4.1 A silver Miliaresion issued under Emperor Leo V (813–820)

Things continued to improve under Leo's son and successor, Constantine V (741–775). He had a difficult start to his reign when he had to ward off a revolt headed by his brother-in-law, Artavasdos. Once he was established in power, however, he set about restoring Constantinople to its former glory. The repeated sieges of the period of crisis had taken their toll. The city had become depopulated partly because non-essential inhabitants had been moved out to preserve the food supply in the expectation of an Arab attack and partly because of the recurring outbreaks of plague. During the 750s, Constantine brought in settlers from Greece and the Greek islands and overhauled the food and water supply to provide for the growing number of inhabitants. He shipped in large contingents of labourers from other areas to restore the aqueduct of Valens, which had been destroyed by the Avars during the 626 siege.

Constantine V was probably also responsible for some far-reaching military reforms, although because of the lack of contemporary testimony these have to be pieced together from hints and later evidence. The Theme armies had provided in-depth defence for Asia Minor during the seventh-century crisis but they had certain drawbacks. One of them was that their leaders, the strategoi, had wide powers and considerable independence. They could use those to stage a revolt, as Constantine V knew only too well. Artavasdos, who had challenged him for the throne in 741, had been strategos of the Opsikion Theme. His own father exemplified the problem, for Leo III had been strategos of the Anatolikon Theme before he seized the throne. It was during Constantine's reign, or that of his father, that the larger themes started to be subdivided to avoid too much power being concentrated in the hands of one man.

It would appear that it was also during Constantine's reign that an alternative military force to the Theme armies emerged, the Tagmata. They were an elite of professional soldiers, paid salaries directly from the imperial treasury and so directly dependent on the emperor. Consequently, the Tagmata troops were fiercely loyal to Constantine V, providing him with a personal command that he could lead against his internal and external enemies. In later years, command of the Tagmata came to be delegated to a new high-ranking officer known as the domestic of the Scholai. He was to become the most senior commander in the Byzantine army, outranking the strategos of a Theme. These military reforms came at a very opportune moment, for by 741 the Umayyad Caliphate was spiralling into terminal decline. Riven by infighting, it was no longer able to mount its annual raids across the Taurus Mountains. Instead, Constantine V was able to go on the offensive. He captured Germanikeia in 747 and Melitene in 750. He knew that he could not hold the latter permanently, so he evacuated its population and then destroyed its fortifications before withdrawing westwards. There was no question at this stage of recovering land beyond the Taurus range but the propaganda value of these successes must have been immense.

4.2 Iconoclasm

Given their achievements, one would naturally expect Leo III and Constantine V to have been celebrated in their own time and remembered ever afterwards as the architects of Byzantium's successful fight back against the Arabs. Yet that was emphatically not the case. All our surviving sources, including Theophanes Confessor and the Patriarch Nikephoros, are deeply hostile to them. They often refer to Constantine V by the insulting epithet of 'Kopronymos', which might delicately be translated as 'excrement-name'. The problem was that however effective these emperors were as soldiers and administrators, to later observers their religious opinions were abhorrent. Both emperors have been labelled as iconoclasts, hostile to the veneration of icons of Christ, the Virgin Mary and the saints.

As we have seen, icons had played a significant propaganda role at moments of desperation in Byzantium's struggle for survival during the crisis of the seventh century, signifying the presence of supernatural helpers (see Section 2.3). By the early eighth century, however, some voices were being raised against them, asking whether their veneration did not, in fact, amount to sinful idolatry. During the 720s, the patriarch of Constantinople, Germanos I, became concerned that some bishops were refusing to bow down to icons in church and wrote some stern letters hoping to convince them of the error of their ways. Unfortunately for Germanos, the new emperor Leo III appears to have shared these reservations. He is alleged to have taken down the icon of Christ that was fixed over the main gate of the Great Palace in Constantinople and in 730 he removed Germanos from office and replaced him with Anastasios, an opponent of icon veneration. Matters went further under Constantine V. In 754, he gathered a council of 338 bishops in his palace of Hieria on the Asian side of the Bosporus and these prelates issued a decree that images of Christ, the Virgin and the Saints should not be made, venerated or displayed. In some churches and public places, the mosaic decoration carrying such depictions was removed and replaced with patterns or scenes from nature. Some of those who opposed the new policy were treated very harshly. A monk called Stephen the Younger was allegedly dragged through the streets and beaten to death in 766 for daring to criticise Constantine V and to defend the veneration of icons.

That at least is the version of events given in the sources. Unfortunately, all of them were written by iconophiles and as a result not only are they vehemently biased against the North Syrian emperors, but they also contain large amounts of anecdotal and frankly quite unbelievable material. They also clearly exaggerate the persecutions and desecrations supposedly committed by the iconoclast emperors. While icons, mosaics and wall paintings may have been removed in some churches, there does not seem to have been a clean sweep by any means. Secondly, a careful examination of the brutal treatment of iconophile monks during the reign of Constantine V reveals that most of these incidents took place in 765–7 and were not a constant occurrence throughout the reign. The chances are that these monks were ill-treated not so much because of their support for icons but for their involvement in a conspiracy against Constantine V around that time. All in all, the iconophile bias of our sources has seriously distorted our understanding of these emperors' reigns.

That said, the dispute over icons should not be dismissed as trivial and irrelevant. The ultimate vindication of icon veneration was to prove extremely influential on the development of Byzantine art and culture (see Section 7.2). The most influential voice in the debate was a monk called John of Damascus (d.749). As he was based at the monastery of Mar Saba near Jerusalem, he was outside Byzantine territory and so safe from iconoclast persecution. There he wrote a series of tracts in defence of icons, coming up with some of the arguments that were subsequently to win the day for the iconophiles. He justified their veneration on the basis of two ideas. The first was that the image was a symbol and mediator with a sharp distinction between the icon itself and the person depicted on it. When you venerated an icon, John claimed, that veneration was directed not to the wood and paint of which the icon was made, but to the holy person depicted on it. The act of veneration of an icon was not, therefore, idolatrous but legitimate and praiseworthy. In the second place, John went further and linked icon veneration to the Incarnation. Only by accepting icons could one accept that Christ was God born in human form, for if you denied that he should be depicted in wood and paint, then you denied that he could be present in flesh and bone. Thus the veneration of icons was not just legitimate, but essential to orthodox Christian belief. At the time, these ideas were specifically rejected at the council of Hieria in 754, but they were later to become orthodox doctrine when a new ruler decided to reverse the anti-icon stance of Leo III and Constantine V.

Box 4.1 Iconophile propaganda in *The Letter of the Three Patriarchs*

For an example of the kind of vehemently iconophile texts produced in the ninth century, one has to look no further than *The Letter of the Three Patriarchs.* It purports to be a missive sent by the patriarchs of Antioch, Jerusalem and Alexandria to the iconoclast emperor Theophilos (829–842) in 836. Such a letter may indeed have existed but the text as it survives was clearly doctored, expanded and rewritten later with all the usual hallmarks added: vitriolic abuse of Leo III and Constantine V and endless anecdotes recounting how icons miraculously survived frenzied attempts to destroy them. Here the letter describes how one made its way from Constantinople to Rome to escape destruction with only a little human assistance:

> On a certain occasion, Germanos, the most holy patriarch, because of the destruction of images imposed by the Emperor Leo, with much wailing and mournful tears threw another icon of the Saviour, one which was set up in the holy patriarchate of Constantinople, into the sea at a place called T'Amantiou, [the icon falling] in an upright position. He had written on a tablet the day and hour of this event and attached it to the right hand of the icon, calling out, 'Master, Master, save yourself and us because we perish!' And behold, on the same day in the famous city of Rome, the icon sailed up the Tiber, the river there, standing erect and keeping all but its ankles dry from the salty wetness of the sea, and like a fiery column it shone out above the water for three nights. When His Beatitude Pope Gregory [II] saw it, he got into a boat, went up to the icon and said to it, 'If you have been sent to us, come towards us'. Then the icon, just as the Lord Christ once walked upon the sea, came at a swift pace over the waters and entered the boat of itself. His Holiness the Pope embraced it and took it in his arms … Seated in a chariot he held it upright while the people came running together from all directions towards the miracle. He then placed it in the great church of the Holy Apostle Peter.

The tales spun by the iconophile propagandists have proved enduring. Even today, the church of the Madonna del Rosario in Rome houses an icon of the Virgin Mary which some say was brought from Constantinople in the eighth century by three brothers who were fleeing the persecution of the iconoclast emperors. There is, of course, no evidence to substantiate the legend (see Figure 4.2).

Source: *The Letter of the Three Patriarchs to Emperor Theophilos and Related Texts*, ed. and trans. Joseph A. Munitiz, Julian Chrysostomides, Eirene Harvalia-Crook and Charalambos Dendrinos (Camberley: Porphyrogenitus, 1997), p. 48.

Figure 4.2 Icon of the Virgin Mary from the church of the Madonna del Rosario, Rome

4.3 The reign of Irene (780–802)

Constantine V was succeeded in 775 by his son Leo IV but Leo's reign lasted only until his early death five years later at the age of 30. His successor Constantine VI was only nine at this point, so his mother Irene became head of a council of regency to oversee affairs of state until he was old enough to rule in his own right. In fact, she ran the empire for much longer than that for she was still involved in state affairs after Constantine came of age. Finally, in 797 she took the unprecedented step of deposing her own son, after which she ruled as empress in her own right until 802.

Irene was not necessarily the greatest ruler of Byzantium but her tenure of power was significant for a number of reasons. First, it was on her initiative that the iconoclast policy of her father-in-law Constantine V was reversed. It may have been that Irene had planned this all along as she herself was from an Athenian iconophile family and had never approved of the policy. On the other hand, the deciding factor may have been that the favour that God had apparently been showing the empire over the past 50 years had suddenly appeared to evaporate. With the collapse of the Umayyad caliphate in 750, the new Abbasid regime that had replaced it moved the capital from Damascus to Baghdad. The change brought with it a resurgence in Arab military fortunes, especially under the able Caliph Harun al-Raschid (786–809). The raids into Byzantine territory began again, and the one launched in 782 reached as far as the Bosporus from where the Arabs could gaze enviously across at Constantinople. No longer could the iconoclasts claim that they were earning God's favour by rooting out idolatry.

Whatever the precise motivation, by mid-784 Irene was in contact with the pope about the need to restore icon veneration. In August 786, she gathered a council of bishops in the church of the Holy Apostles in Constantinople, but the meeting never got down to the main business. No sooner had the session begun than soldiers of Constantine V's Tagmata burst in with drawn swords and broke it up, declaring that they would not stand by and see the great emperor's decrees tampered with. Undeterred, Irene reconvened the council the following year in Nicaea (see Figure 4.3), gathering 350

Figure 4.3 The church of Hagia Sophia, Nicaea, the meeting place of the Seventh Ecumenical Council in 787

bishops and numerous monks in this provincial town where their deliberations might be less public. This gathering, now known as the Seventh Ecumenical Council, adopted the arguments put forward by John of Damascus, condemned all hostility to icons as heresy and ordered the destruction of iconoclast writings. Although this was not the definitive end of the argument, it was a significant step to resolving it one way or another.

A second reason why the years 780 to 802 are significant is the progress that was made in reasserting Byzantine authority in Greece and the southern Balkans. The emperors in Constantinople had never given up on the area, even though they had been able to do very little there in the face of the much greater peril in the east. Every now and then they showed the flag. In 688 Justinian II had fought his way through to Thessalonica and Constantine V had launched incursions into Macedonia in the 750s, but neither of them made any attempt to annex the area. Then, in 783, Irene appointed Stavrakios to lead another expedition. This time, though, the expedition did not stop at Thessalonica, for Stavrakios continued his march, turning south until he reached the Peloponnese. Most of the Slavs he found living there seem to have been peaceable farmers who were divided into numerous tribes, so they were not in a position to put up any concerted resistance to Stavrakios' force. They were compelled to acknowledge Byzantine overlordship and to pay an annual tribute.

This restoration of authority in the Peloponnese proved temporary. Once Stavrakios had gone back to Constantinople, the Slav tribes quickly threw off their allegiance and returned to attacking the Byzantine enclaves in the area, such as the port of Patras. In the years immediately after Irene's reign, however, the process of reconquest that she had started was resumed. In 805 a general called Skleros led an army to the Peloponnese to relieve Patras and inflicted a significant defeat on the Slavs. Thereafter the Byzantines gradually began to retake control of Greece as one by one the Slav tribes submitted. The empire's administrative structure was extended over the region and new Themes were established, such as that of the Peloponnese in around 805. Cultural assimilation went hand in hand with this process, as the Slavs gradually converted to Christianity. New bishops were appointed for the reconquered towns, churches were built in the countryside and itinerant missionaries fanned out into the remoter areas. With Christianisation came the Greek language as the Slavonic dialects gradually died out. The process was a slow one though and it was not until the end of the tenth century that all the Slavs within the empire's borders were Christianised. Nevertheless by 850, Greece and the Peloponnese were once again part of the Byzantine empire.

Finally, Irene's period in control is important in retrospect because of what it tells us about women and political power in Byzantium. In theory, she should never have wielded such authority at all. Byzantium was a male-dominated society where the prevailing ethos was that women were inherently weaker than men and that they were therefore more prone to sin. The model here was Eve in the Old Testament, who had succumbed first to the temptation of the serpent and had then tempted Adam. Women therefore had to be kept out of public life to protect both themselves and everyone else. Those of the wealthier classes tended to remain in the home and were often veiled if they went out in public. They were specifically excluded from acting as judges or bankers or even as witnesses in the execution of contracts.

Yet as in most human societies, theory and practice did not always go hand in hand. Women might have been the weaker vessel but some of the most powerful and revered among the empire's saints were female. The obvious example is the Virgin Mary herself, the protectoress of Constantinople, who often seemed to receive more adulation than God or Christ. Iconophile propaganda was full of pious female iconophiles such as St Theodosia, who was allegedly one of a crowd of women who in 726 had rushed to the brazen gate of the Great Palace to save the icon of Christ. Incensed by the sight of a soldier chipping away at the image, she pushed his ladder away so that the unfortunate man plummeted to his death. Theodosia was then beaten to death by his comrades with a ram's horn, thus achieving martyrdom. Now Theodosia may, of course, be purely fictional, but the very fact that she could be conceived of taking such an active part and being praised for it suggests a certain ambivalence about the role of women in society.

It is therefore perhaps not so surprising that in cases of a minority, where the male heir was too young to rule as emperor, it was the practice for his mother, rather than a male relative, to head the council of regency and it was this that brought Irene to power in 780. What happened next, of course, depended on the character and ambition of the regent. Some empresses in this position would have seen their role as simply keeping things warm in preparation for their son's majority. Irene did more than that, changing policy in the case of icons and extending it in the Balkans. She took a prominent leadership role, personally heading an expedition into Thrace in 784. So prominent a role in fact that Constantine VI's 18th birthday came and went without any sign of her relinquishing her guardianship. Only when the army intervened and proclaimed Constantine as sole emperor was she forced to step down and retire to private life. She was not sidelined for long because Constantine soon ran into trouble. He had divorced his wife and quickly married again, bringing down on himself the condemnation of the church. His armies had suffered defeats in the field at the hands of the Arabs and Bulgars. In 793 Irene was recalled from exile, probably because Constantine realised that he needed her advice and expertise. Once back in power, she started plotting against her son. Taking advantage of his being distracted by grief at the death of his infant son, in the summer of 797 she had him seized and blinded. She even went so far as to have this act carried out in the purple chamber of the imperial palace, the same room in which she had given birth to him 26 years before.

This atrocity did not call down the chorus of condemnation that might be expected. The iconophiles who have provided us with our sources for her reign were simply too grateful to her for restoring the icons to rock the boat. So Irene was left to rule alone for five years. On her coins she was described as *Basilissa* (empress), rather than just *Despina* (lady, mistress) as was usual for female regents (see Figure 4.4). However, in two laws that were issued during her reign, she was called *Basileus* (emperor or perhaps 'ruler'). This was because the emperor was the source of all law, so to describe Irene differently might call into question the legitimacy of the decree. Be that as it may, Irene was as vulnerable to the vagaries of Byzantine politics as any male head of state. In October 802, she was overthrown by one of her own officials, the finance minister, Nikephoros. She escaped blinding but was packed off to a convent on the island of Lesbos where she died less than a year later aged about 51. Her son, the blinded Constantine VI, lived on until 805 but he had no hope of returning to power. Thus the North Syrian dynasty founded by Leo III came to an end.

Figure 4.4 Gold nomisma of Empress Irene from between 797 and 802 (© Dumbarton Oaks, Byzantine Collection, Washington, DC)

Box 4.2 Charles Diehl (1859–1944) and the *Figures byzantines*

On 26 December 1884 a new play opened at the Porte Saint-Martin theatre in Paris. Written by Victorien Sardou and boasting the celebrated Sarah Bernhardt in the lead role (see Figure 4.5), *Théodora* was a melodrama set in sixth-century Byzantium, centring on the life of Empress Theodora (d.548), consort of Justinian I. Much of the sensational action was based on the work of the Byzantine writer Procopius whose *Secret History* recounted Theodora's scandalous life as an actress before she became empress, which probably accounts for the huge success of Sardou's play, which ran for 257 performances. Among the audience on the opening night was Sigmund Freud, who was so smitten with Bernhardt that he later kept a photograph of her in her Theodora costume on the wall of his consulting room in Vienna.

Not everyone was impressed. A young student called Charles Diehl considered that the play was an 'intolerable literary distortion'. It was not just that Sardou felt entirely at liberty to depart from the historical record: he wrote a completely fictional death scene for the lead character in which she was publicly strangled rather than expiring mundanely of cancer. What Diehl really disliked was Sardou's sensationalised and voyeuristic portrait of Theodora with its focus on her sexuality and gender. Twenty years later he launched an attack on the play in the preface to a biography of the empress:

> Back in those days Procopius, rather foolishly, told how the honest folk of Constantinople would studiously move aside when they encountered [Theodora] in the street, fearing that they might be contaminated by this impure contact. In our century, we no longer have the same fears and prejudices: on the contrary the whiff of scandal that floats around Theodora draws us to her. She has … haunted the creative imagination of a Sardou, seduced the magnificent inventiveness of a Sarah Bernhardt.

This could be interpreted as the kind of prudery more associated with Victorian Britain than France under the Third Republic and Diehl has been accused of trying to make Theodora conform to bourgeois morality. Closer examination shows a different agenda:

> There is another [Theodora] who is less well known and who is attractive and interesting in quite a different way: a great empress who occupied an influential place at Justinian's side and who often played a decisive role in government; a woman of superior intellect, of unusual intelligence, strong willed, a despotic, haughty, harsh and passionate individual, complicated and often unnerving, but always endlessly fascinating.

Diehl was, in fact, something of a pioneer in that he presented Theodora and other Byzantine imperial women as political figures in their own right without constant reference to their gender. Shortly afterwards, he produced what was to become his best-known work: *Figures byzantines*. It was a two-volume study of prominent Byzantine personalities, but what made it unusual was that almost all the individuals chosen were women, mainly empresses. Here he sums up the career of Empress Irene:

> History owes Irene less indulgence and more justice. We can understand and, if we wish, excuse the mistake of honest people, who turned a blind eye to her actions on account of party allegiance but we do not have the right to do the same ourselves. In truth, this famous ruler was essentially a political woman, dedicated and ambitious, who was led to crime by her lust for power. The impressive results of her policies in a way make up for the horror of her deed. By her intrigues she reopened for eighty years the era of palace revolutions which her glorious predecessors, the iconoclast emperors, had previously closed for nearly a century.

Diehl thus lays stern criticisms at Irene's door but he does so without reference to her gender or sexuality.

Sources: Charles Diehl, *Théodora: imperatrice de Byzance* (Paris: Eugène Rey, 1904), pp. 6–7; Charles Diehl, *Figures byzantines* (Paris: Armand Colin, 1906–1908), vol. 1, p. 109 (author's translations).

Further Reading: Elena Boeck, 'Archaeology of Decadence: Uncovering Byzantium in Victorien Sardou's Theodora', in *Byzantium / Modernism: The Byzantine as Method in Modernity*, ed. Roland Betancourt and Maria Taroutina (Leiden and Boston MA: Brill, 2015), pp. 102–32.

Figure 4.5 Sarah Bernhardt as Theodora, a photograph published in 1890

4.4 The limits of revival: Bulgaria

The resumption of Arab raids into Byzantine Asia Minor under the Abbasid Caliphate showed just how fragile the revival was. The same lesson had to be learned in the Balkans, for while the Byzantines were reconquering Greece, to the north they were to suffer a series of severe defeats at the hands of the Bulgars. Following the Bulgar victory at Ongala in 680, they had been forced to accept the presence of a powerful unitary state between the Danube and the Balkan Mountains and had to bide their time until the opportunity came to push them back over the Danube. That opportunity seemed to have arrived after 756 when war broke out over some Byzantine forts that had been constructed along the border between the two powers. Constantine V invaded Bulgaria in 759 by land and sea, ravaging the country and routing a Bulgar army, though his own force was mauled as it withdrew through a pass in the Balkan Mountains. Four years later, he inflicted a serious defeat on the Bulgars at Anchialos, capturing huge numbers of prisoners whom he then had executed in Constantinople. So outraged were the Bulgars at this reverse that they rose in revolt against their khan, Teletz, and murdered him.

But in spite of this reverse, the Bulgar state did not collapse. Constantine V launched three more expeditions against it but none of them achieved any decisive success. It was in the course of the last of these that Constantine V fell ill and died, and his successors proved less adept at dealing with their troublesome neighbour. In 789, during the regency of Irene, the strategos of the new Theme of Thrace was ambushed and killed along with a large part of his force. Constantine VI led campaigns against the Bulgars in 791 and 792 but they culminated in a significant Byzantine reverse. Meanwhile events further afield altered the balance of power in the region. In 796, after five years of war, the Avar khanate surrendered to the Frankish king Charlemagne and accepted his overlordship. The Avars occupied the lands north of the Danube and their surrender revealed a weakness that the Bulgars were quick to exploit. Under their new khan, Krum, they had by 805 pushed their borders far west into what is now Hungary, more than doubling the size of their territory. Initially all this worked to the advantage of the Byzantines, as it diverted the energies of the Bulgars away from their borders, but the overall result was to leave them facing a much larger and more powerful khanate.

Perhaps in the hope of pushing the Bulgars over the Danube into their new territories, Emperor Nikephoros I invaded Bulgaria in 807. The campaign had to be aborted because Nikephoros discovered that a plot was being hatched against him among certain officers of the Tagmata and he returned across the Balkan Mountains to deal with it. It had the effect of provoking Krum to mount a reprisal raid in 809, when he crossed into Byzantine territory and surprised the Thematic army just as its soldiers were receiving their pay. Having killed the strategos and many of the soldiers and seized the payroll, the Bulgars took and sacked the town of Sofia. Nikephoros responded promptly and marched out against Krum but once more had to turn back to deal with a mutiny: his strict financial policies had made him very unpopular. It was not until July 811 that Nikephoros was finally able to mount a major campaign against Krum. He personally led an invasion of Bulgaria, ravaged the land and captured and sacked Pliska. Then as his army, heavily laden with loot, marched home through the Balkan Mountains, it found itself trapped in one of the passes which the Bulgars had blocked at either end. After leaving the Byzantines encircled for three days, Krum ordered the attack and allowed his army to wipe out the panicking enemy. Nikephoros I himself was among the thousands killed and

Figure 4.6 The ruins of Pliska: the first Bulgar capital

Krum celebrated his victory by having the emperor's head cut off and his skull made into a cup from which the khan was accustomed to toast his friends. The news of the disaster caused shock and terror in Constantinople. It was seen as a divine punishment and helped to trigger a second bout of iconoclasm between 815 and 843. Krum was quick to exploit his victory, appearing with his army before the walls of Constantinople. Fortunately, the Bulgar khan died suddenly of a cerebral haemorrhage and his less aggressive successor concluded a treaty with the emperor in 816. Peace followed for several decades but the Byzantines now had not only to recognise that they were sharing the Balkans with the Bulgar khanate but also to pay an annual tribute to purchase immunity against future aggression.

4.5 The limits of revival: Italy

The Byzantines were also to lose ground in Italy during this period when they were ousted from the north of the peninsula first by the Lombards and then by the Franks. The process began in 727, when the relative stability in the area came to an end because the Lombard King Liudprand decided to revive the old ambition to dominate the whole peninsula. He began to encroach on the strip of territory that ran between Rome and Ravenna, capturing a string of fortresses, laid siege to Ravenna itself and burned the nearby port of Classis. Liudprand had chosen his moment very carefully, because the pope and people of Byzantine Italy were at that moment once more at loggerheads with the emperor in Constantinople. Emperor Leo III was just making his initial moves against the veneration of icons and he allegedly wrote to Pope Gregory II demanding that all images be removed from the churches of Rome. Gregory refused to comply and in November 731 his successor gathered a synod, which condemned all iconoclasts as heretics. The popes seem to have had a good deal of popular support for their iconophile stance. When news came that the emperor had sent an assassin to Rome to deal with the recalcitrant pontiff, the chief men of the city rallied to his support and declared themselves ready to die for his safety. In Venice, when the Byzantine-appointed duke died, the inhabitants did not wait for a replacement to be sent but elected their own governor, the first doge. There was even opposition in Ravenna itself where opponents of the iconoclast policy rose up and murdered the Exarch Paul. Some of the insurgents talked of appointing an emperor in Italy in opposition to Leo but the pope forbade that. Leo III seems to have held the pope responsible for the insubordination and took revenge by removing Apulia, Calabria and Sicily from papal jurisdiction and putting them under the patriarch of Constantinople. Papal estates were confiscated and Leo also diverted the tax revenues from the areas round about, which had formerly gone to the pope, into his own treasury.

Box 4.3 Paul the Deacon and the situation in Italy (727)

Paul (c.720–799) had been a figure of some importance at the court of the Lombard King Liudprand and his successors, but when in 774 the Frankish ruler Charlemagne destroyed the kingdom of the Lombards, Paul became a monk and entered the monastery of Monte Cassino. It was probably there that he wrote his *History of the Lombards*, which traces his people's fortunes down to the death of Liudprand in 744. His work naturally seeks to portray the Lombards in the best light as friends and not enemies of the pope. This passage describes the events of 727, laying stress on the reprehensible iconoclasm of Leo III to suggest that Liudprand and the pope were allies against the Byzantine emperor:

> At this time, King Liudprand besieged Ravenna and took Classis and destroyed it. Then Paul the patrikios sent his men out of Ravenna to kill the pope, but as the Lombards fought against them in defence of the pope and as the Spoletans resisted them on the Salarian Bridge as well as the Tuscan Lombards from other places, the design of the Ravenna people came to nought. At this time the Emperor Leo burned the images of the saints placed in Constantinople and ordered the Roman pontiff to do the like if he wished to have the emperor's favour, but the pontiff disdained to do this thing. Also the whole of Ravenna and of Venetia resisted such commands with one mind, and if the pontiff had not prohibited them they would have attempted to set up an emperor over themselves.

Also King Liudprand attacked Feronianum (Fregnano), Mons Bellius (Monteveglio), Buxeta (Busseto) and Persiceta (San Giovanni in Persiceto), Bononia (Bologna) and the Pentapolis and Auximun (Osimo) fortresses of Emilia. And in like manner he then took possession of Sutrium (Sutri) but after some days it was again restored to the Romans. During the same time the Emperor Leo went on to worse things so that he compelled all the inhabitants of Constantinople either by force or by blandishments to give up the images of the Saviour and of his Holy Mother and of all the saints wherever they were, and he caused them to be burned by fire in the midst of the city.

Source: Paul the Deacon, *History of the Lombards*, trans. William D. Foulke (Philadelphia PA: University of Pennsylvania Press, 1907), pp. 289–93 (spelling adapted).

With the imperial authorities, the Church and the people of Italy divided on the iconoclast issue, it was hard to make a concerted response to Liudprand's aggression. Not surprisingly, though, the pope viewed the expansion of Lombard power with some alarm, even though Liudprand, as a good Catholic, did everything he could to avoid any impression that in encroaching on Byzantine territory he was attacking the papacy. His forces approached Rome in 729, but he immediately withdrew when the pope emerged from the city in person and begged him to desist. When the king captured the town of Sutri from the Byzantines, as Paul the Deacon describes, he handed it over to the pope as a gift. But he could not hide his hopes of acquiring the city of Rome and Pope Gregory III felt that he should take steps to frustrate that ambition. The obvious protector of the papacy was the exarch in Ravenna, but thanks to the rift over iconoclasm his help could not be relied on. So in 739, Gregory took the radical step of making a direct approach to the ruler of another country. He wrote to Charles Martel, mayor of the palace and the most powerful man in the kingdom of the Franks, complaining about Lombard attacks and begging for his assistance. After all, there was much to recommend the Franks as potential saviours of the papacy. Not only had they proved their military prowess by inflicting a defeat on the Arabs at Poitiers in 732, but they also had impeccable religious credentials. They had been Catholics ever since their leader Clovis had been baptised back in the fifth century and had been untainted by Arianism, as the Lombards had, or by iconoclasm, as the Byzantine emperor currently was. But Charles did not comply with Gregory's request, for he had no quarrel with the Lombards who had recently sent him valuable help when the kingdom of the Franks had been invaded by the Arabs of Spain.

Matters took a decisive turn in 751, when Liudprand's successor Aistulf finally realised the Lombard dream and captured Ravenna, putting an end to the Byzantine exarchate. With the possibility of any Byzantine aid now very remote, Pope Stephen II decided to renew the appeal to the Franks, not by letter but by travelling to their kingdom to make the appeal in person. He arrived in January 754 and met near Paris with Charles Martel's son Pepin, who was now king of the Franks. Pleased and flattered by the appearance of the successor of St Peter in his kingdom, Pepin agreed to help and to make war on the Lombards. The following year, he duly fulfilled his undertaking by leading his army over the Alps, sweeping aside the Lombard army and laying siege to Pavia. Holed up in the town, with no options left to him, King Aistulf surrendered and agreed to a treaty which bound him to respect the lands of the papacy and to hand over to the pope a number of cities that he had taken, including Ravenna. It would seem that Pepin made this last requirement at the request of Stephen. The pope had presented him with a document known as *The Donation of Constantine*, which purported to be a letter of the first Christian emperor, Constantine. In it, Constantine, grateful for being cured of leprosy, supposedly granted the pope lands in Italy and it was on this basis that Stephen claimed that Ravenna and other towns rightfully belonged to him.

With the campaign over, Pope Stephen was escorted back to Rome and Pepin's army withdrew. The Frankish king then sent an embassy to Constantinople to announce what had happened. Constantine V is hardly likely to have been pleased by the treaty that Pepin had concluded with the Lombards. Ravenna was, after all, a Byzantine city which should properly have been returned to him and not given to the pope. So he decided to send envoys to Pepin to negotiate. By the time that they reached Italy in the summer of 756, Aistulf had reneged on the treaty and Pepin had marched back across the Alps to renew the war. Constantine V's envoys intercepted the Frankish king while he was encamped at Pavia and they offered him generous gifts if he would hand Ravenna and the other towns over to the emperor rather than to the pope. Pepin, however, refused to deviate from the undertaking he had made to Stephen. War against the Lombards was renewed and Aistulf was once more bludgeoned into submission. This time the treaty was implemented. Ravenna and the other areas were handed over to Pope Stephen forming the basis of a Papal State that was to last until 1870.

It was not the outcome that Constantine V had hoped for but as the struggle with the Bulgars and Arabs as always had to have priority, he continued to make diplomatic efforts to recover Ravenna. In 757, he sent a friendly embassy to King Pepin, bearing an organ as a gift, but at the same time he put out diplomatic feelers to the defeated Lombards with a view to an anti-Frankish alliance. It all proved unavailing and Byzantine influence in northern Italy was replaced by that of the Franks. In 773, Pepin's son Charlemagne invaded Italy in response to attempts by the Lombard King Desiderius to encroach on the Papal State. This time, rather than merely bringing the Lombards to heel, Charlemagne deposed Desiderius in June 774 and incorporated the Lombard kingdom into his own. As a result, what remained of Byzantine holdings in Italy, notably Venice in the north and Apulia and Calabria in the south, were now close neighbours of the powerful so-called Carolingian empire. There was a real fear in Constantinople that Charlemagne would now try to bring the whole of the peninsula under his control. As regent, Empress Irene tried to defuse the possible threat by proposing a marriage alliance between Charlemagne's daughter Rotrude and her son Constantine VI. When the protracted negotiations led nowhere, in 789 she financed a landing in Italy by Adelgis, the son of the ousted Desiderius, in a bid to stir up a revolt against Frankish rule but it was soon snuffed out by Charlemagne's troops.

The establishment of Frankish power in northern Italy posed a threat not just to Byzantium's territory but also to its political ideology. As Roman emperor, charged with the protection of the Church, the Byzantine ruler was also responsible for guarding Rome and the papacy. Now that role had been taken over by the king of the Franks. Pope Hadrian I (772–795) was the first pope to reflect this, by issuing coins that bore his name alone, removing that of the emperor. Finally, on 25 December 800, his successor Pope Leo III took the next logical step and crowned Charlemagne as Emperor of the Romans in St Peter's Basilica in Rome. Both the pope and Charlemagne seem to have expected that the Byzantines would recognise the Frankish ruler's title and equal status. Charlemagne even opened negotiations with Empress Irene with a view to his marrying her. That door was firmly closed in late 802 when Irene was overthrown by Nikephoros I who then dragged his feet on making a settlement. In frustration, Charlemagne sent a force to attack the nominally Byzantine town of Venice in 810. The catastrophic defeat and death of Nikephoros at the hands of the Bulgar Khan Krum in 811 meant that the Byzantines had no choice but to settle with Charlemagne. An embassy travelled to Charlemagne's capital at Aachen the following year and there recognised his title of emperor, thereby ensuring the security of the remaining Byzantine territories in Italy at the cost of a minor ideological concession.

Points to remember

- The obsession of the primary sources with the controversy over icon veneration makes it tempting to see this period solely in those terms.
- In fact, putting the religious controversy aside, it is possible to see the first glimmerings of the changes that were later to underpin Byzantium's revival as early as the 740s.
- The decline of the Umayyad caliphate was to Byzantium's advantage but its replacement by the Abbasids saw it thrust back on to the defensive.
- Although the Byzantines had some success against the Bulgars in the eighth century, after 811 they had to accept that they were facing a formidable military power that could only be held in check by the payment of an annual tribute.
- In Italy, the Byzantines lost their influence in the north to the Franks and were henceforth largely confined to the south of the peninsula.

Suggestions for further reading

Brubaker, Leslie. (2012), *Inventing Byzantine Iconoclasm* (London: Bristol Classical Press). Brubaker does a fine job of showing how our primary sources have grossly exaggerated the significance of the dispute over icons and played down other aspects of the period.

Herrin, Judith. (2000), *Women in Purple: Rulers of Medieval Byzantium* (London: Phoenix Press). Gives a very effective account of the reign of Irene but also considers the whole question of female power in Byzantium, its extent and its limits.

Noble, Thomas F. X. (2009), *Images, Iconoclasm and the Carolingians* (Philadelphia PA: University of Pennsylvania Press). Considers the impact of Byzantine iconoclasm on relations with the West where there was a similar debate on the legitimacy of venerating religious images.

Treadgold, Warren. (1988), *The Byzantine Revival, 780–842* (Stanford CA: Stanford University Press). Takes issue with earlier works which connected the Byzantine revival with the end of the second bout of iconoclasm in 843, although signs of renewal can be detected even before Treadgold's start date of 780.

Wickham, Chris. (1981), *Early Medieval Italy Central Power and Local Society, 400–1000* (London: Macmillan). See Chapter 3 on 'Romans, Lombards, Franks and Byzantines', which unravels the complex ethnic and cultural mix that characterised Italy in this period.

PART II

Reconquest and hegemony 820–1045

5   Major literary sources for the period 820–1045

From the early tenth century onwards, a great deal more historical writing was produced in Byzantium, recording events of the authors' own times and the decades before. There had been historians at work during the previous century, such as Theognostos the Grammarian who was writing in the years immediately after the death of Theophanes Confessor in 818. Unfortunately his work has not survived. Another noticeable development in the tenth century was that historical analysis became more sophisticated, with authors seeking more concrete causes for events than divine reward or retribution. Both the wider production of historiography and the more critical engagement with the past were part of the general revival of education and literature which has been termed the 'Macedonian Renaissance'.

5.1 The 'Macedonian Renaissance'

During the seventh and eighth centuries, as Byzantium fought for its very survival, it would appear that educational activity was at a very low ebb, although basic literacy probably remained more widespread than in the contemporary West. Literary production dropped off and what was written largely emerged from the monasteries, the work of men like Theophanes Confessor. That began to change as the direct threat receded and increased prosperity provided greater means and leisure. People began once more to read and engage with Byzantium's intellectual heritage – the literature of classical Greece, although as ever their favourites were Homer's *Iliad* and *Odyssey* (see Section 1.1).

This renewed interest in ancient literature is sometimes referred to as the 'Macedonian Renaissance', in reference to the famous revival that took place in Italy in the fourteenth and fifteenth centuries. The term is rather misleading, however, as it connects the revival with the accession of Basil I and the Macedonian dynasty in 867 (see Section 6.2). In fact, just like the military and political revival discussed in the previous chapter, it can be discerned much earlier than that. The first sign of it was two significant developments from around the year 800 that made the dissemination of books much easier. The first concerned the material on which books were written. Previously they had been copied by scribes onto papyrus, which is made from the stem of a reed that only grows on the banks of the River Nile. After the Arab conquest of

Egypt in 642, papyrus had to be imported from a hostile power, which added greatly to its expense. Arab manufacturers also liked to place texts from the Quran in their papyri which made the Christian Byzantines all the more reluctant to use them. Fortunately, an alternative was now becoming available in the form of paper, which had long been used in China as a material for letters and books. It could be manufactured from linen rags and was therefore considerably cheaper than rare papyrus. The second development was the emergence of a new Greek script. The traditional script, known as uncial, was just large capital letters (see Figure 5.1). It took up a great deal of the page because of the spaces between the letters and it was very slow to write because the scribe had to lift the pen from the page after forming each letter. From about 800 on, books began to appear in minuscule, a joined-up script which had completely replaced uncial by the mid-tenth century (see Figure 5.2). Like paper, the new form of writing made books much cheaper as hourly paid scribes did not take as long to copy them. Moreover, the new script included accents and punctuation marks and it gave some indication of where words began and ended, which made it much easier for readers whose Attic Greek was not absolutely perfect.

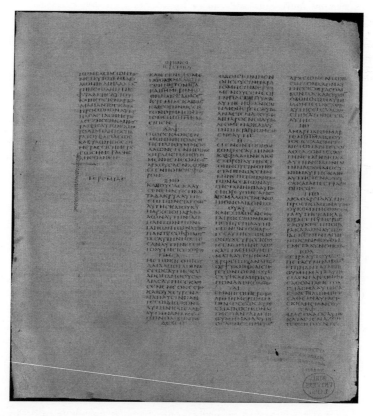

Figure 5.1 The Codex Sinaiticus, a fourth-century uncial manuscript of the Bible, now in the British Library, London

Figure 5.2 Ninth- or early tenth-century minuscule manuscript of the *Elements* of Euclid, from the Bodleian Library, Oxford

One of the central figures in the revival of interest in ancient Greek literature was the future patriarch Photios (c.810–c.895) (see Section 6.3). He was the author of a work known as the *Biblioteca* in which he provided a guide to ancient literature through a series of book reviews often commenting on the language used by the authors. The Athenian orator Aeschines (c.397–c.322 BCE) he praised to the skies because his prose was 'spontaneous and impromptu' and he recommended the grammarian Aelius Dionysius (fl.150 CE) because he was a useful source of Attic expressions and vocabulary. Another bibliophile of the period was Arethas, who was archbishop of Caesarea in Asia Minor from 902 until 945 and built up an impressive library. He was a wealthy man who could afford to have his books copied onto parchment made of animal skin rather than onto paper and, although they were written in minuscule, Arethas insisted that wide margins be left all around, so that he could record his own comments on the text. Evidently a man of meticulous habits, he would make a note of the copyist's name, the cost of the parchment, the copyist's fee and the date he acquired the book. His collection included works by Euclid, Plato and the rhetorician Lucian of Samosata (c.125–c.190 CE), as well as Christian writers such as Eusebius of Caesarea (d.338) and the Church Father Clement of Alexandria (c.150–c.215). Arethas' comments in the margins make interesting reading. When Clement of Alexandria opined that keeping children short of food was good for them, Arethas scribbled down that this was sound advice if you did not want them to grow!

Alongside the interest shown by individuals, the educational system based on the study of the Greek classics also revived (see Section 1.1). During the period of crisis in the seventh and eighth centuries, many cities that had been centres of education had been lost and while Constantinople had beaten off the Arab sieges, its university seems to have ceased to function at some point. In around 857, however, the university was refounded by Caesar Bardas who was the effective ruler of the empire during part of the reign of Emperor Michael III (842–867) (see Section 6.1). It was provided with teaching space in the Magnaura Hall of the Great Palace and one of the first teachers was Bardas' friend Photios. It provided higher education for laymen over the age of 14 and the curriculum was based on reading and imitating the style of the Greek classics, just as it had been in the past.

With the old system of higher education re-established, it became once more the norm for anyone connected with the Byzantine court to write in Attic Greek, whether they were composing letters, treaties, histories or panegyrical speeches given in honour of the reigning emperor on feast days. A court official called Symeon Metaphrastes even spent his spare time 'translating' homely biographies of saints that had been composed by less educated men in previous centuries from everyday Greek into Attic. This obsession with the language of the past and a refusal to allow the contemporary language to be used for official or literary purposes has struck some commentators as being deeply unattractive. The Byzantines have been accused of loving the language of the ancients and assiduously preserving their work while completely failing to grasp their spirit. One such critic was Paul Speck, who identified the ninth century as a pivotal moment in the development of Byzantine literary culture. Rather than allowing the emergence of any vernacular literature, the Byzantines committed 'cultural suicide' by yoking themselves permanently to what was effectively a dead language. It could be countered that such views are guilty of measuring the Byzantines up to cultural standards other than their own. It was not uncommon in premodern societies for the language of literary and elite political circles to be completely different from that spoken by the mass of the population. In contemporary Western Europe, Latin was the literary idiom, rather than the Germanic or Romance dialects that have since developed into modern languages. In China, there was a wide gulf between the Mandarin used at court and the everyday language of the people. Moreover, merely because the Byzantines imitated classical language did not mean that they could not use it to express original ideas of their own. It was just the frame in which they presented their thoughts. Some of the historians writing in the period were able to weave subtle and creative analysis behind the stiff façade of formal language.

Box 5.1 A political speech in Attic Greek

In October 927, after decades of war, the Byzantine emperor Romanos I Lekapenos (920–944) made a lasting peace and marriage alliance with Peter, tsar of Bulgaria (927–969) (see Section 6.4). To mark this auspicious event, a courtier named Theodore Daphnopates was commissioned to make a speech celebrating the restoration of amity after so long and, as required, he did so in Attic Greek. In the translated extract from the speech below, the archaic English gives a flavour of how the classical Greek would have sounded to tenth-century Byzantine ears. Here, Daphnopates is addressing the personification of Peace and hailing her return after such a long absence:

> Where, o holy one in name and deed, hast thou tarried so long until now? Where hast thou sat in counsel apart from thine own? Or didst thou, clad, as they say, in white garments, fly up to Olympus, because thou hatedst the hatred among us? Thou wast loved by us above the haven from the tempest, above the sun undimmed by snow clouds. For so long as thou wast far from us and dwelledst apart like the blue moon of Acesius, and our state knew, like Endymion, no awakening, and we were crushed down in squalor, then was I like one who speaks – as the proverb says – with Stentor, then was I silent as the son of Croesus with the gong of Dodona and became more voiceless than fishes. For I was grieved in soul like Jacob and shed tears in rivers.

Apart from the language, the speech also reflects Byzantium's classical heritage in its references to Greek mythology and literature. Daphnopates asks Peace whether, in the years of her absence, she was living on Mount Olympus, the home of the gods. Acesius was one of the names of the god Apollo, to whom days with a full moon were sacred. Daphnopates asks Peace whether she was hidden away on a blue moon, an additional full moon that occurs during the lunar year, and so a metaphor for somewhere remote and inaccessible. He declares that the long war with Bulgaria felt like the sleep of Endymion which will supposedly continue for ever. As for himself in that unhappy period, his voice was sometimes as loud as that of Stentor, the herald of the Greeks in the Trojan War, whose voice, according to Homer, was as loud as those of 50 men combined, presumably raised in complaint. But often he was as quiet as one of the two sons of Croesus, the king of Lydia (c.560–c.546), who is described by Herodotus as being both deaf and dumb from birth. Note though that Daphnopates did not restrict himself to classical allusions, as there are numerous references to the Bible in the speech as well. He compares himself to the patriarch Jacob in Genesis 37:34–5 who grieved inconsolably for the loss of his son, Joseph. This is a good illustration of the way that the classical and the Christian had become completely enmeshed in Byzantine literary culture.

Source: Ivan Dujčev, 'On the treaty of 927 with the Bulgarians', *Dumbarton Oaks Papers* 32 (1978), 217–95, at 255–7.

5.2 Historians at the court of Constantine VII (945–959)

The fourth emperor of the Macedonian dynasty, Emperor Constantine VII was a literary figure in his own right. He seems to have had a particular interest in the preservation of knowledge and is credited as the author of a number of manuals that describe Byzantine court ceremonial, Theme administration, military tactics and foreign policy, although he doubtless had a team of ghost writers to do the hard graft for him. The influence of the classical heritage is less evident in these works, which were designed for practical use, but it is still there. In his *De Administrando Imperio*, a manual of foreign policy written for his son and successor Romanos II, the emperor managed to drop in the occasional reference to Homer.

Box 5.2 Constantine VII on the preservation of knowledge

The Book of Ceremonies was one of the manuals produced under Constantine VII's auspices, describing the protocols to be followed on state occasions in the Great Palace in Constantinople. In his opening remarks, the emperor tells his son, the future Romanos II (959–963), why the preservation of state ceremonial was so vital.

> Perhaps this undertaking seemed superfluous to others who do not have as great a concern for what is necessary, but it is particularly dear to us and highly desirable and more relevant than anything else because through praiseworthy ceremonial the imperial rule appears more beautiful and acquires more nobility. And so is a cause of wonder to both foreigners and our own people. Over a long time, many things can disappear which, while achieved in that time, are also consumed by it. Among these was the treatise outlining the imperial ceremonial, something valuable and important. Because this had been neglected and become, so to speak, moribund, the imperial power was in fact unadorned and unattractive to look at … Therefore, so that this should not be the case and we should not seem to be acting in a disorderly fashion to be insulting to the imperial majesty, we believed it was necessary to collect with unremitting effort from many sources those things that were devised by earlier generations and were made known by those who had seen them, and to set them out in the present arrangement and to record for those who come after us, in the form of an easily comprehended account, the tradition of our ancestral customs that have been neglected … So that the text will be clear and easily understood, we have used both ordinary and quite simple language and the same words and names applied and used for each thing from of old.

Two points are worth noting here. First, contrary to appearances, this concern for the customs of the past was not mere antiquarianism. As the emperor notes above, visual ceremonial and spectacle had the practical purpose of enhancing Byzantine prestige both at home and abroad. Secondly, Constantine's point about simple language reflects the practical nature of the handbook he was producing. Although it is written in Attic grammar, the text is straightforward and unadorned, unlike Theodore Daphnopates' 927 speech (See Box 5.1).

Source: Constantine VII Porphyrogennetos, *The Book of Ceremonies*, trans. Ann Moffatt and Maxeme Tall, 2 vols (Canberra: Australian Association of Byzantine Studies, 2012), pp. 3–5.

It was only natural that a man so obsessed with preservation and codification should take an interest in the past as well. Constantine VII is credited with commissioning and planning the *Historical Excerpts*, a compilation of passages from classical and earlier Byzantine historians, grouped according to subject. Then in around 950, Constantine asked one of his courtiers, Joseph Genesios, to resume where Theophanes Confessor left off in 813 and to take the story up to the death of Constantine's grandfather, Basil I, in 886. The result was not entirely satisfactory. Genesios worked hard to give his work literary polish by freely quoting Homer and other ancient authors, but he made numerous grammatical mistakes as he struggled with formal, classical Greek and he often got his facts muddled as well.

That probably explains why Constantine asked somebody else to do the job all over again. This time we do not know the name of the author, so he goes by 'Theophanes Continuatus', although he may well have been the Theodore Daphnopates who gave the speech on the treaty with Bulgaria in 927 (see Box 5.1). Whoever the historian was, he covered the period 813 to 948 much more lucidly and elegantly than Genesios had and with a wider range of sources. Moreover, although the work describes itself as a continuation of Theophanes, it is structured in a very different way: as a series of imperial biographies rather than year-by-year annals, and it lacks the earlier historian's strident religiosity. When it comes to the period 867 to 886, the reign of Constantine VII's grandfather Basil I, the work suddenly becomes much more detailed and one suspects that Constantine VII himself had a much greater hand in this section. That was because a sensitive topic was covered here: the murder of Emperor Michael III and the establishment of Constantine VII's Macedonian family as Byzantium's ruling dynasty (see Section 6.2). Constantine and his anonymous assistant had to work hard to present this violent usurpation as justified and beneficial. So, even though the reign of Michael III had been covered already, it was recounted again, with lurid descriptions of Michael's immorality and impiety. Moreover, Theophanes Continuatus claims that Basil played no part in Michael's murder in September 867, and that he only replaced the victim as emperor because he was unanimously acclaimed by the people. Once in power, he is presented as the perfect emperor who has the interests of the state and its people at heart. The pro-Macedonian agenda is obvious but, unlike Theophanes Confessor's crude invective against the iconoclasts, this gentle distortion worked well. In spite of his ruthless crime, Basil I has enjoyed a high reputation ever since.

5.3 Leo the Deacon

By the late tenth century, the Byzantines were producing historiography that was closely modelled on ancient Greek writers such as Thucydides and Polybius, both in its language and its outlook. A good example is the work of Leo the Deacon. Originally from Asia Minor, Leo was sent to Constantinople as a young man to be educated and that was his stepping stone to becoming a deacon and a member of the clergy of the Great Palace under Basil II (976–1025). During that time, he wrote an account of events between 959 and 976, with two forward flashes to 978–9 and 986, using a high standard of Attic Greek.

The influence of Leo's education with its emphasis on the Greek classics is apparent in his work. He specifically mentions not just Homer but also Herodotus and Arrian and he refers obliquely to many more ancient authors. These references are not mere window dressing but do help to add colour to the account, as when Emperor John I Tzimiskes (969–976) is compared to the Trojan war hero Odysseus. Other features of the work are reminiscent of classical historiography. Leo includes character sketches and descriptions of physical appearance, something that is completely absent in Theophanes Confessor or Genesios. Although a clergyman, he is extremely informative and accurate on military matters. Lastly, like his classical models, he tends to attribute events not to the will of God but simply to fortune. That seems odd for a Christian clergyman since the existence of an omnipotent God would preclude anything happening merely by chance. Thus Leo's use of the word should perhaps be seen merely as a literary convention, designed to give his work a classical gloss. There can be no doubt that he himself was a Christian for he tells conventional miracle stories of the kind that can be found in Theophanes. One example is his anti-Semitic tale of a Jew who stabbed an icon of the crucifixion only to be horrified as it gushed out blood. In one respect, though, Leo was a much less effective historian than Theophanes. In contrast to the monk's carefully worked out chronology, the Deacon's work contains only four specific dates, by year of the world and indiction, but only one of them is entirely correct. Even so, he is a vital source for the period of expansion at the end of the tenth century.

5.4 Michael Psellos

Genesios, Theophanes Continuatus and Leo the Deacon are all obscure individuals about whom little is known. Michael Psellos, by contrast, was a prominent figure in eleventh-century Byzantium and one of the foremost intellectuals of his age (see Figure 5.3). Born in Constantinople in around 1022, he was not from a noble or wealthy family but his unusual intelligence attracted attention, for by the age of ten he could recite the whole of Homer's *Iliad* by heart. Consequently, he was able, like Leo the Deacon, to enter higher education and study under John Mauropous, a notable scholar of the day. He went on to become the centre of a circle of intellectuals who set the cultural agenda in eleventh-century Constantinople, and when, in 1045, the university of Constantinople was reorganised, it was Psellos who was put in charge of the faculty of Philosophy with the title 'Consul of the Philosophers'. He wrote numerous books, devoted to subjects as diverse as theology, astrology, demonology and science, along with many letters and speeches, but his main interest was philosophy. In Byzantium, that meant studying the works of Plato and Aristotle, although the latter was generally preferred as his explanations of the natural world were easily reconcilable with Christian doctrine. Psellos, however, preferred Plato and his later followers, the so-called Neoplatonists, who were more concerned with metaphysical matters, those that stand beyond the physical senses, and he later claimed that he single-handedly revived their study. But even for someone as eminent and well-connected as Psellos, it could be dangerous to show too great an attachment to Platonic philosophy, which probed into matters such as reincarnation that were very difficult to reconcile with Christian doctrine. In the 1070s, Psellos was accused

Figure 5.3 Michael Psellos with Emperor Michael VII Doukas (1071–1078) from a manuscript in the Austrian National Library, Vienna

of being too enthusiastic about Plato and was summoned to explain himself before the patriarchal synod. Such was his towering reputation that no action was taken.

Psellos' career as an academic would have been enough to secure his posthumous reputation but he dominated the political as well as the intellectual life of his times. He secured a minor post at court as a secretary during the 1030s and rose to prominence during the reign of Constantine IX Monomachos (1042–1055), who came to rely on him for advice and to draft letters, speeches and treaties (see Section 10.1). Although he fell out of favour at the end of Constantine IX's reign, he was able to return and to resume a position of influence at the court of Theodora (1055–1056). In fact, he showed a remarkable ability to remain influential as short-reigned emperors came and went. He served under Michael VI (1056–1057) but when Michael was overthrown and replaced by Isaac I Komnenos (1057–1059), Psellos remained in the Great Palace. When Isaac I abdicated, Psellos became adviser to the next emperor, Constantine X Doukas (1059–1067).

This scholar and statesman was responsible for a remarkable work of history known as the *Chronographia*. It has two clearly identifiable sections. The first, covering 976 to 1059, was written between 1059 and 1063. The second, covering 1059 to around

1075, was probably composed during the reign of Michael VII Doukas (1071–1078). For the period up to 1034, as Psellos admits, he was dependent on what he had heard from others for information. For events after that, he was able to use his own experience for he was often an eyewitness and sometimes even a participant in them. That gives his work an immediacy and intimacy which is lacking in the works we have looked at so far, but it also narrows its scope to some extent. The emphasis is on Psellos himself and his career and the action is closely focused on Constantinople and the court, with events in the provinces seldom even being mentioned. There is no chronological framework, apart from the comings and goings of emperors, and Psellos almost never gives a date, in contrast to the careful annalistic structure of Theophanes Confessor.

Psellos' intellectual interests ensured that he produced a very different type of history from that of Theophanes in other ways too, because as a student of philosophy he was accustomed to using his senses and intellect, rather than revelation or scripture, to arrive at a conclusion. He tried to find rational, earthly explanations for why events occurred. His preferred explanation was human character so he gives detailed sketches of some of the major political players of the period, balancing their strengths and weaknesses and displaying an astonishing critical insight into human personality. Like Leo the Deacon, he clearly believed that human character could be read in the face and so he gives a detailed account of the physical appearance of some of his subjects. When discussing the reign of Emperor Basil II, Psellos connects the turning point of his reign in 985 with a change in his character and then goes on to describe how his face reflected his natural nobility: his eyebrows were well arched, indicating his pride, but his eyes were neither too deep set, a sign of cunning, nor too prominent, a sign of frivolity.

Box 5.3 Psellos on character: John the Orphanotrophos

Psellos' fascination with human character is apparent in this description of the eunuch John the Orphanotrophos who was the brother of Emperor Michael IV (1034–1041) and the most important member of the administration during that reign:

> I saw the man myself and I heard him speak and witnessed his actions. I marked his disposition closely, and I am aware that although some of his deeds are praiseworthy, there are other things in his life, which cannot meet with general approval. At that time there were many sides to his character. He had a ready wit and if ever a man was shrewd, he was; the piercing glance of his eyes betrayed those qualities. His experience in all branches of government was great but it was in the administration of public finance that his wisdom and shrewdness were especially evident. He bore no one ill will; yet at the same time he was irritated if anyone underestimated his importance. If he did no harm to a soul, yet in his dealings with the people, he assumed a fierce expression which terrified one and all. Thus John was a veritable bulwark to the emperor and a real brother, for he never relaxed in his vigilance, either by day or by night. He never forgot his zeal for duty, even at the times which

he devoted to pleasure or on those occasions when he took part in banquets and public festivals and ceremonies … Once embarked on drink – a besetting sin in his case – he would plunge headlong into all kinds of indecency. Even then, though, he did not forget the cares of empire, nor relax that fierce-beast look on his face or the sternness of his expression. It has often been a cause of surprise to me, when I have sat with him at banquets, to observe how a man, a slave to drink and given to ribaldry as he was, could bear the burden of power. In his cups he would carefully watch how each of his fellows behaved. Afterwards, as if he had caught them red-handed, he would submit them to questioning and examine what they had said and done in their drunken moments.

Other chroniclers described character but usually in a rather one-dimensional way. Note how Psellos does not merely describe John but weighs up the positive and negative sides of his personality, in order to explain his actions and the role that he played in the history of Byzantium.

Source: Michael Psellos, *Fourteen Byzantine Rulers*, trans. E.R.A. Sewter (Harmondsworth: Penguin, 1966), pp. 92–4.

These features of the *Chronographia* make it tempting to see Psellos as some kind of secular rationalist or even a religious sceptic, something that has been suggested by Anthony Kaldellis. However, like Leo the Deacon, Psellos frequently expressed himself in conventional religious terms. Along with all his other works, he wrote a description of a miraculous icon that was kept in one of Constantinople's churches, that of the Virgin at Blachernae. It therefore seems unlikely that the *Chronographia* was an attempt to present a new understanding of Byzantium's past, freed from the shackles of religious convention. The motivation behind the work was probably something much more down to earth: the need to justify the conduct of Psellos and that of his wealthy patrons in the Doukas family, just as Theophanes Continuatus had justified the usurpation of Basil I. The name Doukas recurs again and again in Byzantine history, usually among generations of soldiers who led the army on the eastern frontier. When he was a young hopeful in the 1040s, Psellos met the wealthy Constantine Doukas, who took a liking to him and gave him his unwanted possessions. When Doukas moved into a new house, Psellos was allowed to take over the old one. Meanwhile, political events moved on. In 1057, Doukas took part in the coup which brought Isaac I to power and when Isaac abdicated two years later, Doukas became Emperor Constantine X (see Section 10.2). Psellos played a leading role in bringing about this transfer of power and became one of the new emperor's closest advisers. Constantine X appointed Psellos as tutor to his young son, Michael, and when his pupil became Michael VII, Psellos occupied a similar position as he had under Michael's father. The second section of the *Chronographia*, which was probably written during Michael's reign, displays overt partiality for the Doukas family, quietly ignoring the disasters that occurred during their tenure of power. However, it is often overlooked that the first section, which covers the years 976 to 1059, also has a strong pro-Doukas bias. By stressing the incompetence of earlier emperors, especially Constantine IX Monomachos, Psellos sought to deflect blame for the chaos of the 1070s away from his political masters. As he himself put it, 'the gathering of the clouds in those days presaged the mighty deluge we are suffering today'. Sad to say, Psellos the historian was not a detached philosopher but an adept and ruthless politician.

5.5 Another kind of source: letters

About 150 collections of letters survive from the Byzantine period and on the face of it these should be a treasure trove of personal and historical information. Unfortunately they are not. They were exchanged between members of the Byzantine literary elite who wrote them in laboured Attic Greek. It was considered bad style to impart any concrete facts in the letters. Instead their authors tended to restrict themselves to generalised remarks about perennial concerns such as friendship, exile, sickness and death. No less than 273 letters written by Patriarch Photios of Constantinople survive but a large proportion of them are devoted to lamenting his fate and the loss of his friends after his deposition and exile by Emperor Basil I in 867; there is no specific discussion of the events that landed him in that situation (see Section 6.3). On the other hand, as is the case with many types of Byzantine source, behind the formal façade, Byzantine letters can sometimes be very informative. That is certainly the case with those left by Photios' pupil and friend, Nicholas Mystikos, who was not only patriarch of Constantinople but at times the effective ruler of Byzantium in the early years of the tenth century (see Section 6.4). Consequently his letters are addressed not just to his circle of intellectual friends but to important figures outside Byzantium such as the Arab emir of Crete and Tsar Symeon of Bulgaria. The letters to Symeon were written when the tsar was at war with Byzantium and constantly threatening to march on Constantinople. In one, the patriarch threatens the tsar with the wrath of God, reminding him of the fate of the Persians, Avars and Arabs who had dared to attack the Byzantine capital. In another, he adopts the tone of a concerned father and urges him to make peace with Emperor Romanos I. In this way, Nicholas gives a real insight into the political events of his day in which he himself was a participant.

Points to remember

*   The ninth century saw a revival of interest in the literature of classical Greece and of the higher educational system based on it.
*   From this period on, Byzantine historians wrote in Attic Greek and focused increasingly on human character to explain events.
*   Their works were not detached and neutral enquiries into the past but were often designed to justify and praise whoever was in power at the time that they were composed.
*   Abundant letters survive from the Byzantine period but it can be hard to use them as historical sources.

Primary sources in English translation

Constantine VII Porphyrogennetos. (1967), *De Administrando Imperio*, ed. Gyula Moravcsik and Romilly J.H. Jenkins (Washington, DC: Dumbarton Oaks).

Genesios, Joseph. (1998), *On the Reigns of the Emperors*, trans. Anthony Kaldellis (Canberra: Australian Association of Byzantine Studies).

Leo the Deacon. (2005), *The History of Leo the Deacon*, trans. Alice-Mary Talbot and Denis F. Sullivan (Washington, DC: Dumbarton Oaks).

Nicholas I Mystikos. (1973), *Letters*, ed. and trans. Romilly J.H. Jenkins and Leendert G. Westerink (Washington, DC: Dumbarton Oaks).

Psellos, Michael. (1966), *Fourteen Byzantine Rulers (Chronographia)*, trans. E.R.A. Sewter (Harmondsworth: Penguin).

Symeon the Logothete. (2019), *The Chronicle of the Logothete*, trans. Staffan Wahlgren (Liverpool: Liverpool University Press). An important source as it includes some information that is critical of Basil I and the Macedonian dynasty.

Theophanes Continuatus. (2011), *Chronographiae Quae Theophanis Continuati Nomine Fertur Liber Quo Vita Basilii Imperatoris Amplectitur*, trans. Ihor Ševčenko (Berlin and New York: De Gruyter). This volume covers the reign of Basil I (867–886). The rest of Theophanes Continuatus remains untranslated at present.

Theophanes Continuatus. (2015), *Chronographiae Quae Theophanis Continuati Nomine Fertur Libri I-IV*, trans. Jeffery M. Featherstone and Juan Signes-Codoñer (Berlin and Boston MA: De Gruyter). This volume covers the years 813 to 867.

White, Despina S. (1981), *Patriarch Photios of Constantinople: His life, Scholarly Contributions, and Correspondence* (Brookline MA: Holy Cross Orthodox Press). Contains translations of 52 of Photios' 273 extant letters.

Suggestions for further reading

Kaldellis, Anthony. (1999), *The Argument of Psellos' Chronographia* (Leiden and Boston MA: Brill). Sees Psellos as a nominal Christian who believed that the doctrine that the Byzantine emperor was the representative of God was merely a useful tool for instilling obedience into the populace. Kaldellis' thesis remains controversial.

Speck, Paul. (1998), 'Byzantium: Cultural Suicide?', *Byzantium in the Ninth Century: Dead or Alive?*, ed. Leslie Brubaker (Aldershot and Burlington VT: Ashgate, 1998), pp. 73–84. This is where Speck argues that the revival of higher education in the ninth century had the effect of stifling Byzantine literary culture by tying it to the Attic version of the Greek language.

Treadgold, Warren. (1984), 'The Macedonian Renaissance', *Renaissances before the Renaissance. Cultural Revivals of Late Antiquity and the Middle Ages*, ed. W. Treadgold (Stanford CA: Stanford University Press, 1984), pp. 75–98. An important article which defines what the 'renaissance' was and what it was not.

Treadgold, Warren. (2013), *The Middle Byzantine Historians* (Basingstoke and New York: Palgrave Macmillan). Discusses Byzantine historians writing from the ninth to the thirteenth century.

Wilson, Nigel G. (1996, 2nd revised edition), *Scholars of Byzantium* (London and Cambridge MA: Duckworth and Medieval Academy of America). Focuses primarily on how Byzantine intellectuals read and understood classical Greek literature, with sections on Photios, Arethas and Psellos, among others.

6 Amorians, Macedonians and Lekapenids (820–959)

The ninth and the first half of the tenth century form something of an interim period. The military revival that can first be detected in the later eighth century continued but Byzantium was not yet at the stage where it could go over to the offensive against its external enemies. Consequently, the Byzantines developed further techniques for managing the world and peoples around them without the need for direct military confrontation. Of equal significance is Byzantium's constitutional development at this time. It was to acquire a stable dynasty that was to last for nearly two hundred years, yet for a large part of that period the incumbent emperor was a mere figurehead, with power delegated to his mother, to a court eunuch or even to a co-emperor from another family. The relative authority of Church and state were tested to the limit as emperors explored just how far their status as the representative of God would allow them to go.

6.1 The Amorian dynasty (820–867)

In the early hours of Christmas Day 820, Emperor Leo V was assassinated while attending a service in one of the churches within the precincts of the Great Palace. The conspirators were acting on behalf of a man called Michael the Amorian, a former comrade-in-arms of Leo V, who had fallen foul of the emperor's suspicions and was languishing in prison on a charge of treason. He was quickly released and acclaimed emperor as Michael II. One of his first acts was to promote a eunuch called Theoktistos to the rank of Keeper of the Inkstand, in recognition of the role he had played as intermediary between the imprisoned Michael and his supporters on the outside, and he was to be an influential voice at the Byzantine court for over 30 years. Theoktistos held the same position under Michael's son and successor, Theophilos, and his star rose higher still when Theophilos died in 842, for the new emperor Michael III was still a child. As when this situation had last arisen in 780, a council of regency was formed, headed by the boy's mother, Theodora. The council included her brother Bardas, who held the office of Caesar, along with some other members of their family, but it was on Theoktistos that Theodora chiefly relied for advice, making him the most powerful man in Constantinople.

Theoktistos was just one of many eunuchs who played a central part in Byzantine politics and their prominence requires some explanation. They were probably employed as administrators by the emperors because they could not father children: it was their perceived dedication to the job, undistracted by family responsibilities, that enabled them to rise so high and so fast. They had the added advantage that they were debarred from the throne on the grounds that they were not physically whole so there was no danger of their having designs on the top job. For these reasons, being a eunuch conferred a distinct career advantage and in the provinces some families would deliberately have one of their sons castrated in order to give him the opportunity to travel to Constantinople and make his fortune at court. Others were imported as children from as far afield as the Caucasus to be specially raised for a life of dedicated service.

In reality, of course, eunuchs were no more trustworthy than anyone else. Merely because they could not become emperor themselves did not stop them from involving themselves in political intrigues on the side of someone else who could. The betrayal of Leo V by Theoktistos is a good example. Similarly, eunuchs, like everyone else, were vulnerable to the sometimes vicious politics of the Byzantine court. Bardas deeply resented Theoktistos' influence and hatched against him exactly the same kind of plot that Theoktistos had connived in against Leo V. In November 855, the eunuch was ambushed as he emerged from a council meeting, pursued through the corridors of the Great Palace and finally despatched as he vainly sought safety under a bench. Bardas now replaced Theoktistos as the main power behind the throne, for Empress Theodora was so upset by the eunuch's murder that she suffered some kind of breakdown and she retired to a convent the following year. Bardas remained at the helm even after Michael III grew up, for the young emperor turned out to have no interest in, or aptitude for, the demands of his office. Instead, he occupied himself with diversions such as chariot racing, which he indulged in at his own personal stadium at St Mamas, on the Bosporus north of Constantinople.

This long tale of plot, counter-plot, ruthless ambition and heedless self-indulgence may sound like a recipe for weak government and chaos, but it was not. It was a fact of Byzantine political life that, while emperors and their advisers might come and go, there was a basic continuity of policy, whoever was at the helm, thanks to the existence of an educated, secular bureaucracy, some of whom were eunuchs, some not. So in spite of the infighting behind the scenes, the reign of the puppet emperor Michael III (842–867) witnessed some signal successes. It was in this period that the controversy over icons was finally resolved. Leo V, Michael II and Theophilos had all been of the iconoclast persuasion and so that had remained the official policy, even if it was not implemented as zealously as it had been in the days of Constantine V. Theodora and Theoktistos reversed that. In March 843, they organised a Church synod which reinstated the decrees of the 787 Seventh Ecumenical Council and declared the veneration of holy pictures to be legitimate and orthodox. There was a certain amount of vocal opposition but for the most part the issue now disappeared, partly thanks to Theodora's sensible decision not to persecute the defeated iconoclasts.

The reign of Michael III also saw the empire's prospects improving in its endless struggle against external enemies. Under the first two Amorian emperors there had been a string of defeats at the hands of the Arabs. In 838, the Abbasid caliph Al-Mu'tasim had captured and sacked Amorion, the capital of the Anatolikon Theme, where the ruling dynasty had its roots. As late as 844, the Arabs were planning another attack on

Constantinople and they were gaining ground in areas that had previously not been threatened. In 826, the island of Crete was lost to an Arab invasion force and the following year an expedition sent by the Aghlabids of Tunisia had landed on Sicily and had begun to occupy parts of that island. In addition, the reigns of Michael II and Theophilos were marred by rather more serious internal upheavals than merely a few individual emperors and eunuchs being assassinated. A renegade soldier called Thomas the Slav led a rebellion between 820 and 823, claiming to be Constantine VI, the ousted son of Irene. He besieged Constantinople for over a year before he was finally captured and executed. After about 850, the pendulum began to swing in Byzantium's direction. The Abbasid caliphate was beginning to be troubled by dynastic instability and internal revolts. The regency in Constantinople was quick to take advantage. In May 853, when Theoktistos was still in power, a fleet was sent to the mouth of the Nile to sack the town of Damietta, the first time a Byzantine force had operated in that region for over two centuries. Ten years later, Bardas' brother, Petronas, achieved a significant victory over the armies of the Arab emir of Melitene at the battle of Poson, or Bishop's Meadow. The emir was killed and his entire army was annihilated. There were hopeful signs in Italy too. Although the arrival of the Arabs in Sicily had introduced a new threat to the Byzantine holdings there, the accession of the Western emperor Louis II in 855 was a positive development. Although he was a great grandson of the formidable Charlemagne, Louis ruled only the north of Italy, for the great Carolingian empire had by now broken up. He represented less of a threat and a potential ally against the encroaching Arabs.

The greatest success of all was in Bulgaria. The two powers had largely been at peace since 816 but by 852 the relationship was once again becoming strained. Khan Boris viewed the evident military revival of Byzantium with some alarm while the regency in Constantinople strongly disapproved of Boris' drive for westward expansion. The ultimate provocation came in 864 when it is likely that Bardas discovered that Boris had entered into negotiations with Louis the German, ruler of the East Franks and another descendant of Charlemagne. The prospect of Carolingian influence spreading to the Balkans as it had to Italy was too much and Byzantine troops were moved to the border. The threat came at a particularly bad time for Boris, for an outbreak of plague and a famine were sweeping his country so he was in no position to resist an invasion. He therefore sued for peace and in earnest of his goodwill he undertook to convert to Christianity. He was duly baptised in September 865, along with 30 of his nobles, by a bishop specially sent from Constantinople. It was a considerable triumph for Bardas and Michael III, who regarded the baptism as tantamount to acceptance of the suzerainty of the emperor.

The reign of Michael III did not have an unblemished record of military success. In June 860, Constantinople was attacked by a Russian fleet that had sailed down the River Dnieper from Kiev and then across the Black Sea. Descendants of Scandinavian Vikings who had migrated to the east, the Russians were formidable warriors but more to the point no one in Constantinople had prepared for an assault from that direction. Although they could not hope to break through the Land Walls, the Russians thoroughly pillaged the suburbs and had already departed long before the Byzantine army was able to return from Asia Minor. That reverse aside, the years from 842 to 867 were remarkably successful in spite of the apparent weakness at the top.

6.2 Basil I and the Macedonian dynasty (867–912)

During the years when Michael III officially, and Bardas effectively, ruled the empire, an impecunious young man called Basil set out for Constantinople from his home in Thrace to seek his fortune. Thanks to his charm, good looks and muscular physique, he was able to secure a position in a nobleman's household where he came to the attention of Michael III. The emperor took a fancy to him and gave him the office of Protostrator with the job of accompanying Michael on his daily horse rides. In 866, Caesar Bardas and Michael III gathered an expedition with a view to recovering Crete but while the fleet was at anchor off the coast of Asia Minor, Bardas was set upon by assassins and knifed to death. It is not difficult to guess who was behind the murder, for just over a month later, in May 866, Basil was crowned co-emperor, effectively replacing Bardas as the power behind the throne. Nor was Basil content to stop there. On the night of 24 September 867, Michael III was murdered by his own guards in his bed chamber in the palace of St Mamas and the next day, Basil was proclaimed sole emperor.

The death of Michael III marked the end of the Amorians and the advent of Basil I as the first emperor of the Macedonian dynasty. The name is inappropriate: Basil was in fact a Thracian of Armenian descent, but it has stuck. The Macedonians proved to be one of the most enduring Byzantine dynasties, lasting for 189 years until 1056. At the time of Basil's accession, however, there was no guarantee that he would not suffer the same fate as Leo V, Theoktistos, Bardas and Michael III and that power would not quickly pass to someone else. So from the very beginning of his reign, Basil and his advisers waged a dedicated propaganda campaign to convince his subjects that henceforth only he was entitled to rule. They were well aware that the new emperor's humble origins might be held against him, so in their public announcements they compared him to the Old Testament King David who had similar humble origins. At the same time, they concocted a family tree, linking him back to the kings of ancient Armenia, thus showing that he was of royal blood after all. Above all, they pushed the message that it was not just Basil himself but his whole family who were the legitimate rulers of Byzantium. Basil commissioned family portraits in mosaic of himself with his wife, Eudokia, and their children, to adorn the Great Palace and other public places, while on some issues of his gold coins Eudokia and his eldest son Constantine were depicted on the reverse. That way everyone could see the emperor's family and know who was to follow him on the throne. To make it absolutely clear, shortly after his accession, Basil had his eldest son Constantine crowned as co-emperor and in 870 the second son Leo was crowned too.

Another pillar of Basil's political platform was the message that he represented exemplary piety and traditional morality, in contrast to the hedonistic and irreligious Michael III and Bardas. He provided tangible evidence of his respect for religion by his ostentatious care for Constantinople's church buildings. He commissioned a splendid new edifice in the precincts of the Great Palace, known as the Nea Ekklesia or New Church, and following an earthquake in 869 he repaired Hagia Sophia and other churches that had been damaged. Basil also went out of his way to show that he was an ideal ruler with the interests of the people at heart. One way of doing that was to show concern for justice. Hence Basil's new legal compilation known as the *Epanagoge* which followed on from law codes issued by Justinian I and Leo III (see Box 6.2). The propaganda effort to assert the Macedonian dynasty's right to rule was to continue after Basil's death in the work of Theophanes Continuatus (see Section 5.2).

At the end of the day though, the safest way to deliver permanence for the Macedonian dynasty was through the kind of spectacular military victories that had earned Constantine V such popularity. Basil clearly aspired to that level of adulation, for unlike his immediate predecessor, he often led his armies in person. His reign did see some notable successes. In Asia Minor, the most pressing threat at the time of his accession was not the Arabs but the Paulicians, a Christian sect who rejected the teachings of the official Church. The Paulicians might have lived inconspicuously and harmlessly if they had been left alone, but in 844, Empress Theodora had ordered a massacre of them and thereby had driven them to insurrection. They had established a separate state in eastern and central Asia Minor and under their leader Chrysocheir they allied themselves with the Arabs and raided deep into Byzantine territory as far as Nicaea. On Basil's succession, the tide changed dramatically. In 872, a Byzantine army crushed the Paulicians and killed Chrysocheir, whose head was sent to Basil in Constantinople. With the Paulicians disposed of, Basil went on the offensive against the Arabs and captured some important fortresses, although he did not succeed in his main goal of taking Melitene.

Italy was also under threat during Basil's reign, for in 868 the Arabs crossed from their base in Sicily to the mainland and seized the port of Bari. Like his predecessors, Basil had no intention of leading an army there himself so he entered into an alliance with the Carolingian emperor, Louis II. Louis succeeded in ejecting the Arabs from Bari in 871 but having done so was reluctant to hand it back to the Byzantine emperor. It was only after Louis' death in 875 that Byzantine forces were once more able to occupy the port and to take back Taranto in 880. In 885, Basil appointed Nikephoros Phokas as domestic of the Scholai in the region, where he was able to reassert the emperor's authority throughout Apulia and Calabria. These successes were gratifying but Basil and his supporters must have known that depending on military victory for security and popularity was risky as things could very easily go wrong. That was exactly what happened in 878. Ever since their first landing in 827, the Tunisian Arabs had been slowly conquering the island of Sicily, but the city of Syracuse on its eastern side held out (see Figure 6.1). In 877, Basil received news that an Arab fleet was gathering on the Syrian and Egyptian coasts to make an attack, although no one knew as yet what its target might be. So the emperor gathered a fleet in Constantinople in readiness. To keep the crews busy while they waited for news of the enemy's movements, Basil put them to work on the construction of his new church, the Nea Ekklesia. Spring came and a report arrived that the Arab attack had been called off so Basil decided to send the ships to Sicily instead, placing it under the command of an admiral called Adrian. The fleet set sail but encountered stormy weather so it put in at a harbour in southern Greece and waited for a favourable wind. It was still there when dispatches arrived with the news that Syracuse had fallen on 21 May 878. Basil's victorious reputation had suffered a severe blow. People remembered the sailors working on the church and connected that with the fleet's late arrival. It was only to be expected that the historiography produced at the Macedonian court would play down the disaster. The responsibility was placed on the shoulders of Admiral Adrian for lingering too long in harbour. The moment the fleet arrived back in Constantinople, Adrian fled to the cathedral of Hagia Sophia for sanctuary but was dragged out and sent into exile. Even so, some of the blame was bound to stick to Basil.

Figure 6.1 Syracuse and its defences

Box 6.1 Theodosios the Monk on the fall of Syracuse (878)

Theophanes Continuatus, keen to preserve Basil I's reputation, goes into little detail about the Arab capture of Syracuse, although he does admit that 'the enormity of the mishap sorely tore at the vitals of the emperor'. Just how enormous the disaster was emerges from a letter written in Latin shortly afterwards by an eyewitness, the monk Theodosios. He makes it clear that a sudden Arab attack caught the defenders by surprise with fearful consequences for everyone inside the city:

> For when the stern displeasure of God against us had scattered hither and thither the stoutest of those who resisted the enemy, and had called away our famous Patrikios with his companions from the walls to their own houses, in order that they might take some food for their bodies' sake, then it was put into the hearts of the barbarians to renew the attack at that fatal tower of which I have spoken; and when they had advanced those engines which they used for throwing stones, the murderous traitors who invaded our city enjoyed the spectacle. Nor had they

undertaken a hard matter, since but a few soldiers were guarding the tower, and the citizens did not suppose that it was a time for fighting, so our defenders felt safe and thought of nothing less than of going to the ramparts. Therefore, while the enemy were hurling stones into the city in a fearful manner, and compassed it all round about, a certain wooden ladder, over which the half-ruined tower was usually reached by the garrison, was broken down, and thereupon a great din arose; when the Patrikios heard this, he sprang up at once from the table without finishing his meal, full of great anxiety for the ladder. As soon as the barbarians perceived that the ladder was broken down, for they were hurling their stones in its vicinity, they approached the walls with the greatest alacrity, and seeing but a few men guarding the tower, vigorously drove them back and slew them ... After this they ascended without opposition and took possession of the place, and thence they spread through the city like a river in the sight of those who were gathering together to defend it. First they slew to the last man those who were drawn up in line against them at the porch of the Church of the Saviour, and with a great rush they opened the doors and entered the temple with drawn swords, as they panted for breath, to emit fire from their nostrils and eyes. Then indeed people of all ages fell in a moment by the edge of the sword, princes and judges of the earth, as we sing in the psalms, young men and maidens, old men and children, both monks and those joined in matrimony, the priests and the people, the slave and the free man, and even sick persons who had lain a long time in bed. Merciful God, the butchers could not even spare these ...

It was not just that the Byzantines had lost one of their major strongholds in the West. The disaster was a milestone in the slow Arab conquest of the whole of Sicily which was completed in 902 with the fall of Taormina. No wonder the details were suppressed in Constantinople.

Source: Francis Marion Crawford, *The Rulers of the South*, 2 vols (London: Macmillan, 1901), vol. 2, pp. 79–99, at 86–8 (spelling adapted).

In spite of the reverse at Syracuse, the efforts of Basil and his supporters to establish the right of his family to rule paid off in the end. When he died in 886, apparently in a hunting accident, his eldest surviving son Leo replaced him without any question. That was some achievement, given that there were persistent rumours that Leo was not Basil's son at all but the offspring of the murdered Michael III. Leo VI (886–912) enjoyed a long reign and died in his bed of natural causes. In spite its bloody and completely illicit origins, the Macedonian dynasty was there to stay.

6.3 Church and state under the Amorians and early Macedonians

By now, one of the curious contradictions in Byzantine political ideology will have become apparent. In theory, the emperor was the representative of God on earth and his office was supposedly a sacred one, which was why he was usually portrayed in mosaics and on coins with a halo (see Section 0.3). Nevertheless, for all the mystical aura that surrounded them, emperors were regularly deposed, blinded and even, as in the cases of Leo V and Michael III, murdered. The relationship between the emperor and the Church was equally contradictory. In theory, the emperor followed as religious a calling as any priest, monk or bishop. Indeed, Leo III had once boasted to the pope that he was both ruler and priest. He and many others considered that emperors had as complete a power over the Church as over the rest of society. So on the face of it, the emperor could just dismiss any priest who displeased him, even a patriarch of Constantinople. In 730, Leo III had deposed Patriarch Germanos who opposed his stance on icons and replaced him with the more compliant Anastasios. In 843, Empress Theodora had likewise dismissed the iconoclast Patriarch John the Grammarian and replaced him with the iconophile Methodios. In practice though it was not always that easy. Emperors sometimes ran into implacable clerical opposition and found that they had their hands very full indeed trying to control the Church.

During the reign of Michael III, Caesar Bardas, who was an emperor in all but name, took a strong dislike to Patriarch Ignatios. An austere monk who had been appointed in 847, Ignatios publicly voiced his disapproval of the murder of Theoktistos and the side-lining of Theodora. He even went so far as to criticise Bardas' private life, accusing him of incest with his own daughter-in-law and barring him from receiving communion. So in 858, Bardas had the patriarch arraigned on a trumped-up conspiracy charge and instructed the soldiers who arrested him to give him the roughest treatment. They dragged the elderly cleric to the church of the Holy Apostles, stripped him naked and locked him inside the empty marble sarcophagus of the long-dead iconoclast emperor Constantine V. There he had to stay all night in the depth of winter, before next morning being taken off to exile in a monastery in the nearby Princes Islands. To replace Ignatios, Bardas chose a friend of his, the worldly and academic Photios who was not even a priest (see Section 5.1). Such a trifle was not allowed to stand in the way: Photios was simply ordained through all the ranks of the clerical hierarchy on successive days, to emerge as patriarch shortly after Christmas. Bardas clearly thought that as the secular ruler of the empire he could get away with anything.

He soon discovered his mistake, for he had stirred up a hornets' nest. Many monks, priests and bishops flatly refused to accept the unjust deposition of Ignatios and the irregular appointment of Photios. In February 859, they gathered in the church of St Irene and declared Photios deposed and Ignatios restored to office. They appealed over Bardas' head to the pope in Rome who was regarded as having a senior position in the Church (see Section 0.3). Pope Nicholas I backed the Ignatian case, declaring Photios to have been appointed illegally and excommunicating him. Both Bardas and Photios simply ignored the decree and the dispute might have gone on indefinitely had it not been overtaken by political events. Bardas was murdered in April 866 and in September the following year Basil I seized power. The new emperor had no love for Photios, a protégé of his enemy Bardas, so shortly after his violent accession, he deposed the patriarch, brought back Ignatios from his island exile and reinstated him. Envoys were sent to Rome to heal the breach and before long complete amity with the pope had been restored.

Although it was resolved, the incident had revealed that the emperor could not do anything he wanted with the Church and should have acted as a salutary warning to subsequent rulers to handle ecclesiastical matters with care. Unfortunately, so intertwined were Church and state in Byzantium that it was impossible to stand aloof. Basil I found that while the deposition of Photios in 867 might have satisfied the pope, the Byzantine Church remained divided. On one side were the now-victorious Ignatians, fundamentalist zealots who opposed secular learning and compromise. On the other were the Photians, men of education and culture, who were as familiar with the works of Aristotle as they were with the Bible and the Fathers of the Church. With their champion Photios now in exile, they lobbied behind the scenes for his return, or at least for him to be allowed access to his precious books. In time, the weary emperor relented and by 876 Photios was back in Constantinople and even working as a tutor to Basil's sons. When Ignatios died in 877, Photios stepped back into his former place in the patriarchal residence by Hagia Sophia. He became an important part of Basil's governing circle, helping to form the emperor's benign image and wash away the stain of the murder of Michael III. The Ignatians were now once more excluded and left resentful.

When Leo VI succeeded in 886, he may not have wanted someone who had been so influential over Basil I's latter years to remain in one of the highest offices in the land. So he deposed Photios and replaced him as patriarch with his own brother Stephen. The emperor got away with it this time although he did not have his own way entirely. A show trial designed to convict Photios of treason collapsed for lack of evidence and his supporters were able to present him as a dignified and wronged old man. In 901, Leo appeased the Photians by appointing one of their number, Nicholas Mystikos, as patriarch. Leo may have felt that he now had a safe and compliant individual in office and that probably would have been the case, had it not been for the thorny issue of the emperor's fourth marriage.

Leo VI suffered some extraordinarily bad luck in his personal life. Married three times and widowed three times between 882 and 901, he had no male heir apart from his younger brother Alexander. The future of the Macedonian dynasty was beginning to look rather uncertain. When in September 905, Leo did become the father of a son called Constantine there was a problem: he was not married to the boy's mother, Zoe Karbonopsina. At this point Leo doubtless reasoned that as emperor he could do anything he liked, so he married Zoe in April 906. He assumed that Patriarch Nicholas would obediently accept the marriage and announce that Leo's heir was legitimate. Unfortunately, the emperor had reckoned without the Eightieth Canon of St Basil of Caesarea which prohibited fourth marriages. The patriarch had no other option than to refuse to recognise the marriage to Zoe and although he baptised little Constantine, he stoutly refused to consider him legitimate. He severely disciplined the priest who had officiated at the offending nuptials and when on Christmas Day 906 the emperor, putative empress and their retinue turned up for the morning service at Hagia Sophia, the patriarch ordered the doors to be closed and refused to allow them in.

Nicholas though was not the stuff of martyrs and behind the scenes he was secretly searching for some kind of compromise which would allow the Church to recognise Leo's fourth marriage. Sadly, he was thwarted at every turn by the monks, priests and bishops of the Ignatian tradition who insisted that any accommodation of the emperor's demand would be a sinful betrayal of the faith. Finally, Leo VI lost patience and deposed Nicholas in February 907, replacing him with Euthymios. On the face of it, the appointment was a risky one, for Euthymios was a monk of the Ignatian mould, not given to compromise. But he was an old friend of Leo's and sympathised with the emperor's plight. He arranged for a dispensation, in return for penance on Leo's part, and in 908 little Constantine was proclaimed co-emperor and thus the heir presumptive. On the face of it, Leo had won but even Byzantine emperors could not control events from beyond the grave. When Leo died in 912, there was still a large body of opinion that the now seven-year-old Constantine was not legitimate. So it was Leo's younger brother Alexander who took over as emperor with Constantine VII relegated to co-emperor. The boy's mother Zoe was sent away from the Great Palace. Patriarch Euthymios was ritually defrocked at an ecclesiastical gathering, the assembled clergy kicking and punching him and pulling out the hairs of his beard, while Nicholas Mystikos returned triumphantly to office.

The dealings of Bardas, Basil I and Leo VI with the Church all reveal that there were certain limits on how far the emperor could go in imposing his will, but the lessons of these bruising encounters did not go unlearned. A few years later another emperor, Romanos I Lekapenos (920–945), was eager to appoint someone compliant to the office and his candidate was a certain Theophylact. Romanos knew that this appointment was likely to run into opposition because not only was Theophylact the emperor's own son, but he was only 16. Undaunted, Romanos might well have reasoned that the great mistake of Bardas and Leo VI had not been so much what they did but the high-handed and arbitrary manner in which they did it. Romanos went out of his way to make his actions seem legal and constitutional. The sitting patriarch, Tryphon, was apparently induced to resign voluntarily and the emperor then wrote to the pope asking for a dispensation to allow the Theophylact to succeed. Pope John XI, hard pressed by factional politics in Rome, happily agreed and the young patriarch was ordained in February 933. There were a few complaints. It was murmured that Theophylact preferred racing horses to church services and that he would break off in the middle of a liturgy and rush to the stables if he heard that one of his mares was giving birth. But there was nothing on the scale of the outcry that greeted the installation of Photios. Theophylact proved a loyal ally to his father for the rest of the reign. Romanos had need of the support because he was not a member of the Macedonian dynasty. How he came to be at the helm at all will be considered next.

Figure 6.2 Alexander leaves power to his nephew in 913; illustration from a thirteenth-century manuscript of Skylitzes in the National Library of Spain, Madrid

Box 6.2 The *Epanagoge*

The *Epanagoge* (Restatement) should more properly be called the *Eisagoge* or Introduction, because it was a handbook promulgated in around 886 to serve as a concise introduction to the legal code known as the *Basilika*. Photios was probably a major influence on its compilation during his second tenure of the patriarchate when he was in high favour with Basil I. Along with many other topics, the *Epanagoge* grapples with the issues of the exact powers of the emperor and the patriarch and the relationship between them. Here are some of the powers and responsibilities of the emperor. Note how they include some matters that one might assume to have belonged more properly to the Church and how §7 provides a limit on how far he can go. That might have influenced Romanos I in his careful process for appointing his son to the patriarchate:

II. §1. The emperor is a legal authority, a blessing common to all his subjects, who neither punishes in antipathy nor rewards in partiality, but behaves like an umpire making rewards in a game.

§5. The emperor must be most notable in orthodoxy and piety, and to be famous for holy zeal, both in the matter of the doctrines laid down about the Trinity and in the matter of the views most clearly and surely defined about the nature of the being of our Lord Jesus Christ according to the flesh …

§6. The emperor must interpret the law laid down by the men of old; and he must in like manner decide the issues on which there is no law.

§7. In his interpretation of the laws he must pay attention to the custom of the state. What is proposed contrary to the cannon [of the Church] is not admitted as a pattern [to be followed].

Regarding the powers of the patriarch, §8 sets out the ideal relationship between him and the imperial incumbent. §4 makes it clear, though, that the emperor is to be opposed if he violates the teaching of the Church, as Bardas and Leo VI discovered:

III. §4. The attributes of the patriarch are that he should be a teacher; that he should behave equally and indifferently to all men, both high and low; that he should be merciful in justice, but a reprover of unbelievers; and that he should lift up his voice on behalf of the truth and the vindication of the doctrines [of the Church] before kings and not be ashamed.

§8. As the constitution consists, like a man, of parts and members, the greatest and most necessary parts are the emperor and the patriarch. Wherefore the peace and felicity of subjects, in body and soul is [i.e. depends on] the agreement and concord of the kingship and the priesthood in all things.

Source: Ernest Barker, *Social and Political Thought in Byzantium from Justinian I to the Last Palaeologus* (Oxford: Oxford University Press, 1957), pp. 89–92.

6.4 Romanos I and the Lekapenid interlude (912–945)

Only a year after his accession, Emperor Alexander sickened and died unexpectedly in June 913. He made it clear on his deathbed that he wanted his nephew Constantine to succeed him as sole emperor, whatever the doubts as to his legitimacy (see Figure 6.2). So a council of regency was formed to govern until the boy was old enough to rule, even though Leo VI's widow, Zoe, was passed over as the head of the council. The Patriarch Nicholas Mystikos took charge instead but he still had doubts about the boy's right to be considered an emperor at all. Before the summer was out, the regency was facing a grave threat from the khan of Bulgaria, Symeon (893–927), the son of Boris who had converted to Christianity in 865 (see Section 6.1). During his brief reign, Alexander had given Symeon a pretext to attack by refusing to pay the annual tribute with which the Byzantines had for decades purchased peace with their troublesome neighbours. In August 913, the Bulgar khan arrived before the Land Walls with a large army. As the effective ruler, Patriarch Nicholas had to decide how to respond. It was unlikely that Symeon would be able to breach the Land Walls, but he could hardly be left in possession of Thrace indefinitely, so he would have to be bought off somehow. Certainly by September some kind of agreement had been reached, for the Bulgar army was packing up and heading for home. What is not entirely clear from the sources is what it was that Nicholas did to induce Symeon to leave. Theophanes Continuatus describes how Symeon's two sons were admitted to Constantinople where they dined with young Constantine VII. Then Patriarch Nicholas went outside the Land Walls to Symeon who knelt down before him. The patriarch was about to place a crown on the khan's head but at the last moment, he switched the crown with his own monastic cowl. After this, Symeon left Constantinople with his army, laden with gifts.

This description, like that of the fall of Syracuse, is clearly another example of the pro-Macedonian historiography manipulating the record to avoid an unpalatable subject. Symeon would hardly have broken off the siege for a free dinner and a new hat. Some kind of major concession must have been made and from other sources it is possible to work out what it was. Nicholas probably agreed to crown Symeon as emperor and to bless a marriage between Constantine VII and one of Symeon's daughters. Certainly from this time on, Symeon took to referring to himself as 'Tsar', a Slavonic word derived from 'Caesar' which was effectively the equivalent of the word that the Byzantines used for their emperor: *basileus*. Some of his seals carried an inscription in Greek: 'Many years to Symeon, peace-making *basileus*'. This all arose from the fact that Symeon was a very different kind of enemy from those who had threatened Byzantium in the past. He was not the product of an alien culture or religion. He was a Christian who had been educated in Constantinople, who spoke Greek fluently and was well acquainted with the ceremonial and spectacle of the Byzantine court. Indeed he admired what he had seen and sought to emulate it in his homeland. He moved his capital from Pliska to Preslav (see Figure 6.3) where he built a splendid palace for himself alongside the so-called Golden Church, a huge domed building in imitation of Hagia Sophia. Thus Symeon had no intention of destroying Byzantium but he did want to dominate it and possibly incorporate it into his own khanate. The marriage alliance and the imperial title were the first step towards that.

Figure 6.3 Column from Symeon's capital of Preslav

As it happened, the agreement made between Symeon and Nicholas was never put into effect. Many people seem to have been very uneasy at the far-reaching concessions that the patriarch had made and the following year, he was ousted from the regency. Zoe, Constantine's mother, took over and she quickly put paid to the plan to marry Constantine VII off to a Bulgar princess. Not surprisingly, Symeon was incensed at this U-turn and retaliated by invading Byzantium, overrunning Thrace and briefly capturing Adrianople in September 914. In response, Empress Zoe opted for the military option, confident that as the larger and richer society, Byzantium was bound to prevail. Certainly when the two armies clashed near Anchialos on 20 August 917, the Byzantines came off best at first and looked likely to push the Bulgars off the battlefield. Then a rumour started to circulate in the Byzantine ranks that their commander was dead. Noticing the ensuing panic, the Bulgars counter-attacked and largely wiped out the opposing army. It was a disaster on the same scale as that of 811 (see Figure 6.4).

No one could hope to survive politically after a defeat like that. In March 919, the admiral of the Byzantine fleet, Romanos Lekapenos, overthrew the regency of the empress Zoe and the following year had himself crowned emperor. That should have been the end of the

Figure 6.4 The defeat at Anchialos in 917, from the Madrid Skylitzes

Macedonian dynasty, just as 867 had been of the Amorians, but things had changed. Emperor Romanos was acutely aware that while he was of humble origins, the Macedonian family had come to be regarded as Byzantium's legitimate ruling dynasty. That precluded his merely brushing Constantine VII aside and instead he kept him in place as junior emperor. Romanos arranged that Constantine should marry his daughter Helena, so that he could then be linked to the Macedonian house. The two emperors appeared together on the coinage, although Romanos' figure was larger and his name came first in the inscription. Doubtless, Romanos planned to substitute his own family in due course, hence his coronation of his eldest son Christopher as co-emperor in 921. Constantine's image then disappeared from the coinage and was replaced by that of Christopher. But for the time being, the Lekapenids remained a parallel dynasty, ruling alongside the Macedonians.

The eventual establishment of Romanos' family was made much more likely by a number of military successes. It was Romanos who finally blocked the ambitions of Symeon of Bulgaria. With the military option ruled out, he resorted to the 'war by other means' at which the Byzantines excelled. He embarked on a diplomatic offensive to try to isolate the Bulgarian ruler. Learning that Symeon had sent envoys to al-Mahdi, the Fatimid caliph in North Africa, to ask for naval help in an attack on Constantinople (see Figure 6.5), Romanos sent ambassadors of his own to outbid the Bulgarians and keep the Tunisian ships in port. He encouraged the prince of Serbia to throw off his allegiance to Symeon, embroiling the Bulgars in a disastrous war in the mountains of Croatia in 926. Then in 927, Symeon died suddenly. Later that year, a treaty was made with the new tsar, Peter, who had no desire to prolong the conflict. Peter married Romanos' granddaughter and received recognition of his title of tsar. The peace was to hold for 40 years.

The settlement with Bulgaria allowed Romanos to pursue a more active policy in Italy and the east after 927. In Italy, the Byzantine position was once more under threat both from Arab raids from Sicily and from the rebellious Christian vassals, the princes of Capua and Salerno. By 935, Romanos had forged an alliance with the Frankish king of Italy, Hugh of Provence, and he sent a considerable force to the region to reassert

Figure 6.5 Tsar Symeon sends envoys to the Fatimid caliph, illustration from the Madrid Skylitzes

Byzantine authority. On the eastern frontier, Romanos inherited the old Byzantine ambition to recapture Melitene, the city which had for centuries been the base for Arab raids deep into Asia Minor (see Section 3.3). In 926, a Byzantine force succeeded in breaking into the city for a short time before being repulsed, but in 934 it was finally captured and was to remain in Byzantine hands for a century and a half. For the next ten years, the Byzantines mounted a series of successful raids across the Taurus range into Arab territory, reaching as far as Edessa in 944. The greatest success of Romanos' reign came in June 941 when a Russian fleet that had attacked Constantinople was completely destroyed in the Bosporus. Romanos must have hoped that with this kind of track record, he could quietly retire his scholarly co-emperor, Constantine VII.

Box 6.3 Letter of Muhammad al-Ikshid to Romanos I (938)

In spite of the religious divide and the frequent wars, the Byzantines were in regular diplomatic contact with their Arab neighbours. Envoys were constantly passing between Constantinople and the Abbasid capital of Baghdad, usually to negotiate truces and prisoner exchanges. By the 930s, however, the Abbasid caliph had become a weak and ephemeral figure, preoccupied with the revolt of the Shi'ite Qaramatians, barely able to pay his own army and in constant danger of being overthrown by his own Turkish bodyguards. It was much more profitable for the Byzantines to negotiate with those who held the real power, the governors of the provinces. Muhammad al-Ikshid administered Egypt between 935 and 946, ostensibly as an appointee of the caliph but in reality as an independent ruler. It was to him that Romanos Lekapenos sent envoys in 938, hoping to set up an exchange of prisoners. Note how al-Ikshid in his reply begins with the rhetoric of holy war before readily agreeing to Romanos' proposal:

Muhammad ibn Tugi al-Ikshid, servant of the Leader of the Faithful, to Romanos, great leader of the Romans and his associates, greetings in accordance with your merits. As for us, we give praise to God, apart from whom there is no god and we ask Him to confer His blessing on Muhammad, His servant and messenger: May God grant him blessings and peace!

Regarding the ransoming of prisoners and the views that you have expressed on the subject of their release, we are certain that those who are in your hands long only for victory or martyrdom. We know exactly their feelings on that point and their confidence in a good death and a fine reward, as they know what is coming to them. For these are men who prefer the miseries of imprisonment and the hard tests of adversity to the softness and pleasure of an easy life because they have the certainty of a magnificent hereafter and a splendid reward. They know that Almighty God, while he keeps their souls safe from harm, does not preserve their bodies.

However, we also have an exact knowledge of what the imams of former times and our pious predecessors have said on this matter. We find that these judgments are in harmony with what you ask and do not contradict what you desire. We also rejoice that everything can easily be achieved. Thus we have sent letters and messengers to the governors of all our provinces and we have asked them to gather together all the prisoners in their care, along with their dependants and to have them set out in complete safety. We have invested all possible effort on this and we waited before we answered your letter, so that our deeds came before our words and our fulfilment preceded our promise. You will soon see the outcome which will afford you the greatest satisfaction, if it please God! ... We have granted to your ambassadors the opportunity of selling the goods that you sent with that intention. We have permitted them to sell and to buy everything that they wish and desire. We have in fact found no religious or political reason that forbids that. More than any other ruler, we are anxious to be on friendly terms with you and with those who have come on your behalf. We wish also to nurture and maintain the relations that you have established with us and to make the seed that you have broadcast grow. God will help us to achieve our good intentions and to complete the good work to which we are strongly attached.

The clause at the end is instructive as well. While Byzantines and Arabs fought bitterly on the Asia Minor border, their merchants happily traded with each other. There was even a mosque in Constantinople specially provided for the use of visiting Arab traders (see Box 7.1). The rhetoric of holy war and religious difference was only part of the story.

Source: Marius Canard, 'Une lettre de Muhammad ibn Tugi al-ihsid, émir d'Egypte à l'empereur Romain Lécapène', in Marius Canard, *Byzance et les musulmans du proche orient* (London: Variorum, 1973), No. VII (author's translation from the French).

6.5 The Macedonians restored (945–959)

Although Romanos Lekapenos proved himself to be one of the most able Byzantine emperors, his dynasty never succeeded in establishing itself. His eldest son Christopher, whom he had crowned as co-emperor and doubtless expected to succeed him, died before his father in 931. Romanos' youngest son Theophylact had become patriarch, but he had two others, Stephen and Constantine, who were now given precedence over the Macedonian Constantine VII on state occasions. Nevertheless, Romanos did not announce specifically that Stephen was to succeed him, and by December 944, he was obviously in ill health. Stephen and Constantine took their chance and overthrew him, sending him off to a monastery on one of the islands in the Sea of Marmara. The obvious next step would have been to remove Constantine VII, but when news came of Romanos' overthrow a large crowd gathered outside the Great Palace, demanding to see the Macedonian emperor. The brothers then tried to set up an arrangement similar to that used by their father, with Constantine VII as a figurehead while they held real power. But by then, it was too late. Constantine VII had allied himself with the new domestic of the Scholai, Bardas Phokas, and they had Stephen and Constantine arrested in January 945, sending them into exile in the same monastery as their father.

Now that he had finally achieved sole power at the age of 39, Constantine VII was understandably bitter against his father-in-law Romanos, who had very nearly deprived him of his birth right. He took a literary revenge, branding the ex-emperor as a 'common ignorant fellow' in one of the manuals produced during his reign (see Section 1.4). Nevertheless, the policies that he pursued followed much the same pattern as those of his predecessor, especially when it came to affairs in the east. The run of military successes continued with a number of border towns being retaken, although an attempt to seize back Crete in 949 proved a failure. Like Romanos, Constantine VII was aware of the increasing fragmentation of the Abbasid caliphate and he reflected that in his diplomatic dealings with the Muslim world, exchanging envoys with the rulers of Cordova, Damascus, Tunisia, Aleppo and Tarsus rather than Baghdad. There was, however, one significant result of the weakness of the caliphate. In response to Byzantine attacks on the Taurus Mountains border, it was decided to create autonomous districts on the frontier so that defence could be organised locally. The cities of Tarsus and Melitene had had their own autonomous emirs for years and that practice was now extended to northern Mesopotamia where the Hamdanid family established themselves as emirs first at Mosul and then at Aleppo. The Byzantines soon found that their attempts to push further east were parried by the formidable Hamdanid emir, Sayf ad-Dawlah (945–967), who also mounted regular raids into Byzantine territory. In 954, as he returned from one of these expeditions, Sayf was intercepted by a numerically superior force led by the domestic Bardas Phokas. The fierce attack of the Hamdanid cavalry unnerved the Byzantine troops who abandoned their commander. Bardas was wounded in the face and only just escaped himself. For the time being the old equilibrium on the eastern frontier remained in place.

Points to remember

- The political events of this period demonstrate that power was by no means concentrated in the hands of the emperor. The patriarch, empress, eunuchs, generals and even the ordinary people of Constantinople could play a part.
- Although Byzantine politics have a reputation for bloodshed, there were limits. Basil I seized the throne in 867 by murdering his predecessor but that was not enough to make his dynasty permanent. He had to establish his legitimacy with the help of a carefully orchestrated propaganda campaign.
- Romanos I tried to follow the same path but was ultimately unsuccessful and the Macedonian dynasty returned to power.
- The treaty of 927 with the Bulgars brought a lasting peace to the Balkans, allowing the Byzantines to concentrate their military efforts in Italy and on the eastern frontier.
- Byzantine fortunes on the eastern frontier in this period were closely tied to the strength and weakness of the Abbasid caliphate.

Suggestions for further reading

El-Cheikh, Nadia Maria. (2004), *Byzantium Viewed by the Arabs* (Cambridge MA: Harvard University Press). Containing numerous translated extracts from contemporary Arabic sources, this book demonstrates how the Arabs viewed Byzantium not only with hostility but sometimes with sympathy and admiration.

Nicol, Donald M. (1988), 'Byzantine Political Thought', in *The Cambridge History of Medieval Political Thought C.350-c.1450*, ed. J.H. Burns (Cambridge: Cambridge University Press), pp. 51–79. This article provides a very useful overview, even if it tends to present Byzantium's ideology as rather static and unchanging.

Tougher, Shaun. (1997), *The Reign of Leo VI: Politics and People* (Leiden and Boston MA: Brill). An authoritative and thorough investigation of the reign with an especially helpful chapter on the stand-off over Leo's fourth marriage or *tetragamy*.

Tougher, Shaun. (2008), *The Eunuch in Byzantine History and Society* (Abingdon and New York: Routledge). Considers the whole question of when and why eunuchs came to play such a central part in Byzantine politics and includes a useful appendix with biographies of some of the most prominent.

7   Economy and culture

It is easy to dismiss economic and cultural matters as peripheral to the history of a medieval society such as Byzantium, because the surviving literary sources largely ignore them, focusing instead on religion, politics and war. Yet Byzantium's survival and military recovery would not have been possible without the parallel economic upturn and that in turn fuelled a cultural revival. Nor should developments in art and architecture be seen as mere add-ons, the wallpaper behind the 'real' political history. Byzantine culture played a pivotal role in the establishment of the empire's hegemony and was to have a lasting influence on its neighbours.

7.1 Economic revival

Even in the darkest times of the crisis in the seventh and eighth centuries, Byzantium had retained certain economic advantages, one of which was preservation of the gold coinage (see Section 3.4). While the copper coin or follis ceased to circulate in some parts of the empire during the seventh century and silver coins disappeared altogether, the gold nomisma continued to be minted and it served as a recognised and sought-after means of exchange throughout the world. Surviving examples have been found in hoards and burial sites as far afield as Scandinavia and China. Such was its international reputation that when the Umayyad caliph, Muawiyah, minted his own gold coin in the 660s, his subjects initially refused to accept it because its design differed from that of the nomisma.

As the military situation improved, the silver and bronze coinage returned. Herakleios had minted some silver coins in 615 but it was Leo III who reinstated the silver denomination permanently in 720 when he began minting the miliaresion, 12 of which made up one nomisma. Numbers of the copper follis in circulation increased dramatically after 800. There were 288 of them to the nomisma and 24 to the miliaresion, so they were used for everyday purchases, such as buying bread or fish at a local market. The larger quantities being produced would therefore suggest that many more transactions were taking place. Given that they were now circulated so widely, the miliaresion and follis were also useful tools for disseminating a message among the mass of the population. They generally carried a portrait of the reigning emperor but subtle changes were often made to the design for political reasons. For example, during the reign of Michael I (811–813) the inscription on the miliaresion was changed from just 'emperor'

Figure 7.1 Follis of Constantine VII (945–959). The inscription reads: 'Constantine, in God, Emperor of the Romans'

to 'emperor of the Romans'. The same change was later made on the follis. This was doubtless a response to the coronation of the Frankish ruler Charlemagne as emperor in Rome in 800. The Byzantines had reluctantly recognised his title but they insisted that only their ruler was emperor of the Romans (see Section 4.5 and Figure 7.1). Then, during the reign of John Tzimiskes (969–976), the design of the follis was more radically changed. The imperial portrait was replaced by that of Jesus and the inscription on the back became 'Jesus Christ, King of Kings' (see Figure 7.2). The change was probably once again designed to demonstrate the uniqueness of Byzantium as the state on earth ordained by God: Christ was its real ruler.

The wider circulation of coinage and the revival of economic activity would have greatly increased the income that the state received through taxation. A land tax was levied on all landowners, the rate depending on the size and quality of their holding. Peasants did not pay the tax individually: the village itself was assessed and the inhabitants clubbed together to make up the amount, the so-called *allelengyon*. There were all kinds of other imposts as well: a hearth tax and a tax on bees and other animals. These were paid in coin but there were also requirements for compulsory labour, such as repairing

Figure 7.2 Follis of John I Tzimiskes with Christ as ruler

bridges and roads. Not everyone was liable to all these dues. Some peasant households, which were instead responsible for supporting one of their number who served in the army, were exempt, as were most monasteries (see Section 7.3).

There was, however, another source of income in the kommerkion, a customs duty of 10 per cent of the value of cargoes, whether imports or exports. Ships coming to or sailing from Constantinople had to pay the duty at either Hieron on the Bosporus or at Abydos on the Dardanelles, and similar levy was made at other Byzantine harbours such as Almyros and Trebizond (see Figure 7.3). The kommerkion was a particularly valuable source of revenue as there was a marked increase in international trade after about 800. Constantinople stood at the end of the overland silk road that ran from China through Central Asia via the Abbasid caliphate, so cargoes of silk, spices, glass and porcelain regularly reached it by this route as well as by sea from Syria. From the north, Russian

Figure 7.3 Byzantine kommerkion seal. Lead seals were used to close letters prior to despatch. This one belonged to an official who administered the collection of the kommerkion from vessels that passed through the Dardanelles at Abydos. The text reads 'Lord, help your servant Andrew, imperial kommerkiarios and paraphylax of Abydos' (© Dumbarton Oaks, Byzantine Collection, Washington, DC)

and Bulgarian merchants brought furs, honey and amber, while Italian merchants shipped in cargoes of wool, tin and timber. Only a small proportion of all these imports would have remained in Constantinople. Most would have been bought up by merchants to fill their ships for the return journey. Furs commanded a high price in the markets of Baghdad. Silk and spices could be sold on at astronomical prices in Italy and Western Europe beyond the Alps. Constantinople was thus an entrepôt, a place where goods from one part of the world could be brought to be sold on and taken to another. Some of this trade was in the hands of Byzantine merchants but the bulk of it was handled by foreigners, especially Arabs, Russians and Italians from cities such as Amalfi, Pisa and Venice. The Byzantines benefited by taxing every cargo that came in and everything that went out.

This reliable income stream enabled the Byzantine emperors to buy alliances and truces with foreign powers, to fund complex projects such as the movement of entire populations to resettle deserted lands and later to pay for the aggressive wars of the later tenth and early eleventh century that are described in the next chapter (see Section 8.2). The greater wealth of the state and of Byzantine society in general were also reflected in the advances in education that were taking place at this time (see Section 5.1) and in developments in art and architecture.

Box 7.1 The Serçe Limanı ship

In around the year 1030, a Byzantine merchant ship was heading northwards up the Aegean towards Constantinople on its way back from Syria. It was a small two-masted vessel, probably measuring only about 15 metres in length and 5.3 metres across. The crew would have lived and slept on the deck since all the space in the hold would have been occupied by the cargo. It would seem that as darkness was falling and the wind was rising, the captain decided to drop anchor for the night, inside a natural harbour on the Asia Minor coastline, opposite the island of Rhodes. Unfortunately, when the anchor was dropped, its shank broke off. With nothing to hold it, the ship was dashed up against the rocky coast and sank with its entire cargo. Perhaps some or all of the crew managed to swim or wade ashore, perhaps not.

Rediscovered in the twentieth century, the wreck was excavated by a team from the Institute of Nautical Archaeology at Texas A&M University during the summers of 1977–1979. Known as the Serçe Limanı ship, from the place on the Turkish coast where it sank, it is now preserved in the Museum of Bodrum (see Figure 7.4). Inside the hull were discovered numerous personal effects of the crew: a pair of scissors, a comb, an earring, a sword, several axes and some gaming pieces that were doubtless helpful in whiling away the long hours on deck. Fish and pig bones gave a clue to what the crew ate for their last meal. Even more intriguing was the cargo, which was surprisingly intact, given that it consisted of ceramics and glass. Analysis of the items suggested that they had been manufactured in Syria and were thus tangible proof of the trade between Byzantium and the lands of the Abbasid caliphate which was mentioned in the 938 letter of Muhammad al-Ikshid to Emperor Romanos I (see Box 6.3). They included glazed bowls, amphorae for wine, glass bottles and weights. There was also a certain amount of broken glass but it had not been smashed in the wreck. It was cullet, fragments that were being imported as a raw material for Byzantine glass manufacturers and thus an early example of recycling. The Serçe Limanı ship was just one of thousands that doubtless made their way up the Aegean every year, passing through the Dardanelles to reach Constantinople's harbour, the Golden Horn, providing an important income stream for the Byzantine treasury.

Further reading: George F. Bass et al., *Serçe Limanı: an Eleventh-Century Shipwreck*, 2 vols (College Station TX: Texas A&M University Press, 2004–9).

Figure 7.4 The remains of the Serçe Limanı ship, in the Bodrum Museum, Turkey

7.2 Art and architecture

Just as commerce and education had been neglected during the period of crisis, so had art. The production of illustrated manuscripts, icons, ivories, mosaics and other expensive artefacts seems to have dropped off steeply during the later seventh and eighth centuries. Byzantium's straitened political and economic circumstances probably ensured that there was little money to spare for such things, even on the part of the emperor. Of what was produced almost nothing has survived. We know, for example, that Constantine V adorned the Milion arch in Constantinople with a painting of his favourite charioteer, but both arch and painting have long since vanished. As regards religious art, the dispute over icon veneration caused some uncertainty as to what could or could not be depicted. Some, although by no means all, of the decoration in churches was destroyed by the iconoclasts, but they did replace it with designs of their own that featured trees, birds and animals rather than human figures. Again, none of this work has survived apart from a large cross in the apse of St Irene in Constantinople which may date from the iconoclast period (Figure 7.5).

As the crisis passed and conditions became more settled, emperors and wealthy patrons could once more commission both secular and religious art and architecture. Around 830, Emperor Theophilos gave orders for a new summer residence to be built on the Asian side of the Bosporus, the Bryas palace. For the Great Palace, he ordered a tree made of gold with birds perched on its branches that could be made to sing, probably by some kind of steam power. Books began to be produced in greater numbers: it was in the later

Figure 7.5 Cross from the apse of the church of St Irene in Constantinople

ninth century that Byzantine intellectuals such as Arethas and Photios began to commission and collect manuscripts of classical Greek texts (see Section 5.1). Illustrated religious texts came to be in demand as well. For example, in around 880, Basil I commissioned a copy of the Homilies of St Gregory Nazianzus, accompanied by richly coloured scenes from the Old and New Testaments (Figure 7.6).

For those who had the resources, a favourite act of patronage was the building (or rebuilding) of churches and the decoration of their interiors. An early example is Caesar Bardas' renovation of the Pharos chapel in the Great Palace, which housed the True Cross, in around 860. Later emperors did not content themselves with merely restoring but wanted to leave a monument to themselves with a completely new church. Basil I built the Nea Ekklesia, or New Church, within the precincts of the Great Palace (see Section 6.2) and Romanos I Lekapenos built the Myrelaion just down the hill from it, intending it to become the burial place for his family (Figure 7.7).

None of these churches was particularly striking when viewed from the outside. The Byzantines tended not to adorn them with ornate carvings of the kind that are found on the outer walls of Western medieval churches or to build on the scale of the great Romanesque or Gothic cathedrals. Rather, they poured all their energies into the interior decoration, which was usually done in mosaic where the image was built up with thousands of tiny cubes of different-coloured marble. A surviving mosaic from the ninth century is the Virgin and Child in the apse of Hagia Sophia which was finished in 867 (Figure 7.8).

Figure 7.6 The homilies of St Gregory of Nazianzus from the Bibliothèque Nationale, Paris

Isolated examples like that, however, do not do justice to the impact that the decoration would have had. The entire wall, roof and dome space would have been covered with depictions of scenes from the life of Christ and the Virgin and an army of saints and martyrs. Whether viewed by flickering candlelight or by the sun shining in through the upper windows, the effect of the glittering light on these mosaics must have been stunning. Basil I's Nea Ekklesia no longer stands, but Theophanes Continuatus described it as being 'resplendent with beautiful images as with stars'. One of the best-preserved Byzantine churches is that of the monastery of Hosios Loukas near Steiris in central Greece (Figure 7.9). Founded in the mid-tenth century by a hermit called Luke of Steiris (c.900–953) (see Box 7.2), it was rebuilt on a lavish scale in the early eleventh century. It typifies the square design with no long nave leading to a distant altar. Byzantine churches were designed in this way to reflect the dictum of St John of Damascus that the veneration of an image passed beyond it to the holy person depicted. The intimate space was intended to surround and enfold the congregation, conveying their veneration through the mosaics and icons towards heaven and linking them directly to the metaphysical world.

Figure 7.7 The church of the Myrelaion monastery, now the Bodrum Mosque

Figure 7.8 The apse mosaic from Hagia Sophia

Figure 7.9 The interior of the Hosios Loukas monastery

7.3 Monasteries

More often than not, the churches that attracted the patronage of the emperor and his prominent subject were attached to a monastery or convent. Romanos Lekapenos' Myrelaion stood at the centre of one and the emperor arranged an annual stipend for the maintenance of the monks. It was not only emperors who established and funded these institutions but their wealthy subjects too. In 907, a nobleman called Constantine Lips founded a new monastery in Constantinople and invited emperor Leo VI to its inauguration. Nor was the phenomenon confined to Constantinople. New monasteries were founded in Greece and the southern Balkans in the wake of the restoration of Byzantine rule there. One of the most famous and long-lasting was the Great Lavra on Mount Athos in northern Greece, established in 963 by a hermit called Athanasios with the encouragement and financial backing of Emperor Nikephoros II (Figure 7.10). With the recapture of Crete in 961, the Aegean islands were once more safe from piratical attacks by sea so that Emperor Constantine IX could establish his Nea Moni on the island of Chios in 1044. The monasteries would, of course, have varied in size, depending on

Figure 7.10 The Great Lavra monastery, Mount Athos

the resources available to the founder. Many would have been tiny and housed only a handful of monks or nuns. Whatever the size, founders generally provided their new monastery with a charter or typikon which laid out in detail what lifestyle the monks should follow: there was no universal rule like that of St Benedict in the West. Individual hermits, who lived outside a monastic community altogether, were regarded as following a higher calling.

For the motives behind all this generosity, we need look no further than a deeply felt religious belief and a genuine admiration for the lifestyle of monks and nuns. Thanks to their unworldly lifestyle, they were believed to possess *parrhesia*, literally 'access' to God, to whom their prayers would be more acceptable than those of everyone else. Thus they acted as a kind of bridge between God and the mass of the population and could perhaps make the difference between salvation and damnation in the next life. Politicians like Basil I and Romanos I, who had done some unscrupulous things in their quest for power, hoped to atone for their misdeeds by supporting the godly lifestyle of monks and nuns. There was, of course, the added advantage that giving help to monks enabled them to present themselves as pious and virtuous and so justified in their seizure of supreme power.

Even if their deep admiration for the monastic life is taken into account, the sheer number of monasteries being set up from the ninth century onwards and the expense lavished on them might seem excessive. One twentieth-century historian estimated that there were around 7,000 monasteries and about 150,000 monks in the Byzantine empire by 1000 CE: the Great Lavra on Mount Athos alone had 700. They must therefore have constituted a significant proportion of its population, which cannot have been more than about 20 million people. Given that these men were thus removed from military service and agriculture and that monasteries and their land often enjoyed tax exemption, monasticism might be seen as a massive drain on wealth and manpower. There are indications that some people thought so at the time. Even though he was the devoted patron of the Great Lavra, in 964 Emperor Nikephoros II introduced a law decreeing that those who wanted to promote the monastic life should restore existing establishments rather than set up new ones. Instead of giving land to monasteries, they should sell it and use the money to provide the monks with sheep, oxen and other animals. At the end of the day though, such reservations were not the norm. Nikephoros II's law was only in force for a few years until 988, when it was repealed by a later emperor, Basil II. The monastic ideal was too deeply embedded in the Byzantine psyche to be restricted in that way.

In any case, monks and nuns were by no means idle drones who made no contribution to society. In a world where there was neither state social security nor private insurance, they offered a wide range of services, free of charge for those who needed them: care for orphans, the disabled, lepers, the insane and the elderly. They provided poor relief, medical care and ultimately the decent burial of those who died without means or family. All the great imperial monasteries were designed not only to look grand but also to provide some or all of these services in the complex of buildings around the main church. There was a hospital and an old people's home at the Myrelaion monastery and every day some 30,000 loaves of bread were distributed there to the poor (see also Box 11.3). That was, of course, exceptionally generous because the Myrelaion was a very well-endowed institution, but most monasteries and convents did something similar for anyone who asked for help at the gate. They usually provided hospitality to travellers as well and financial assistance to orphans, prisoners and women who could not afford a dowry.

Box 7.2 Admiration of the Holy Man: the life of Luke of Steiris

Reverence for the monastic life was a feature of all levels of Byzantine society. Emperors and noblemen might build new monasteries and endow them with lands, but the poor and obscure paid their respects in their own way too. In this passage, it is the year 953 and news has spread through the neighbourhood of Steiris in central Greece that the hermit Luke was dying.

> When those who dwelt in the villages round about learned this, even though there was a terrible storm and indescribable snow was falling, so that the roads were nearly impassable and the people housebound, nevertheless nothing could prevent them from travelling to see him. All of them gathered together and remained by him until the ninth hour, paying no attention to food or to returning home; they all stood attentively looking at his gentle face, hoping to hear his beloved voice and last words and to receive his blessing. Indeed they were

unable to tear themselves away from the bed and to stop looking at him and go home, for they were feeling the blow of the final separation, the one after death, and their tears which flowed without ceasing showed how their souls suffered on his account; finally, kissing all of them and praying for good things, he dismissed them, even though they were reluctant, groaning sadly and profoundly grieving ... At dawn, [after Luke had died] the priest called the villagers from the neighbourhood and, digging out the spot and embellishing it as best he could, completed the customary service; and he placed the sacred body in it as if it were great wealth ...

There is no reason to doubt the text's account of the grief of the villagers for Luke's passing but inevitably not everyone reverenced all monks all the time. Two brothers who lived near Chrysopolis, across the Bosporus from Constantinople, became embroiled in a property dispute with their neighbour, a monk called Symeon the New Theologian, and even came to blows with him. Incidents like that are irrelevant here. The ideal of the individual who by their self-denying lifestyle drew closer to God than the mass of humanity remained a compelling one, even if very few people ever lived up to it.

Source: *The Life and Miracles of St Luke*, trans. Carolyn L. Connor and W. Robert Connor (Brookline MA: Hellenic College Press, 1994), pp. 107–9.

7.4 Cultural influence

The value of monks went a lot further than just their charitable work. They played an integral part in the way Byzantium used its religious, literary and artistic heritage to advance its political interests. One way in which they did that was to help to integrate reconquered territories. From 780 on, the Byzantines had been able to reassert their control over Greece and the southern Balkans and during the 880s, the domestic of the Scholai, Nikephoros Phokas, had re-established control in southern Italy. Similarly in 961 Crete was finally reconquered after being under Arab rule since 820 (see Sections 3.5, 6.2 and 8.2). While these victories were heartening, they brought within the borders populations that did not necessarily identify with the government in Constantinople. During the nearly 200 years of separation, Greece and the southern Balkans had been occupied by large numbers of pagan Slavs. Not all of them were happy to submit to Christian rule and they rose in revolt in around 840. On Crete, there had been inevitable conversions to Islam during nearly a century and a half of Arab rule while in southern Italy the period of Byzantine weakness must have impelled many people to look to the Carolingian ruler in the north as a better protector.

It was not enough simply to import existing administrative structures and to set up new Themes in the reconquered areas: something had to be done to win over hearts and minds. Itinerant hermits such as Luke of Steiris (see Box 7.2) travelled around Crete and

Greece, preaching and converting the empire's new subjects to Christianity. They founded monasteries, like that of the Virgin at Myriokephala on Crete and Hosios Loukas in central Greece. They helped to spread the use of the Greek language which ultimately replaced the Slavonic dialects in the Peloponnese. In southern Italy, a similar function was performed by Neilos of Rossano (c.910–1004) and others. By spreading Byzantine monastic practices and the Greek liturgy they reinforced the cultural links of Apulia and Calabria with Constantinople as opposed to Rome and the Latin north.

Monks also had a role to play outside the empire, helping to bring potentially hostile countries inside the Byzantine cultural orbit. In 865, the Byzantines appeared to have scored a major diplomatic triumph when their former enemy, Boris the khan of the Bulgars, accepted baptism as a Christian from priests sent from Constantinople (see Section 6.1). But rejoicing at having drawn Bulgaria into the Byzantine fold proved rather premature. Boris faced considerable internal opposition to his new religion and his conversion was immediately followed by a revolt among some of the leading Bulgar clans. There was a widespread perception that Bulgarian independence was threatened and that acceptance of Byzantine Christianity would lead to political and cultural absorption as was happening to the Slavs in the southern Balkans. Boris began to demand a separate patriarch for Bulgaria, so that it would not be under the ecclesiastical domination of Constantinople. When it became clear that the patriarch of Constantinople had not the slightest intention of granting his request, he expelled all Byzantine missionaries and sent an embassy to Rome asking the pope to send his own preachers of the faith. There was a real danger that Boris would align himself with the pope and the king of the East Franks and thus present an even greater threat to Byzantium's northern border.

The Byzantine response was to develop a strategy completely different from the one that they were using to reintegrate the southern Balkans: they aimed to present the Christian religion in a way that was not culturally alien to the Bulgars. When, in 886, Boris relented and once more allowed Byzantine missionaries into Bulgaria, a group of monks was despatched under the leadership of Clement (840–916), who become the first archbishop of Bulgaria, based at Ohrid. Clement and his followers brought with them something that the missionaries sent from Rome did not have: Glagolitic script. It was an alphabet designed specifically for the Slavonic language that the Bulgars spoke. It had been developed during the 860s by two Byzantine monks, the brothers Cyril and Methodios, who were from Thessalonica and had grown up bilingual in Greek and Slavonic. The new alphabet allowed them to translate the Gospels and liturgy from Greek into an idiom comprehensible to all Slavonic speakers, which became the official language of the Bulgarian Church. From his base at Ohrid, Clement organised Slavonic-speaking preachers and the dissemination of the Slavonic liturgy and scriptures so that by 900 Bulgaria had been effectively Christianised. He even improved on the Glagolitic script and ultimately developed a replacement for it, known as Cyrillic, which is still in use today. By not attempting to impose Greek, Clement and his followers helped to foster a distinct Bulgarian religious culture. Khan Symeon's capital of Preslav became a centre for the translation of Greek texts into Slavonic.

While an adjustment was made for the Bulgarian context in the matter of language, when it came to ecclesiastical art, Byzantine traditions could be imported without change. For monks not only preached Christianity and developed the Slavonic script, they were also the artists who created the mosaics and frescoes that adorned Byzantine churches. They were often also the architects that designed them and the workmen that built them too. The images that they created were a powerful weapon. According to one story, Khan Boris was persuaded to convert by seeing a wall painting of the Last Judgement by a Byzantine monk. The story is probably apocryphal but it does bear witness to the impact that art could have in a world where man-made visual imagery was rare. Archbishop Clement saw to it that the town of Ohrid was provided with a cathedral, dedicated to the Holy Wisdom like its counterpart in Constantinople, and constructed and decorated in the Byzantine style (Figure 7.11). Other churches and monasteries were also built there, the archbishop overseeing the construction of St Panteleimon himself. The frescoes that survive inside these churches were probably the work of Byzantine monks, painted in the eleventh century under Archbishop Leo, another monk from Constantinople.

Byzantine religious and cultural influence was not restricted to Bulgaria. The Serbs accepted baptism in the 870s so that Byzantine art and the Cyrillic script were introduced there as well. The Russians took much longer to join the Byzantine fold. From their capital at Kiev, they made regular excursions down the River Dnieper and across the Black Sea to Constantinople, usually to trade, but sometimes to make piratical attacks on the city's undefended suburbs as they did in 860 and 941. Olga, the wife of Prince Igor of Kiev, was baptised in Constantinople in 957 but her son Svyatoslav held resolutely to the old gods of his Nordic ancestors and came into conflict with Byzantium over Bulgaria in

Figure 7.11 Cathedral of the Holy Wisdom, Ohrid

967–971 (see Section 8.2). It was only under Svyatoslav's son Vladimir I, who ruled Kiev from 980 to 1015, that Russia became a Christian country. There were doubtless very good political and strategic reasons for doing so. Vladimir had forged close ties with the Byzantine emperor Basil II (see Section 8.3 and Box 0.1), sending him military aid during a civil war and marrying his sister Anna, so it made sense to enter into the Byzantine sphere and enjoy the prestige and economic benefits that came with it. As in the case of Boris of Bulgaria, however, the impact of Byzantine art may also have played a role. According to one story, some envoys returning from Constantinople reported to Prince Vladimir that when they entered the churches there 'we knew not whether we were in Heaven or on earth. For on earth there is no such splendour or such beauty'. That allegedly clinched it for Vladimir. As in Bulgaria, with conversion came the Cyrillic script and Byzantine art. No sooner had the old temples been demolished than Vladimir commissioned a church dedicated to the Virgin Mary, bringing in Byzantine monks to do the job. Under his son Yaroslav (1019–1054) the cathedral of the Holy Wisdom went up

Figure 7.12 Virgin praying from the cathedral of the Holy Wisdom, Kiev. Note the Greek letters behind the head of the figure which stand for 'Mother of God'

in Kiev. Much of its original mosaic and fresco decoration survives (see Figure 7.12) and is very much in the Byzantine tradition. Byzantine monastic life was also deeply influential in Russia. The Pechersky Monastery was established in imitation of Mount Athos in some caves just outside Kiev and its daily routines were based on those of the Constantinopolitan monastery of St John Stoudios.

It was not only monks who disseminated Byzantium's cultural influence beyond its borders, however, and in some circumstances their involvement was not required. When it come to the Islamic world, the Byzantines were facing a society that already had its own highly developed monotheistic religion and was every bit as wealthy and powerful. There was no question of converting the Abbasid caliphate or drawing it into the cultural orbit. On the other hand, the intellectual elites of the two societies did have something in common: an interest in ancient Greek literature. The expansion of Islam had brought numerous centres of Greek learning under Arab rule and had given them the impetus to study works of the ancient authors and to translate them into Arabic. They were particularly interested in philosophy, mathematics and medicine. Under Caliph Harun al-Raschid, Baghdad became a centre for the study and translation of the ancient scientific texts. This shared interest was to have an impact on diplomatic contact with Byzantium and helped to build bridges between the two societies. Caliph al-Ma'mun (813–833) allegedly wrote to Emperor Theophilos offering 2,000 pounds of gold and eternal peace, if he would only allow his best scholar, Leo the Mathematician, to reside a short time in Baghdad. Theophilos declined on the grounds that it would be unwise to hand over such an asset to the enemy. On other occasions, though, the Byzantines were willing to share if they could reap some advantage. Constantine VII sent a copy of the *Materia Medica* of Dioscorides as a diplomatic gift to the Umayyad Caliph of Spain at Cordova. It is worth bearing in mind, though, that the cultural influence in this context was a two-way street. Emperor Theophilos' new Bryas palace on the Asian side of the Bosporus was inspired by a breathless account of the beauties of the caliph's palace brought back by his ambassador to Baghdad.

Box 7.3 Dimitri Obolensky (1918–2001) and the Byzantine Commonwealth

Born shortly after the Bolshevik revolution, Obolensky was the son of a Russian prince and could claim descent from the first Christian prince of Kiev, Vladimir. Not surprisingly, his family left Russia shortly after his birth and he grew up in France and England. It was as professor of Russian and Balkan medieval history at Oxford that he published *The Byzantine Commonwealth* in 1971. Obolensky argued that Byzantium's influence outside its borders depended on four things: acceptance of Christianity as practised by the Byzantine Church, recognition of the primacy of the patriarch of Constantinople, acknowledgement that the Byzantine emperor was endowed with authority and the adoption of Byzantine artistic styles. Those societies that did so, notably Bulgaria, Russia and Serbia, formed a distinct cultural bloc which he described as a commonwealth.

Inevitably the book and its central thesis have had their critics over the years. Academic reviewers have professed themselves uneasy with the very broad chronological sweep and pointed out the unsubstantiated assertions that wide-ranging books like this inevitably make. They have also questioned whether the word 'commonwealth' was an appropriate one in this context and wondered whether Obolensky, who had adopted British nationality in 1948, had not been unduly influenced by the British Commonwealth which had emerged from the decolonisation of the 1950s and 1960s. Perhaps most important of all, they have challenged Obolensky's apparent tendency to make the emergence of Slavic culture solely dependent on Byzantium.

All these criticisms have some validity although, as regards the last point, Obolensky was well aware of the limitations of Byzantine 'soft power' and devoted plenty of space to those who, like Khan Symeon of Bulgaria, came into conflict with the empire. Above all, the book's fluent and authoritative style, its command of the historical geography of the Balkans and above all its formulation of a clearly expressed and easily graspable thesis have made it a classic that still features on university reading lists and doubtless will continue to do so for some time.

Further reading: Dimitri Obolensky, *The Byzantine Commonwealth: Eastern Europe, 500–1500* (London: Weidenfeld and Nicholson, 1971); Christian Raffensperger, 'Revisiting the idea of the Byzantine Commonwealth', *Byzantinische Forschungen* 28 (2004), 159–74.

7.5 Urban life

Constantinople dominates our perception of Byzantium. That is partly a result of most of our literary sources being written there by people who knew little about the world outside its gates, but also because Constantinople undoubtedly overshadowed every other Byzantine city thanks to its size, wealth and sheer beauty. Unlike so many Byzantine towns, it had escaped being captured and destroyed, so the monumental architecture put up by Constantine the Great and his successors was still intact and a source of awe and wonder to visitors. It is impossible to assess exactly how many people lived there at any one time, but the number definitely increased after 800 and may have reached as many as 375,000 by about 1050. Supplying their daily needs was a considerable challenge, requiring water to be piped in from distant rivers via aqueducts, mountains of grain to be trundled in by cart or shipped in by sea and thousands of animals to be driven in every day for slaughter. It was the preferred residence of anyone of wealth and importance and those among the educated elite who found themselves posted to the provinces on state or Church business complained bitterly about the experience in their letters home. Michael Choniates, who was sent to Athens to be its archbishop in around 1175, lamented his intellectual isolation there: 'I sing to myself and no one answers, except the echo'.

Politically, economically and culturally dominant as Constantinople was, that did not mean that there were no provincial towns of importance. Like the capital, their populations had shrunk during the period of crisis and they had been often relocated to a more defensible position around a hilltop kastro (see Section 3.4). Now as the threat of attack receded, they were beginning to expand once more. Archaeological excavations have revealed that areas beyond the city centres that had been deserted for centuries were being reoccupied and built over, and suburbs were springing up outside the walls. Amorion, sacked by the Arabs in 838, was soon rebuilt and the devastated areas covered once more with streets and houses. The remains of its main church have been excavated and show that it was burned down at some point (probably in 838) but rebuilt in the late ninth or early tenth century. Athens, once an isolated bastion in the midst of Slav territory, had grown so much by about 1050 that a new wall had to be built to enclose the new developments. Nearby Thebes, which had retreated to just the Kadmeian hill during the period of crisis, was now strung out between several hills.

In spite of the economic dominance of the capital, these towns shared in the rising prosperity and were by no means the wretched backwaters they were sometimes portrayed as by supercilious Constantinopolitans. Lakedaimon in the Peloponnese, or Sparta as it is better known, was just a small provincial town and not the powerful city-state that it had been in ancient times. Even so, the large numbers of coins from this period unearthed there by archaeologists suggest that it was a prosperous enough place and its inhabitants could afford to build a new bridge across the Eurotas River in 1027. At the other end of the scale was Thessalonica, Byzantium's cosmopolitan second city. It had beaten off numerous sieges by the Avars and Slavs in the sixth and seventh centuries, only to fall victim in 904 to an Arab raiding force from Crete which captured and sacked the city and dragged a large proportion of its inhabitants off to be sold as slaves. In spite of that setback, the city showed signs of increasing prosperity throughout this period. Its church of Hagia Sophia was rebuilt at the end of the eighth century, and during the following century, when the controversy over icons had been resolved, it was provided with rich mosaic decoration. Like Constantinople, Thessalonica benefitted from the upsurge in trade because it was both a port and a staging post on the Via Egnatia, the main East–West land route across the Balkans. It hosted an annual fair, held every 26 October in honour of the city's patron saint, Demetrius. Local farmers and merchants from Bulgaria would bring produce and merchandise to the fair to be sold on. Thessalonica was also a tourist destination thanks to the shrine of St Demetrius in its main church. The tomb of the fourth-century martyr exuded a sweet-smelling myrrh which was supposed to have healing properties and which drew in pilgrims from a wide area.

A similar urban centre in Asia Minor was Ephesus. The city had moved inland to a more defensible site during the seventh century (see Section 3.4) but its harbour still functioned until the tenth century when it silted up and ships moored at nearby Phygela instead. Like Thessalonica, Ephesus had an annual fair and a flourishing pilgrimage trade thanks to the tomb of the apostle St John the Evangelist in the city's central church. At 130 metres long and 65 wide, the building rivalled the great church of the Holy Apostles in Constantinople. Some Byzantine towns based their prosperity on manufacture rather than trade or pilgrimage. At Corinth, glass and metal furnaces and lime and pottery kilns grew up and the town also became a centre for silk manufacture, as did Thebes. The settlement, which had

Figure 7.13 The ancient city of Corinth with the Acrocorinth behind

retreated during the period of crisis to the top of the nearby Acrocorinth, now returned to level ground and the site of the ancient Greek city (Figure 7.13).

7.6 Rural life

In spite of the size of Constantinople and the recovery of the provincial cities, the vast majority of the Byzantine population would have lived in the countryside and made their living by working on the land. Every now and then one of them made it to prominence: Emperors Leo III, Basil I and Romanos I Lekapenos were all from rural, peasant backgrounds. It was said that when he was a baby, Basil was placed in a shelter of corn sheaves to protect him from the midday sun while his parents gathered the harvest. An eagle was seen perching on top of the shelter, an omen of the child's future greatness. The biography of St Theodore of Sykeon contains a great deal of information about rural life (see Section 1.4). For the most part, though, the farm workers of the countryside formed a silent majority who are seldom documented or even mentioned in the literary record.

While it is hard to trace individuals, it is safe to say the countryside experienced the same crisis in the seventh and eighth centuries as the towns did, followed by revival in the ninth and tenth. An early tenth-century treatise on taxation mentions that exemptions were given to peasants living in areas that had suffered invasion, suggesting that this happened frequently and seriously disrupted agricultural production. On the other hand, archaeology has demonstrated that from about 850 on, land that had been abandoned began to be resettled and brought back into cultivation, such as the Pylos and Mani areas in the Peloponnese. In other areas, such as Apulia in Italy, forested land was brought into cultivation for the first time.

By about 950, the most fertile areas within the Byzantine borders were Thrace (the area immediately west of Constantinople), southern Italy and western Asia Minor, especially the valley of the River Meander, south of Ephesus. These regions produced huge surpluses of fruit and corn which could be used to feed the population of Constantinople. Central Greece and the interior of Asia Minor were better for the raising of cattle and sheep. The Peloponnese produced olives and mulberry trees. The leaves of the latter were essential for the silk industry and the area's alternative name of 'Morea' is derived from the Greek word for the mulberry tree (see Figure 7.14). Wine was produced everywhere although that from Crete and from some of the vineyards on the northern shore of the sea of Marmara were particularly prized. The Byzantines used a two-field rotation system, allowing some land to lie fallow each year or switching the crop planted there to help it to recover its fertility. They were aware of the benefits of manuring and stockpiled poultry droppings and horse and donkey manure for this purpose. Given the climate of the eastern Mediterranean, the management of water was the key to successful agriculture. Irrigation was widely used in Asia Minor and watermills would have dotted

Figure 7.14 Tenth-century Byzantine silk from the treasury of the church of Sainte-Foy, Conques, France

the landscape. These techniques, and the tools used to till the land, were much the same as those of Roman times.

There was, however, one major difference between Byzantine rural life in this period and that which had existed before 600. The land was generally distributed between small village communities rather than large estates. The latter had probably fallen victim to the unsettled conditions of the seventh century, when a great deal of land had gone out of cultivation. Moreover, the land was tilled not by serfs or slaves but by a free peasantry who owned their fields. That much is clear from a legal treatise known as the *Farmer's Law* which was written in around 700. Some historians, particularly George Ostrogorsky, have idealised this state of affairs, contrasting the free and happy Byzantine peasants with their enslaved and downtrodden counterparts in the contemporary 'feudal' west (see Box 3.3). The arrangement was not necessarily advantageous though. Small peasant communities had flourished when there was more land than people to till it but, by the tenth century, much more land was back under cultivation so that demand was starting to outstrip supply. The great estates were coming back, many of them belonging to monasteries which had received donations of land from pious well-wishers. Wealthy and powerful individuals were starting to acquire more land on their own account too. The village communities were particularly vulnerable to the vagaries of climate because their resources seldom rose above subsistence level. One drought or hard winter and they were likely to face destitution. In those circumstances, their inhabitants had little option but to sell their land, usually to a larger landowner.

The government is Constantinople seems to have viewed this development with disfavour and in 922 Emperor Romanos I passed a law restricting acquisition of land. He complained about people he referred to rather cryptically as 'the Powerful' (*Dynatoi*) who had apparently been using their wealth, influence and even a certain amount of intimidation to persuade peasants to sell. So Romanos laid down that if for some reason the lands of a peasant came up for sale, there was a fixed ranking of people who were allowed to buy it, ranging from relatives to those with adjoining land. Only if these were unwilling or unable to buy it was anyone else to be allowed to. The law seems to have been widely ignored, especially during the harsh winter of 927–928 when the earth was frozen solid for 120 days and famine followed. Some landowners took advantage by snapping up land at bargain prices. Romanos tried to stem the practice by ordering that land for which less than half the just price had been paid was to be returned without compensation. It is unlikely that the law was very effective as Constantine VII had to legislate on the same issue in 948. It could well have been that in the new climate of prosperity the peasant holdings were simply no longer viable. The possible deeper motives behind the emperors' efforts to stem this trend will be discussed in the next chapter (see Section 8.1 and Box 8.3).

Points to remember

- Byzantium revived economically after 800 as more settled conditions boosted the emperor's tax income.
- The building of churches and production of luxury items was a reflection of that greater prosperity.

- The architecture and decoration of Byzantine churches reflected the theology of the icon developed by St John of Damascus in response to iconoclasm.
- Monasteries were not just safe retreats from the world: they played a central part in Byzantine life and even foreign policy.
- Although Constantinople was culturally, politically and economically dominant, many provincial towns enjoyed greater prosperity after about 850.
- Byzantium's agricultural land became more productive from around 850 but that was accompanied by social change in the countryside.

Suggestions for further reading

Grierson, Philip. (1999), *Byzantine Coinage* (Washington, DC: Dumbarton Oaks). A short and very accessible introduction.

Harvey, Alan. (1989), *Economic Expansion in the Byzantine Empire, 900–1200* (Cambridge: Cambridge University Press). A survey of Byzantium's urban and rural economic revival which synthesises otherwise inaccessible archaeological evidence.

Humphreys, Mike. (2017), *The Laws of the Isaurian Era: The Ecloga and Its Appendices* (Liverpool: Liverpool University Press). Includes a translation and discussion of the *Farmer's Law*.

Laiou, Angeliki E. and Morrisson, Cécile. (2007), *The Byzantine Economy* (Cambridge: Cambridge University Press). A concise and extremely clear survey of Byzantine trade, agriculture, revenue, coinage and production from the sixth to the fifteenth century.

Mango, Cyril. (1986), *Art of the Byzantine Empire, 312–1453* (Toronto: University of Toronto Press). A particularly useful book as it provides translations of passages from Byzantine sources that describe now-vanished works of art.

Morris, Rosemary. (1995), *Monks and Laymen in Byzantium, 843–1118* (Cambridge: Cambridge University Press). Investigates the complex relationship between Byzantine religious houses and their lay founders and patrons.

8   Expansion and social change (959–1045)

This chapter examines a very uncharacteristic period in Byzantium's history when the empire was expanding rather than struggling to protect its beleaguered frontiers. It is tempting to see these years in triumphalist terms as a series of glorious victories and there is no doubt that there were some extraordinary successes. It should be remembered, however, that the expansion both drove and was driven by far-reaching changes in Byzantine society that were to create tensions and difficulties in the future.

8.1 The rise of a landed, military aristocracy?

We have already seen how, in the late ninth and early tenth centuries, the Byzantines had begun to be more successful against their Arab opponents on the eastern frontier. There was a number of factors behind this accelerated offensive. One was the peace that was made with Tsar Peter of Bulgaria in 927 which freed the Byzantines from any threat from their formidable western neighbour for 40 years and allowed them to concentrate their resources in the east. Another was the increasing weakness of the Abbasid caliphate (see Section 6.1). These factors are not enough in themselves, however, to explain the sudden run of Byzantine success. Tension with Bulgaria resurfaced from 967 and many of the Muslim states that established themselves on former Abbasid territory, such as the Hamdanid emirate and the Fatimid caliphate, were formidable adversaries.

So in explaining Byzantine success, another factor has to be taken into consideration. It is very noticeable that the gains of the early tenth century were made by armies which were not led by the emperor in person. After Basil I, no Byzantine emperor of the Macedonian dynasty marched at the head of his troops until his great-great-grandson Basil II. So a significant defeat inflicted on the Arabs at Germanikeia in 904 has to be credited to a certain Andronikos Doukas, not the ruler at the time, Leo VI. The temporary and final captures of Melitene in 926 and 930 were the work of the domestic of the Scholai, John Kourkouas. One name in particular crops up again and again: that of Phokas. The domestic of the Scholai responsible for restoring the Byzantine position in Apulia and Calabria was called Nikephoros Phokas. His son, Bardas, held the office of domestic after him and made his name campaigning against Arab raiders in eastern Asia Minor. He could also claim a record of loyalty to the Macedonian dynasty for he had supported Constantine VII in his coup against the Lekapenids in 945. Bardas' sons Leo and

Nikephoros in turn succeeded to lead the army. It was Leo who ambushed and mauled a retreating Hamdanid raiding party in 950. Another domestic, John Tzimiskes, was the nephew of Leo and Nikephoros Phokas, as well as being related to John Kourkouas, the conqueror of Melitene. It would appear that war had become a family business, passed down from father to son.

It was Bardas' son Nikephoros Phokas who was to achieve some of the greatest military successes after being appointed domestic of the Scholai by Constantine VII in 955. After Constantine's death in 959, his son and successor Romanos II commissioned Phokas to make yet another attempt to regain Crete. A Byzantine force stormed ashore on the island in July 960 and within weeks the Arabs had been driven back into their capital of Chandax. After a long siege, the city fell in March 961, restoring Crete to Byzantine rule after a century and a half. The following year, Phokas moved to the eastern frontier to settle accounts with the Hamdanid emir, Sayf ad-Dawlah, whose daring raids had long plagued Asia Minor. Marching across the Taurus Mountains and deep into Syria, he captured and sacked Aleppo, an event which marked the beginning of the decline of the Hamdanid dynasty (see Figure 8.1). These two successes earned Nikephoros Phokas the nickname of 'White death of the Saracens' and the adoration of his troops.

Given that the Phokas and other families were leading this successful offensive, it seems logical to credit them with something that was happening at the same time: the reorganisation of the Byzantine army and the way that it fought. It was operating increasingly in enemy territory east of the Taurus range, often far from its own homeland. Under these

Figure 8.1 The citadel at Aleppo

conditions, the Theme troops, levied for purposes of defence, were no longer adequate. Instead, a larger proportion of the army came to be filled with professional troops, either from the tagmata or else mercenaries recruited from outside the empire, for the improved economic situation and higher tax receipts meant that there were funds available to pay them. The largest group of foreign mercenaries in the tenth century was the Russians, even before Vladimir converted to Christianity in 989. No less than 700 of them took part in an unsuccessful attempt to retake Crete in 911. They had proved their prowess in damaging attacks on Byzantium, so it made sense to hire them and turn them against the Arabs.

Alongside the increasing professionalisation of the army, new tactics were being developed. During the first decades of the tenth century, the old defensive, shadowing procedures that had proved effective in the days of the great Arab raids across the Taurus Mountains were abandoned in favour of something more aggressive, which required expensive equipment, discipline and co-operation. Heavily armoured horsemen or *kataphracts*, who had disappeared from the ranks after the late sixth century, now returned (see Figure 8.2). There were new infantry contingents as well, such as the *menavlatoi*, so-called from the short, stabbing spear that they carried, the *menavlion*. The idea was that there should be a close co-operation between infantry, archers and the kataphracts. The cavalrymen were to make the initial charge against the enemy front rank, causing as much damage as they could, while the footmen and archers followed behind. Once the momentum of the charge was lost, or the kataphracts found themselves attacked by enemy cavalry, the foot soldiers were to form a square, leaving gaps in the ranks through which the kataphracts could retreat. From inside the square, they could safely regroup for the next charge, while the infantry and archers fended off the enemy. No one knows exactly when and how these tactics were introduced but they can be dated to the tenth century because they are described in a series of manuals of military practice that were written around that time. The earliest to do so is the anonymous *Sylloge Tacticorum* from around 930. They are also discussed in a work from the 960s known as the *Praecepta Militaria*, which was apparently composed under the auspices of Nikephoros

Figure 8.2 Kataphracts in action against the Bulgars at the battle of Sperchios in 997, from the Madrid Skylitzes

Phokas. He was certainly a great believer in heavy cavalry and used them to good effect on his campaigns. When his army landed on Crete in 960, his kataphracts charged onto the beach, already mounted, down ramps from the specially adapted ships that had ferried them and their horses down the Aegean, to the consternation of the Arab defenders.

Box 8.1 The new Byzantine tactics in the *Sylloge Tacticorum*

The *Sylloge Tacticorum* is a Byzantine manual of military tactics, written in Greek in around 930. It might have been commissioned by Emperor Romanos I Lekapenos and then completed and revised under Constantine VII. The name of the author is unknown. It is the earliest Byzantine military manual to mention the new infantry tactics where the soldiers operated in close formation to confront cavalry. The first of the two paragraphs below advises how the tagmata, composed of menavlatoi (spear-bearing infantrymen), should be deployed. The second describes how the cavalry should co-operate with slingers when charging, but if they are repulsed by the enemy cavalry they should retreat within the infantry square. Note that the author sometimes refers to tagmata in the singular form of 'tagma':

> So, there is one tagma of the banner-guards of the general's banners of fifty heavy infantry and one tagma of those who [stand] in the eight major intervals of eight hundred men, all light [infantry]. These eight hundred will be drawn up in the aforementioned intervals, in order to fill the space between the tagmata. They will not, however, have the same front as the others but they will be drawn up towards the inside, aligning with the last rank of the tagmata, so as to always keep an eye on those who want to break in through the intervals. The third tagma is of the so-called menavlatoi, comprising three hundred shield-bearers. The menavlatoi are first set in the intervals of the front side. But when the enemy approaches at a distance of a bowshot … their task is courageously to pierce the horses of the enemy kataphracts with their menavlia.
>
> The cavalry must be drawn up close to the outmost flanks of the infantry tagmata for the following reason. Since the infantry army is small, it is extremely likely that it will be encircled on account of its shortage [of men]. The cavalry will easily guard against the enemy encirclements, and if the time calls for it, it will encircle the enemy for they are horsemen and they conduct charges from an advantageous position, just as we discussed for the outflankers and the flank-guards … In this case then, the cavalry begin the battle, followed by the infantry bearing their slings. If they are repulsed, they retreat to their previous position and they fight together with their *defensores* and the infantry tagmata.

Source: *A Tenth-Century Byzantine Military Manual: The Sylloge Tacticorum*, trans. Georgios Chatzelis and Jonathan Harris (London and New York: Routledge, 2017), pp. 77, 80.

The victories of John Kourkouas and Nikephoros Phokas were naturally greeted with jubilation in Constantinople. Kourkouas' successful 944 Syrian campaign was celebrated with a magnificent reception for a relic that he had captured, the Mandylion of Christ. When Phokas returned from Crete in 961, he made a triumphant entry into Constantinople and the loot that he had brought back with him was put on public display in the Hippodrome. Yet even as they rejoiced, the emperors and their advisers were wary. History was littered with examples of victorious generals who had then used their popularity with the troops to make a bid for the throne: this was the old danger that had attached to the wide powers given to the strategos of a Theme. That suspicion of over-mighty warlords may lie behind the series of laws that were passed between around 922 and 948 by Romanos I and Constantine VII, which restricted the right of individuals and institutions to purchase agricultural land (see Section 7.6). Yet it is by no means clear that was the motive. Romanos may have been acting purely out of a humanitarian desire to protect his less affluent subjects. The wording of Constantine VII's law, on the other hand, suggests that he was concerned that buyers were taking over land that had been given to soldiers to provide for their maintenance and that troop numbers for the Byzantine army might be affected. Another concern might have been that monasteries were acquiring too much land, for Constantine VII listed them among the likely buyers. However, Constantine also mentioned *dynatoi*, or 'powerful people', as the villains of the piece and there is a wide gulf in modern historiography when it comes to defining exactly who it was that the emperor meant here.

George Ostrogorsky, and those historians who were strongly influenced by him (see Box 3.3), unhesitatingly identified the 'powerful people' with the emerging military families like that of Phokas. As well as monopolising the office of domestic of the Scholai, they must have been building up large estates in Asia Minor, storing up immense reserves of wealth and creating their own political powerbases. Thus the laws of Romanos I and Constantine VII were partly aimed at ensuring that victorious generals were starved of the resources that they might use in a bid for the throne but also to protect the Theme armies which Ostrogorsky considered to be the basis of Byzantine military strength. Ostrogorsky and his followers went further and argued that this 'military aristocracy' that was based in Asia Minor was slowly growing apart from the 'civil aristocracy' of Constantinople. While the former were enhancing their power with military victories and voracious acquisition of land, the latter were doing so through holding office in the civil administration in the capital. Both the civil aristocrats and the emperors viewed the aggrandisement of the military aristocrats with alarm. So after Melitene had been recaptured in 934, Emperor Romanos I saw to it that the land around the city became property of the state. He had no intention of allowing John Kourkouas to add land to his already considerable powerbase. In the autumn of 944, he dismissed Kourkouas from his office of domestic, in spite of all his achievements. The legislation to prevent acquisition of peasant land by the 'powerful' was therefore part of this policy of clipping the wings of the military aristocrats, or so the theory went.

More recent historians, such as John Haldon, Catherine Holmes, Anthony Kaldellis and Paul Lemerle, have raised doubts about this version of events. They have pointed out that there is little specific evidence that military families like the Kourkouas or Phokas were acquiring or even attempting to acquire vast rolling acres in Asia Minor. We know the name of one eager land buyer of the 970s – Basil Lekapenos – but he was a eunuch administrator based in the Great Palace, not a military man. Significantly the laws of Romanos I and Constantine VII make it plain that by 'the powerful' they did not mean only military men: the term included civic office holders, bishops and monasteries. These historians are also opposed to pigeonholing members of the Byzantine ruling classes into a neat division between 'civil' and 'military'. They point out that individuals from the same family, such as that of Doukas, were to be found holding both government posts in Constantinople and military ones in the provinces. They argue that political power in Byzantium continued to be based solely on office holding at court and the salaries that went with it, in spite of the conquests of the 960s. There was no alternative power structure emerging out in Asia Minor and no specifically military aristocracy.

The debate is a technical and rather arid one, but it is an instance where the revisionists have not completely carried their point. Even if there is a lack of evidence for powerful families in Asia Minor acquiring land, it is hard to believe that they did not do so, for even in a money economy like that of Byzantium, possession of property must have conferred great economic and political advantages. It is noticeable that the Phokas family enjoyed a high level of support in the area around Caesarea in Cappadocia: can we really believe that they had no property there? Even if there was no rigid distinction between civil and military aristocracy, there could well have been individuals and families that were powerful either because they owned land or because they held office or because they had both. In the latter case, if they could also deliver military victory and command the loyalty of the army, then they were in a very strong political position indeed. Finally, it is difficult to explain internal developments in the tenth and eleventh centuries without recognising that there was some kind of tension between capital and provinces. Consequently, this book will use the term 'military aristocracy' to denote a particular group, while acknowledging that it was not perhaps as strictly defined as Ostrogorsky suggested.

8.2 The soldier emperors (963–976)

In March 963, Emperor Romanos II died unexpectedly. He left as heirs to the throne two small sons: Basil II, aged three, and Constantine VIII, who was hardly a year old. Their mother Theophano became head of the usual council of regency but she must have been aware that moves were afoot to proclaim Nikephoros Phokas, the conqueror of Crete, as emperor. She made the politically astute move of entering into secret correspondence with him and when he marched on Constantinople with his army, she and her supporters welcomed him into the city. Phokas was duly crowned emperor as Nikephoros II in August 963 and the following month he married Theophano to give legitimacy to his takeover. An arrangement was now put in place similar to that which had existed during the reign of Romanos I. Nikephoros II was to be senior emperor, and guardian of his stepsons, the legitimate emperors Basil and Constantine. For supporters of the Macedonians, the advantage was that Nikephoros had no living sons of his own, so he would not be tempted to try and replace the dynasty with his own family as Romanos Lekapenos had been.

The regime that came to power after 963 was very different from what went before. No longer did the emperor remain in Constantinople and leave his generals to head the army. Nikephoros II himself directed a series of aggressive campaigns on the eastern frontier with impressive results. In 965, he captured the long-coveted stronghold of Tarsus, deploying the devastating combination of kataphracts and infantry to destroy an attempted counter-attack by the city's garrison. That victory gave the Byzantines their first foothold east of the Taurus Mountains and a base for further eastward expansion. In the same year, Cyprus, which had long been uneasily shared between Byzantium and the Abbasid caliphate, was restored to sole Byzantine rule. In 966, Nikephoros marched into Syria and besieged the town of Hieropolis (Manbij). Three years later, the Byzantine presence in northern Syria became permanent when they recaptured Antioch, which had last been under Byzantine rule in 639.

These successes earned Nikephoros considerable popularity in the provinces. There is a visible monument to that in the cave chapel known as the Pigeon House Church at Çavuşin in Cappadocia. There are fresco portraits in the apse of Nikephoros, his wife Theophano and other members of the Phokas family with an inscription that reads: 'Lord preserve at all times our pious majesties, Nikephoros and Theophano our lady'. Nowhere are the Macedonian junior emperors, Basil and Constantine, depicted or even mentioned, suggesting that people in that part of the world would probably have been perfectly happy for Nikephoros to have swept away the remnants of the old dynasty. The new emperor could also count on devoted support in the army and he repaid that by diverting all the resources that he now had at his disposal for military purposes. He made no secret of his partiality. When, following his assumption of power in 963, some of the soldiers he had brought with him misbehaved and looted thousands of houses in Constantinople, he refused to discipline them, merely remarking that there were bound to be a few bad characters among such a large body of men. He even asked the patriarch whether those of his men killed in action against the Muslim enemy could be declared martyrs with a guarantee of a place in Heaven, though the patriarch refused to comply with his request.

In Constantinople, it was different. There Nikephoros' blatant favouritism ensured that he was deeply unpopular and a longstanding attachment to the side-lined Macedonian dynasty doubtless added to that. There were loud complaints that taxes had been increased and that the receipts were all being handed over to the soldiers, especially Nikephoros' beloved kataphracts. On one occasion, he was jeered and pelted with mud and stones by the crowd as he rode through the streets, so shortly afterwards he ordered that a stout wall be built around the Great Palace in case of an insurrection. So it is now, in the late tenth century, that the gap between capital and provinces that was to become so marked later on can first be discerned. Those who wish to play down that gulf often point to Nikephoros' legislation on land acquisition. Given that a member of one of the great military families of Asia Minor was now in power in Constantinople, it might be expected that Nikephoros would repeal the laws of Romanos I and Constantine VII restricting the acquisition of peasant land. In fact, he did no such thing. In 967, he promulgated his own law in which he expressed his sympathy with those impeded by the restrictions but did not remove them. Instead he merely made a token gesture by limiting the rights of those further down the social scale to acquire land, ostensibly in the interests of equality. Revisionist historians have seized on this as evidence that Nikephoros was not part of a landowning class. It could, of course, be interpreted in another way. The Phokas family might well have been landowners, whose powerbase in Asia Minor had greatly assisted their rise to power, but they had no intention of allowing others to imitate their success. Nikephoros kept the legislation in place in order to pull the ladder up after him.

If that was his intention, it did not work, for he was toppled after six years on the throne by another soldier, his own nephew, John Tzimiskes. One night in December 969, a group of assassins, aided and abetted by Empress Theophano, assassinated him in his bedroom in the Great Palace. The plan was that Tzimiskes would himself marry Theophano but it was foiled by the patriarch who refused to allow the match after he had heard about Nikephoros' brutal end. Theophano ended up being exiled to a convent for the rest of her life and Tzimiskes had to purchase his legitimacy elsewhere by marrying Theodora, a daughter of Constantine VII. That seems to have satisfied the patriarch so that he then could be crowned as John I. There was no objection to the coup from the people of Constantinople, who had hated Nikephoros, but the Phokas family were unlikely to take it lying down. Another nephew of the late Nikephoros, Bardas Phokas, did contest it from Cappadocia but he was soon overpowered and exiled.

John I's reign followed a very similar course to that of his ill-fated uncle, with a series of relentless military campaigns. It was in the west that John had to operate initially because the peace that had been concluded with the Bulgars in 927 had finally broken down. In 966, Nikephoros II had stopped paying the annual tribute and war had broken out. Distracted by his campaigns in the east, Nikephoros decided to fall back on other tactics and paid 1,500 pounds of gold to the Russian prince Svyatoslav to attack Bulgaria. Svyatoslav fulfilled his side of the bargain but once he had invaded and occupied Bulgaria, he showed no desire to leave. So on his accession, John inherited a situation where a relatively weak and unthreatening Christian northern neighbour had been replaced by a strong, pagan one. He could hardly let that situation stand. In the spring of 971, he crossed the Balkan Mountains with a picked band of 5,000 men, while the bulk of the army followed on behind. This vanguard moved so swiftly that it was almost at the walls of Preslav before news reached Svyatoslav of its approach. The city was stormed and taken, with the Golden Church and much of Tsar Symeon's monumental architecture going up in smoke. The campaign culminated at Dristra in June where the Russians were overwhelmed by a kataphract charge. After Svyatoslav had sued for peace and withdrawn (see Figure 8.3), John was left in possession of a large part of Bulgaria, which he had no intention of handing back to the Bulgar Tsar. Instead he did what his predecessors had dreamt of for centuries and brought the Byzantine frontier back to the Danube. He constituted his conquests into the Theme of Paristrion, with its capital at Ioannopolis, the new name for Preslav. The Bulgarian patriarchate, set up by Tsar Symeon, was downgraded to the status of an archbishopric.

Figure 8.3 John Tzimiskes discusses peace terms with Svyatoslav after the battle of Dristra in 971, from the Madrid Skylitzes

Southern Italy presented a similar problem inherited from Nikephoros and here too John I found a solution, albeit by different means. The king of the East Franks, Otto I (936–973), had occupied northern Italy, deposing its king, Berengar II. Then, taking up the mantle of Charlemagne, he had had himself crowned Emperor of the Romans by the pope in 962. Claiming overlordship of the whole of Italy, in 968 Otto had invaded Apulia and laid siege to Bari. He may not have intended to capture the town, but only to make a demonstration to strengthen his bargaining position. He sent an envoy, Liudprand, bishop of Cremona, to Constantinople to negotiate, offering to make peace in return for Byzantine recognition of his imperial title and a marriage alliance between his son and Anna, the sister of the Macedonian emperors Basil II and Constantine VIII. Nikephoros II received the envoy very frostily and Liudprand left Constantinople some months later with nothing to show for his efforts. It was left to John I to resolve the stand-off in Italy. He knew perfectly well that it could not be ended by military means, given his commitments in Bulgaria and the resources that Otto had at his disposal. So when a new envoy from Otto arrived in Constantinople at the end of 971, John brokered a compromise. Rather than the Macedonian Anna, he offered his own niece Theophano as a bride to Otto's son. The offer was accepted, if somewhat grudgingly, and Otto I agreed to respect Byzantine possession of Apulia and Calabria. The treaty kept Byzantine Italy safe for another 50 years.

Box 8.2 An interview with Nikephoros II Phokas (968)

Bishop Liudprand of Cremona wrote a remarkably detailed account of his mission to Constantinople on behalf of Emperor Otto I in 968. Not surprisingly, given Otto's attack on Bari, his reception was chilly to say the least. In this passage, he records his first conversation with the emperor:

[Nikephoros II:] 'It would have been right for us, nay, we had wished to receive you kindly and with honour; but the impiety of your master does not permit it since, invading [Italy] as an enemy, he has claimed for himself Rome; has taken away from Berengar [II] and Adalbert [Berengar's son] their kingdom, contrary to law and right; has slain some of the Romans by the sword, others by hanging, depriving some of their eyes, sending others into exile; and has tried, moreover, to subject to himself by slaughter or by flame cities of our empire. And, because his wicked endeavour could not take effect, he now has sent you, the instigator and furtherer of this wickedness, to act as a spy upon us while simulating peace'.

I answered him: 'My master did not by force or tyrannically invade the city of Rome; but he freed it from a tyrant, nay, from the yoke of tyrants … You neglected it, my master did not neglect it. For, rising from the ends of the earth and coming to Rome, he removed the impious and gave back to the vicars of the holy apostles their power and all their honour …'.

'Well', he said, 'he may, as you say, have done this justly. Explain now why with war and flame he attacked the boundaries of our empire. We were friends, and were expecting, by means of a marriage to enter into an indissoluble union'.

'The land', I answered, 'which you say belongs to your empire belongs, as the nationality and language of the people proves, to the kingdom of Italy. The Lombards held it in their power, and Louis, the emperor of the Lombards, or Franks, freed it from the hand of the Saracens … Nor would it until now have passed from the yoke of his servitude or that of his successors, had not the emperor Romanos [I Lekapenos], giving an immense sum of money, bought the friendship of our king Hugh [of Provence] … But, in order that now all deceit may be laid bare and the truth not be hidden, my master [Otto I] has sent me to you, so that if you are willing to give [Anna] the daughter of the emperor Romanos [II] and of the empress Theophano to my master his son …, you may affirm this to me with an oath; whereupon I will affirm by an oath that, in return for such favours, he will observe and do to you this and this. But already my master his given to you, as to his brother, the best pledge of his friendship in restoring to you, by my intervention, at whose suggestion you declare this evil to have been done, all Apulia which was subject to his sway …'.

'The second hour', said Nikephoros, 'is already past. The solemn procession to the church is about to take place. Let us now do what the hour demands. At a convenient time we will reply to what you have said'.

Note that Nikephoros did not reject the proposed marriage alliance outright, his tactic being to string out the negotiations in the hope of extracting further concessions from Otto. In the end, no agreement was reached and an angry Liudprand left Constantinople in October 968.

Source: Ernest F. Henderson, *Select Historical Documents of the Middle Ages* (London: George Bell, 1910), pp. 444–6 (spellings adapted).

For the last years of his reign, John I campaigned on the eastern frontier. He made at least one foray into Abbasid territory in 972 and so pushed the Byzantine frontier to the River Euphrates. He may have returned two years later and advanced into Mesopotamia and the Tigris valley. However, the main opponent in the region was now the Fatimid caliphate of Egypt which had occupied Palestine and much of Syria in 969. Shi'ite rather than Sunni Muslims, the Fatimids were deadly rivals of the Abbasids in Baghdad but they also posed a threat to the Byzantine position in Antioch and northern Syria. It was probably as a display of strength that, in 975, John marched south from Antioch, reaching as far as Caesarea in Palestine. Nikephoros II had already tried to give a religious tone to his wars but the trend was even more marked under John I. In his eastern campaigns, he gathered relics as he went, including what purported to be the sandals of Christ and the hair of John the Baptist. There was even talk of his recapturing the holy city of Jerusalem. It would be unwise to put too much emphasis on that aspect of his campaigns though, for these were not proto-crusades. John made no attempt to take Jerusalem and the evidence that he considered doing so is very late and unreliable. The chronicler Leo the Deacon, who was a contemporary, does not mention it. One gets the impression instead that John I was more interested in extorting money than fighting for the faith. When he reached Damascus in the summer of 975, he accepted a payment of 60,000 Dinars to move on and leave the city in peace. There was a certain stark practicality in the way the Byzantines waged war, even under two of the most militaristic emperors they ever had.

8.3 Basil II (976–1025)

John Tzimiskes died in Constantinople in January 976, probably of dysentery picked up on the Syrian campaign. Many people assumed that some other warlord would now step forward to take up the role of emperor and protector of the Macedonian heirs, even though Basil was now 18 years old. John I left no son, so the obvious candidate was his brother-in-law, Bardas Skleros, who had an outstanding military record. He might indeed have become emperor, had he enjoyed the support of the powerful eunuch Basil Lekapenos. An illegitimate son of Emperor Romanos I, Lekapenos fulfilled the same role that Theoktistos had during the reign of Michael III, effectively a kind of prime minister who ran the administration in Constantinople while the emperor was concerned with other matters. He had been helped by Nikephoros Phokas and John Tzimiskes to come to power but now, for reasons that are not entirely apparent, he decided to bring the dominance of the warlords to an end. He had Skleros relieved of his command and Basil II and Constantine VIII proclaimed sole emperors, although it was understood that Lekapenos was to be the power behind the throne. The coup was not likely to go unchallenged. Bardas Skleros launched a revolt and was only stopped when Lekapenos recalled Bardas Phokas, the nephew of Nikephoros II, from exile and sent him to deal with the rebel. Skleros was defeated in battle and fled to Baghdad, leaving Lekapenos and Phokas as the last two men standing, rivals for dominance over the apparently feeble Macedonian dynasty. At this point, though, the unexpected happened. The young Basil II suddenly asserted himself. In 985, he dismissed Lekapenos and sent him into exile. When Phokas revolted and proclaimed himself emperor, Basil called in the help of a large contingent of Russians sent by Prince Vladimir and put the rebel force to flight at Abydos in 989. Vladimir's reward was the hand of Basil's sister Anna, the same one who had been denied to Otto I's son, and it was at this point that the Russian ruler converted to Christianity (see Section 7.4).

For the first time in decades, an emperor of the Macedonian house was once more in undisputed control in Constantinople. In theory, Basil II reigned jointly with his brother Constantine VIII, but the easy-going Constantine was relegated to purely ceremonial tasks. Basil soon gained the reputation for ruling without anyone's advice, and although that was not entirely the case, throughout his long reign the emperor imposed his will ruthlessly. Above all, he led the army in person, the first Macedonian emperor to do so since Basil I, for he must have been acutely aware that it was the control of the military force that had allowed Nikephoros II and John I to eclipse the rightful emperors. Fortunately, Basil turned out to be an efficient and successful military leader.

On the eastern frontier, Basil II's campaigns were much less ambitious than those of his two predecessors and were mainly designed to counter the Fatimid threat. Nevertheless, they gave Basil the opportunity to prove his mettle as a general. In late 994, after the Fatimids had defeated a Byzantine force and started to threaten Antioch, the governor of the city sent an urgent message to Basil begging him to send help. The people of Antioch were astonished when the emperor appeared with his army the following spring, much sooner than anyone had expected, having broken off his campaign in Bulgaria and force-marched across Asia Minor. For the next few years, Basil campaigned in the east, laying siege to Tripoli in December 999. He did not take the port, but he had done enough to show the Fatimids that he could seriously jeopardise their position in Syria. In 1001, a ten-year truce was concluded between Basil II and the Fatimid Caliph Hakim and the two powers were seldom in conflict again.

By making the truce with the Fatimids, Basil II had drawn a line against any further territorial gains in Syria. However, the Byzantine eastern frontier was greatly extended further to the north during his reign, at the expense of the small Armenian kingdoms and principalities. These gains were achieved through negotiation rather than conquest. In 990, Basil II made threatening moves towards David, prince of Tao in the Armenian–Georgian borderlands, because he was furious at David's support for Bardas Phokas' revolt in 987–989. To avoid confrontation, the childless David changed his will and bequeathed his lands to the Byzantine emperor. Basil duly annexed them after David's death in 1000. That set a precedent for similar arrangements. In 1022, Basil II was contacted by Senek'erim, king of Vaspurakan, who offered to hand over his lands to the south and east of Lake Van in return for estates inside the Byzantine empire. Around the same time, John-Smbat III, king of Ani, bequeathed his lands to the emperor in the same way that David of Tao had, although he outlived Basil by some years. Exactly why these Armenian potentates were so ready to hand over their kingdoms and the consequences of their doing so will be discussed later (see Section 10.1), but for the time being suffice it to say that these annexations pushed the Byzantine border far further to the east than it had ever been before.

It was in Bulgaria rather than Syria and Armenia that Basil II's military reputation was really made, earning him the epithet of the 'Bulgar Slayer'. With the death of John

Tzimiskes, the Bulgars immediately shook off the recently imposed Byzantine administration, under the leadership of Samuel, the son of a provincial governor. With the political uncertainty in Constantinople, the response was long in coming and when Basil did take to the field against Samuel in 986, he was roundly defeated at the battle of Trajan's Gate. The entire achievement of John Tzimiskes in the Balkans now crumbled away. Samuel re-established an independent Bulgaria with its own patriarchate and in 997 proclaimed himself tsar. The revived state took control of a huge swathe of the Balkans.

Basil refused to accept the independence of Bulgaria. In 1001, following the truce with the Fatimids, he resumed the war, but he employed rather less flamboyant tactics than those of his Syrian campaign. He mounted annual raids and encouraged Bulgaria's Hungarian neighbours to invade from the west. On the face of it, Basil was using war by attrition to grind the country down, but a later source, John Skylitzes, records one pitched battle which was fought at Kleidion on 29 July 1014 where Samuel's army was completely defeated. According to Skylitzes, Basil afterwards had all 15,000 prisoners blinded, except every hundredth man who lost only one eye. The one-eyed men were then made to lead their comrades back to Tsar Samuel who is supposed to have collapsed with the shock when he witnessed the gruesome procession and to have died two days later. The story is very suspect, since there is no contemporary evidence for it. Skylitzes was writing up to 80 years after the episode and was probably just passing on a tale that had been modified and exaggerated in the telling. So while it is likely that Basil won a victory and Samuel did die, the casualty figures have been grossly exaggerated. There were plenty more Bulgarians to take the field and the war went on. It took a further four years to finally subjugate Bulgaria. Only when Tsar John Vladislav was killed near Dyrrachion in 1018 did the struggle come to an end as the surviving members of Samuel's family surrendered to Basil. Bulgaria was then once more incorporated into the Byzantine empire and divided into the Themes of Paristrion and Bulgaria.

While the conquest of Bulgaria accounts largely for Basil II's later reputation as a strong and uncompromising ruler, he is also remembered for issuing two edicts which appear to have extended and strengthened the land laws of his predecessors. The first was issued in January 996 and was portentously entitled 'New Constitution of the pious emperor Basil the Young, by which are condemned those Rich Men who amass their wealth at the expense of the poor'. It put up further impediments against the acquisition of peasant land, decreeing that any land acquired illegally since the 920s was now liable to restitution without compensation.

Box 8.3 Basil II's land law of 996

Basil II's famous edict is very direct in its language and makes a point of parading the emperor's righteous anger against some of his wealthier subjects. He even seems to have added a private note to the text, naming and shaming two particular families, one of which was that of Phokas:

For we have been much disturbed on this account by the poor and passing through the Themes of our empire and going on expeditions we have seen with our own eyes the acts of greed and injustice daily inflicted on them. For how, as has happened, shall time be absolutely efficacious, when one who is powerful practices greed against the poor man ... Then shall we not hinder them, and affirm the right belonging to the poor, of which they were basely robbed and defrauded? ... Should we not do this, we would give an excuse to the grasping individual to say that, since today I am well off and the poor man is not able to act against me ... greed is profitable to me.

[*Marginal note, perhaps by the emperor:* This is clear from the family of Maleinos and likewise of Phokas. For the patrikios Constantine Maleinos and his son, the magister Eustathios enjoyed wealth which extended back from them a hundred or even a hundred and twenty years. The Phokas family, much more than they, for their grandfather, then the father, and thereafter his sons had, so to speak, almost perpetual authority up to our day ...]

Source: Charles M. Brand, *Icon and Minaret: Sources of Byzantine and Islamic Civilisation* (Englewood Cliffs NJ: Prentice-Hall, 1969), pp. 91–7, at 92 (spelling adapted).

A second edict was issued by Basil in 1004 and changed the way that the tax known as the allelengyon was collected. In the past a shortfall on the part of any one individual had had to be made up by the other members of the village community, but Basil's decree made it the responsibility of any great landowner who had bought up property in the district.

The provisions of these two edicts have been interpreted in various ways. Ostrogorsky and his followers saw them as an attack on an entire class: the military, landed aristocracy of Asia Minor whom Basil feared and hated as a threat to the Macedonian dynasty. The land law was designed to prevent them from adding to their power by expanding their estates and the tax law hit them financially. The second law also provided the government with greater security for the collection of the tax. It is noticeable too that Basil II chose to resettle Armenian princes such as Senek'erim of Vaspurakan and their followers in Cappadocia, perhaps to dilute the influence of the great magnates there. Catherine Holmes and others have questioned this interpretation, arguing that Basil may have been aiming only to punish certain families rather than a whole class. Certainly, the marginal note in the 996 law singles out two particular families for opprobrium and it is hardly surprising to find the Phokas dynasty as one of them. Basil never forgave Nikephoros II for elbowing him aside in 963 and elsewhere in his legislation referred to him as the 'interloper'. Also named is the family of Maleinos, in whose house Bardas Phokas had been proclaimed emperor in 987. Basil was later to take his revenge on the head of the clan. He invited Eustathios Maleinos to Constantinople, then imprisoned him for life. After his death, the emperor expropriated Maleinos' estates. Those individuals aside, Holmes argues, it would have been unwise to antagonise an entire group, as Basil still needed them. He may have ruled alone and personally led the army, but he could not be in two places at once and had to delegate on occasions. Both lines of argument have their merits, but it is difficult to explain what occurred later without accepting that Basil's legislation may have helped to widen the gulf between the government in Constantinople and the prominent families of the provinces.

8.4 After Basil (1025–1045)

The death of Basil II in December 1025 has often been seen as a radical turning point in Byzantium's destiny. Many modern historians have seen it as the moment when the old emperor's dynamic military campaigns and stern internal rule were abandoned by his weak and feckless successors, leading to an inevitable decline. It is unlikely that contemporaries would have seen it like that as, in many ways, life went on exactly as before with the Byzantine army still expanding the borders. Only after 1071 did people look back and discern the beginning of decline at the time of Basil's passing. They may have been wrong to do so because some of the seeds of Byzantium's eleventh-century crisis were sown before Basil's reign and some while he was still alive.

It is true that the sequence of five emperors who ruled after Basil could not match his achievements, lasted for much shorter reigns and were much less secure on the throne. That to some extent was Basil's own fault. It is decidedly perplexing that a man who was apparently deeply concerned with the rights and dignities of the Macedonian dynasty should do almost nothing to ensure its continuation. He never married or had children of his own, so his heirs were the three daughters of his brother, Constantine VIII. He did very little to find them husbands so that they could continue the line. It would appear from Western sources that the middle daughter Zoe was betrothed in 1001 to the Western emperor Otto III but he died before the marriage took place. So none of Basil's nieces was married by the time of his death: the eldest was a nun and Zoe and the youngest, Theodora, were by then middle-aged. Constantine VIII succeeded his brother as sole emperor and it was only when he was dying in 1028 that Zoe was married to Romanos Argyros, governor of Constantinople, who thus succeeded as Romanos III. After six years, Romanos drowned mysteriously in his bath, probably murdered on the orders of Zoe so that she could marry her lover, a guardsman who became Michael IV. Michael suffered from epilepsy and after seven years it was clear that he had not long to live. So his brother, John the Orphanotrophos, the most powerful eunuch at court (see Box 5.3), persuaded Zoe to adopt their nephew, so that when Michael IV died in December 1041, the nephew became Michael V. He lasted only a matter of months. An ill-judged attempt to sideline Empress Zoe led to a popular revolt in support of the Macedonian dynasty and Michael was overthrown. Zoe then ruled jointly with her sister Theodora for three months, until June 1042 when she married her third and final husband Constantine Monomachos, who became Constantine IX (see Figure 8.4).

All the chopping and changing sounds like a recipe for political instability and weakness but that was not the case. The conquests of Basil II's reign did not evaporate the moment he died, as had those of John I Tzimiskes. That was partly thanks to Basil himself who had been careful to make a magnanimous peace settlement with Bulgaria, showing respect for Bulgarian traditions by allowing them to pay their taxes in kind rather than in coin as they had under their own rulers. The Bulgarian Church was allowed to be independent, although its head was downgraded to an archbishop whom the emperor appointed. There was a revolt in 1040, when the Bulgars took

Figure 8.4 Emperor Constantine IX (1042–1055) and Empress Zoe, a mosaic in Hagia Sophia

exception to a new tax regime and proclaimed Peter Delyan as tsar, but it was put down by swift action on the part of Emperor Michael IV. Thereafter, Bulgarians generally accepted Byzantine rule and their nobility integrated into the empire's hierarchy.

Similarly, on the eastern frontier, Basil's treaty with the Fatimids was renewed by Constantine VIII in 1027. The stability in northern Syria was jeopardised a few years later when Emperor Romanos III and his advisers considered that the time had come to annex Aleppo, which was already nominally under Byzantine overlordship. They offered first to buy the city and when its emir refused, Romanos invaded in the summer of 1030. The campaign went badly to start with when Romanos' army fell into an ambush and he himself barely escaped from the rout. Matters improved the following year, after the emperor had handed over command to the strategos of the Theme of Teleuch, George Maniakes. After a devastating Byzantine raid north of Aleppo, the emir sued for peace and resumed paying an annual tribute. Byzantine possession of Antioch was thus secured and Basil II's territorial gains in Armenia also survived his passing.

In fact, as well as retaining Basil II's conquests, Byzantium was still expanding after 1025. In October 1031, George Maniakes seized the town of Edessa from the neighbouring Marwanid emirate. In Italy, the Byzantines were hoping to recover Sicily, which had been lost at the beginning of the previous century. At the very end of his reign Basil II had been contemplating sending a fleet there, but he died before he could put the plan into effect. The task was taken up

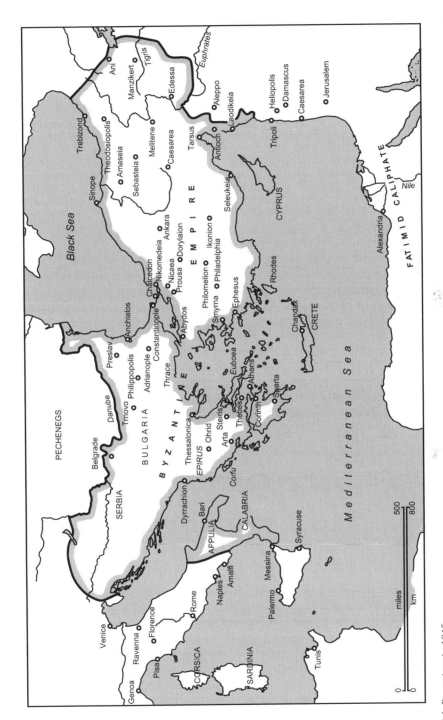

Map 8.1 Byzantium in 1045

by his successor Michael IV, who in 1038 despatched an expeditionary force under Maniakes to intervene in a civil war between the emir of Sicily and his brother. By 1040, much of the eastern side of the island had been occupied, including Syracuse, the loss of which in 878 had been such a blot on the record of Emperor Basil I (see Section 6.2). The last addition to the empire before the crisis came was the small Armenian kingdom of Ani. It had been bequeathed to the Byzantine emperor by its king, John-Smbat III, in a will made in 1021. When the king finally died in 1040, however, his nephew Gagik II ignored the will and established himself as ruler of Ani. Emperor Constantine IX refused to accept this coup and in 1045 sent an army to conquer the territory. Gagik submitted and was pardoned, being given a court title and estates in Cappadocia to make up for losing, Ani which was now incorporated into the Byzantine Theme of Iberia. With hindsight, of course, it is easy to see that these gains were ephemeral and that the brief age of expansion was coming to an end.

Points to remember

*   There was a marked increase in Byzantine military success after 959.
*   The success can partly be attributed to the decline of the Abbasid caliphate and to the new equipment and tactics adopted by the Byzantine army.
*   Recent historians have been reluctant to attribute this success to an identifiable group, the military aristocracy of the provinces, as opposed to the civil aristocracy of the capital.
*   Nevertheless, there are definite signs in this period of a cultural and political gap between Constantinople and the provinces.
*   The death of Basil II in 1025 did not necessarily mark a turning point: the roots of the crisis that Byzantium was to face after 1045 went much deeper than the removal of one particularly able emperor.

Suggestions for further reading

Haldon, John. (2009), *A Social History of Byzantium* (Oxford: Wiley-Blackwell). This is an edited volume with chapters by different authors. See Haldon's summary of the civil versus military aristocracy issue on pp. 182–7.

Holmes, Catherine. (2005), *Basil II and the Governance of Empire* (Oxford. Oxford University Press). Currently the most detailed examination of Basil's reign. Holmes argues against the idea that Basil was waging a war against the military aristocracy of Asia Minor.

Kaldellis, Anthony. (2017), *Streams of Gold, Rivers of Blood: The Rise and Fall of Byzantium, 955 AD to the First Crusade* (New York: Oxford University Press). This author is also opposed to the idea of a landowning, military aristocracy in Asia Minor and argues against the claim that the death of Basil II in 1025 was a turning point in the empire's fortunes.

McGeer, Eric. (1995), *Sowing the Dragon's Teeth: Byzantine Warfare in the Tenth Century* (Washington, DC: Dumbarton Oaks). As well as providing an analysis of Byzantine military tactics and campaigns, this book also contains translations of some of the key primary texts, including Nikephoros II's *Praecepta Militaria*.

Stephenson, Paul. (2000), *Byzantium's Balkan Frontier: A Political Study of the Northern Balkans, 900–1204* (Cambridge: Cambridge University Press). Includes a very detailed account of Byzantium's relations with Bulgaria in this period and the annexation of the latter in 1018.

PART III

Contraction, recovery and calamity 1045–1204

9 Major literary sources for the period 1045–1204

This period produced some of the greatest works of Byzantine historiography. One of them, the *Chronographia* of Michael Psellos, has already been discussed (see Section 5.4). It is a very important source for events after 1050 but it becomes increasingly partisan in its account after 1059 when Psellos' friend Constantine Doukas became emperor. Fortunately, there is a corrective in the work of Michael Attaleiates, a judge and courtier who wrote an account of the years 1040 to 1079. Attaleiates was no friend of the Doukas family. His first patron was Romanos IV Diogenes (1068–1071) who was overthrown and cruelly blinded by Andronikos Doukas, cousin of Emperor Michael VII. Later Attaleiates was a supporter of Nikephoros III Botaneiates (1078–1081) who overthrew Michael VII and the Doukas dynasty. That does not mean that Attaleiates was any less partisan than Psellos, for his history is as much a eulogy of Nikephoros III as Psellos' is of Constantine X and Michael VII. He does, however, give a very different perspective on events. He was by no means as fixated on Constantinople as Psellos was as he often travelled beyond its walls, taking part in Romanos IV's campaign in Armenia in the summer of 1071. Perhaps most helpful of all, he reveals all kinds of inconvenient details that Psellos would much rather have left buried.

9.1 Historians at the Komnenian court

Between 1081 and 1185, Byzantium was ruled by emperors of the Komnenos family. In its first decades the dynasty encouraged an austere military ethos and the Platonic studies that had flourished under Psellos were firmly discouraged (see Section 5.4). The writing of history, however, flourished. Nikephoros Bryennios, the son-in-law of Emperor Alexios I (1081–1118), wrote an account of the years 1070 to 1080 and would have continued further had he not died in 1138 of an illness contracted while on campaign in Syria. Not surprisingly, his work casts a laudatory light on the Komnenos family and their rise to power. By contrast, John Zonaras, a court official who published a history in around 1130, included some negative judgements about Alexios I. His monumental work runs from the Creation of the world up to 1118, and thus provides a useful corrective to the pro-Komnenos work of Bryennios and his wife, Anna (see Section 9.2).

Also active at the court of Alexios I was a certain John Skylitzes who was a judge and official in the 1080s. Between 1092 and 1094, he compiled what he described as a *Synopsis of Histories*. The title is a helpful one because Skylitzes' aim was to provide an accurate and detailed record of events since 811 by epitomising and synthesising the work of other historians. Although he made some errors, generally Skylitzes carried out this task very well and in doing so preserved much material from works that are now lost, such as those of Nikephoros the Deacon and Demetrius of Cyzicus. The *Synopsis* ends in 1057, but Skylitzes later wrote a continuation which took the story up to 1079. Oddly, given that he was alive during this latter period, he takes much of his information directly from Michael Attaleiates and only occasionally gives his own opinion. He makes it quite clear though that he deeply disliked Michael Psellos.

In stark contrast to the work of Skylitzes is that of John Kinnamos, who was the personal secretary of Emperor Manuel I Komnenos (1143–1180). Kinnamos covers only the period from 1118 to 1176 and he was an eyewitness to some of the events he describes, for he accompanied Manuel on a number of his campaigns. As with all Byzantine historians, Kinnamos displayed a marked political bias in favour of his paymaster, praising Manuel's every deed, including his grasp of philosophy, his intellect, his bravery in combat, his humanity and even his medical skill. He is more neutral in his account of the reign of Manuel's father, John II Komnenos (1118–1143) but much less minutely informed as well. These weaknesses aside, Kinnamos' work is a vital source of information on the reigns of these emperors and an important supplement to the evidence of Niketas Choniates (see Section 9.3).

9.2 Anna Komnene and the *Alexiad*

One historian who wrote during the Komnenos period stands out from all the others because she was female. Byzantine historiography was usually the work of men who had generally passed through the traditional course of higher education but that route was not open to women, even if they were members of the royal family. Anna Komnene was the daughter of Emperor Alexios I and she was educated up to the age of 14 but her parents did not want her to proceed any further. She managed to get around this prohibition by secretly taking lessons from one of the palace eunuchs. After her marriage, she continued her education openly, progressing to the study of philosophy and becoming the centre of a circle of scholars who were writing commentaries on the works of Aristotle. She was well acquainted with the whole range of ancient Greek literature and the influence of her education is obvious throughout the work, which is written in Attic Greek. She made frequent allusions to ancient authors, especially Homer.

Her history, the *Alexiad*, shares many features of male-authored historiography. There is an obvious political bias. She presents her father as the ideal Christian emperor: pious, merciful and humane, concerned only with the common good, stoical in adversity and ultimately victorious in battle. She extended that praise to other members of Alexios' family, such as his brother Isaac and his mother, Anna Dalassena, who is depicted not only as a woman of exemplary piety but as Alexios' chief political supporter during his early years as emperor. His wife Irene is portrayed as beautiful, pious, brave, resolute and very well read. Since Anna was half-Doukas through her mother Irene, members of that family are also singled out for praise, such as John Doukas, the brother of Emperor Constantine

X, who aided Alexios during his rebellion in 1081. Some historians have argued that the bias went deeper than the usual partiality for those who were in the same political grouping and have seen her work as an attempt to criticise and undermine Alexios' successors, her brother John II and her nephew, Manuel I. Anna was Alexios and Irene's oldest child. Soon after her birth, she was betrothed to Constantine Doukas, the son of the former emperor Michael VII, as part of Alexios I's efforts to gain legitimacy for his seizure of power by linking himself to the previous ruling dynasty. Constantine Doukas became Alexios' heir and so for the first few years of her life, Anna was a prospective empress. That all changed in 1087, when Empress Irene bore a son John, who displaced Constantine as heir. In any case, Anna never married Constantine Doukas, who died in 1094, and two years later Nikephoros Bryennios became her husband. It has been claimed that she never forgot that for a brief period she had been in line for supreme power. According to John Zonaras and Niketas Choniates, when Alexios was on his death bed in 1118, she and her mother Irene tried to persuade him to change the succession in favour of Anna's husband. Choniates further claims that she was implicated in plans to have her brother John murdered. Although she was pardoned and allegedly reconciled with John, it is noticeable that direct mentions of him in the *Alexiad* are few and unflattering. Anna complains at one point that she lived a sequestered life and was not allowed to see anyone, suggesting that she was out of favour. Consequently, the *Alexiad* has been seen as an attempt to hijack Alexios' legacy and to present Anna as the only one who was true to it. She certainly claims that after his death all the benefits that he brought to Byzantium were squandered by the stupidity of his successors.

This picture of Anna as ambitious and embittered has recently been challenged by Leonora Neville and, even if it were true, too great an emphasis on it can have the effect of diverting attention from the real significance of the *Alexiad* as an extraordinary work of literature that uses subtle techniques to sway the reader in the required direction. Like Leo the Deacon and Psellos, Anna Komnene was fascinated by human appearance, providing physical descriptions of her father, mother and husband and several other individuals. When it comes to character, though, her approach is different to that of Psellos. She does not weigh it up as a possible cause of events but rather constructs it to fit the individual into the part they are to play in the story. The most striking example is her portrait of the Norman leader Bohemond. Tall and imposing, possessed of limitless courage and daring, he is at the same time cunning, manipulative and deceitful. It is not difficult to discern Homer's Odysseus as the prototype and Komnene has clearly used that model to create a kind of super-villain, a worthy adversary for Alexios who inevitably triumphs in the end. She has other failings as a historian. Her dates are sometimes wrong or left incomplete to be filled in later. Events are narrated out of chronological sequence. She is often the only source for much of what she describes, but on a few occasions, when there are other sources against which she can be checked, she can sometimes be convicted of having subtly manipulated the record. A prime example is her insistence that Alexios deeply mistrusted Bohemond when he arrived in Constantinople with the First Crusade in 1097. Latin sources suggest that at that stage the two men were allies and that they only fell out later over Bohemond's seizure of Antioch. Similarly her account of the battle of Dyrrachion in 1081 puts a heroic gloss on a disastrous defeat (see Box 10.3).

These flaws, which Komnene shared with other Byzantine historians, do not detract greatly from the value of the *Alexiad* as history. The book was evidently based on painstaking research that went beyond synthesis of previous histories or personal experience. By her own account she derived much of her information from Alexios himself from listening to his conversations, from other members of the family and from the accounts of old soldiers who had served under him. She clearly had access to official archives because she gives the full text of two treaties and one of Alexios' decrees. Like Psellos, whom she had read and admired, Komnene devoted a great deal of space to plots and intrigue but she was by no means so fixated on Constantinople and the affairs of the court there as he had been. She provides a great deal of detail on military matters, as Leo the Deacon did, and her descriptions of battles are helpful and convincing. At the end of the day, it is not that Komnene is any more honest or impartial than other Byzantine historians, but she does appear to have been both extremely well informed and very dextrous in her use of language. That gave her the ammunition to make her eulogy of her father far more convincing than Psellos' attempt to whitewash the Doukas family. For all its faults, the *Alexiad* of Anna Komnene stands head and shoulders above the other works of history produced between 1081 and 1185.

Box 9.1 Anna Komnene's historical method

In this very unusual passage, Anna Komnene reveals her sources:

> I most certainly do not describe and write of these things in order to favour my father. And, wherever I perceive that my father made a mistake, I unhesitatingly transgress the natural law and cling to the truth, for though I hold him dear, I hold truth dearer still … And the proof is close at hand; for I am not writing about things of ten thousand years ago, but there are many still living to-day who knew my father and tell me of his doings; and no small part of my history has been gathered from them, for one will relate one thing which he happens to remember and another another, and all are of the same opinion. And as a rule I was with my father and mother and accompanied them. For it was not my lot to be kept at home and brought up in the shade and in luxury … Part of my history, as I said, I derive from my own memory and part from the men who accompanied the Emperor on his expeditions and told me divers things about them, and who by means of ferrymen conveyed the news to us of what had happened in the wars; but most I gathered first-hand as I often heard the Emperor and [his brother-in-law] George Palaiologos talking about them. In this way I collected much of my material, but most during the reign of the third successor to the imperial throne after my father, when all flatteries and lies about his grandfather had expired together, for the whole world was flattering the present occupant of the throne and nobody shewed any sign of adulation for the departed, but related the naked facts, and spoke of things just as they had received them.

But now I am bewailing my own misfortunes and lamenting the deaths of three Emperors, my Emperor and father, my Empress and mistress-mother [Irene], and alas! my own husband and Caesar [Nikephoros Bryennios]; so I mostly keep in a corner and occupy myself with books and God. And I shall not allow even the most insignificant of men to approach me unless they be men from whom I can learn of things which they happen to have heard of from others, or they be my father's intimate friends. For during these last thirty years, I swear it by the souls of the most blessed Emperors, I have neither seen nor spoken to a friend of my father's, this is due partly to many of them having died and partly to many being prevented by fear. For the powers that be have condemned us to this ridiculous position so that we should not be seen, but be a general object of abhorrence.

This is an interesting passage as it sums up both the strengths and weaknesses of the *Alexiad*. It reveals the author to have been a conscientious researcher and although a protestation that the author was going to tell the truth was a standard feature of Byzantine historical works, to list the sources of information in this way is unique. On the other hand, Komnene's political agenda emerges here too when she asserts that she has been sequestered and kept out of public life. Many modern historians are sceptical of her claims to ill-treatment after 1118 and interpret them as part of her presentation of herself as the true heir of Alexios I.

Source: *The Alexiad of the Princess Anna Comnena: Being the History of the Reign of her Father, Alexius I, Emperor of the Romans, 1081–1118 A.D.*, trans. Elizabeth A. Dawes (London: Routledge and Kegan Paul, 1967), pp. 380–2 (spellings adapted).

9.3 Niketas Choniates

All Byzantine historians reflected their life experience and political views but Niketas Choniates lived through a trauma so profound that it required a complete revision of his work. Born at Chonai in Asia Minor in around 1155, he was sent to Constantinople for the usual course of higher education and then entered the civil service as a minor tax official sometime before 1182 (see Figure 9.1). With the accession of Isaac II Angelos (1185–1195), he became a secretary and began to climb the career ladder. The overthrow of Isaac II by his brother Alexios III (1195–1203) made no difference to Choniates, for around that time he reached the prestigious rank of Grand Logothete. Then on 13 April 1204, his successful career and prosperity came to an abrupt end. The army of the Fourth Crusade stormed the Sea Walls of Constantinople and poured into its streets. Choniates' splendid mansion was ransacked and then burned down and he had to take refuge with his family in the house of a Venetian wine merchant. A few days later he was able to get his wife and children out of the city but he himself returned later, probably in the hope that he could find some kind of post under the new Latin regime. Like many

Figure 9.1 Lead seal of Niketas Choniates bearing the image of the Virgin and Child and the inscription: 'I seal the letters of Niketas Choniates' on the other side (© Dumbarton Oaks, Byzantine Collection, Washington, DC)

other Byzantines, he was disappointed and by 1206 he had moved to Nicaea where Theodore Laskaris had established a government in exile. There he seems to have lived a wretched existence in makeshift accommodation by the lake, lobbying for a post at Theodore's court which never materialised.

These experiences were reflected in Choniates' *Chronological Narrative*. He wrote it in Attic Greek while working at the court of the Angelos emperors, starting with the death of Alexios I in 1118 and taking the story down to 1202. Following the cataclysm of 1204, he decided to revise and rewrite it, extending the coverage to 1207. Only this second version survives but by a careful analysis of the manuscripts, scholars have been able to reconstruct some of the changes that the author made. The main difference was a more critical approach towards Isaac II and Alexios III, the emperors under whom Choniates had flourished and prospered. When the first version was written, Alexios III was still on the throne, so Choniates probably gave an account of the deposition of his brother Isaac which suggested that he was not involved. The second version, penned after Alexios' fall from power, denounces him for his brother's blinding and both Isaac and Alexios are excoriated from beginning to end. Saying one thing about an emperor when he was alive and another once he was removed was very common in Byzantium and does not detract from the value of Choniates' history, which ranks alongside the *Chronographia* and *Alexiad* as an enduring work of literature. It is one of the most important sources of information on Byzantium in the twelfth century and it is the only one that gives the Byzantine version of the Third and Fourth Crusades. The coverage of John II and Manuel I is obviously derivative because Choniates was not born during the reign of one and was only a child in that of the other, but it still contains numerous insights to lay alongside Kinnamos' narrative. For the period after 1185, he was an eyewitness and participant. In 1187, for example, he accompanied Isaac II on a campaign against the Vlach-Bulgarian rebels and witnessed the near-disaster which followed. As governor of the city of Philippopolis in 1189, he was personally involved in the passage of the German emperor Frederick Barbarossa through the Balkans during the Third Crusade. He recounts how he and others tried to persuade Isaac to abandon his resistance to the Crusade, and succeeded in getting the emperor to release Barbarossa's envoys, whom he had taken into custody. These personal appearances have no element of self-promotion as they do in Psellos and Komnene. On the contrary, Choniates seems to present himself as a helpless onlooker as the catastrophe unfolded. Describing how he and other prominent Byzantines met in Hagia Sophia in January 1204 to elect a new emperor, he says that they dithered for three days before finally, under pressure from the mob, forcing the crown on a reluctant young man called Nicholas Kannavos. The unfortunate Kannavos was flung into prison a few days later when Alexios Mourtzouphlos seized power. It is this rueful tone that characterises both Choniates' history and the times in which he lived, his sometimes bitter and denunciatory tone probably reflecting the deep disillusionment that he felt at the end of his career.

Box 9.2 Alexander Kazhdan (1922–1997) and homo Byzantinus

Born in Moscow, Kazhdan studied at the city's university where he completed his PhD on agrarian conditions in the later Byzantine period in 1952. His early career was difficult, because in the Stalinist era his Jewish and 'bourgeois' background was held against him, but in 1956 he secured a post teaching in the Institute of History at the Soviet Academy of Sciences. In 1978, he left the Soviet Union and moved to the United States where he became a research associate at the Dumbarton Oaks Center for Byzantine Studies in Washington, DC. By then, he had developed his own very particular approach to the study of Byzantium. In the first place, he was deeply opposed to the idea, still found in secondary works, that Byzantium's political, literary and religious culture was created in the late antique period (300–600 CE) and remained static and unchanged throughout its 1,000-year history. Secondly, he strongly believed that the job of a historian was not to uncover new 'facts' but to develop new understandings of what has long been known. Much of his research involved reading the vast corpus of neglected Byzantine texts which he felt should be considered as literature in their own right and not merely as sources of information. Finally, like the great French historian Marc Bloch (1886–1944), Kazhdan thought history should not just be about momentous events or the experiences of a few elite individuals, but the lives, attitudes and beliefs of all people. Consequently, he sought to uncover the experiences and outlook of *homo Byzantinus* or the 'Byzantine person':

> No one will deny that *homo Byzantinus*, like people of all times, had two legs, needed food, married and raised children. But does this mean that people at all times have been the same? … People always needed food, but there were different means of providing it at different times and different attitudes towards it; they concluded their marriages differently, and their children were brought up differently in order to conform to specific social standards and values. In studying the Byzantine model not only the traits common to mankind in general must be dealt with but also the particular features of the Byzantine way of life. The only means of reaching a solution is to keep in mind the complex duality of the problem and to study both the common and the particular features in the social structure of the time and in the human psyche.

So what were the particular features of Byzantine life? One that Kazhdan discusses is a longing for stability and continuity:

> Whereas power in Byzantium was ideal, unattainable and alien, in the West there was an illusion of participation in the administrative activity. This gap between authority and subject, combined with the lack of social relationships, resulted in the constant instability of the Byzantine way of life. The subjects of the Byzantine emperor were defenseless in the face of corporal punishment, confiscation of property or banishment. The only restriction on governmental executions was the morality of the ruler … The threat of ruin, whether or not it was realized, hung over society, and its existence forced Byzantine men and women into a pattern of political and cultural conformity … The alienation both from social ties outside the nuclear family and from power primarily accounted for this social fear, but it was also strengthened by other reasons ranging from human defenselessness before disease and starvation to frequent and dangerous invasions.

Not everyone would accept Kazhdan's bleak picture of Byzantine society, which may have been influenced by his own experiences in Stalin's Russia. There is also in his words a deep irony of which he was well aware. The very fallacy about Byzantium that he disliked the most, its supposedly stiff and unchanging nature, has its roots in the Byzantines' own perception of themselves and their society.

Source: Alexander P. Kazhdan and Giles Constable, *People and Power in Byzantium: An Introduction to Modern Byzantine Studies* (Washington, DC: Dumbarton Oaks, 1982), p. 22, 35–6.

9.4 Other sources: political speeches and views from the West

The period 1045 to 1204 may have seen great political upheavals but it was also a flourishing one for literature. Quite apart from the major histories, large numbers of poems, hagiographies, commentaries on classical texts and speeches survive. The court of Manuel I Komnenos was particularly productive and in some ways very innovative. There was a general loosening of the stays after 1143, perhaps in reaction to the austere morality of his grandfather Alexios I and father John II, and authors were emboldened to express themselves in ways that would not have been approved of in previous decades. A favourite genre was the racy romance, such as Theodore Prodromos' *Rhodanthe and Dosikles*. They usually told the tale of a pair of lovers who had to go through various trials and tribulations before being finally united, laced with a generous helping of ribaldry, eroticism and the occasional pagan god. Perhaps most shocking of all, they were written not in Attic but in the kind of Demotic Greek that had replaced Koine as the everyday language. They may also have been the product of Western influence brought to Constantinople by mercenaries and crusaders and are thus a reminder that Byzantine culture, like that of all societies, was constantly in flux.

As far as historical evidence is concerned, the surviving speeches are very informative. We have already seen how panegyrical speeches were given at the Byzantine court in honour of the reigning emperor on feast days and on special occasions (see Box 5.1). One of the people who gave them during the reign of Manuel I was Eustathios, who was archbishop of Thessalonica from around 1178. He made a speech to welcome the French bride of Manuel's son Alexios II to Constantinople in 1179 and he regularly gave the traditional address at Epiphany (6 January) when the visit of the Magi to the infant Christ was celebrated. The one that Eustathios gave in January 1174 is particularly informative as it celebrates two Byzantine victories from late the previous year. Typically neither was achieved by committing Byzantine armies to a pitched battle. In the first, Manuel I had succeeded in persuading the Seljuk Turkish sultan Kilij Arslan II to turn back with his army from Philadelphia in Asia Minor. In the second, a German army had laid siege to Ancona, an important Byzantine ally in Italy. After seven months, Byzantine gold induced an Italian countess, Aldruda of Frangipane, to lead an army to the rescue and force the Germans to withdraw. Eustathios waxed lyrical about Ancona's saviour, comparing her both to the biblical Judith and to Queen Artemisia of Halicarnassus who helped the Athenians at the battle of Salamis in 480 BCE. His speech supplements the information given about these incidents in the works of John Kinnamos and Niketas Choniates. Eustathios also wrote a detailed account of the Norman capture of Thessalonica in 1185, a work which was probably expanded from a speech in praise of Emperor Isaac II Angelos.

As the period 1045 to 1204 coincided with the era of the Crusades, there was a great deal more direct contact between the Byzantines and their co-religionists in Western Europe than there had been in previous centuries. That in turn led to Byzantium featuring more frequently and prominently in historical works written in Latin and Western vernacular languages such as Old French. The anonymous *Gesta Francorum*, for example, gives an account of the passage of the First Crusade through the Byzantine Balkans, Constantinople and Asia Minor in 1096–1097. The work of the French abbot

Odo of Deuil likewise recounts that same journey that was followed by the Second Crusade in 1147–1148. Both works are extremely hostile towards the Byzantines. The *Gesta* describes Alexios I as *iniquus* (hostile or unjust) while Odo denounces what he saw as the betrayal of the Second Crusade by the treacherous Byzantines. Both authors reflect the widespread view that the Byzantines had not helped, and had sometimes positively hindered, the cause of capturing and holding the holy city of Jerusalem. Not all Western views of Byzantium were so negative, however. There survive numerous accounts by pilgrims who passed through Constantinople on their way to Jerusalem and who were overwhelmed by the size and beauty of the city and of its churches. The Anglo-Norman chronicler Orderic Vitalis likewise has many good things to say about Byzantium (see Box 9.3). Historians are therefore now rather wary of using Latin sources as evidence for a mounting hostility that led inevitably to the sack of Constantinople in 1204.

Box 9.3 Orderic Vitalis and the Varangian guard

Orderic Vitalis spent most of his life as a monk at the abbey of Saint-Evroul in Normandy but he was originally from Shropshire in England and was taken to Saint-Evroul as a child of 11. That is why his chronicle is quite sympathetic towards the Anglo-Saxons, whose country was conquered by William, duke of Normandy following his victory at the Battle of Hastings in October 1066. It might also account for Orderic's relatively favourable attitude towards Alexios I Komnenos and the Byzantine Empire. He denies Alexios his proper title, calling him 'emperor of Constantinople', and he labels his subjects as 'Greeks', but these were standard conventions in Latin literature of the time. Here Orderic describes how his compatriots sought political asylum in Constantinople following their defeat by the Normans:

> And so the English groaned aloud for their lost liberty and plotted ceaselessly to find some way of shaking off a yoke that was so intolerable and unaccustomed. Some sent to Swein, king of Denmark, and urged him to lay claim to the kingdom of England which his ancestors Swein and Cnut had won by the sword. Others fled into voluntary exile so that they might either find in banishment freedom from the power of the Normans or secure foreign help and come back to fight a war of vengeance. Some of them who were still in the flower of youth travelled into remote lands and bravely offered their arms to Alexios, emperor of Constantinople, a man of great wisdom and nobility. Robert Guiscard, duke of Apulia, had taken up arms against him in support of Michael [VII Doukas] whom the Greeks – resenting the power of the senate – had driven from the imperial throne. Consequently the English exiles were warmly welcomed by the Greeks and were sent into battle against the Norman forces, which were too powerful for the Greeks alone. The Emperor Alexios laid the foundations of a town called Civitot for the English, some distance from Byzantium [i.e. Constantinople]; but later when the Norman threat became too great he brought them back to the imperial city and set them to guard his chief palace and royal treasures. This is the chief reason for the Anglo-Saxon exodus to Ionia; the emigrants and their heirs

faithfully served the holy empire, and are still honoured among the Greeks by Emperor, nobility, and people alike.

Anglo-Saxon volunteers were enrolled into the Varangians, the emperor's personal security guards, but they also served in the main body of the Byzantine army. In October 1081, they had the opportunity to avenge the defeat at Hastings when Emperor Alexios confronted the invading Normans at Dyrrachion in what is now Albania (see Section 10.5 and Box 10.3). Sadly, the fighting soon turned against the Byzantines and many of the English volunteers took to their heels and sought refuge in a church. Rather than flush them out, the Normans simply burned down the building over their heads.

Source: Orderic Vitalis, *Ecclesiastical History*, trans. Marjorie Chibnall, 6 vols (Oxford: Oxford University Press, 1980), vol. 2, pp. 203–4 (spellings adapted).

Figure 9.2 The Varangian guard from the Madrid Skylitzes. The scene depicts the overthrow of Emperor Michael V (1041–1042) who is being dragged out of the monastery of St John Stoudios prior to being blinded. Note that the Varangians are brandishing their favourite weapon, the axe

Points to remember

- This period produced some of the finest works of Byzantine historiography by Michael Psellos, Anna Komnene and Niketas Choniates.

- Alongside these major works, there are numerous surviving speeches, letter collections and shorter histories.
- There is much more source material in Latin and Western vernacular languages for this period and it is no longer restricted to affairs in Italy.

Primary sources in English translation

Anonymous. (1962), *Gesta Francorum: The Deeds of the Franks and the Other Pilgrims to Jerusalem*, trans. Rosalind Hill (Oxford: Oxford University Press).

Attaleiates, Michael. (2012), *The History*, trans. Anthony Kaldellis and Dimitris Krallis (Cambridge MA and London: Harvard University Press).

Choniates, Niketas. (1984), *O City of Byzantium. Annals of Niketas Choniates*, trans. Harry J. Magoulias (Detroit MI: Wayne State University Press).

Eustathios of Thessalonica. (2008), *The Capture of Thessaloniki*, trans. J.R. Melville-Jones (Canberra: Australian Association for Byzantine Studies).

Eustathios of Thessalonica. (2013), *Secular Orations 1167/8 to 1179*, trans. Andrew F. Stone (Brisbane: Australian Association for Byzantine Studies).

Kinnamos, John. (1976), *The Deeds of John and Manuel Comnenus*, trans. Charles M. Brand (New York: Columbia University Press).

Komnene, Anna. (2009), *The Alexiad*, trans. E.R.A. Sewter and Peter Frankopan (London: Penguin). There is another more literal translation by Elizabeth A. Dawes. (1967), *The Alexiad of the Princess Anna Comnena: Being the History of the Reign of her Father, Alexius I, Emperor of the Romans, 1081–1118 A.D.* (London: Routledge and Kegan Paul).

Odo of Deuil. (1948), *De Profectione Ludovici VII in Orientem*, trans. Virginia G. Berry (New York: Norton).

Skylitzes, John. (2010), *A Synopsis of Byzantine history, 811–1057* (Oxford: Oxford University Press).

Zonaras, John. (2009), *The History of John Zonaras from Alexander Severus to the Death of Theodosius the Great*, trans. Thomas M. Banchich and Eugene N. Lane (London and New York: Routledge). This is a translation of only a part of Zonaras' work and does not include the period 602–1118.

Suggestions for further reading

Gouma-Peterson, Thalia. (2000), *Anna Komnene and Her Times* (New York: Garland). A collection of essays. See especially the contributions of Paul Magdalino, who argues for Anna's political agenda, and Ruth Macrides, who refutes the argument that Anna Komnene's *Alexiad* was written by her husband.

Kazhdan, Alexander P. and Epstein, Ann Wharton. (1985), *Change in Byzantine Culture in the Eleventh and Twelfth Centuries* (Berkeley CA: University of California Press). Aims to show how Byzantine society, art and literature developed during this period, as a result of the growth of provincial towns and of a military aristocracy.

Neville, Leonora. (2016), *Anna Komnene: The Life and Work of a Medieval Historian* (Oxford: Oxford University Press). Discusses how Anna Komnene constructed herself as a historian within an overwhelmingly masculine literary genre.

Simpson, Alicia J. (2013), *Niketas Choniates: A Historiographical Study* (Oxford: Oxford University Press). Explores the first and second versions of Choniates' historical work and the differences between them.

10 The eleventh-century crisis (1045–1091)

At the beginning of this period, Byzantium was still expanding its borders, incorporating the small Armenian kingdom of Ani. Forty years later, it was once more on the defensive, having lost control of most of the eastern Themes in Asia Minor, and was fighting desperately to hold on to the Balkans and to stave off threats to Constantinople itself. Not surprisingly, generations of historians have sought to discover what brought about this dramatic reversal of fortune. For a long time, the obvious answer seemed to lie in the incompetence of the emperors who ruled after the death of Basil II in 1025 and in the policies of one of them in particular.

10.1 The watershed moment? The reign of Constantine IX (1042–1055)

As we have seen, Constantine Monomachos became emperor rather unexpectedly in June 1042, when the Macedonian empress Zoe summoned him back to Constantinople from exile and married him. He reigned for 13 years before dying of natural causes, much to the grief of Psellos' friend John Mauropous, who described him as 'the marvel of the earth'. The next generation of Byzantines was less impressed. Writing at the end of the eleventh century, John Skylitzes claimed that it was from Constantine's reign that 'the fortunes of the Romans began to waste away' and that damning verdict can also be found in the pages of Michael Psellos, Michael Attaleiates and others. Given the almost unanimous chorus of disapproval in the primary sources, it is hardly surprising that Constantine IX is generally presented very critically in secondary work as well, even if there are those, notably Michael Angold and Anthony Kaldellis, who are prepared to defend him.

Attaleiates, Psellos and Skylitzes bring a number of charges against Constantine. For a start, they claim that he ruined the empire financially by his irresponsibility and prodigality. Basil II had built up an enormous financial surplus by the time of his death in 1025 and it was all stored in the form of gold coins in huge vaults underneath the Great Palace. Constantine IX is alleged to have squandered much of this treasure on gifts for his mistresses and on frivolous extravagances such a new a pond in the palace gardens. His costliest project was the foundation of a new monastery of St George in Mangana whose astronomical cost spiralled because the emperor kept changing his mind on the design. So lavish was Constantine's expenditure that he had to seek out new sources of income.

Taxes were raised, oppressive collectors unleashed on the population and trumped up charges brought against wealthy victims as a way of extorting even more money. There seems to have been another contrivance that the contemporary sources do not mention but which can be detected by weighing and analysing the surviving coins from the period. By the end of Constantine IX's reign, the gold content of the nomisma had reduced to 87 per cent and its purity to 18 carats. Presumably this debasement was an economy measure, designed to make the treasury's reserves of gold go further (see Figure 10.1).

At first sight the case against Constantine IX looks watertight, until one remembers that most of the charges made against him in the sources had also been levelled at his predecessors. Nikephoros II Phokas had been accused of excessive taxation. John I Tzimiskes had expended large sums on rebuilding the church of the Saviour above the Brazen Gate to the Great Palace. Nor is debasement something that can be laid solely at Constantine's door. Nikephoros II had already tampered with the coinage by introducing the 22-carat tetarteron that circulated alongside the full-weight coin. During the reign of Michael IV (1034–1041), the nomisma's gold content had already declined from 94.4 per cent to 90 per cent. Moreover, while Constantine may well have been rather free with his money, it is hard to believe that his gifts to his mistresses were so generous as to bankrupt the state.

Box 10.1 The debate on debasement

For many historians, the dwindling gold content of the nomisma was both a symptom and a cause of Byzantium's decline in the eleventh century. For the economic historian Robert S. Lopez (1910–1986), the nomisma was the 'dollar of the Middle Ages' and by resorting to debasement for short-term financial relief, Constantine IX and other emperors fatally damaged not only the empire's economy but also its international prestige. The coin was, he claimed, 'the ambassador of the chosen people to the other nations of the world'.

There is, however, a radically different interpretation, that of Cécile Morrisson. She pointed out that a similar debasement was happening elsewhere over the same period. In Western Europe, the silver denier lost 50 per cent of its precious metal content and in the Abbasid caliphate the dinar was also debased, indicating that the phenomenon did not necessarily arise as a response to events within Byzantium alone. Rather it was a reaction to the wider expansion in trade, increase in population and economic upturn that was taking place across the Mediterranean during the eleventh century. In these conditions, there were more transactions so more coins were needed than could be provided if the original precious metal content were adhered to. So, far from being wasteful and irresponsible, Constantine IX was pursuing a sensible economic policy by providing more coins when they were needed. Given that there were no complaints about debasement at the time nor any discernible evidence of economic damage, Morrisson argued that debasement during Constantine's reign was actually a sign of prosperity. She termed it a *dévaluation d'expansion*, something that should be carefully distinguished from the *dévaluation de crise* (crisis devaluation) which occurred later, after 1071.

Although accepted in some quarters, notably by Michael Angold and Paul Lemerle, Morrisson's theory has not gone unchallenged. Costas Kaplanis has questioned the idea of a 'benign' debasement of the nomisma before 1071. He argued that Constantine's action here was no carefully thought out fiscal measure but a panicky *dévaluation de crise*, prompted by the need for cash during the Pecheneg War of 1046–1053.

Sources: Robert S. Lopez, 'The dollar of the Middle Ages', *Journal of Economic History* 11 (1951), 209–34; Cécile Morrisson, 'La devaluation de la monnaie byzantine au XIe siècle: essai d'interprétation', *Travaux et mémoires* 6 (1976), 3–30; Costas Kaplanis, 'The debasement of the "dollar of the Middle Ages"', *Journal of Economic History* 63 (2003), 768–801.

Figure 10.1 Nomisma of Constantine IX

Another development during Constantine's reign that has been held against him was that the long period of relative immunity from invasion that Byzantium had enjoyed since 1018 finally came to an end. Three dangerous enemies, one Christian, one pagan and one Muslim, started to threaten the borders. The Christians were the Normans who were slowly eroding the Byzantine position in southern Italy. The pagans were the Pechenegs, another Turkic people from beyond the Danube, who invaded Byzantine Bulgaria during the winter of 1046–1047, when the river froze over. The most dangerous enemy of all was the Muslim one, for here the Byzantines faced a new major power. In 1040, the Seljuk Turks had gained control of Iran and lands up to the borders of Armenia so their territories now met the extended Byzantine frontier. During Constantine's reign, subjects of the Seljuk sultan made some damaging incursions across that border.

These attacks cannot be blamed on any policy of Constantine IX for the roots of the problem went far further back, into the reign of Basil II. The Normans had first appeared in Italy in 1017, when a Byzantine governor asked some passing knights to help him to put down a rebellion. It was their descendants and families that were now slowly conquering Byzantine territory. The Pechenegs likewise did not appear out of the blue in 1046. For years the Byzantines had used them as allies against the Russians and Bulgars. The trouble was that as a result of Basil II's annexation of Bulgaria in 1018, the Byzantines and the Pechenegs now shared a border along the Danube and any instability among the Pechenegs was likely to spill over into Byzantine territory. Similarly, by annexing large parts of Armenia, Basil II had effectively eliminated the buffer states that screened Byzantine Asia Minor from peoples migrating westward from Central Asia and made it vulnerable to attacks from Seljuk territory.

It should be pointed out too that Constantine IX's response to the incursions was by no means incompetent. In Italy, as ever, resources were limited and Constantine did what his predecessors had done and sought allies on the spot. He entered into negotiations with Pope Leo IX who was as alarmed about Norman expansion as he was. In accordance with the agreement, in 1053 a papal army moved south to confront the Normans at Civitate. As it happened, the pope's German troops were scattered by the Norman cavalry and he ended up being taken prisoner, but that can hardly be blamed on Constantine. In the East, the Byzantine response to the Seljuk incursions was effective at this stage. When the Seljuks sacked the Armenian town of Artze in 1048, a Byzantine force under Kekavmenos Katakalon quickly attacked them and forced them to withdraw. Constantine's reaction to the Pecheneg attacks was probably the least effective. After several years of fruitless attempts to push them back over the Danube, the emperor was forced to make a treaty with them in 1053, allowing large numbers of Pechenegs to settle on land in the Theme of Paristrion. They were later to become a thorn in the side of his successors.

Even if Constantine's response to the threats is regarded as acceptable, there remains another serious charge: that he deliberately allowed the army and the defences to be run down and thus paved the way for the collapse of the Byzantine eastern frontier after 1071. He has often been portrayed as the archetypical 'civilian' emperor who hated and mistrusted all things military. Certainly, he never even attempted to lead his armies in person and spent his entire 13-year reign safely in Constantinople. For a ruler whose talents did not run to military leadership that was perhaps sensible, but it did leave the danger that military glory would go to someone else. In the 1030s and early 1040s, it was all being scooped up by George Maniakes, the conqueror of Edessa and western Sicily. So in 1043 Constantine relieved him of his command (see Figure 10.2). This action pushed Maniakes to rebellion and he crossed the Adriatic from Italy with his army and marched on the capital. Fortunately for Constantine, Maniakes was killed by a stray arrow in a skirmish and the revolt petered out. Another rebellion occurred in 1047. Leo Tornikios,

Figure 10.2 Arrest of George Maniakes, from the Madrid Skylitzes

strategos of the Theme of Iberia, was relieved of his command and forced to become a monk. He escaped and gathered an army to march on Constantinople. Once again, Constantine IX survived, thanks to the strength of the Land Walls.

These events could be interpreted as a civilian emperor at odds with his generals but the facts do not always stack up. The revolt of Maniakes was partly precipitated by the machinations of another military man, a member of the Skleros family who owned adjoining lands in Anatolia and had a longstanding feud with his neighbour. Since Constantine's mistress was a member of the same family, Skleros was able to persuade the emperor to dismiss Maniakes, thus provoking his rebellion. With Tornikios, there seems to have been a similar personal grudge behind the revolt as he deeply resented the emperor for breaking up a love affair with Constantine's sister Euprepia. These rebellions may therefore not signify any particular alienation between the emperor and the army.

There is, however, something else that does smack of indifference to the army and defence. At some point during his reign, Constantine decided to disband the army of the Theme of Iberia. The Theme had been set up during the reign of Basil II along the border between Armenia and Georgia when the lands inherited from David of Tao came under Byzantine control. The army had supposedly consisted of some 50,000 men, probably peasant farmers who held land in return for military service. Now they were expected to pay money taxes instead. Iberia was, of course, the very area which was shortly to suffer the raids of the Seljuk Turks so on the face of it, robbing it of a significant element of its defence seems little short of suicidal. Contemporaries were certainly very critical of the move. Attaleiates even went so far as to claim that the demobilised troops made common cause with the Seljuk raiders instead.

On closer examination, though, even here something might be said in Constantine's defence. After all, we know nothing about the army of Iberia and how effective it was. It may only have existed on paper. On the other hand, we do know that for years the emperors had been placing greater reliance on professional paid troops, either the tagmata or foreign mercenaries who may well have been much more effective than part-time farmers. In that scenario, cash from taxes would have been a great deal more valuable than their military service. There is, moreover, no evidence whatsoever that this was a general policy or that any other Theme armies were disbanded.

At the end of the day, the evidence for the reign of Constantine IX can be read two ways. He can be dismissed as an idle incompetent who allowed the empire's defences to weaken or exonerated as a man who did what seemed to be the reasonable thing at the time. Whichever view is taken, it is hardly convincing to blame everything that happened later on one individual. To do so is to fall into the trap set by writers such as Psellos and Skylitzes who wanted to divert any opprobrium away from their masters of the Doukas and Komnenos families.

10.2 The end of the Macedonian dynasty (1055–1067)

Constantine IX died in January 1055. At first there was some uncertainty as to who his successor would be. He had only been emperor by virtue of his marriage to Zoe, Basil II's niece, and she had died some five years previously. A group of courtiers took it upon themselves to elevate Zoe's sister, Theodora, to be sole empress. She held power for only 18 months but during that time, according to Psellos, 'the empire prospered and its glory increased'. The threats to the frontiers died down. The Pechenegs settled in Byzantine territory were quiescent for the time being and in Italy the Normans, rather embarrassed by their capture of the pope, did not follow up their victory at Civitate. Apulia was now largely under their control, but Bari still held out and Calabria remained in Byzantine hands. There was one significant foreign policy success. During the summer of 1055, Theodora's representatives concluded a treaty with the Seljuk sultan Tughrul, who had no interest in making war on Byzantium. His ambition was to control Baghdad and the Abbasid Caliphate, a goal that he realised the following December. So the Byzantine eastern frontier was now secure against further attack from that direction.

This period of calm came to an end when Theodora died in August 1056. With her passing the Macedonian dynasty finally came to end and the issue of who was to succeed became acute. The decision was made ten days later by the palace eunuchs and other administrators, who selected a man called Bringas to take the throne as Michael VI. In doing so, they may well have thought that they were appointing someone who would take energetic action against the Pechenegs, for according to Skylitzes, Michael had been a military man in his youth. But to many, including Psellos, it looked as if they had raised up one of themselves, an elderly Constantinople-based bureaucrat who would be indifferent to the fate of the provinces.

The new emperor confirmed that impression by falling out with some of elements of the military within weeks of his accession. In March 1057, a delegation of army commanders from Asia Minor came to Constantinople, led by Katakalon Kekavmenos, the man who had driven off the Seljuk Turks in 1048. They came in the hope of the promotion and gifts that were generally distributed on the accession of a new emperor but were cruelly disappointed. Michael VI refused to reward them and even berated them on their poor performance. The fact was that in spite of the 1055 treaty, unruly subjects of the Seljuk sultan had continued to make incursions into Armenia and northern Syria and Michael did not think that his generals' response had been energetic enough. Sending them away empty-handed was a fatal mistake, for the disgruntled leaders returned to Asia Minor and there proclaimed one of their number, Isaac Komnenos, as emperor the following June. Michael VI was forced to abdicate when the citizens of Constantinople came out onto the streets in support of the rebellion and Isaac was crowned emperor in September 1057.

Despite the efforts of historians to play down the gulf between the military of the provinces and the court in Constantinople, it was clear that a very different kind of regime had come to power with Isaac I. On his gold coins, he was depicted as a full-length figure, clutching a drawn sword, a type of portrait that had never appeared on the coinage in the past. His economic policies matched the image, for he aimed to restore the empire's finances so that a larger army could be paid for. He commanded that all arrears of taxation should be collected immediately, he curtailed pensions paid to court dignitaries and he rescinded grants of property made from the imperial estates. Even the monasteries were not spared as Isaac returned to the policy of Nikephoros II and sought to restrict the amount of land they owned and even confiscated some of it. Such drastic austerity would inevitably provoke opposition and the attack on the monasteries brought Isaac into conflict with the patriarch of Constantinople, Michael Keroularios. Matters came to a head when Keroularios bluntly told Isaac that his authority as a priest exceeded that of the emperor. Isaac promptly had him arrested, threatening that if he did not resign he would be brought to trial. When the patriarch died not long after, Isaac was left looking like an oppressor of the Church, but he was at least able to appoint a more emollient individual to the vacant post.

None of this would have mattered if Isaac had been able to deliver an impressive victory against the Seljuk Turks or Pechenegs. In fact, his reign witnessed a significant deterioration in the military position. Just six months after his accession, in February 1058, a group of Turks crossed the border, moved beyond Armenia over the Taurus Mountains and sacked the city of Melitene. The news came as a terrible shock in Constantinople. Melitene was the city which had once been such a bone of contention between Byzantines and Arabs and whose capture by John Kourkouas in 934 had symbolised Byzantium's resurgence in the East. It was, moreover, not in Armenia but deep in Byzantine territory to the west of the Taurus range. Isaac was also faced with a revived threat in the Balkans. The Pechenegs who were settled in the Theme of Paristrion had taken to raiding the lands round about, often in alliance with the neighbouring Hungarians. The situation at least gave Isaac the opportunity to prove his mettle. In the summer of 1059, he marched out to confront the Pechenegs but he found it very difficult to get to grips with the enemy because they avoided battle and fled at his approach, leaving him only with the satisfaction of capturing their camp and destroying their tents. At the end of the campaign, his army was caught in a storm as it was crossing a swift-flowing river and many of his men were drowned. It was not the glorious return to Constantinople that he had hoped for. Shortly afterwards, Isaac fell ill and, fearing that he was likely to die, was persuaded to abdicate in favour of Michael Psellos' old friend Doukas, who became Constantine X (see Section 5.4).

Constantine X's short reign is not as well documented as Isaac I's but it could be seen as exemplifying the problems that Byzantium was facing in the second half of the eleventh century. Some historians have contrasted the new emperor unfavourably with Isaac I as an ineffective, 'civilian' emperor. In fact, the two men were of much the same background and Constantine had supported Isaac during the 1057 coup. Their policies were broadly similar. Constantine X continued the financial restraint and was rigorous in collecting taxes. On the other hand, unlike Isaac, he was careful to avoid making enemies, restoring to office those who had been ousted by his predecessor. He had a tendency to micromanage, often personally supervising the administration of justice. Some said that he did so in order to levy large fines and so benefit the treasury.

These were all sensible policies but there was a more controversial aspect of his reign. According to Attaleiates, Skylitzes and even the pro-Doukas Psellos, for all Constantine's financial prudence, he was unwilling to spend money on the army and defence. On the face of it, it seems inconceivable that any ruler would cut back on military spending at a time when the frontiers were under attack, yet that appears to be what Constantine X did. Perhaps the financial crisis had become so acute that he had little choice, but there may be another explanation. With the end of the Macedonian dynasty, there was no longer any family which had an obvious legitimate right to the throne. It was open to being grabbed by anyone, much as Isaac Komnenos had taken it in 1057 and Constantine X himself in 1059. It could easily happen again and the most likely contenders would be generals in command of an army, therefore Constantine may have been reluctant to hand to anyone the wherewithal to overthrow him. To some extent the policy paid off, for there were almost no rebellions during his reign, which would indicate that he enjoyed a broad measure of support. He doubtless hoped that in time the Doukas family would come to achieve that aura of legitimacy once enjoyed by the Macedonians.

The drawback, of course, was that the scaled-down defences left the frontiers open to attack. In Italy during the 1060s, the new Norman leaders, Robert Guiscard and his brother Roger, went on the offensive, taking numerous fortresses in Calabria. In the Balkans, the preoccupation of the Byzantine forces with the Pechenegs gave other enemies the chance to breach the frontier. In 1064, two other Turkic groups, the Uzes and the Cumans, crossed the Danube and ravaged Bulgaria. Constantine did respond to these attacks but by the time that he had arrived with an army, the raiders had already crossed back over the river. In Asia Minor, the raids by Seljuk bands whom the sultan could not control continued. In the summer of 1059, a group of them raided into Asia Minor, capturing and sacking the city of Sebasteia. Shortly afterwards, a new development made the eastern frontier even more vulnerable. The new Seljuk sultan, Alp Arslan, decided that since his predecessor had been unable to check the raids into Byzantine territory, he would join them and abandon the 1055 treaty. In July 1064, the sultan captured and sacked Ani, the city that had come under Byzantine rule in 1045 (see Figure 10.3). There was little resistance. Attaleiates recounts how an Armenian called Pangratios had promised the emperor that he could defend the city without the need for extra resources and Constantine naturally took him up on this offer. When the siege began, the garrison in the citadel might have held out, but they soon ran short of supplies as no stockpiles had been made. They had no choice but to surrender.

Figure 10.3 The walls of Ani

Constantine X might have reasoned that such reverses were acceptable, provided he could establish a stable dynasty in Constantinople, but his calculations went awry here as well. In October 1066, he fell ill and was no longer able to govern the empire. From his sickbed he saw the danger. His son and heir, Michael, was only in his teens so there would almost certainly be a bid for power by some well-established military man. Doubtless with the precedent of Theophano and Nikephoros II Phokas in mind, Constantine made his wife Eudokia swear that she would never remarry and would guard the throne for Michael. When the emperor finally died in May 1067, Eudokia became the head of the council of regency that also included the patriarch and Constantine's brother, John Doukas. She may well have hoped to fulfil her promise but events forced her hand. During the summer of 1067, a powerful Turkish raiding force crossed the Taurus Mountains and marched west to Caesarea, the old heartland of the Phokas family. The city was captured, many of the inhabitants were massacred and the cathedral of St Basil was desecrated and looted. It had been centuries since anything like this had happened in the centre of Asia Minor and the news was a measure of just how grave the crisis had become. In the circumstances, Eudokia had little choice but to remarry, even if doing so would put the continuation of the Doukas dynasty into question. She decided to promote a successful general called Romanos Diogenes to the throne by making him her husband and guardian to her son Michael VII.

Box 10.2 Eudokia breaks the news to Michael Psellos

The decision to remarry in spite of her oath to her late husband must have been a very difficult one for Empress Eudokia. It was politically sensitive too, as supporters of the Doukas family into which she had married were likely to interpret it as betrayal. She therefore moved cautiously and secretly and only revealed her marriage to Michael Psellos, an influential courtier and lifelong friend of Constantine X, after it had already been arranged. Here he describes the interview:

> That evening the empress sent for me. When we were alone, she spoke to me with tears in her eyes. 'You must be aware', she said, 'of our loss in prestige and the declining fortunes of our empire, with wars constantly springing up and barbarian hordes ravaging the whole of the east. How can our country possibly escape disaster?' I knew nothing of the things that had been going on, nor that the future emperor was already standing at the palace doors, so I replied that it was no easy matter to decide. 'It requires careful consideration', I said, 'Better propose today and listen tomorrow, as the proverb says.' 'But deliberation is superfluous now. The matter has been considered already and the decision is made. Romanos, the son of Diogenes, has been invited to rule as emperor, in preference to all others.' The words filled me with instant consternation. I could not conceive what would become of me. 'Well then', I said, 'tomorrow I too will give my advice on the matter.' 'Not tomorrow', she replied, 'but now. Give me your support.' I returned to the attack with just one question: 'But your son, the emperor [Michael], who will presumably one day govern the empire alone – does he know what has happened too?' 'He is not entirely in the dark, although he does not yet know all the details', she said, 'However, I am glad you mention my son. Let us go up to him together, and explain how things stand.'

The bleary-eyed boy was roused from his bed and taken down to meet his new stepfather Romanos, whom he embraced with conspicuous ill grace. It was not an auspicious start to the new reign.

Source: Michael Psellos, *Fourteen Byzantine Rulers*, trans. E.R.A. Sewter (Harmondsworth: Penguin, 1966), pp. 348–9 (spellings adapted).

10.3 Romanos IV and the battle of Manzikert (1067–1071)

The new emperor married Eudokia and was crowned in January 1068. His short reign marks the moment when the problems facing Byzantium in the late eleventh century escalated from a crisis to a catastrophe. It began well. The new emperor decided to give priority to the Seljuk threat and, in the summer of 1068, campaigned in Asia Minor, chasing off incursions in the area around Sebasteia. In the autumn, he switched location to northern Syria, bolstering the defences of Antioch which had been the target of Turkish and Arab attacks from Aleppo. The following summer found him in Asia Minor once more but he had some difficulty actually finding the Turkish raiders. They would often strike unexpectedly when he was hundreds of miles away and be long gone by the time he arrived. Thus he was unable to prevent the sack of Ikonion in 1069. So when, on his third expedition in August 1071, Romanos IV encountered the army of the Seljuk sultan Alp Arslan, close to the town of Manzikert in Armenia, it seemed that he at last had an opportunity to strike a decisive blow. His force greatly outnumbered the sultan's so that he felt confident enough to reject his offer of peace. In the ensuing battle, however, the Byzantine army was routed and Emperor Romanos ended up as a prisoner of the sultan.

This unexpected outcome could have been the result of simple bad luck, for it is very easy for battles to go wrong on the day. In the initial clash, the Turks pulled back before the Byzantine onslaught and were pursued. After a time, the emperor called a halt to the chase and ordered the banners to be turned around to signal a withdrawal. Unfortunately, the soldiers at the rear read this as a sign that the vanguard had been defeated. They panicked and started to flee. That gave the Turks the chance to come between the vanguard and the main body of the army, overwhelming and capturing the emperor. Most historians, however, have argued for deeper causes behind the defeat, though they have disagreed on what those were. Some have fastened on to the remark of Skylitzes that the Byzantine army was 'a dreadful sight', its soldiers elderly, infirm and badly equipped, in order to argue that the defeat at Manzikert was the outcome of the neglect of the army by previous emperors. The weakness in this line of argument is that contemporary evidence suggests that while the army may have been understrength at the beginning of Romanos' reign, it had greatly improved by the time of Manzikert. Attaleiates describes how Romanos on his accession set about a recruiting drive and soon brought the army up to strength so that when he marched out against the Turks in 1071, he had so many good troops that he sent away those whom he felt did not made the grade. Thus Skylitzes may well have been referring to the army as it was in 1068, not 1071.

Others have detected treachery, the kind of 'stab in the back' that is so often used to both explain and excuse defeat. It has been suggested that some Armenians, resentful at attempts to impose Byzantine religious practices on their Monophysite church, betrayed their fellow Christians. Yet there is little specific evidence for it and some contrary examples of Armenians fighting bravely on the Byzantine side can be found. More common is the claim that the treachery came from Romanos' own camp. There can be no doubt that some members of the Doukas family were horrified at Eudokia's decision to break her oath and remarry, since they feared that Romanos would one day push Michael VII aside and substitute his own family as the ruling dynasty. According to Attaleiates, it was Andronikos Doukas, a cousin of Michael VII, who deliberately spread the rumour that Romanos was dead and led his contingent away from the battlefield. At first sight, Attaleiates' evidence is damning, for he was personally present at the battle, but he does make it clear that this is something he heard about rather than saw. It was a rumour he was only too happy to pass on, as he was a friend and protégé of Nikephoros Botaneiates, who was later to overthrow the Doukas family. Nevertheless, this explanation ties in with the endemic political rivalry that had plagued Byzantium since the end of the Macedonian dynasty in 1056.

The one last possibility that historians have always fought shy of is that Romanos himself was in any way responsible. Perhaps the image of the noble hero betrayed by lesser men is just too compelling. Yet he certainly made some errors in the lead-up to the battle. He was not aware that the sultan's army was in the vicinity until it was almost on top of him. Under the impression that he was dealing only with small bands of raiders, he split his forces, sending a large contingent off in a different direction. Those men would have been very useful to him in the engagement with the sultan. Romanos could also be accused of rashness in taking a position at the front of his army and thus exposing himself to capture. The sultan wisely watched the whole thing from a safe distance. These criticisms were made by a contemporary, Michael Psellos, but his testimony is usually dismissed because of his virulent pro-Doukas bias. Yet there is no reason why the views of the equally virulent and anti-Doukas Attaleiates should be preferred.

10.4 The fall of Asia Minor (1071–1081)

The defeat at Manzikert is often seen as the moment when Byzantium's status as a great power began to wane and Asia Minor started to become Turkey. With hindsight, that view is not unreasonable, but on closer inspection it appears that the defeat was by no means as serious as some others in Byzantine history. Humiliating though it was, it did not involve casualties on the scale of those suffered at Anchialos in 917 when the Bulgars had wiped out an entire Byzantine army. Two very large contingents of Romanos IV's command, the troops sent off in a different direction and the rearguard commanded by Andronikos Doukas, escaped completely unscathed. Nor was the defeat followed by punitive concessions imposed by the victors. Sultan Alp Arslan had no interest in making conquests in Armenia or Asia Minor. His main anxiety was to be free to take up the more important struggle against the Fatimids of Egypt, his bitter rivals for leadership in the Islamic world. He therefore made a very generous treaty with the captured Romanos. It would seem that the emperor handed over some Armenian fortresses, agreed to release his Muslim prisoners and promised the sultan military assistance in the future. He was then given his liberty after promising to raise a large ransom payment. So the defeat at Manzikert could have been no more than an untoward event from which Byzantium quickly recovered. It was not in itself the reason why the Byzantines were to suffer such a huge loss of territory in the decade that followed.

It was continuing internal political instability that was to prove fatal in Asia Minor. When the news of Romanos' capture had arrived in Constantinople, Michael Psellos and the Doukas family took immediate advantage by proclaiming Michael VII as sole emperor and declaring Romanos IV to be deposed. When they learned that Romanos had unexpectedly been released, they were not prepared to back down. Andronikos Doukas was sent with an army to arrest Romanos and, after some fighting, the emperor surrendered and agreed to renounce the throne and retire to a monastery, receiving in return a guarantee that no harm would come to him. Tragically, the agreement was not adhered to and Romanos was blinded by his captors once they had him in their hands. It was done so ineptly that he never recovered from his injuries and he died in the summer of 1072. Common though this fate was in Byzantine politics, it would seem that public opinion in this case was outraged at Romanos' treatment, at least if Attaleiates is to be believed. It is likely that the atrocity tainted the Doukas regime and was a factor in the continuing civil unrest.

Had the regime that had come to power in Constantinople in 1071 gained widespread respect and popularity by being seen to deal effectively with the crisis, it might have weathered the storm, but it failed to do so. Michael VII soon revealed himself to be too inexperienced and naïve to deal with the crisis. Real power soon passed into the hands of others, first his uncle, Caesar John Doukas, then a eunuch called Nikephoritzes, who did attempt to resolve the situation. With refugees crowding into Constantinople from Asia Minor, Nikephoritzes attempted to maintain the food supply by taking control of the grain market, stockpiling corn at the port of Rhaidestos. There were unfortunate economic results. The price of grain sky-rocketed and workers demanded higher wages in order to be able to pay for it. Matters were compounded by the fact that the nomisma had lost a great deal of its value thanks to debasement while the tax revenues from Asia Minor were dwindling as the Byzantines lost control of the area.

Dissatisfaction soon expressed itself in a rash of military revolts. In 1075, Nestor, governor of Dristra rebelled, joined forces with the Pechenegs and marched on Constantinople. In 1077, Nikephoros Bryennios was proclaimed emperor at Adrianople and Nikephoros Botaneiates, who was related to the Phokas family, was proclaimed emperor in Asia Minor. Beleaguered on all sides, in March 1078, Michael VII abdicated and became a monk. In April 1078, Botaneiates entered Constantinople and became Nikephoros III but that did not end the upheavals. Nikephoros III had been a great commander in his day but he was now rather elderly and was not up to the challenge. So the revolts continued. In the summer of 1078, Nikephoros Basilakios was proclaimed emperor in the Balkans but his revolt was crushed by an army led by one of Nikephoros III's generals, Alexios Komnenos, nephew of the short-reigned Isaac I. In early 1081, Nikephoros Melissenos was proclaimed emperor in Asia Minor, but a few months later it was someone else, the young general Alexios Komnenos, who finally toppled Nikephoros III.

It was largely as a result of these civil wars and general instability that the government in Constantinople lost its authority in Asia Minor. It was not that the area was invaded by the Seljuk sultan. Alp Arslan adhered to the treaty that he had made with Romanos and, in any case, he died the following year. What actually happened was that various disparate groups filled the power vacuum in different areas, whether Latins, Armenians or Turks. The Latins were Western European Christians who had increasingly been used as mercenaries in the Byzantine armies during the eleventh century. In 1073, one of them, a Norman called Roussel of Bailleul, commanded a troop of 400 Western mercenaries in an expedition into Asia Minor under the command of Isaac Komnenos, domestic of the Scholai and older brother of Alexios who later became emperor. However, when they got to Ikonion, Roussel and his contingent mutinied and left the army. He set himself up as an independent ruler in the area around Amaseia. In this case, the annexation of territory was short-lived. Roussel was defeated and captured by Alexios Komnenos in 1075 but his short career prefigures the later Norman seizure of Antioch in the wake of the First Crusade (see Section 11.2). The Armenians were to carve out a much more enduring home for themselves in Byzantine Asia Minor. Since Basil II's annexations, Armenians, like Latins, had played an important role in the Byzantine army. Philaretos Brachomios had been a prominent officer, but when he saw the downfall of Romanos IV he no longer wanted to serve, as he had been very loyal to that particular emperor. So he seized

Antioch and a swathe of land in south-eastern Asia Minor, the area known as Cilicia. Although the Armenians were to lose Antioch to the Turks in 1084, by the early twelfth century an independent Armenian principality had emerged and it was to last until the fourteenth century.

Then there were the Turks. When Alp Arslan had led his army out of Armenia after his victory, independent bands took advantage of the Byzantine civil wars to resume their incursions in the area. It was to counter these that Michael VII sent Isaac Komnenos into Asia Minor in 1073 but the force was badly mauled in an encounter with a band of Turks and Isaac himself was captured. No further Byzantine armies were sent into the region and so the raiders ceased to withdraw after their attacks and began to settle on the land. One group, the Danishmendids, established themselves in north-eastern Asia Minor around the town of Sebasteia. Suleyman ibn Qutulmush, a cousin of Sultan Alp Arslan, took control of a band of Turks in western Asia Minor. They supported Nikephoros Botaneiates in his revolt against Michael VII and that enabled them to acquire an important prize. Botaneiates used them to garrison the towns that he captured during his march on Constantinople, including Nicaea. Since Botaneiates never came back to claim the towns, Nicaea became the centre of a territory under Suleyman's rule. From about 1081, he was styling himself 'Sultan' and his successors called themselves 'Sultans of Rum', that is to say of Rome. Having a non-Christian ruler established in a historic town so close to Constantinople does not seem to have given rise to the anxiety that one might expect. It would seem the Byzantines still regarded the Turks as potential allies and not as alien occupiers of their lands. That was probably because by 1081, the Byzantines were facing an even graver threat in the Balkans.

10.5 The struggle for the Balkans (1081–1091)

The accession of Alexios I Komnenos as emperor in April 1081 is often taken as a turning point, the moment when an able emperor restored Byzantine military prowess and defeated its invading enemies. In fact, there were few signs of revival in the early years of his reign and things got worse, not better. There was a real danger that the Balkan provinces would be lost in the same way that Asia Minor had been. The main threat did not come from the Pechenegs, for although they were still entrenched in Bulgaria, they were relatively quiescent in the early 1080s. Nor did it come from the other enemies in the region, who had been quick to take advantage of Byzantium's evident weakness after Manzikert. In 1072, the Hungarians had crossed the Danube while the Bulgarians had revolted against Byzantine rule and captured Ohrid, proclaiming their leader as tsar. The response of Michael VII and his advisers in this case had been very effective. They put down the Bulgarian revolt by force of arms in 1073 and they defused the Hungarian threat by more subtle means. They backed one contender in a civil war so that when Géza I was victorious and became king of Hungary in 1074, he adopted a more friendly approach, even marrying the daughter of a Byzantine aristocrat (see Figure 10.4).

The real danger to the Balkans came from across the Adriatic, from Italy. Even before the defeat at Manzikert, the Byzantine position there had collapsed, for in April 1071 the Normans under Robert Guiscard had taken Bari, last Byzantine stronghold in Apulia. Bowing

Figure 10.4 Crown sent by Michael VII to Géza I of Hungary, now in the Hungarian National Museum, Budapest

to the inevitable, Michael VII had made a peace treaty with Robert in 1074, recognising the Norman duke's possession of Apulia and Calabria, agreeing the marriage of Robert's daughter Helena to his son Constantine, and providing for Robert to act as an ally of the emperor in time of need. The plan was doubtless to enlist Norman aid against the Pechenegs and Turks. Unfortunately, Michael VII's policy unravelled when he was overthrown in 1078 and the treaty was shelved. With his ambitions to ally himself with the ruling Byzantine dynasty frustrated, a furious Robert Guiscard prepared for war. Claiming to be acting on behalf of the ousted Michael VII, he led an army across the Adriatic in June 1081 to invade the Byzantine Balkan provinces. The recently acceded Emperor Alexios I was quick to respond, gathering an army and marching west to confront the invader. But when he met Robert Guiscard in battle at Dyrrachion in October 1081, he suffered a catastrophic defeat that was far more serious than that at Manzikert.

Box 10.3 Disaster at Dyrrachion (1081)

Unlike at Manzikert, Byzantine casualties at Dyrrachion were heavy, but at least this time the emperor escaped capture. According to Anna Komnene he only did so by the skin of his teeth, hotly pursued by the Norman cavalry.

> After showing his pursuers his back for some considerable time, he turned upon them and encountering one of them, ran his spear through his chest, and the man fell backwards to the ground. Then the emperor turned his horse again and

held on his former way. And so he met a number of the Franks who before had been chasing the Roman troops. When they saw him in the distance, they formed in close order and halted, partly to wind their horses, but also because they were anxious to take him alive and carry him off as booty to Robert [Guiscard]. But when he saw that besides the men pursuing him there were now others in front as well, he had well-nigh despaired of safety; nevertheless he collected himself and noticing a man amongst the foe whom from his stature and gleaming weapons he judged to be Robert, he set his horse straight at him; and the other aimed his spear at him. So both joined combat, and launched themselves the one against the other in the intervening space. The emperor first directing his hand aright, struck at his opponent with his spear, which passed right through his breast, and out at the back. Straightway the barbarian fell to the ground and gave up the ghost on the spot, for the wound was mortal. And next the emperor dashed right through the middle of the company and rode away, for by slaying that one barbarian he had gained safety for himself. As soon as the Franks saw their hero wounded and hurled to the ground, they crowded round the fallen and busied themselves about him. And when those who had been pursuing the emperor saw them, they, too, dismounted, and on recognizing the dead man, began beating their breasts and wailing. However, the man was not Robert, but one of the nobles, second only in rank to Robert. While they were thus occupied, the emperor continued his flight.

Readers may be sceptical as to whether Alexios personally killed two Norman knights, one of whom was allegedly Robert Guiscard's second-in-command, especially as Komnene is the only one to report this encounter. Her contemporary, John Zonaras, merely says that Alexios' departure from the battlefield was 'ignominious'. Komnene's lengthy account of his daring escape helps to cover the fact that he presided over one of the worst defeats in Byzantine history.

Source: *The Alexiad of the Princess Anna Comnena: Being the History of the Reign of her Father, Alexius I, Emperor of the Romans, 1081–1118 A.D.*, trans. Elizabeth A. Dawes (London: Routledge and Kegan Paul, 1967), pp. 112–13 (spellings adapted).

The following spring, the Normans marched eastwards and looked likely to take Thessalonica. With the possibility of ejecting the Normans by force of arms now ruled out, Alexios reverted to the tried and tested policy of looking for allies whom he could persuade or bribe to attack his Norman enemies. He attempted to enlist the Western emperor, Henry IV, to attack Guiscard's lands in Italy and made a treaty with the Venetians, who could use their fleet to cut off reinforcements and supplies crossing from southern Italy to Guiscard's army (see Section 12.2; see Figure 10.5). He also made contact with Sultan Suleyman in Nicaea and persuaded him to send a contingent of 7,000 Turks to fight on the Byzantine side. Slowly the tide began to turn. In April 1082, Robert Guiscard had to return to Italy to counter Emperor Henry IV's invasion, leaving

Figure 10.5 The church of St Mark, Venice, where the style of decoration reflects the city's long-standing
political and commercial links with Constantinople

his son Bohemond in command in the Balkans. The Normans continued to gain ground until October 1083 when Alexios inflicted a significant reverse on them at Larissa. The death of Robert Guiscard in 1085, when he was on his way back to the Balkans, caused the Normans to lose heart and withdraw.

Alexios had little time to rejoice in his victory, for almost immediately the Pecheneg raids resumed, reinforced by further groups crossing the Danube into Byzantine land. In 1087, Alexios received a bruising defeat at their hands at Dristra in Bulgaria. Matters also took a turn for the worse in Asia Minor. With the death of Sultan Suleyman in 1085, other Turkish groups began to challenge for land in western Asia Minor. One of them, led by Chaka, occupied the port of Smyrna and there used local labour to construct a fleet, which they sent to prey on shipping in the Aegean. By the winter of 1090–1091, Byzantium was once more in a very dangerous position. The waters off Constantinople were being blockaded by Chaka's fleet while the Pechenegs had advanced into Thrace and were threatening the capital from the landward side.

From this nadir, matters suddenly improved in the spring of 1091. Allying himself with another Turkic group, the Cumans, Alexios surrounded and almost completely annihilated a large army of Pechenegs at Mount Levounion, putting an end to their incursions for a generation. The following year, he despatched a fleet under the command of his brother-in-law, John Doukas, which drove Chaka's forces off the Aegean islands that he had seized. Shortly afterwards, the troublesome Chaka was murdered on the orders of the new sultan of Nicaea, Kilij Arslan I. At last, the Balkans were secure and the naval threat to Constantinople neutralised. The immediate crisis was over.

Points to remember

*   Many historians have blamed the successors of Basil II, especially Constantine IX, for causing the eleventh-century crisis by incompetent government. That might be a little simplistic.
*   Some of the problems facing Byzantium after 1025 had their roots in the reign of Basil II.
*   The end of the Macedonian dynasty in 1056 was a factor in the crisis as it fuelled internal instability.
*   The defeat of Manzikert was not in itself decisive but with Byzantium riven by civil wars, various group were able to take over large tracts of territory in Asia Minor.
*   The accession of Alexios I in 1081 was not the moment when recovery began. That did not happen for another ten years.

Suggestions for further reading

Angold, Michael. (1997, 2nd revised edition), *The Byzantine Empire, 1025–1204: A Political History* (London and New York: Longman). A critical survey of the entire period, taking into account the arguments of Morrisson (see Box 10.1) and Lemerle (see Box 11.1).

Beihammer, Alexander D. (2017), *Byzantium and the Emergence of Muslim-Turkish Anatolia ca. 1040–1130* (London: Taylor and Francis). Shows how eleventh-century Asia Minor was not so much invaded as infiltrated by various Turkic groups.

Haldon, John. (2001), *The Byzantine Wars: Battles and Campaigns of the Byzantine Era* (Stroud, Gloucestershire and Charleston SC: Tempus). Includes useful analyses of the Manzikert and Dyrrachion campaigns.

Hillenbrand, Carole. (2007), *Turkish Myth and Muslim Symbol: The Battle of Manzikert* (Edinburgh: Edinburgh University Press). Presents translations of Muslim and Christian primary sources for the battle with a very useful commentary.

11 Stability under the Komnenos dynasty (1091–1180)

Having restored Byzantium's position in the Balkans, Alexios I Komnenos went on to reign for 37 years and to establish a dynasty that was to last for over a century, the longest tenure of power by one family since the end of the Macedonians in 1057. Under his two successors, Byzantium seemed to have recovered the wealth and prestige that it had enjoyed in the days of Basil II and to have resumed its dominance in the region. What needs to be considered now are the ways in which these three rulers achieved their military victories and established internal stability.

11.1 A new style of government under Alexios I

When Alexios Komnenos seized power in the spring of 1081, he had little to distinguish him from all the other ambitious military leaders who were marching on the capital. True, he was the nephew of Emperor Isaac I, but Isaac had himself been a usurper and his reign had been brief. So Alexios had to find a way to give himself some fig leaf of legitimacy to justify his occupation of the throne as opposed to that of anyone else, just as Basil I had after 867. A standard way of doing that was to create a marriage alliance with a previous dynasty. Alexios was helped in his coup by John Doukas, brother of Emperor Constantine X and shortly before his accession he married John's granddaughter Irene, daughter of the Andronikos Doukas who had allegedly deserted Romanos IV at Manzikert in 1071. Alexios had, after all, overthrown Nikephoros III, the deposer of Michael VII, and so could now pose as the avenger of the Doukas family and as someone who had restored things to the way they should have been.

Not everyone was convinced. There were numerous plots and rebellions throughout Alexios' reign, including one led by Nikephoros Diogenes, son of Romanos IV, in June 1094. So Alexios and his advisers had to do more to gain widespread acceptance that imperial power was reserved for his family, whether by blood or by marriage. One of the first tasks in 1081 was to neutralise one of his rivals for power, Nikephoros Melissenos, who was still sitting near Nicaea with a large army. Rather than confront him militarily, Alexios reminded him that he was his brother-in-law, since Melissenos had married Alexios' sister Eudokia. He persuaded his rival to abandon his bid for the throne and, in return, conferred on him the title of Caesar, effectively making him deputy emperor, along with extensive estates around Thessalonica. The threat of Melissenos had thus been defused by absorbing him into the imperial family.

In the years that followed, Alexios went further in reserving imperial power for his own kin, keeping all the highest ranks and dignities for members of his family, which had never been the case before. He achieved this by subtly downgrading many of the old titles and offices that had existed since late Roman times, and by creating instead a whole new series of honours based on the Greek word *sebastos* or 'augustus'. His brother Isaac was made sebastokrator, a rank higher than that of the old Caesar that promoted him over the head of Nikephoros Melissenos. His brother-in-law, Michael Taronites, became protosebastos. The same applied to military appointments. When the domestic of the West was killed fighting the Pechenegs in 1086, Alexios replaced him with his brother Adrian. Another of his brothers-in-law, Michael Doukas, was appointed second in command of the land forces, and yet another, John Doukas, held the office of grand duke of the Fleet. This was, of course, systematic nepotism, but the reservation of offices and titles for those whom Alexios could trust did address the problem of the successful general using his prestige and army to make a bid for the throne. It seems to have worked in the long run, for although Alexios' reign was troubled by conspiracies and rebellions, those of his two successors were relatively free of them.

Another strategy used by Alexios was to occupy the moral high ground. That was made easy by the catastrophic events of the 1070s, which many pious Byzantines would have believed to have been a divine punishment for moral laxity. From the outset, Alexios presented himself as the man who was going to bring the empire back to the paths of righteousness that earlier emperors had forsaken, in the same way that Basil I had denigrated his predecessor Michael III and stressed his own sober virtue (see Section 6.2). Alexios delegated part of this task to his mother, Anna Dalassena, who took it upon herself to reform the morals of the Great Palace. Out went the free and easy life which had held sway under Constantine IX, who openly flaunted his mistresses. The palace, according to Anna Komnene, became more like a monastery with set times for prayers and hymn singing. Alexios himself acted to ensure strict adherence to religious orthodoxy as defined by the Byzantine Church and dealt harshly with anyone who deviated. Michael Psellos had been able to get away with his open admiration for Plato and the Neoplatonists, but his successor John Italos was not. He was put on trial and disgraced in 1082. Towards the end of his reign, Alexios had the leader of the heretical Bogomil sect publicly burned at the stake in the Hippodrome. Such drastic punishments were rare in Byzantium and distinguish Alexios' reign from the more tolerant regime which preceded it. Finally, a new and austere ethos that put value on military prowess and manly virtues can also be discerned. The influence of eunuchs, who had once dominated the court, began to wane during the twelfth century.

Box 11.1 Paul Lemerle (1903–1989) on Alexios I Komnenos

While most historians regard the reign of Alexios I as marking Byzantium's recovery from the eleventh-century crisis, some have questioned just how beneficial his advent to power really was. After all, they argue, we mainly know about his reign from the laudatory work of Anna Komnene and that has inclined us towards a favourable assessment. One of these doubters was the French Byzantinist Paul Lemerle, who argued that Alexios' coup in 1081 put an end to a promising constitutional development. Byzantium still possessed a body known as the Senate, although it was no longer a legislative assembly as it had been in the days of the Roman Republic. Rather, it formed the emperor's council of advisors and was composed of his most prominent and influential subjects. During the eleventh century, the membership of the Senate was widened, especially under Emperors Constantine IX Monomachos and Constantine X Doukas. Contemporaries such as Michael Psellos railed bitterly against this development, claiming that the institution was being watered down by the inclusion of 'rascally vagabonds of the market'. For Lemerle, however, it was a positive move. Like Cécile Morrisson (see Box 10.1), Lemerle saw the first half of the eleventh century as a time of economic expansion and prosperity and he interpreted the expansion of the Senate as reflecting that situation: the emperors were widening their circle of advisers to include men with commercial experience. All that was brutally cut short in 1081, when Alexios' coup brought to power a landed aristocrat who was determined to concentrate power in the hands of his own class:

> Matters changed completely with Alexios I and not only because the senatorial class had been favourable to [Nikephoros III] Botaneiates. A curious passage in Zonaras tells us that when they entered Constantinople, Alexios' men 'threw any senators whom they met off their mules, sometimes even stripping them of their clothes, leaving them half-naked and on foot in the middle of the street'. The same author claims elsewhere that Alexios did everything he could to humiliate and oppress the senatorial class. That body was effectively absent from the major events of the reign, apart from occasionally being informed of, but not consulted about, dire emergencies. Similarly it does not feature in the work of Anna Komnene. Everything suggests that Alexios aimed to restrict the Senate to a purely ceremonial role.

This is, of course, Lemerle's personal interpretation. The soldiers might well have attacked the senators to rob them rather than to make any political point. There can be no doubt though that after 1081, political power in Byzantium was much more closely linked to particular families. For better or worse, the days when a complete outsider like Basil I could seize the throne were over.

Source: Paul Lemerle, *Cinq études sur le XIe siècle byzantin* (Paris: Centre National de la Récherche Scientifique, 1977), pp. 309–10 (author's translation).

Astute use of propaganda and family ties helps to explain why Alexios I succeeded in establishing his dynasty, but his long reign does raise another important question. How did the emperor not only survive his terrible defeat at Dyrrachion in 1081 but go on to rebuild his army and defeat the Normans, the Pechenegs and Chaka's Turks? The answer is not immediately apparent, for it is not a topic that Anna Komnene engages with at any length. Consequently, historians have had to base their theories on the interpretation of a very limited body of evidence.

One thing that we can be sure about is that Alexios made a great effort to attract and recruit foreign mercenaries and he cast his net very wide. He sent English volunteers against the Normans at Dyrrachion in 1081 (see Box 9.3) and faced with Robert Guiscard's smashing victory, he induced Suleyman of Nicaea to send Turkish soldiers to swell his depleted ranks. After his defeat of the Pechenegs in 1091, he had duly enrolled many of the survivors in his own service and they were to be an important element in the Byzantine army for years to come. But although mercenaries were usually very good troops, they had one major drawback. They were expensive because they had to be paid and permanently maintained by the treasury. In the difficult economic situation of the late eleventh century, Alexios had had difficulty mustering the necessary resources and he had to resort to requisitioning ecclesiastical treasures. Although Herakleios had done the same in a similar period of crisis, Alexios found himself under severe censure from Bishop Leo of Chalcedon for robbing the Church, something that sat awkwardly with his carefully cultivated image of a pious and moral emperor.

Faced with this moral and economic pressure, Alexios may have looked for ways of providing soldiers more cheaply. After all, in earlier centuries that had sometimes been done by giving them land rather than pay. Those old Thematic troops, already obsolete by the late tenth century, seem to have vanished by Alexios' day but George Ostrogorsky argued that he developed an alternative system: grants of land known as 'pronoia'. The emperor would allow the beneficiary to hold the land for his lifetime with the obligation that in return he should serve with a certain number of troops in the Byzantine army when required. Thus pronoia differed from earlier military grants of land which were made to individual soldiers, rather than to commanders. Ostrogorsky argued that these grants helped to provide Byzantium with the troops that it needed and they explain why the emperors of the Komnenos dynasty were able to field such large armies. Just like his theories on the Themes, Ostrogorsky's ideas on pronoia have attracted criticism. He seems to have assumed that if the word 'pronoia' was used in a grant of land, then military service had to be part of the agreement. Mark Bartusis has shown that the meaning of the word was never as closely defined as Ostrogorsky suggested. It could be used to describe any grant of land, such as those that Alexios made to reward his supporters for helping him to power in 1081. So although there were pronoia grants in return for military service, they were probably not made on a scale that amounts to a completely new way of financing the Byzantine army.

The reality is in all likelihood rather more mundane. In the desperate years between 1081 and 1091, Alexios probably managed to hang on by raising what revenue he could from a number of sources. Zonaras lists appropriating church treasures, debasing the nomisma, inventing new taxes, melting down bronze statues and confiscating the property of his enemies. After 1092, with the Balkans pacified, Alexios attempted to restore the finances by issuing a new gold coin, the hyperpyron, which weighed 4.55 grams and had a fineness of 20.5 carats, and a new silver one, the trachy. He overhauled the taxation system by appointing a new official, the grand logariast, to co-ordinate and supervise collection. By 1109, matters had stabilised enough for a new tax register to be drawn up, outlining how many coins needed to be paid for each tax. The collection system became more efficient and Alexios and his successors received the sums they needed to pay for the huge armies that Byzantium fielded during the twelfth century. Nevertheless, Alexios might still have been seeking to find some other way to attract mercenaries into his service, one that offered some lure other than money. If so, it would help to explain what is undoubtedly the best-known event of his reign.

11.2 Alexios I and the First Crusade (1091–1118)

By the mid-1090s, the crisis that had nearly brought Byzantium to its knees was over but much of Asia Minor was still in the hands of Turkish emirs and Armenian warlords. Alexios was now making plans to reassert his authority in the area and just as he had brought in outside help to defeat the Normans and Pechenegs, so he planned to do so again. Clearly Turks and Turkic Cumans could not be used in Asia Minor as they might be sympathetic to the enemy. So the obvious source of manpower was Western Europeans, or Latins as the Byzantines tended to call them, who had successfully served as mercenaries in the Byzantine armies for decades.

Alexios was aware, however, that there was an impediment to help reaching Byzantium from Western Europe. Although both societies were Christian, there had been disagreements between the leaders of their Churches over the years, such as those over Monotheletism and Iconoclasm. Those disputes had been resolved but more intractable issues had arisen since then. During the ninth century, patriarch Photios had effectively accused the pope of heresy when he discovered that some versions of the Latin Creed used in the West had added an extra word, *filioque* ('and from the Son'). He had also challenged the claim of the pope to have jurisdiction over the entire Church. The dispute had led to a brief schism in August 867 but when Basil I became emperor, he had quickly dismissed Photios and patched up relations with Rome. The issues of papal authority and the filioque had cropped up again in 1054 when some papal legates had angrily excommunicated the patriarch of Constantinople, Michael Keroularios. Eager to heal the breach, in 1089 Alexios started to make overtures to the papacy. For his part the reigning pope, Urban II, was very receptive to Alexios' advances as he was currently embroiled in a long-running dispute with the Western emperor, Henry IV, and needed all the friends he could get. So in the spring of 1095, the emperor sent envoys to meet the pope in the town of Piacenza where he was chairing a synod, although there is some doubt as to exactly what message they carried (see Box 11.2).

Box 11.2 What did Alexios I ask for at the Council of Piacenza?

Anna Komnene makes no mention of her father's 1095 embassy to Pope Urban II, so we are dependent on a few terse accounts in Western chronicles. Here is the version of events given by a German monk called Bernold of St Blasien:

> Since God and St Peter favoured him, the Lord Pope [Urban II] had the upper hand almost everywhere and he announced that he would hold a general synod

in the middle of Lombardy, in the city of Piacenza [in March 1095], in the territory of the schismatics [i.e. the adherents of Western Emperor Henry IV] and directed against them ... A legation from the emperor of Constantinople likewise arrived at this synod and humbly implored the Lord Pope and all Christ's faithful people to give him some help against the pagans in defence of Holy Church, which the pagans had already almost destroyed in that region, having seized that territory up to the walls of the city of Constantinople. The Lord Pope, therefore, encouraged many men to give this help, so that they even promised on oath that with God's help they would go there and with all their might give their most faithful help against the pagans to that emperor.

It is interesting though that nowhere in Bernold's account does Alexios offer money for this service. Instead it is presented as a moral imperative: a duty that Christians should help their co-religionists. While we can never be sure whether the Byzantine envoys said precisely what Bernold says they did, it could be that Alexios was trying out another inducement to lure Western knights to Constantinople, by presenting the forthcoming campaign in Asia Minor as a kind of righteous war. If so, he played a major part in what was going to happen, even if he could not possibly have envisaged its scale and outcome.

Source: Bernold of St Blasien in I.S. Robinson, *Eleventh Century Germany: The Swabian Chronicles* (Manchester: Manchester University Press, 2008), pp. 323–4.

Whatever it was that the Byzantine envoys said at Piacenza, they seem to have made an impression on Urban II. The following November, at Clermont in France, the pope preached a sermon to an audience of thousands, in which he urged them to go to the aid of the Byzantine emperor. But Urban did not stop there. He went on to urge his listeners to liberate the holy city of Jerusalem from Muslim rule. It is a matter of debate why it was that Urban suddenly introduced Jerusalem into the equation. Many historians, such as Steven Runciman (see Box 12.2), have argued that it was something that Emperor Alexios never mentioned or envisaged. He only wanted the pope to use his moral influence to urge a few contingents of Western knights to fight under Byzantine command against the Turks. A dissenting voice is that of Peter Frankopan, who claims that it was Alexios who proposed Jerusalem as the ultimate goal and that he deliberately asked for large armies under their own commanders. The idea is intriguing and provocative but it has little evidence to substantiate it and it makes it very difficult to explain Alexios' subsequent behaviour towards what has become known as the First Crusade.

Whoever introduced Jerusalem as the goal of the expedition, it proved wildly popular. In a world obsessed with the consequences of sin, it was widely believed that travelling to the place where Jesus Christ rose from the dead would secure God's forgiveness and entry into paradise. In the months after the Clermont sermon, many thousands of Western knights took a vow to travel east, to fight for the Christian faith and to recapture the holy city. Several large armies were formed and the first stage of their planned route was across Byzantine territory in the Balkans to Constantinople. Alexios' response to their advent is instructive. Anna Komnene claims that he dreaded their arrival which is odd if, as Frankopan claims, he proposed and orchestrated the entire expedition. Rather, his actions suggest that he aimed to limit the damage of this unforeseen inundation and to derive as much benefit from the crusaders' presence as possible, regardless of whether they reached Jerusalem or not. When the first contingent under Peter the Hermit reached Constantinople in August 1096 and started to loot the suburbs outside the Land Walls, Alexios had the unwelcome visitors shipped over to Asia Minor, where they were quickly massacred by the Turks. The main contingents arrived in the winter and spring of 1096–1097, under prominent leaders such as the duke of Lower Lorraine, Godfrey of Bouillon, and the count of Toulouse, Raymond IV. The fact that one of the leaders was Bohemond, son of Robert Guiscard, against whom Alexios had fought in 1081–1083, was irrelevant at this stage. The Byzantines had long seen the wisdom of converting former enemies into allies. Alexios demanded that all these leaders swear an oath to him, promising to return any cities that they might capture that had formerly been Byzantine territory, in return for his supplying them with food and guides.

With the oath in place, Alexios shipped the crusade armies over the Bosporus and unleashed them against Nicaea, which was still in Turkish hands after being handed over to them by Nikephoros III Botaneiates in 1078. Rather than let the crusaders capture the city, however, Alexios entered into negotiations with the Turkish garrison who gratefully surrendered to him. When the crusaders began the next stage of their journey to Jerusalem, they asked Alexios to accompany them but he declined, providing them only with a token force and promising to follow later with his main army. It is quite clear why he held back. After the crusaders had smashed the Seljuk army at Dorylaion in July 1097, Alexios took advantage by sending his brother-in-law, John Doukas, to recover western Asia Minor. By the end of 1098, Smyrna and the fertile Meander valley were once more in Byzantine hands. Alexios' actions here leave no doubt that his main interest was to recover as much of Asia Minor as he could in the wake of the passing crusade, regardless of its ultimate outcome.

There was one particular city that Alexios would have dearly liked to get back, and that was Antioch (see Figure 11.1). Recovered in 969 and lost again in 1084, the city had been the centre of Byzantine administration in northern Syria. During the autumn of 1097, the crusaders arrived and mounted a siege but the Turkish garrison doggedly resisted, taking advantage of the fact that the city's walls were so long that it was impossible for the crusaders to blockade their entire length or to cut off supplies from outside. Instead, the crusaders themselves ran short of provisions and endured great hardship during the winter of 1097–1098. Things became so bad that the leader of the Byzantine contingent abandoned the army and sailed for Cyprus. In the early summer of 1098, Alexios did set out from Constantinople with his army to assist, but when he was halfway to Antioch he received news that a Turkish relieving force had got there first. He therefore turned around and headed home. Heroics were not on his agenda, only the recovery of what territory he could easily take. So when, against all expectations, the crusaders succeeded in capturing Antioch and in driving off the relieving force, the emperor was left in an embarrassing position. The crusade leadership did send an envoy to Alexios and invite him to come and take over Antioch in accordance with their oath, but in December 1098 Bohemond pre-empted him and seized the city for himself.

Figure 11.1 The citadel at Antioch

For the crusaders, their expedition ended in triumph when they captured Jerusalem on 15 July 1099. Four Latin states emerged in the territory that had been conquered, the largest being the kingdom of Jerusalem and the closest to Byzantine territory being the principality of Antioch under Bohemond. Alexios was perfectly content for the crusaders to have Jerusalem but Antioch he regarded as a prize that had been unjustly withheld from him, given the oath that Bohemond had sworn. Before long, Byzantine forces were being mobilised on Cyprus with a view to retaking Antioch by force. Realising that he could not take on the emperor alone, Bohemond returned to Europe to gather an army. In October 1107, he invaded the Byzantine Balkans across the Adriatic, but this second Norman invasion proved less dangerous than the first. Bohemond's army was surrounded near Dyrrachion and forced to lay down its arms. Antioch, however, remained in the hands of Bohemond's nephew, Tancred, and was to be a bone of contention for decades to come.

11.3 After Alexios: John II (1118–1143)

When Alexios died in August 1118, he was succeeded by his eldest son, John II Komnenos. John's reputation has suffered from his not having a laudatory biographer in the way that his father had Anna Komnene and his son Manuel had John Kinnamos. His sister disliked him and even claimed that he had squandered all their father's achievements. That was evidently unfair for even from the rather short accounts of his reign, John emerges as an extremely effective ruler (see Figure 11.2).

Figure 11.2 Emperor John II and Empress Irene, a mosaic in Hagia Sophia

Although the later years of Alexios' reign had been relatively peaceful, there was soon an opportunity for John to show his mettle. In late 1121, a large raiding force of Pechenegs crossed the Danube and pushed down into Macedonia and Thrace, looting and burning as it went. The following spring, John moved his armies into the area, even before the campaigning season had begun, and surrounded the raiders as they withdrew through Bulgaria. The Pechenegs created a makeshift fort with their wagons to fend off the attackers but the emperor's Latin mercenaries cut through the barrier with their axes and the Pechenegs laid down their arms. The victory marked the end of the Pecheneg threat in the Balkans. John also fought a short war with the Hungarians in 1127–1128 which saw him leading his army across the Danube in retaliation for an earlier sack of Belgrade. He also had to mount a campaign against the Serbs, who were normally a quiescent client state.

By 1130, with the Balkans secure, John was in a position to turn his attention to Asia Minor. Thanks to the passage of the First Crusade, the Byzantines had recovered the fertile western regions but the central Anatolian plateau was still held by the Seljuk Sultan of Rum, who had moved his capital to Ikonion after the loss of Nicaea in 1097. The northern areas along the Black Sea were part of the Danishmendid emirate, while Cilicia in the south-east was held by the Armenian prince Leo. In a series of campaigns, John II pushed the Byzantine frontier eastwards at the expense of the Danishmendids and in 1137 he invaded Cilicia. Following in the footsteps of Nikephoros II, he recaptured Tarsus and then took the Armenian prince Leo prisoner. Declared deposed, Leo was taken off to exile in Constantinople and Cilicia was now in theory returned to Byzantine rule.

The 1137 campaign in Cilicia brought John II within striking distance of Antioch. That was no accident for John had for some time been hoping to reassert his authority over the city. Back in 1130, when news came in that the city's ruler, Bohemond II, had been killed in an ambush, John II had hoped to resolve the issue by marrying his son Manuel to

Figure 11.3 Isaac Komnenos, brother of John II, mosaic from the Chora church in Constantinople

Bohemond II's heir, his daughter Constance. That plan fell through when Constance took a French nobleman called Raymond of Poitiers as her husband instead. So while he was in Cilicia in 1137, John decided to make a show of force, appearing before Antioch with his army at the end of August. Although he did not try to capture the city, he did compel Raymond of Poitiers to recognise his overlordship and from the military and internal political points of view the campaign was a success. Diplomatically, however, there were unfortunate consequences because John's actions helped to exacerbate the growing divide between Byzantium and the West. When the pope heard about the emperor making war on Christians rather than helping them against infidels, he issued an encyclical letter calling on all Latin mercenaries in John's army to desert. The dispute over Antioch also highlighted the gulf that had opened up between the Byzantine and Latin Churches. One of the first actions of Bohemond I after he had seized it in 1099 had been to eject the Byzantine patriarch and replace him with a Latin. Henceforth there were two patriarchs of Antioch, a Latin in the city itself and a Byzantine in exile in Constantinople. John did not succeed in getting the Byzantine claimant reinstated but he did eject Latin bishops from the towns that he conquered in the vicinity, replacing them with Byzantines. Again, public opinion in the West reacted very negatively to his actions here.

11.4 'Most happy emperor of illustrious memory': Manuel I (1143–1180)

In April 1143, John II died of an injury sustained while out hunting. He was in Syria at the time, once more attempting to impose his will on the principality of Antioch. Of his four sons, two had predeceased him and the eldest survivor, Isaac, was far away in Constantinople. It was his youngest son Manuel who was accepted by the army as his successor and during the long march back to the capital, Manuel sent a message ahead ordering his brother Isaac to be placed under arrest. It was a kind of usurpation but a very benign one by Byzantine standards. Isaac was later released unharmed and two of his daughters went on to be queens of Jerusalem and Hungary.

Manuel I had not been in power for very long when he learned a lesson that was to influence his outlook and policy for the rest of his reign. In September 1147, the armies of the Second Crusade passed through Byzantine territory on their way to the Holy Land. Led by the King of France, Louis VII, and the ruler of Germany, Conrad III, the two armies aimed to avenge the recent loss of Edessa to Zengi of Mosul. Manuel handled their transit much as his grandfather Alexios had the First Crusade, aiming to reap whatever advantage he could from the enterprise. That policy soon gave rise to a perception among the crusaders that the Christian Byzantine emperor was not wholly behind, and possibly even working against, the enterprise. Their fears seemed to be confirmed when they discovered that Manuel had recently made peace with their enemy, the Seljuk Sultan of Ikonion, through whose territory they would have to pass in order to reach the Holy Land. Clashes took place with Byzantine troops and an attack on Constantinople was urged by some in the French army. In the end, the crusade passed through without a major confrontation, but when the expedition ended in failure many people blamed the Byzantine emperor and urged that an attack be made on Constantinople. The danger never materialised but the incident starkly revealed how vulnerable Byzantium could be to Western aggression, especially given its reliance on Latin mercenaries.

So after 1147, Manuel actively worked to counter the image of the Byzantine emperor as hostile to the crusades and to Latins in general. He made a point of employing Latins as interpreters and advisers and went out of his way to show that he was interested in Latin customs and way of life, introducing jousts and tournaments in Constantinople, something that had not been part of Byzantine culture before. He promoted ecclesiastical dialogue, inviting delegations of Latin clergy to Constantinople in the hope of ending the schism. He entered into friendly relations with Western rulers, even those whose lands lay far away like Henry II of England. He took Latin wives: first the German Bertha of Sulzbach and then Maria of Antioch. He married members of his family to Latins: two nieces to kings of Jerusalem; his daughter Maria to Renier, son of the marquis of Montferrat; and his son Alexios to Agnes, daughter of Louis VII of France, a clear sign that the breach over the Second Crusade was healed. He made sure that he was seen to support the Latin Kingdom of Jerusalem and its Christian ruler. He paid the ransoms of crusaders who had been taken prisoner and joined with the king of Jerusalem; in an attack on Egypt in 1169.

Overall, the policy seems to have worked. Manuel came to enjoy a high personal reputation in Western Europe and in the Latin east where 'Greeks' were often the object of scorn and mistrust. It was a Latin archbishop who after his death described him as the 'most happy emperor of illustrious memory'. By presenting his actions in the right way, Manuel was able to impose his will on the principality of Antioch without incurring Western opprobrium in the way that John II had. He chose his moment carefully, when the pope was distracted by a dispute with the Western emperor in Italy. He made sure that he had a legitimate pretext too, since the prince of Antioch, Reynald of Châtillon, had mounted a raid on the Byzantine island of Cyprus. So when Manuel took his army to Antioch in 1159 and forced Reynald to accept his overlordship in a humiliating public ceremony and agree to the restoration of the Byzantine patriarch, there was not a murmur of criticism in the West.

It was not that Manuel had departed from the policies of Alexios I and John II. Like them, he aimed to advance Byzantine interests by any means possible. The difference was that he did so in ways that were less likely to outrage Latin opinion. By remaining on good terms with the papacy and most Latin powers, he was able to act against those that he regarded as a threat. At the beginning of his reign, the Norman kingdom of southern Italy and Sicily appeared to pose the greatest danger. In 1147, while the Second Crusade was passing through Byzantine territory, the Norman king, Roger II, had launched a naval attack on Greece, sacking the prosperous towns of Corinth and Thebes and occupying the island of Corfu. Manuel used Venetian help to eject the Normans from Corfu and then in the spring of 1155 he sent a small expedition to the Italian Adriatic coast. The invaders were soon joined by local rebels and they marched south towards Bari and Apulia. Manuel's motives in mounting this invasion are not entirely clear. It might have been merely to destabilise the Norman kingdom rather than to reconquer the Italian lands that had been lost in 1071. If he had wanted to achieve the latter he should have sent a larger force. As it was, the small army was easily crushed by the new Norman king, William I, in May 1156.

It is in his reaction to this minor reverse that Manuel's ability as a strategist and diplomat emerges. Rather than continue to pursue a vendetta against the Normans, he decided to use them against a new danger. During the 1150s, the German emperor, Frederick I Barbarossa, was seeking to impose his will on the city-states of northern Italy and on the papacy. Once he had achieved that, he was likely to do what his predecessor Otto I had done and push south. The thought of the whole of the Italian coast facing the Byzantine Balkans coming under the rule of a major power was a very worrying one. In response, Manuel swung round and concluded a treaty with his former enemy, William of Sicily. At the same time, he made friendly overtures to the pope, Alexander III, who was so apprehensive about Barbarossa's ambitions that he even at one point considered crowning Manuel emperor of the West. Manuel sent generous financial aid to the Lombard League of Italian cities that were opposing Barbarossa and who ultimately frustrated his ambitions at the battle of Legnano in 1176.

The reign saw many other successes against Byzantium's enemies. A series of wars with Hungary culminated in a spectacular victory in 1167 when 15,000 Hungarians are said to have perished. On this occasion though the commander was not Manuel himself but his nephew, Andronikos Kontostephanos, who attacked the enemy in defiance of the emperor's specific orders. In 1172, when the Serb ruler Stephen Nemanja attempted to throw off Byzantine overlordship, Manuel swiftly crushed him and made him grovel publicly before the emperor's throne, barefoot with a halter round his neck in exactly the way that the prince of Antioch had. In Asia Minor, attempts by the sultan of Ikonion, Kilij Arslan II, to chip away at Byzantine territory were firmly resisted. As in the case of Barbarossa, Manuel used diplomacy to isolate and undermine Kilij Arslan, allying himself with the sultan's eastern enemies, the Danishmendid emir and the sultan of Syria, Nur ed-Din. In the end, Kilij Arslan had to come to Constantinople in 1161 to make peace with the emperor.

Yet for all the apparently brilliant achievements of Manuel's reign there were persistent signs that all was not well and that Byzantium was not as powerful as it seemed. It was having increasing difficulty making its authority felt in its outposts a long way from Constantinople. The emperor might turn up with an army and enforce his will, but no sooner was his back turned than matters went back to the way they were before. John II had supposedly put an end to the Armenian enclave of Cilicia in 1137 when he deposed its ruler Leo and took him as a prisoner to Constantinople, but in 1143 one of Leo's sons, Thoros, escaped back to Cilicia, led a revolt and had soon re-established himself as ruler of the area. The prince of Antioch had grovelled before Manuel in 1159 when the emperor was there with his army. Once he was gone Reynald's successor, Bohemond III, slowly distanced himself from Byzantine overlordship, restoring the Latin patriarch in 1170 and in 1180 repudiating his Byzantine wife. The sultan of Ikonion accepted peace in 1161 but continued to probe the Byzantine border. In September 1176, Manuel's all-out attack on the sultanate ended in disaster when his army was trapped by the Turks in a narrow gorge at Myriokephalon and it suffered heavy casualties before it was able to withdraw. The defeat was by no means a decisive one. No territory was lost as a result, and the following year a Turkish raiding force in the Meander valley was destroyed by another of Manuel's nephews, John Vatatzes. But from a long-term perspective, it does raise questions about how long Byzantium could have continued to maintain its international prestige and hegemony, even if the gifted and brilliant Emperor Manuel had not died in 1180.

11.5 Art and architecture under the Komnenos dynasty

With hindsight, it is easy to see the chinks in Byzantium's armour as the twelfth century went on, but at the time it looked like a place of almost limitless affluence and power. A Spanish Jew called Benjamin of Tudela, who visited Constantinople in around 1161, marvelled at the towering buildings and conspicuous affluence on display there and on the city's flourishing markets and trade. The prosperity of Byzantium under the Komnenos emperors meant that there was no shortage of commissions for new works of art, many of them designed to promote and publicise the dynasty's achievements. John II ordered mosaics depicting his father, Alexios I, to adorn the Great Palace and Manuel I had similar images placed in the renovated palace of Blachernae near the Land Walls, although these apparently featured Manuel himself rather than his predecessors. The establishment of new monasteries and churches was a more subtle form of self-promotion, displaying the family's piety and leaving a tangible monument to remember them by. Irene, the wife of Alexios I, founded the convent of Our Lady Full of Grace in around 1110 and her son

John II established the monastic complex of the Pantokrator in 1136 (see Box 11.3). John II's brother Isaac (see Figure 11.3) paid for the refurbishment of the Chora monastery, close to Constantinople's Land Walls (see Section 14.5). New foundations were not confined to the capital. The Kosmosoteira monastery at Feres in Thrace (see Figure 11.4) and that of St Panteleimon at Nerezi in Macedonia were both paid for by members of the Komnenos family in the mid-twelfth century. The monastery of Asinou on Cyprus was founded in around 1099 by Nikephoros Euphorbenos, a son-in-law of Alexios I (see Figure 12.1).

The churches of all these institutions would have been richly adorned on the inside, either with mosaic or with fresco, but this decoration has not always survived. From what does remain, some art historians have discerned a new, naturalistic aspect to Byzantine art of the twelfth century. Certainly the cycle of 20 scenes from the Passion of Christ at Nerezi display an extraordinary emotional intensity, with the grief-stricken apostles bent double over Jesus' body (see Figure 11.5). The problem with such judgements, however, is that they are based on the very limited number of examples that have survived and they are therefore very much a matter of opinion. For the most part, artistic trends seem to have been a continuation of those of previous centuries, but if some artists were trying new techniques then that would neatly parallel literary developments of the period where the demotic language was coming into wider use (see Section 9.4).

Figure 11.4 The church of the Kosmosoteira monastery (1152)

Figure 11.5 Scene from the Passion of Christ from the church of St Pantaleimon, Nerezi (1164)

Given Byzantium's strength and prestige for most of the twelfth century, it is only to be expected that its styles of art and architecture would remain influential, especially in those countries whose Churches were linked to the patriarchate of Constantinople. During the 1100s Byzantine monks travelled from Constantinople to execute the mosaic decoration in the Pechersky monastery in Kiev. The surviving mosaics in the church of the Archangel in Kiev might also be the work of Byzantine artists, which would explain why there are mistakes in the Slavonic inscriptions. Similarly in the West, Venice, a long-standing ally and trading partner, looked to Byzantium for the most prestigious styles of art. A series of mosaics in the Byzantine style was commissioned for the city's main church of St Mark following a fire in 1100 (see Figure 10.5). The Venetians seem also to have purchased art from Constantinople. When the Pala d'Oro, or altarpiece of St Mark's, was remodelled in around 1105, the work was either carried out in the Byzantine capital and shipped out or completed in Venice by Byzantine artists. Made of gold and silver, and adorned with enamel plaques and gems, the altarpiece as it survives today carries a portrait of Irene, the wife of Alexios I, and so probably originally had one of the emperor as well, now lost (see Figure 12.5). Artistic influence tended to follow political influence. By the 1150s, the kingdom of Jerusalem and other states of the Latin east were very dependent on Byzantine military and financial aid. As a visual symbol of his patronage, Manuel I had the church of the Holy Nativity in Bethlehem redecorated with mosaics which included several portraits of himself.

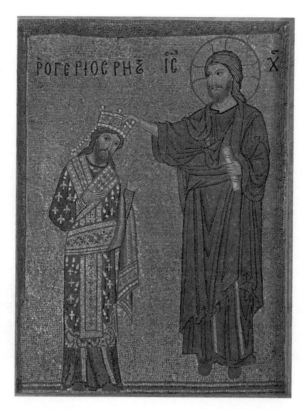

Figure 11.6 Roger II of Sicily (1130–1154) from the Martorana church, Palermo. The inscription is in Greek letters but spells out 'Rogerios Rex' in Latin, i.e. King Roger

Even enemies adopted Byzantine styles. The Normans who took over the old provinces of Apulia and Calabria, and later ejected the Arabs from Sicily, reflected the culture of the former owners. King Roger II had himself depicted in a mosaic in almost exactly the same guise as a Byzantine emperor with Christ placing his hand on his crown (see Figure 11.6). The only thing missing is the halo (see Introduction 0.3). When he wanted to build a palace of appropriate splendour for himself in Palermo, Roger brought in Byzantine artists to decorate it, though he never lived to see it finished. Churches and monasteries elsewhere in southern Italy and Sicily continued to be decorated in the Byzantine style, long after the emperor's political domination in the region had come to an end. The cathedral of Monreale, founded in 1174 just outside Palermo, is decorated with mosaics that look very Byzantine, though in conformity to Western tradition, Christ Pantokrator appears not in a central dome but in the apse above the altar (see Figure 11.7). It is tempting to conclude that Byzantium's artists and craftsmen made a greater impact on the world than its soldiers and statesmen.

Figure 11.7 Christ Pantokrator from Monreale, Sicily

Box 11.3 The Monastery of the Pantokrator (1136)

John II chose the site for his new foundation of Christ Pantokrator (i.e. 'the ruler of all') with great care, placing it very prominently on the summit of one of Constantinople's seven hills where it could be seen from miles around (see Figure 11.8). It was designed to be the special monastery of the Komnenos dynasty and a lasting monument to its achievements. Alongside its two churches, there was a funerary chapel, which was, in the fullness of time, to house John's tomb and those of other members of his family. John's son and successor, Manuel I, greatly increased the monastery's prestige by securing a precious relic for it: a slab of red marble on which Christ had supposedly lain after his crucifixion. He had it shipped to Constantinople from Ephesus and, when it arrived, carried it up the hill from the harbour to the Great Palace on his own back. After Manuel's death in 1180, the slab was used to surmount his tomb in the funerary chapel.

Given the monastery's connection to the royal family, huge sums were spent on the interior decoration of its churches and funerary chapel. The window panes were filled with stained glass and its central dome was supported by columns of rare red marble. The walls and dome would have been covered in mosaic but sadly, although the churches and the chapel have survived, the mosaics for the most part have not. Today, the three conjoined buildings are a working mosque, known as Zeyrek Camii, and under the carpets that cover the floor of what was once one of the churches is hidden what must have been a striking feature: a floor made of cut marble featuring colourful geometric patterns.

Like all Byzantine monasteries, the Pantokrator provided a range of social services for the rest of the population. It had an old people's home which provided its residents with food, oil, firewood, a clothing allowance and two baths a month. There was a leper sanctuary and a hospital of 50 beds where poor patients were treated free of charge. We are relatively well informed about this hospital as it is described in great detail in the typikon. It was no mere hospice where the sick were merely made comfortable, but was specifically organised to treat fractures and to cure disorders of the stomach and eye. There were five wards, each presided over by two doctors and seven other staff. One ward was reserved for women and was run by female doctors. No one knows whether this was a unique and particularly well-run hospital or whether all the others were organised along the same lines. Nor is it possible to assess whether the regime outlined in the typikon was actually adhered to. What can be said with certainty is that while royal monasteries like the Pantokrator were monuments to the political ambitions of their founders, they were also designed to bring tangible benefits to the less fortunate of the emperor's subjects.

Further reading: John Freely and Ahmet S. Çakmak, *The Byzantine Monuments of Istanbul* (Cambridge: Cambridge University Press, 2004), pp. 211–20.

Figure 11.8 The domes of the Pantokrator Monastery

Points to remember

- Alexios I Komnenos succeeded in making his dynasty endure by greater reliance on ties of kinship to erode the idea that the throne was available to anyone strong enough to seize it.
- Many older books devote a good deal of space to pronoia and the 'feudalisation' of Byzantium under the Komnenos dynasty. These should be treated with caution.
- It is unlikely that Alexios expected the First Crusade to arrive in the form that it did, but he may have unwittingly contributed to the notion of holy war that underpinned it.
- The reign of John II is not well documented but it would seem that he was an effective military leader, if perhaps lacking the diplomatic finesse of his predecessor and successor.
- Manuel I's reign saw further spectacular successes but there were clear limits on what he could achieve.
- The twelfth century was a vibrant period for both visual and literary culture, with Byzantium's influence extending far beyond its borders.

Suggestions for further reading

Bartusis, Mark C. (2012), *Land and Privilege in Byzantium: The Institution of Pronoia* (Cambridge: Cambridge University Press). Bartusis argues against the idea of a pronoia 'system' spreading under the Komnenos dynasty, arguing that it was simply a continuation of tax exemptions given to monasteries by previous emperors.

Bucossi, Alessandra and Suarez, Alex R. (2016), *John II Komnenos: Emperor of Byzantium in the Shadow of Father and Son* (London and New York: Routledge). A collection of essays that throw a great deal of light on this important but neglected emperor.

Frankopan, Peter. (2012), *The First Crusade: The Call from the East* (London: The Bodley Head). Advances the controversial and questionable thesis that Alexios I proposed the First Crusade's expedition to Jerusalem and even organised the route.

Harris, Jonathan. (2014, 2nd revised edition), *Byzantium and the Crusades* (London and New York: Bloomsbury). Puts Byzantium's interaction with the First and subsequent crusades into the context of its long-standing approach to dealing with foreign powers.

Magdalino, Paul. (1993), *The Empire of Manuel I Komnenos, 1143–1180* (Cambridge: Cambridge University Press). Definitive and exhaustive treatment of Manuel's reign.

Mullett, Margaret and Smythe, Dion. (1996), *Alexios I Komnenos* (Belfast: Belfast Byzantine Enterprises). A collection of essays: see especially the contribution by Paul Magdalino on 'innovations in government'.

Neville, Leonora. (2012), *Heroes and Romans in Twelfth-Century Byzantium: The Material for History of Nikephoros Bryennios* (Cambridge: Cambridge University Press). Explores the muscular military ethos of the Komnenos period through the prism of unfinished history written by the husband of Anna Komnene, arguing that it drew inspiration from the ancient Roman concept of manly virtue.

12   The road to catastrophe (1180–1204)

In the 25 years that followed the death of Emperor Manuel I in 1180, Byzantium's power unravelled with astonishing speed, culminating in the events of 1204 when Constantinople was stormed and captured and the provinces were occupied and dismembered. Political instability, economic and social issues, personal incompetence of Byzantium's rulers as well as outside aggression all need to be considered in order to explain this rapid turn of events.

12.1 Instability returns (1180–1185)

By restricting the most prestigious offices and commands to members of his own family, Alexios I had largely put an end to the frequent bids for the throne made by military leaders in the provinces that had been such a feature of the Macedonian period. The reigns of his son and grandson were largely free from such challenges. On the other hand, there was now a new potential source of instability in disgruntled members of the ruling dynasty. John II had to deal with plots by his older sister Anna and his younger brother Isaac throughout his reign. Manuel I effectively side-lined his older brother, another Isaac, to become emperor in 1143. These internal rivalries only became acute after 1180.

The catalyst, as ever, was a minority and a regency. Manuel's successor, Alexios II, was only 11 at the time of his accession, so his mother Maria of Antioch headed the regency council along with the patriarch of Constantinople and a nephew of the late emperor, the Protosebastos Alexios Komnenos. Before long, a faction opposed to the regency emerged, led by Manuel I's daughter by his first marriage, Maria the Porphyrogenita, and her husband Renier of Montferrat. They believed that the Protosebastos was the empress' lover and that he had designs on the throne for himself. When a plan to assassinate the Protosebastos went wrong, Maria the Porphyrogenita and her supporters fled to Hagia Sophia and fighting broke out in the streets. She sent a message asking for help to her father's cousin, Andronikos Komnenos, who entered Constantinople with an army in April 1182.

Thus far, events had followed a familiar pattern but they now descended into a savagery not experienced since the reign of Emperor Phokas. Determined to take the imperial office himself, Andronikos proceeded to liquidate anyone in his path. The Protosebastos was blinded and the Empress Maria of Antioch was strangled, but his former allies Maria the Porphyrogenita and Renier of Montferrat fared no better. Both were murdered within a few months, probably by poison and doubtless regretting that they had invited Andronikos to Constantinople in the first place. The young Alexios II was first pushed aside when Andronikos was proclaimed emperor in September 1183 and shortly afterwards was strangled with a bowstring and his body dumped in the Bosporus. The only member of the immediate imperial family to survive was Alexios' young French wife, Agnes, and that was only because Andronikos needed to marry her to give his coup at least a patina of respectability.

Once in power, Andronikos I Komnenos' reign was brief and bloody. The emperor devoted his energies to a purge of Manuel's appointees and indeed of anyone whom he considered to pose a threat. Among his victims was Andronikos Kontostephanos, the man who had led the Byzantines to victory against the Hungarians in 1167, whom Andronikos had blinded. In the spring of 1184, he marched out into Asia Minor to punish the towns of Nicaea and Prousa, whose inhabitants had refused to accept his accession. After Prousa had been taken by storm, he had several of the defenders impaled as a punishment for their defiance. The reign of terror came to an abrupt end in September 1185 when Andronikos' henchmen tried to arrest a young nobleman called Isaac Angelos. He succeeded in escaping their clutches and found himself the centre of popular demonstrations against the emperor. When Andronikos, sensing the way things were going, tried to flee Constantinople, he was captured, dragged into the Hippodrome and lynched by the crowd. Meanwhile there were jubilant scenes in Hagia Sophia as the patriarch crowned Isaac II, that same young man whose dramatic escape from death had started the chain of events leading to the tyrant's downfall.

12.2 Alienation in the provinces

Dramatic and shocking though the events of 1180–1185 were, they probably had no long-term impact. The murder and mayhem were largely confined to the ruling classes in Constantinople, although the people of Nicaea and Prousa suffered too. Far more important in explaining Byzantium's rapid decline were developments that went back long before 1180, although, as ever, historians have not been unanimous in identifying what they were. For Donald Nicol and many others, one ominous change was the central role that the Italian maritime republic of Venice had come to play in Byzantine economic life and that can be discerned as far back as the reign of Alexios I Komnenos. In around 1082, eager to obtain naval support against the Norman duke, Robert Guiscard, Alexios had made a treaty with Venice (see Section 10.5). He had granted the city's merchants exemption from paying harbour tolls and customs duties such as the kommerkion in nearly every Byzantine port and given them their own quarter alongside the Golden Horn in Constantinople. The loss to the Byzantine treasury must have been considerable but in the crisis of the 1080s sacrifices were necessary. Doubtless the emperor expected that these privileges could be quietly rescinded once the crisis was over. That proved easier said than done. On his accession in 1118, Alexios' son, John II, refused to renew the treaty but the Venetians swiftly responded with force. Their fleet, which was on its way to help establish the kingdom of Jerusalem, was diverted to mount raids on Byzantine ports and islands in the Adriatic and Aegean. There was no defence against these kinds of unpredictable attacks and so John was forced to back down and to renew the treaty with its generous tax exemptions. It was left to Manuel I to take more drastic action. In 1171, he ordered the arrest of all Venetians in the empire and the confiscation of their goods. This time, the emperor got away with it. The crews of the Venetian fleet that was sent to attack the Byzantine Aegean islands contracted some kind of sickness while wintering at Chios and had to return to their home port.

The efforts made by John II and Manuel I to abrogate the treaty with Venice certainly seem to suggest that the position that Venetian merchants had established for themselves had come to be regarded as a danger. Consequently many modern historians have characterised the Venetians as greedy bloodsuckers who drained Byzantium of its tax revenues and were happy to undermine it to protect their own trade. It was no coincidence, they claim, that it was Venetian ships that brought the Fourth Crusade to Constantinople in 1203 and ferried the crusaders across the Golden Horn to attack the Sea Walls the following spring: it was in their interest to ensure that Constantinople was captured to protect their trade and to guard against a repetition of the events of 1171.

Figure 12.1 Interior of the church of Panagia Phorbiotissa Asinou, Nikitari, Cyprus

These arguments have been successfully challenged. After all, if the Venetians were really such a burden why did the emperors keep renewing the treaty with them? Although his strike against the Venetians in 1171 had apparently been a complete success, within a few years Manuel was seeking to patch up relations with them. In 1184, Andronikos I invited the Venetians back to Constantinople with the same concessions and privileges as before, even offering them compensation for their losses in 1171. Thereafter the treaty was renewed regularly, right up to 1198. In fact, the emperors even made similar treaties with other Italian trading cities, such as Pisa from 1111 and Genoa from 1155. The Byzantine emperors must have been receiving something of value from these cities to make these tax concessions worthwhile. Part of it was the need for supporters in Italy, in the face of the threat from the Normans and from Frederick Barbarossa. But there were also sound economic considerations behind these treaties. The Italians were needed to run Byzantium's internal trade for it was their ships that supplied Constantinople with much of its food and wine, shipping it in from provincial towns and ports such as Corinth, Dyrrachion and Thebes. They also dominated the Italy–Egypt–Constantinople trade triangle, so that for Byzantine merchants the easiest way to ship goods for export would be to entrust them to a Venetian who would carry them to Alexandria and sell them on for a very reasonable commission. Thus the Venetians and other Italians conferred benefits that well repaid their tax exemption. Manuel's high-handed action of 1171 therefore might not have been motivated by concerns about Venice's economic role but by annoyance over the republic's encroachment onto Byzantine territory on the Adriatic coast. Finally, the argument that blames the Venetians for diverting the Fourth Crusade to Constantinople does not hold water either, as we shall see (see Section 12.5).

For other historians, the most significant change during the twelfth century was what they termed the 'feudalisation' of Byzantium. The ever-influential George Ostrogorsky and others traced this development to the reign of Alexios I Komnenos who, they claimed, had augmented the number of troops available to his armies by making grants of pronoia where a tract of land and all its tax revenues were handed over to an individual in return for providing a contingent for the Byzantine army (see Section 11.1). The spread of this practice has been labelled 'feudalisation' because these grants seemed to mirror the fiefs of Western Europe where a vassal held land in return for military service. In the short term, so the argument runs, this policy was beneficial and provided Alexios with the military muscle he needed to save the empire in the late eleventh century. As time went on, however, it became socially divisive. On these properties, the free peasants effectively became serfs or paroikoi who were tied to the land and effectively the property of the pronoia holder. The latter was often a foreign mercenary, who was more interested in squeezing as much tax revenue from them as possible than in participating in the defence of the frontiers. That, at least, was how Ostrogorsky interpreted a passage in the History of Niketas Choniates (see Box 12.1).

Box 12.1 Niketas Choniates on pronoia?

The following passage is central to arguments that grants of pronoia were a factor in weakening the Byzantine empire in the second half of the twelfth century. Niketas Choniates is a difficult writer to follow at times, thanks to his use of a complex Attic Greek, but he seems to be talking about the unfortunate results of land being handed over to soldiers:

> This emperor [Manuel I Komnenos], pouring into the treasuries the so-called gifts of the peasants like water into a cistern, sated the thirst of the armies by the payment of provision money and thereby abused a tactic begun by former emperors and rarely resorted to by those who had frequently thrashed the enemy. He was not aware that he was enfeebling the troops by pouring countless sums of money into idle bellies and mismanaging the Roman provinces. The brave soldiers lost interest in distinguishing themselves in the face of danger, as no one any longer spurred them on to perform glorious exploits, and now the concern of all was to become wealthy. The inhabitants of the provinces, who in the past had had to pay the imperial tax collector, now suffered the greatest horrors as a result of military greed, being robbed not only of silver and obols but also stripped of their last tunic, and sometimes they were dragged away from their loved ones. For these reasons, everyone wanted to enlist in the army and many bade farewell to their trades as tailors and cobblers … Sometimes a Roman of royal bearing would pay taxes to a half-Turkish, half-Greek barbarian manikin who knew nothing of pitched battles even though the Roman was as superior to the tax collector in the mastery of warfare as Achilles was to him … This disorderliness of the troops brought deserved suffering to the Roman provinces; some were plundered by alien peoples and made subject to their rule, while others were devastated, ravaged by our own men as if they were enemy lands.

Source: Niketas Choniates, *O City of Byzantium. Annals of Niketas Choniates*, trans. Harry J. Magoulias (Detroit MI: Wayne State University Press, 1984), pp. 118–19.

Once again, though, these arguments and interpretations can be questioned. In the key passage, Choniates expresses himself in very general terms and nowhere specifically mentions the word pronoia. The arguments of Mark Bartusis have already been outlined. He shows although there are plenty of surviving grants that are described as pronoia, it is by no means clear that they all involved land in return for military service. Many of them seem to have been simple gifts of lands and revenues to supporters of the Komnenos family and they probably were not nearly widespread enough to represent a system (see Section 11.1). Just as pronoia was probably not an ingredient in Alexios I's success, so it seems unlikely that in itself it could have somehow alienated the peasantry from the empire or undermined its defence.

Yet even if Venice and 'feudalisation' are dismissed as elements in Byzantine weakness in the late twelfth century, that does not mean that internal problems did not exist. Byzantine sources from the twelfth century are full of complaints about the heavy burden of taxation. In about 1105, the archbishop of Ohrid wrote to Alexios I's nephew, John Taronites, governor of Dyrrachion, claiming that the people were 'as heavily oppressed by the demands of military service as by taxation'. Inevitably too there were some unscrupulous tax farmers who ensured that they profited in the process. It was probably them, rather than any particular institution such as pronoia, that Niketas Choniates was referring to. His complaint does not seem to be about grants of lands and tax revenues in themselves but rather about the greedy individuals who exploited them for personal gain and neglected their military duties (see Box 12.1). His brother, Michael Choniates, who was archbishop of Athens between about 1175 and 1204, frequently made similar complaints in his letters to high officials, urging that the tax burden on the people of Greece be lightened and that corrupt tax gatherers be brought to justice. Of course, nobody is ever happy about paying their taxes and there had been plenty of complaints in the past, especially against Nikephoros II Phokas, who was perceived to be milking the populace to expand his army. But the frequency and stridency of the protests do seem to be something new. It could be that with a smaller territory to draw income from and enemies all around them the emperors were having to extract more and more just to maintain the borders, expand the army and make the usual payments to foreign allies.

The heavy burden of taxation seems to have led in turn to an increasing alienation between provinces and capital. Again, this was nothing new: we have already discerned it during the tenth century (see Section 8.1). The difference now was that the gulf was an economic one. Magnificent and impressive though the showcase capital might have been, Constantinople was beginning to be regarded as to some extent parasitic on the provinces, drawing in tax revenue but giving very little in return. Curiously, the one man who seems to have realised the danger was the much-vilified tyrant Andronikos I. During his short reign, in contrast to his bloodthirsty massacres in the capital, he put into effect a very sensible policy elsewhere, aimed at securing the well-being of the provincial administration and the peasantry. He overhauled the taxation system, seeking to root out corruption and to ensure that only regular taxes were paid and not the surcharges imposed by the tax farmers. He insisted that revenue collection posts should be awarded on merit and not simply sold to the highest bidder. But although his reforms were well meant, they were carried out far too hastily and he was, in any case, overthrown in 1185. The chance to stop the rot had been lost.

12.3 From alienation to separation: Isaac II Angelos (1185–1195)

In spite of his fairy-tale accession (see Section 12.1), Isaac II has not been treated kindly by posterity. Choniates is scathing about him in his *History*, even though he had held office under him and had frequently given laudatory speeches in his honour (see Section 9.3). Modern historians have followed suit and Isaac's incompetence, along with that of

Figure 12.2 Trachy of Isaac II. Originally a silver coin, by 1185 the trachy was being minted from billon, an alloy of silver and base metal

his brother and successor Alexios III, has been cited as a reason for Byzantium's rapid decline. That may not be entirely fair. Isaac could be seen as the unfortunate individual who was in power when the problems that had been building up for decades became acute and alienation turned into separatism.

At the time, the reign seemed to have begun well. Isaac came to power amid a wave of goodwill as the liberator from the tyranny of Andronikos and he had a legitimate claim to the throne, for he was a great-grandson of Alexios I. His accession had certainly come at a difficult moment. Byzantium's internal disarray under Andronikos had not gone unnoticed by its enemies and they were quick to take advantage. In the summer of 1183, King Béla III of Hungary led his army across the Danube into Byzantine territory and two years later, as Andronikos' regime unravelled, the Normans of southern Italy launched an invasion across the Adriatic and, meeting little resistance, marched east to capture Thessalonica. Once in power, Isaac took effective counter-measures. The Normans were worsted by the Byzantine general Alexios Branas in November 1185 at the River Strymon and they withdrew from the Balkans shortly afterwards. In the aftermath, Isaac laboured to build better relations with the traditional enemy across the Adriatic. In 1193, he concluded a peace treaty with King Tancred of Sicily and married his daughter Irene to Tancred's son Roger. Similarly, at the end of 1185, Isaac signed a treaty and entered into a marriage alliance with the Hungarians, taking as his wife Margaret, daughter of Béla III: as the dowry he received back the lands along the Danube that Béla had seized. The following year, he married his niece Eudokia to the son of Stephen Nemanja of Serbia, thus helping to consolidate Byzantine influence there too and restore its prestige in the Balkans.

Isaac had done much to stabilise the frontiers but already forces were in motion over which he had no control. A first intimation of what was to come was already happening on Cyprus. At the height of Andronikos I's reign of terror in 1184, the island had been seized by Isaac Komnenos, a great-grandson of John II. He refused to recognise Andronikos I as emperor or Isaac II once he had succeeded in 1185. The new emperor despatched a naval expedition to Cyprus to bring the rebel to heel in 1187 but it was destroyed by a roving Norman–Sicilian fleet, so thereafter Isaac Komnenos was left to rule Cyprus unmolested. He proclaimed himself emperor but he made no attempt to make good his claim by marching on Constantinople. He can therefore be seen as the first of a series of leaders who established themselves in a particular locality, gathered the taxes for themselves and ruled there in defiance of the emperor in Constantinople.

Another example was Theodore Mankaphas who was proclaimed emperor at Philadelphia in western Asia Minor in 1188. Like Isaac Komnenos of Cyprus, he might have hoped to capture Constantinople one day but he made no move to do so. In the meantime he seems to have been taking advantage of provincial discontent at the heavy tax burden imposed by the government in Constantinople, which gave back very little in the way of defence in return. So when in June 1189 Isaac II arrived with his army to deal with the rebel, the people of Philadelphia shut their gates and defied him. Pressed by commitments elsewhere, Isaac could not pursue the siege and had to withdraw. Mankaphas was left to rule in just that one town, minting silver coins with his portrait on

Figure 12.3 Trachy of Theodore Mankaphas, issued in Philadelphia

(see Figure 12.3). Four years later, one of Isaac II's generals was able to end the deadlock by striking at the heart of the problem. He made secret payments to Mankaphas' most loyal followers who then abandoned his cause. Mankaphas was forced to take refuge with the Seljuk sultan in Ikonion.

The most serious separatist challenge came from Bulgaria. In the spring of 1186, a revolt broke out there which seems to have been provoked by the imposition of an extra tax to pay for the emperor's wedding to the daughter of the king of Hungary. Its leaders were not Bulgars but two Vlach brothers, Peter and John Asen, and although it began in the old Bulgarian heartland, the uprising soon spread. Before long the rebels had crossed the Balkan mountains and started raiding into Macedonia. Isaac's response was swift and effective, marching north at the head of his army in April 1186. He had soon driven the rebels back over the mountains and then out of the empire across the Danube. Elated by his success, Isaac returned to Constantinople in triumph but he rejoiced too soon. In the autumn, Peter and John Asen returned with a formidable following. They had concluded an alliance with the Turkic Cumans and their joint army routed a Byzantine force led by Isaac II's brother-in-law, John Kantakouzenos. This setback meant that the rebellion was not going to be put down quickly and the war went on for years, sometimes with Isaac enjoying considerable success but often not.

It was probably that failure to crush the Vlach–Bulgar revolt that ended Isaac II's honeymoon as the popular liberator and provoked the first of a long series of challenges to his rule. Following John Kantakouzenos' defeat, Isaac replaced him with Alexios Branas, the man who had routed the Norman army at the River Strymon in 1185. Unfortunately, no sooner was Branas in charge than he proclaimed himself emperor and led his army in a march on Constantinople in the spring of 1187. It had been many years since a military man lacking close kinship to the ruling dynasty had made a bid for power but Branas clearly had a considerable body of support behind him. Isaac II's instinct was to wait behind the walls of Constantinople until the revolt petered out, for the tactic had worked well in the past. His Italian brother-in-law, Conrad of Montferrat, brother of the ill-fated Renier, thought otherwise. He gathered an elite force of 250 cavalry and 500 foot-soldiers and placed this at the centre of an army that he led out against Branas. In the ensuing battle, Conrad and his men fought their way through to where Branas was. Conrad personally knocked the rebel general from his horse and cut his head off.

While Branas' bid for power had been disposed of relatively easily, a spate of others followed. In 1189, a young man appeared in Asia Minor claiming that he was Emperor Alexios II and that he had escaped death at the hands of Andronikos I. His fair hair, which Alexios II had inherited from his mother Maria of Antioch, helped to give credence to the story. He had the backing of the sultan of Ikonion, who provided him with troops, but his career came to an abrupt end when he was assassinated by one of his own supporters. Within days, another alleged Alexios II had emerged and began gathering support in the area bordering the Black Sea until a detachment of troops caught up with him and killed him. In Constantinople, another Isaac Komnenos, a nephew of Andronikos I, escaped from prison and managed to reach Hagia Sophia. Doubtless he was hoping to repeat Isaac II's legendary success and be proclaimed emperor by the crowd. As it turned out, he was quickly restrained and dragged away, dying under torture soon afterwards.

Not surprisingly, the frequency of these rebellions left Isaac II rather paranoid and ready to strike out at anyone against whom there was the slightest suspicion. In 1191, he had the governor of Thessalonica, Andronikos Bryennios, relieved of his command. Bryennios' only crime was being the grandson of Anna Komnene and Nikephoros Bryennios but he was imprisoned and blinded. Afterwards his son also ran to Hagia Sophia and proclaimed himself emperor but again the crowd did not respond in the way he had hoped.

Since, as Choniates put it, these rebellions were a response to what was perceived as 'the feeble manner in which Isaac governed the empire', it was only a matter of time before one succeeded. In April 1195, Isaac II set out on another military expedition against the Vlach and Bulgar insurgents. While the army was encamped in Thrace, Isaac took some companions and went hunting, but while he was away his older brother Alexios seized the imperial regalia and was proclaimed emperor by his supporters. Isaac was apprehended and blinded before being taken back to Constantinople to be imprisoned. During his ten-year reign he had been an energetic and by no means unsuccessful emperor, given the challenges that he had faced, but in the end they had overwhelmed him.

12.4 The threat from the West: Alexios III Angelos (1195–1203)

The replacement of Isaac II with his brother Alexios III conferred no particular benefit and may even have made the situation worse. Isaac had pursued a cautious financial policy and had stockpiled as much money as he could. Alexios now needed to reward his supporters so he cancelled Isaac's projected expedition against the Vlachs and Bulgars and used the funds to hand out titles and sinecures. It was an understandable move to ensure that his accession was permanent, but it did mean that later in his reign he was to lack resources when he needed them. The same concern led him to adopt the surname Komnenos in place of Angelos to emphasise his descent from the great Alexios I. Neither of these measures had the desired effect for Alexios III found himself constantly challenged by would-be usurpers, just as his brother had been. No sooner was he on the throne than another imposter appeared in Asia Minor claiming to be Alexios II. In July 1200 John Komnenos Axouchos, a great-grandson of John II, broke into Hagia Sophia, where an obliging monk crowned him as emperor. He then invaded the palace with a crowd of supporters before the Varangian guard arrived to scatter the mob and kill its leader.

Alexios also had to grapple with the same problems that had bedevilled his brother's reign and he achieved no greater success. The Vlach–Bulgar threat was the most pressing issue so after abandoning the 1195 campaign, Alexios entered into negotiations with Peter and John Asen. The talks broke down when the rebels demanded terms that the Byzantines could not possibly accept. Choniates does not say precisely what they were but in all probability they included full independence for Bulgaria. Since about 1188, both Peter and John Asen had been using the title tsar and thus claiming to be the successors of the rulers of Bulgaria up to Basil II's conquest in 1018. With no treaty in place, during the autumn of 1195 the Vlachs and Bulgars invaded Byzantine Macedonia and put a Byzantine force sent to intercept them to flight. At this point, however, Alexios III was presented with an opportunity to exploit the divisions among his enemies. Early in 1196, John Asen was murdered by his nephew Ivanko. Realising that Peter was likely to take revenge for the deed, Ivanko fled with his supporters to the well-fortified Bulgarian town of Trnovo and he sent a message to Constantinople begging for assistance against his uncle (see Figure 12.4). Alexios responded to the request and sent a force under the command of his cousin, Manuel Kamytzes. Had it reached Trnovo, which was by now under siege by Peter's army, it might well have been able to restore Byzantine rule in Bulgaria, but when it arrived at the Balkan mountains the troops mutinied and refused to go through the passes in which so many of their predecessors had come to grief. In the end, Ivanko fled Trnovo and made his own way to Constantinople.

That was probably the moment at which Bulgarian independence became inevitable, for Alexios made no further serious attempts to reconquer the lands beyond the Balkan range. Tsar Peter was also assassinated in 1197 but he was replaced by a third brother, Kalojan, who turned out to be one of the greatest rulers of medieval Bulgaria. In March 1201, he led his army to capture the last Byzantine outpost in Bulgaria, the port of Varna. Having done so, he had the survivors of the garrison thrown into the moat and buried alive. Early the following year, Alexios concluded a treaty with the tsar, ending hostilities and thereby recognising an independent Bulgaria.

The loss of such a significant tract of territory was bound to damage Byzantine prestige, and long before 1202 its client states were starting to distance themselves. The ruler of Serbia, who in the past had been happy to accept Byzantine overlordship, had

Figure 12.4 The Tsarevets fortress above the town of Trnovo, the new Bulgar capital

thrown it off by the late 1190s and sent his wife, Alexios III's daughter Eudokia, back to Constantinople. The prince of Antioch, Bohemond III, likewise repudiated his Byzantine wife, Theodora, whom he had married during the reign of Manuel I when Byzantine military support was still worth having. The ruler of Cilician Armenia, Leo, sought out a new overlord, sending envoys to the Western emperor Henry VI in 1194, requesting that he be crowned king. The ceremony took place in 1198 with an Armenian and a German archbishop presiding. When Alexios III heard of the coronation, he allegedly sent a crown of his own to Leo but Armenia had already slipped out of the Byzantine orbit. Alexios also had to contend with a rash of rebellious local lords along the lines of Theodore Mankaphas. A Vlach mercenary called Dobromir Chrysos seized a tract of land in Macedonia in late 1196 and holed himself up in the fortress of Prosakos. In 1199, Alexios III's former Bulgarian ally, Ivanko, took control of the city of Philippopolis. Leo Sgouros took over Corinth in 1202 and Alexios and David Komnenos Trebizond in 1204. They probably owed their local support to the fact that they provided better defence against Bulgar or Turkish raids than the emperor did.

Byzantine weakness had also been noticed by the Christian powers of the West but their attention in the late twelfth century was initially focused elsewhere. In the summer of 1187, the sultan of Egypt and Syria, Saladin, had invaded the kingdom of Jerusalem and destroyed its army at the battle of Hattin. By the end of the year, he had retaken Jerusalem and overrun much of the kingdom apart from a few enclaves on the coast. In response the pope launched the Third Crusade and the crowned heads of Europe took the cross and vowed to recover the holy city. In this feverous atmosphere, rumours began to circulate in the West that Byzantium was somehow complicit in the fall of Jerusalem. Two developments fuelled the reports. One had occurred in April 1182, when Andronikos I had seized Constantinople. His troops had run amok through the streets of the city and made common cause with the citizens of Constantinople in an attack on the Genoese and Pisan merchants who lived along the shores of the Golden Horn. Forewarned of the attack, many of them escaped by ship, but those left behind, including old people and children, were killed without mercy as the mob looted and then torched the houses and warehouses. The massacre was seen in the West as evidence of Byzantine hatred of all Latins. The second development took place a few years later. With his empire under attack from Hungarians and Normans, in 1185 Andronikos I entered into negotiations with Saladin. Following the overthrow of Andronikos, Isaac II confirmed a treaty with the sultan. The agreement as finally concluded was probably only the usual limited non-aggression pact that the Byzantines had maintained with the rulers of Egypt since 1001 but the rumour mill converted it into a sinister pact to partition the Holy Land and suggested, entirely falsely, that the emperor had sent naval help to Saladin during his 1187 campaign.

The perception that Byzantium was both weak and colluding with infidels led to some tension during the Third Crusade. Emperor Frederick Barbarossa, with whom Byzantium had had a very tense relationship during Manuel I's reign, led his army through the Byzantine Balkans on his way to the Holy Land in 1189–1190. As during the First and Second Crusades, there were clashes with Byzantine troops and Isaac II was by no means as co-operative as he might have been. Many in the German army urged Frederick to make an attack on Constantinople but in the end he turned aside and took his army across the Dardanelles into Asia Minor. Another crusade leader did not show the same restraint. In May 1191, while he was on his way to the Holy Land by sea, the king of England, Richard I, paused on his journey long enough to invade and occupy Cyprus. The island at that point was still under the control of the rebel Isaac Komnenos and Richard justified this aggression against Christian territory by claiming that Isaac had kidnapped some shipwrecked crusaders and that he was in league with Saladin.

The danger of self-righteous Western aggression became acute during the reign of Alexios III. Following the failure of the Third Crusade to retake Jerusalem, Emperor Henry VI, son of Barbarossa, took the Cross in 1195. He immediately sent a message to the Byzantine emperor demanding that he place his ports in readiness to receive the crusade fleet, that Byzantine ships should join the expedition and that 5,000 pounds of gold be handed over to help him finance the crusade. Henry added that if these demands were not met, he would invade the Byzantine Balkans. He had recently seized southern Italy and put an end to the Norman kingdom, so he was well placed to carry out his threat. Alexios III had little option but to give way and to raise the tribute demanded. A special levy was imposed on the provinces to meet the demand and church treasures were seized and melted down. Fortunately for Alexios, Henry VI unexpectedly died in 1197 and the tribute never had to be paid.

In spite of this lucky escape, the incident starkly revealed the potential danger from the West and Alexios did his best to counter it. He was well aware that, along with the supposed collusion with Saladin, there was another potential pretext for aggression: the schism between the Byzantine and Western Churches. So in 1198, he wrote to the new pope, Innocent III, asking for legates to be sent to Constantinople to discuss reunion. Innocent was only too happy to comply but in the course of his correspondence with Alexios III he revealed himself as a very tough negotiator. He told the emperor that he must bring the Byzantine Church back to Rome 'like a limb to the head and a daughter to the mother' and that he must do much more to aid the efforts being made to recover Jerusalem. Alexios could only temporise and in the end the correspondence was overtaken by events.

12.5 The Fourth Crusade (1203–1204)

The Fourth Crusade was a pivotal event in Byzantine history and yet it was never originally supposed to go anywhere near Constantinople. It was launched in 1198 by Pope Innocent III with a view to recovering Jerusalem, but rather than attempt a direct attack on the Holy Land, the strategy was to land in Egypt and conquer that country first. Ships and men began to gather in Venice during the summer of 1201. By the end of that year, however, plans were already afoot to divert the expedition to Constantinople before moving on to Egypt because its leaders had run into financial difficulty. They had been unable to raise the amount needed to pay the Venetians for the fleet and it was probably late in 1201 that an offer was made by a member of the Byzantine royal family that would enable them to do that.

The offer did not come from Alexios III but from his nephew. When Alexios had seized the Byzantine throne in 1195, he had had his brother Isaac II blinded but thereafter he did not mistreat him and kept him in a comfortable confinement with the freedom to receive visitors. That meant that Isaac was able to get messages out to his daughter Irene. She had been married in 1193 to the Norman prince Roger but following his death and the German conquest of southern Italy, she had become the wife of Philip of Swabia, brother of Emperor Henry VI. She and Philip may well have been behind a plot to spirit Isaac II's son Alexios out of Byzantine territory in a Pisan merchant galley in October 1201. Once in Italy, young Alexios made contact with the crusade leader, Boniface of Montferrat, who had long-standing connections with Constantinople through his brothers Conrad and Renier. The Byzantine prince promised Boniface that if the crusade army would come first to Constantinople to restore Isaac II to the throne, he would resupply the fleet and hand over 200,000 silver marks, enough to cover what was owed to the Venetians with plenty left over. He even undertook to join the expedition to Egypt in person and to put an end to the schism between the Byzantine and Western Churches: the very demands that Innocent III had made of his uncle. Boniface eagerly accepted and although many in the army were unhappy about what they regarded as a deviation from the expedition's main purpose, they were eventually won round. The Byzantine prince joined the Venetian crusade fleet when it had reached Corfu in May 1203 and then sailed with it to Constantinople.

This sequence of events makes it quite plain that the Fourth Crusade did not go to Constantinople with any aggressive intent to sack the city as a result of a long-standing tension between Byzantium and the West. It was invited there by a Byzantine prince who, like so many imperial claimants in the past, was making use of Latin military muscle in a civil war. Its leaders aimed to stay only long enough to bring about a change of rulers and to earn the promised reward, then to proceed to Egypt according to the original plan. There is no substance in the allegation that it was all a sinister plot on the part of the Venetian doge Enrico Dandolo who somehow engineered the diversion in order to take revenge for Manuel I's actions back in 1171. Alexios Angelos approached Boniface and not Dandolo, who merely went along with the plan. Dandolo, it is true, had earlier diverted the crusade to capture the city of Zara in the Adriatic but that was a separate incident, completely unconnected with what was later to happen in Constantinople.

When the fleet arrived in the waters off Constantinople in June 1203, Alexios III tried to brazen it out, even trying to buy the crusaders off, though he could not match his nephew's offer. But after the crusaders had drawn up their forces in front of the Land Walls and the Venetian ships had succeeded in breaking into the Golden Horn, he started to lose heart. He did lead his army out of the Land Walls to confront the crusaders but then quickly retreated before any fighting took place. He probably feared treachery within the city and that someone would open a gate in the walls and let his nephew and his Latin allies in, as had happened in 1057 and 1082. On the morning of 18 July, the palace administrators awoke to discover that the emperor had run away in the night. Interpreting his flight as abdication, they had the blind Isaac II brought from his prison and reinstated on the throne. His son came over from the Venetian fleet to join him and was crowned co-emperor, as Alexios IV.

So far everything had gone according to plan. The crusade leadership now awaited only the promised 200,000 silver marks so that they could honour their commitment to the Venetians and then depart for Egypt. That, unfortunately, was where the difficulties began. Alexios IV discovered that the treasury was empty and that he could not fulfil his undertaking. The sailing to Egypt had to be postponed until the spring while the emperor desperately tried to collect the necessary sum, melting church plate down into coin and introducing new taxes. Needless to say, that did not make him popular with the people of Constantinople. In January 1204, the short-reigned emperor was deposed and murdered by a court official called Alexios Mourtzouphlos. Isaac II died around the same time, though possibly of natural causes, so Mourtzouphlos could take the throne as Alexios V. He immediately cancelled all payments to the crusaders.

Only now did the plan to attack and conquer Constantinople emerge, largely because there was little alternative. The crusade fleet, which was still sitting in the Golden Horn, was running desperately low on provisions because Alexios V had cut off the food supply. On the other hand, it was too early in the year to leave for Egypt because of the likely weather conditions. The only way now to replenish supplies was by taking the city. On 13 April 1204, the Venetian fleet crossed the Golden Horn and the crusaders gained a foothold on the Sea Walls. Alexios V, who had come to the throne with such great promises of seeing the Latins off, fled from the city and the crusaders swept into Constantinople virtually unopposed. Now in control of one of the richest cities in the world, they pillaged it mercilessly.

Figure 12.5 The Pala d'Oro altarpiece from the church of St Mark in Venice, which carries a number of enamel plaques thought to have been looted from Constantinople in 1204

Box 12.2 Steven Runciman (1903–2000) and the sack of Constantinople

One of the most influential twentieth-century historians of Byzantium and of the Crusades, Runciman had a gift for vivid and evocative prose. Here, he describes what happened when the soldiers of the Fourth Crusade burst into Constantinople in April 1204:

> The sack of Constantinople is unparalleled in history. For nine centuries the great city had been the capital of Christian civilisation. It was filled with works of art that had survived from ancient Greece and with the masterpieces of its own exquisite craftsmen. The Venetians indeed knew the value of such things. Wherever they could, they seized treasures and carried them off to adorn the squares and churches and palaces of their town. But the Frenchmen and Flemings were filled with a lust for destruction. They rushed in a howling mob down the streets and through the houses, snatching up everything that glittered and destroying whatever they could not carry, pausing only to murder or to rape, or to break open the wine-cellars for their refreshment.

For Runciman, the sack of Constantinople was the final outcome of a clash of cultures between Byzantium and the West in the period of the crusades:

> The real disaster of the crusades was the inability of western Christendom to comprehend Byzantium. Throughout the ages there have always been hopeful politicians who believe that if only the peoples of the world could come together they would love and understand each other. It is a tragic delusion ... Thousands of soldiers and pilgrims found themselves in a land where the language, the customs and the religion seemed to them strange and incomprehensible and therefore wrong. They expected the peasants and citizens in the territory through which they passed not only to resemble them but to welcome them. They were doubly disappointed. Quite failing to realise that their thieving and destructive habits could not win them the affection and respect of their victims, they were hurt, angry and envious. Had it been left to the choice of the ordinary crusading soldier Constantinople would have been attacked and sacked at a far earlier date.

Compelling though Runciman's words are, they should be treated with caution. He was an avowed philhellene, a passionate admirer of Greek culture, and that led him to idealise the Byzantines as civilised and artistic. Western Europeans, on the other hand, he characterised as brutish and violent, determined to destroy Byzantine civilisation because they did not have the wit or education to understand it. The sack of Constantinople in 1204 was certainly shocking to contemporaries: Pope Innocent III was horrified when he found out. But it was by no means unprecedented. Alexios I's soldiers had pillaged houses and churches in Constantinople after his coup in 1081. Nor was it necessarily the outcome of years of tension between Byzantium and the West, as Runciman suggests, since the Fourth Crusade did not go to Constantinople with any intent of capturing and plundering the city. Perhaps most misleading of all is Runciman's assumption that it is the uneducated who are responsible for intolerance and conflict. History provides plenty of instances of educated elites bringing about wars, leaving the unschooled to fight and die in them.

Sources: Steven Runciman, *A History of the Crusades: Vol. 3 The Kingdom of Acre* (Cambridge: Cambridge University Press, 1954), pp. 123, 475–6; Minoo Dinshaw, *Outlandish Knight: The Byzantine Life of Steven Runciman* (London: Allen Lane, 2016).

Even if the sack of Constantinople was not unprecedented, it was still extremely controversial at the time. After all, the victors were crusaders who had taken a vow to fight infidels, not to attack a Christian city. Just before the final attack, some of the rank and file had had doubts on that score and had hesitated to go into battle. It was only at that last moment that the relations between Byzantium and the West over the past century and a half became relevant. The Latin clergy with the army assured the doubters that it was lawful to attack Constantinople because the Byzantines were faithless and deceitful, having murdered their lawful emperor, Alexios IV, and because they were schismatics, having refused to acknowledge the authority of the pope. Those themes were expanded on when one of the crusade leaders, Baldwin of Flanders, wrote to the pope to justify the attack in May 1204. He made the same points as the Latin clergy and added in Byzantium's supposed alliance with Saladin for good measure. So it would be unrealistic to claim that the sack of Constantinople was completely unconnected with the uneasy relations between Byzantium and the West. They did not cause it but they provided a convenient justification for it.

When Constantinople fell, the Byzantine empire fell with it. In May 1204, Baldwin of Flanders was elected by the victorious crusaders and Venetians as emperor and he then set about enforcing his authority in the provinces. To start with that was not difficult. The local populations often acquiesced in the takeover and even welcomed the Latins. The people of Thessalonica streamed out to meet Baldwin's army and to surrender their city without any resistance. At another town in Asia Minor, the new emperor's representative was met by a procession carrying crosses and Gospel books. A knight called Renier of Trit and his followers were enthusiastically ushered into the city of Philippopolis because the inhabitants hoped that this Latin lord would provide the kind of effective defence against the Bulgars and Vlachs that Alexios III Angelos and his predecessors had conspicuously failed to deliver. Effectively the Latins were taking on the same role as local lords such as Theodore Mankaphas and Chrysos. Discontented minorities also welcomed the new masters. When a crusader force crossed to Asia Minor in late 1204, they found allies there in communities of Armenians who hated the previous Byzantine rulers. At this point it must have seemed that Byzantium was at an end, to be replaced by a new, stronger Latin empire.

In the light of the apparent ease with which the crusaders first took Constantinople and then divided up its hinterland, it might be concluded that they merely finished off a state that was in the throes of collapse anyway. Certainly with Bulgaria lost and with numerous challengers to central authority springing up everywhere, Byzantium was looking very fragile at the end of the twelfth century. On the other hand, Alexios III's

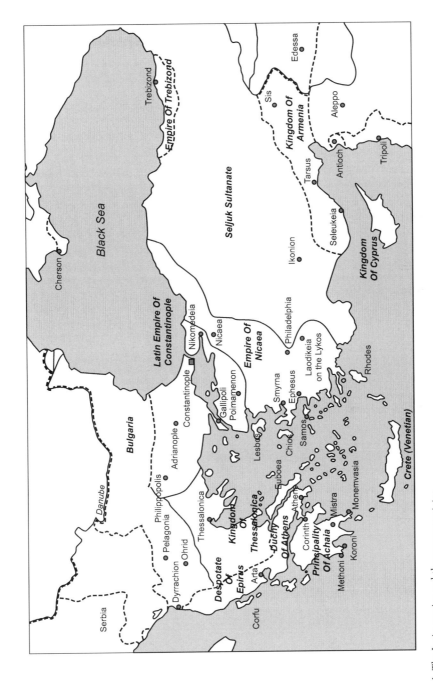

Map 12.1 The Latin empire and the successor states

response to these difficulties was not entirely ineffective. He wisely ended the fruitless Bulgarian war and then concentrated on his other enemies. He managed to dispose of Ivanko by luring him into a trap and executing him and he took the fortress of Prosakos back from Chrysos in 1202. Diminished it may have been but Byzantium's recovery would probably have continued had it not been brutally cut short by the events of 1204.

Points to remember

- Theories about the 'feudalisation' of Byzantium and the sinister role of Venice are now largely discredited.
- Isaac II and Alexios III have been criticised as weak and ineffective but their reigns were not without successes.
- The real problem in late twelfth-century Byzantium was the increasing tax burden as the state struggled to maintain its power and prestige.
- The Fourth Crusade was not planned or diverted with a view to capturing Constantinople and dividing up the provinces.
- On the other hand, issues such as the schism between the churches were used to justify aggression against Byzantium, even if they did not motivate it.

Suggestions for further reading

Brand, Charles M. (1968), *Byzantium Confronts the West, 1180–1204* (Cambridge MA: Harvard University Press). A detailed account of the period, though historians now question its narrative of deteriorating relations leading inevitably to the sack of Constantinople.

Herrin, Judith. (2013), *Margins and Metropolis: Authority across the Byzantine Empire* (Princeton NJ: Princeton University Press). Includes two important chapters on Byzantine society and economy in the late twelfth century.

Nicol, Donald M. (1988), *Byzantium and Venice: A Study in Cultural and Diplomatic Relations* (Cambridge: Cambridge University Press). Provides a comprehensive survey of Veneto–Byzantine relations up to 1453, but tends to present the Venetians in a negative light.

Simpson, Alicia. (2015), *Byzantium 1180–1204: 'The Sad Quarter of a Century'?* (Athens: National Hellenic Research Foundation). A collection of essays that re-examine aspects of the period outside the assumption of 'decline'. See especially the chapters by Alicia Simpson and Vlada Stanković.

PART IV

Decline and disappearance 1204–1453

13 Major literary sources for the period 1204–1453

In many ways, the last phase of Byzantine history is the best documented. There is a succession of literary histories in Attic Greek that cover events up to around 1359 but also a wealth of other material from both inside and outside Byzantium. Even so, there is a gap in the coverage for the later fourteenth century, which remains a difficult and obscure period.

13.1 George Akropolites

In spite of the political earthquake of 1204, there was cultural continuity in one respect: another historian continued the narrative from close to where Niketas Choniates left off in 1207. George Akropolites was born in 1217 in Constantinople, where his father probably held some post with the Latin regime. Disillusioned with his employers, in 1233 he sent his son George to Nicaea with a view to following himself shortly. Unfortunately, he died before he could do so and therefore young George was taken into the court of Emperor John III Vatatzes (1221–1254) and there he completed his education. He later became one of John III's secretaries and held the office of Grand Logothete under John's son and successor, Theodore II (1254–1258). His career reached its height under Michael VIII Palaiologos (1259–1282), to whom he was related by marriage, when he became one of the emperor's main advisers (see Figure 13.1). He helped to reorganise the University of Constantinople after 1261 and led the Byzantine delegation to the Council of Lyon in 1274.

Given that Akropolites was so influential under Michael VIII, it is odd that his history ends in August 1261, just two years into the reign. It is possible that he intended to continue into the 1280s but he might have preferred to end on a high note with the recovery of Constantinople from the Latins. That relieved him of the necessity of having to record Michael VIII's blinding of young John IV Laskaris and his own role in the Union of Lyon. His work is a vital source of information on the empire of Nicaea and on how it developed the wherewithal first to resist and ultimately overthrow the Latin empire of Constantinople. Naturally, Akropolites champions the rulers of Nicaea as the true emperors of the Romans, not only against the Latin emperor but also against their rivals in Epirus and Trebizond. The long shadow of Akropolites' political master, Michael VIII, also reaches back into his account of the exile in Nicaea. The achievements of John III, though diligently recorded, are not acclaimed in the way those of Michael are. Theodore

Figure 13.1 Seal of George Akropolites bearing the image of his patron saint, George. The inscription on the other side reads: 'Martyr, confirm the letters of Akropolites, the Grand Logothete who bears the same name as you' (© Dumbarton Oaks, Byzantine Collection, Washington, DC)

II is portrayed as dangerously unstable as the ground is prepared for Michael VIII's seizure of power and his replacement of the Laskaris dynasty with his own family. Thus Akropolites' work was in the Byzantine tradition not only in terms of its language and style but also of its highly tendentious presentation of events and personalities.

13.2 The last Attic historians

After George Akropolites, three historians took up their pens to produce traditional histories in Attic Greek. None of their works has yet been translated into English in its entirety, although some sections are presented in text boxes in this book (see Boxes 13.1, 14.1 and 15.1). George Pachymeres, a deacon and a pupil of Akropolites, wrote a continuation of his teacher's history covering the years 1255 to around 1308. He gives the most detailed and the only contemporary account of the reign of Michael VIII and a narrative for a large part of that of Andronikos II (1282–1328). As a clergyman, his slant on events was theological rather than political. He was perfectly happy with Michael VIII until 1274, when the emperor agreed to a union with the Church of Rome at the Council of Lyon. Thereafter he was deeply hostile to the emperor. For most readers though his chief drawback is his convoluted version of Attic Greek, which at times makes him very difficult to understand.

Nikephoros Gregoras paralleled Michael Psellos in the range of his interests, for as well as his monumental *Roman History*, which covers the years 1204 to 1359, he wrote on grammar, rhetoric, philosophy, poetry, physics, mathematics, astronomy and theology. His *Method of fixing the Date of Easter* (1324) was later used to formulate the Gregorian calendar, which was introduced in 1578 and is still used today. He was born in Asia Minor in around 1290 and came to Constantinople at the age of 20 where he studied under Theodore Metochites, the most prominent political and intellectual figure of the time (see Figure 13.2). Like Psellos again, Gregoras' writing of history was influenced by his personal experiences and political affiliations. He was in favour at the court of Andronikos III (1328–1341) and a personal friend of the emperor's chief minister, John Kantakouzenos, but his career soon sailed into choppy waters. In 1340, he became involved in the debate over Hesychasm, the mystical practices pursued by monks on Mount Athos (see Section 7.3). For a fastidious intellectual like Gregoras, praying with

Figure 13.2 Theodore Metochites (1270–1332), mosaic from the Chora church in Constantinople

a mantra and claiming to have received ecstatic visions of the emanations of God were the dangerous ravings of uneducated fanatics and he publicly denounced them as such. Then, following the death of Andronikos III in 1341, Byzantium descended into civil war, as John Kantakouzenos did battle with the regent Anna of Savoy. In spite of his friendship with Kantakouzenos, Gregoras sided with Anna and her son, John V, and as it happened the regency council shared his mistrust of Hesychasm. When Kantakouzenos captured Constantinople and was crowned as Emperor John VI in 1347, he organised a synod that declared Hesychasm to be legitimate and orthodox. Gregoras refused to accept the decision and was imprisoned in the monastery of Chora. He was released when John VI abdicated in 1354 and presumably continued to work on the *Roman History* until his death in 1360. The later chapters are taken up with rather shrill denunciations of Kantakouzenos and Hesychasm and are overloaded with official documents, but as a whole his work is vital for our understanding of thirteenth- and fourteenth-century Byzantium. It contains a great deal of information on constitutional, administrative and economic questions and included material that is not given in either Akropolites or Pachymeres.

Finally, there is the *History* of John Kantakouzenos who was none other than Gregoras' one-time friend Emperor John VI (see Figure 13.3). Following his abdication in December 1354,

Figure 13.3 Emperor John VI Kantakouzenos presiding over a synod of bishops from a manuscript in the Bibliothèque Nationale, Paris

he retired to a monastery, living on until 1380 and writing his history and some theological works. Kantakouzenos' history is much more of a personal memoir than those of Pachymeres and Gregoras. It only covers the years 1320 to 1357 and inevitably takes the form of the apologia of a retired statesman. His activities are always presented in the most favourable light and any inconvenient facts are suppressed or glossed over. Yet even if Kantakouzenos' interpretation is highly partisan, his facts are generally reliable and tally with those given by Gregoras. Based on the emperor's diary and often on official documents, it offers a great deal of information and is a vital source for the disastrous civil war of 1341–1347.

Box 13.1 John Kantakouzenos on the Byzantine Civil War of 1341–1347

Writing after his abdication in 1354, former Emperor John VI here opens his account of the civil war that he waged against the regency for John V Palaiologos.

> Since after the death of Andronikos [III] the younger [in 1341] the bitterest war of the Romans against each other ever in memory erupted ... I considered it necessary to set forth what happened during this war as well, not only in order that those hereafter should know envy is the cause of such great evils – utterly destroying not only those envied but also the enviers, just as rust destroys the iron it is begotten from – but also that you, who are present now, may be able to know the truth of these matters and not be led astray by the rumours coming from abroad into believing that which is not, nor pay heed to the babblers from each of the factions, whether flattering themselves or slandering their opponents. It is important to pay careful and not cursory attention to me. For all others, if indeed there are certain persons who wrote about this war, know nothing clear about what happened; either they were entirely absent from these events, or they accepted whatever they heard – whatever the common mob spreads about or certain others have reported – and they passed such things on to later generations, caring nothing for the truth. Or else, even if they campaigned with either of the two emperors – but doubtlessly not participating in their counsels – they were neither confidants in the more confidential matters, nor were they otherwise present at every action, since the war was continuous and long – for it lasted five years. In my case, however, no one could hold me responsible for any such thing. For being present myself with the authors of the actions, I know these things on my own account.

Most Byzantine historians prefaced their work with an avowal that they were going to tell only the truth but in the case of Kantakouzenos, who was a major player in the events he describes, 'the truth' could only be his version of what happened. In the rest of his description of the civil war he stresses how he was forced into proclaiming himself emperor by the aggressive actions of the regency in Constantinople and how he consistently sought to advance not his own ambitions but the good of the state.

Source: John Kantakouzenos, *Historiarum Libri IV*, ed. Ludwig Schopen, Corpus Scriptorum Historiae Byzantinae, 3 vols (Bonn: Weber, 1827–1832), vol. 2, pp. 12–13 (translation by Brian McLaughlin).

13.3 Historians writing after 1453

After Gregoras and Kantakouzenos, the succession of Byzantine historians who chronicled the past in the style of the ancients came to an end. It was only after the final fall of Constantinople in 1453 that a member of the educated Byzantine elite produced a history in the same style, by which time the Byzantine empire had ceased to exist. Michael Kritovoulos wrote a History covering the years 1451 to 1467 which is closely modelled on the work of Thucydides and full of classical parallels and allusions. At first sight, though, its content seems rather different from that of his predecessors. The last Byzantine emperor Constantine XI Palaiologos (1449–1453) does feature but he is killed relatively early in the story. The main focus is on the conquests of the Ottoman sultan Mehmed II, who is presented as a worthy successor to Alexander the Great and Julius Caesar.

This preoccupation with the sultan, however, is all in the good Byzantine tradition of talking up the ruler to whom the author was attached politically. Kritovoulos had taken a decision in 1453 not to resist the Ottoman takeover or to flee to the West, as many of his contemporaries did. He was living on the Byzantine Aegean island of Imbros at the time of the siege of Constantinople and when news arrived that the city had fallen, he initiated negotiations with the commander of the Ottoman fleet at Gallipoli. As a result, the islands of Imbros, Lemnos and Thasos surrendered to the sultan without resistance. Kritovoulos was even happy to hold office under the new regime, serving as Ottoman governor of Imbros between about 1455 and 1466. That did not mean that he was a traitor. He makes clear in his work his belief that acceptance of Ottoman dominion was the best way to preserve Byzantine religion and culture. Unlike the Latins during their period of rule in Constantinople, the Turks were happy for their Byzantine subjects to practise their Orthodox religion. As for the inheritance of classical literature, the sultan himself took an interest in it and even commissioned Greek manuscripts for his library. Kritovoulos' work was probably partly designed to persuade his countrymen to follow his example and accept the new regime.

Another educated Byzantine who wrote after 1453 was Laonikos Chalkokondyles. Born in Athens in about 1427, when it was ruled by the Florentine Acciajuoli family, he was taken as a child to the Byzantine city of Mistra in the Peloponnese and educated there as a pupil of the Platonic scholar George Gemistos Plethon. He had probably left Mistra by the time that Mehmed II conquered the Peloponnese in 1460 but where he went is anyone's guess. He may, like Kritovoulos, have settled in Constantinople, but he may have spent time in Italy, where his cousin Demetrius had taken up residence. Wherever he was, at some point, probably the 1460s, he wrote his *Demonstrations of History* which covers the years 1298 to 1463. As with Kritovoulos, while the archaic language was very much in the Byzantine tradition, the focus was somewhat different. Chalkokondyles aimed to tell the story of the rise and victory of the Ottomans, in conscious imitation of Herodotus who described the rise and ultimate defeat of the Persians. Moreover, while Kritovoulos had called the Byzantines 'Romans', Chalkokondyles only ever refers to them as 'Hellenes' (i.e. Greeks), suggesting that he had abandoned the old Byzantine political ideology. As history, the *Demonstrations* leave a great deal to be desired. The chronology is often wildly inaccurate, especially for the period before 1453, and much of the material included in the work seems to be anecdotal. He does not seem to have had access to official documents nor to the works of previous Byzantine historians. For the period after 1453, he seems much better informed, and provides some very useful information on matters such as Ottoman financial arrangements, for which presumably he had an inside source. His work shows very little overt hostility to the Ottomans, which might suggest that he, like Kritovoulos, felt that the future lay in accepting their rule.

Another member of the Byzantine elite recorded a very different reaction to the Ottoman Conquest, probably because his experience of it was much less pleasant. George Sphrantzes held office first under Manuel II (1391–1425) and then under Manuel's son, Constantine XI. Unlike Kritovoulos, he was in Constantinople when the Ottomans stormed the city in 1453, and he ended up being taken prisoner and sold into slavery, along with his wife and two children. Thanks to the help of friends, he was able to procure his freedom and that of his wife, but his children both died as slaves in the household of Mehmed II. In those circumstances, Sphrantzes and his wife had no desire to remain under Ottoman rule as Kritovoulos did. They went first to the Peloponnese and then to the Venetian-ruled island of Corfu where Sphrantzes died in 1478.

As is only to be expected, Sphrantzes' historical work, known as the *Chronicon Minus*, has a much less optimistic tone than that of Kritovoulos or Chalkokondyles. Written in straightforward Greek with few literary pretensions, it opens with Sphrantzes' heartfelt declaration that he is setting out 'the events that occurred during my wretched life'. It is really a personal memoir of himself and his family rather than a history of the time. Sphrantzes includes all kinds of personal details, such as the birth of his children, gifts conferred on him by emperors and his promotions, but he sometimes misses out wider events of historical significance. Even those that he does include are dealt with very tersely: his account of the fall of Constantinople gives very few specific details. Like other Byzantine historians, he is full of praise for his imperial patrons, Manuel II and Constantine XI, although one might question whether he was as close to them as he suggests, since he is not mentioned in any other contemporary source. A distinction needs to be drawn here between Sphrantzes' *Chronicon Minus* and the *Chronicon Maius* of so-called Pseudo-Sphrantzes. The latter, though bearing Sphrantzes' name, is now known to have been written by a sixteenth-century Greek archbishop called Makarios Melissenos. Some historians, such as Steven Runciman, cite Melissenos' work as if it were by Sphrantzes, but it is not an authentic contemporary source.

Finally, there is the work of Doukas, which covers the years 1341 to 1462, breaking off abruptly in the middle of an account of the Ottoman conquest of Lesbos. It is, however, a moot point whether he can be counted as a Byzantine at all. We know almost nothing about him, not even his first name. His grandfather, Michael Doukas, had been a supporter of John Kantakouzenos in the civil war of 1341–1347 and he had fled from Constantinople to the territory of the Aydın Turks in Asia Minor. So Doukas himself was born and brought up outside Byzantine territory and he later earned his living working for the Genoese rulers of Chios and Lesbos. He was apparently an adherent of the Western rather than the Byzantine Church. By the same token, his history is very different from those produced in Byzantium. He had not received the same higher education in the classics that Kritovoulos and

Chalkokondyles had, for his Greek is an odd mixture of the demotic language with some Attic words and structures thrown in. His information about the period before 1402 is rather sparse and his chronology is obviously awry at times. He is more useful for later events as he sometimes provides information that is obviously derived from Ottoman sources. It is clear that he could speak both vernacular Italian and Turkish and he even occasionally quotes words and phrases in those languages. That would have been unthinkable for Byzantine authors like Michael Psellos or Anna Komnene for whom the purity of Attic prose could not be compromised. Doukas' work therefore marks not just the end of Byzantium as a political entity but also of its literary culture.

13.4 Other sources: Western literary and archival

The wider array of Western source material for the later period of Byzantine history is partly a result of the Latin conquest of a large part of Byzantine territory in and after 1204. One vital source is the compilation known as the *Chronicle of Morea*. Written by an anonymous author during the early fourteenth century, it was subsequently reworked and edited by others and it survives in four language versions: Old French, Italian, Aragonese and Demotic Greek. It tells the story of the conquest and settlement of the Byzantine Peloponnese and the history of the Principality of Achaia. Another body of Western literature that casts light on later Byzantine history is first-hand travel literature whose authors passed through Constantinople on one errand or another. One example is Ramon Muntaner who wrote a detailed account of the Catalan expedition against the Turks in Asia Minor in the early fourteenth century in alliance with the Byzantine emperor Andronikos II.

One abundant source of information about the later period that is not available for earlier centuries is archival documentation. Sadly, none of it emanates from Constantinople. Although archives were certainly compiled and carefully maintained there, their contents have now completely disappeared, probably having been destroyed either in 1204 or in 1453. On the other hand, archive collections in Western Europe preserve a wide range of documentation about Byzantium in the fourteenth and fifteenth centuries. Foremost among them is the State Archives of Venice, which not only houses rich records of the republic's administration of former Byzantine territories such as Crete, but also about its diplomatic dealing with the Byzantine emperor. The Vatican Archives in Rome, where the papal registers contain numerous letters to, from and about the emperor and patriarch in Constantinople, are also a mine of information. Archival sources such as these are especially important for reconstructing events of the second half of the fourteenth century when the Byzantine narrative voice falls silent.

Box 13.2 Pope Urban V to Count Amedeo VI of Savoy (4 November 1369)

In this letter, preserved in the Vatican archives, the pope tells Amedeo about Emperor John V who had visited Rome in 1369 and had made a personal submission to papal authority. Amedeo had earlier sailed to Constantinople and persuaded John to make the journey, so that he could ask for the pope's help against the Ottoman Turks (see Section 15.4).

We are joyfully announcing to you in this letter, in order to increase your happiness, that our most dear son in Christ John Palaiologos, illustrious emperor of the Greeks, your relative, in accordance with what was agreed between him and yourself [in Constantinople in 1367], has reverently approached the Apostolic See, with promises to abjure schism and to profess the Catholic Faith. And after he had given a suitable oath to maintain our mandates and of those of the Church, on 21 October last in the basilica of the Prince of the Apostles [i.e. St Peter's in Rome] we received him solemnly and in paternal charity. Accordingly, the sacred Church of God rejoices in the Lord, hoping that by the act of the same emperor the population subject to him will return to the bosom of the Church.

For the rest, the emperor caused to be set before us that he once lent to you in the city of Pera twenty thousand gold florins or goods to that value, which you promised to return to him within one month. After he had presented himself before us, we saw then that the public document certainly confirmed this, so we affectionately ask and strongly urge you, that you should swiftly give satisfaction to him as regards the aforementioned loan. In this way, you will nobly and faithfully fulfil your promise for your honour and for the relief of poverty, from which you ought to know the emperor suffers greatly. Moreover, we have pleaded with certain kings and other magnates in our letters that, out of reverence for God and for the propagation of the faith, they should give help to the emperor just as to a Catholic prince for the recovery of the lands of his empire occupied by the impious Turks. We hope from the reconciliation of the aforesaid emperor with the help of divine grace that this will come to pass. We exhort you to this even more, in as much as the closeness of blood and the knowledge of the wretched state of that empire, which you have seen with your own eyes but a short time ago, ought to induce you to it more than the others.

Note the allusion to the emperor's poverty and the plea that Amedeo should repay the loan that the emperor had made to him. John was to later experience great difficulty returning to his capital because he was unable to pay his fare for the sea voyage from Venice.

Source: Oskar Halecki, *Un Empereur de Byzance à Rome* (Warsaw: Société des sciences et des lettres, 1930), pp. 378–9 (author's translation).

Points to remember

- The succession of historians writing in Attic Greek continued up to 1359.
- A number of historians wrote in Greek after 1453, although their work differs from traditional Byzantine historiography in various ways.
- The late fourteenth century is poorly documented, but otherwise there is a rich range of sources for the later Byzantine period.
- Western literary and archival sources do much to supplement Byzantine ones for the fourteenth and fifteenth centuries.

Primary sources in English translation

Akropolites, George. (2007), *The History*, trans. Ruth Macrides (Oxford: Oxford University Press).

Anonymous. (2015), *The Old French Chronicle of Morea: An Account of Frankish Greece after the Fourth Crusade*, trans. Anne Van Arsdall and Helen Moody (Farnham and Burlington VT: Ashgate).

Chalkokondyles, Laonikos. (2014), *The Histories*, trans. Anthony Kaldellis, 2 vols (Cambridge MA and London: Harvard University Press).

Doukas. (1975), *Decline and Fall of Byzantium to the Ottoman Turks*, trans. Harry J. Magoulias (Detroit MI: Wayne State University Press).

Kritovoulos, Michael. (1954), *History of Mehmed the Conqueror*, trans. Charles T. Riggs (Princeton NJ: Princeton University Press).

Muntaner, Ramon. (2006), *The Catalan Expedition to the East*, trans. Robert D. Hughes (Barcelona and Woodbridge: Barcino/Tamesis).

Sphrantzes, George. (1980), *The Fall of the Byzantine Empire*, trans. Marios Philippides (Amherst MA: University of Massachusetts Press).

Suggestions for further reading

Chysostomides, Julian. (2011), *Byzantium and Venice, 1204–1453*, ed. Michael Heslop and Charalambos Dendrinos (Farnham and Burlington VT: Ashgate). A series of studies that use Venetian documents to cast light on the complex politics and diplomacy of the late Byzantine world.

Gill, Joseph. (1959), *The Council of Florence* (Cambridge: Cambridge University Press). Uses the Vatican archives to trace ecclesiastical relations leading to the Union of Florence in 1439 and the years after.

14   Exile and restoration (1204–1282)

It is a tribute to Byzantium's political and cultural resilience that even after such a terrible blow as the fall of Constantinople and the partition of the provinces in 1204, it still managed to stage a comeback, so that by the mid-thirteenth century it was once more a power to be reckoned with. The recovery was partly made possible by the weakness of its enemies, but the policies and leadership of some of its rulers played a major part as well. Having re-established itself, Byzantium was then faced with a serious threat from the West but it weathered that too. This was a real revival, not a mere postponement of an inevitable demise.

14.1 The aftermath of the Fourth Crusade (1204–1221)

The proclamation of Baldwin of Flanders as emperor in May 1204 turned out not to be the glorious birth of a new and powerful successor to the worn-out Byzantine state. Less than a year after his accession, in April 1205, the army of the Latin empire was destroyed in a clash with the Bulgarian tsar Kalojan at Adrianople. Baldwin disappeared into captivity and was never seen again. The Latin regime did not collapse at once, for Baldwin's energetic brother, Henry, managed to retrieve the situation, but after his death in 1216, it declined into terminal weakness.

Part of the problem was that the Latin emperor only ever controlled a fraction of the land, and hence the tax revenues, of his Byzantine predecessor: only Thrace, a small part of north-western Asia Minor, some of the Aegean islands and Constantinople itself. In the carve up of 1204, Thessalonica, Macedonia and Thessaly went to Boniface of Montferrat to form the kingdom of Thessalonica. In the Peloponnese, the Latin Principality of Achaia was formed by William of Champlitte, while Athens became the centre of an extensive lordship in Attica and Central Greece. The Venetians took over Crete and a string of ports and islands and they also secured a near monopoly of the Latin empire's trade with complete immunity from paying customs duties. In theory, the rulers of these areas, with the exception of the Venetians, were vassals of the Latin emperor and were obligated to provide military service in return for the land. In practice, that seldom happened.

There were some parts of the Byzantine empire that the Latins never conquered because someone else got there before them. Trebizond on the Black Sea was taken over by Alexios and David Komnenos, grandsons of Andronikos I, in April 1204, a few days before Constantinople fell to the crusaders. In the western Balkans, Michael Angelos, a cousin of the emperors Isaac II and Alexius III, set himself up as ruler in the town of Arta (see Figure 14.1) in late 1204, founding what came to be known as the despotate of Epirus. At Nicaea, Theodore Laskaris, a son-in-law of Alexios III, put up a determined resistance to attempts both by Latin emperors and the sultan of Ikonion to invade western Asia Minor.

Small and weak though the Latin empire was, these mushrooming statelets did not necessarily pose a threat. Trebizond was too far away to give cause for worry and the rulers of Nicaea and Epirus were merely local warlords who had few resources at their disposal. Whenever Emperor Henry met Theodore Laskaris in battle, Laskaris came off worst and he only survived because Henry was constantly distracted by the greater threat from Bulgaria. But the Latin rulers of Constantinople made one fatal mistake that allowed one of these pygmies to become a giant: they alienated their Byzantine subjects. At first, many Byzantines were prepared to accept the new regime: plenty of them turned out to cheer when Baldwin I was crowned in 1204. What they had not bargained for was the intransigence of the Latins in the matter of religion. One of the conquerors' first acts was to appoint a Venetian cleric, Tommaso Morosini, as the first Latin Patriarch of Constantinople and he at once demanded that the Byzantine clergy in the city recognise his authority. This they were unwilling to do, writing to Pope Innocent III to ask if they

Figure 14.1 The Panagia Church in Arta, Epirus

could have their own patriarch. The pope did not reply and in 1213 Morosini closed down all the churches in Constantinople that used the Greek liturgy. Emperor Henry was horrified and quickly had them reopened, but after his death in 1216, the gulf between the Latin conquerors and the Byzantine Orthodox population widened. More and more of them, especially from among the educated elite, started to leave Constantinople and make for either Arta or Nicaea.

Their arrival gave Michael Angelos and Theodore Laskaris a marvellous propaganda boost that enabled them to transform their image from local warlords to emperors in waiting. They could now show that the Latin emperor had no right to the throne, partly because he was an enemy of the true faith and partly because of the way in which he had come to power. It was now that lurid accounts of the sack of Constantinople were written, mainly at Nicaea, sparing no details and emphasising the desecration of churches and holy objects. Niketas Choniates and others recounted how, in April 1204, a group of Latins had broken into the cathedral of Hagia Sophia where they looted ecclesiastical vessels, gospel books and vestments, loading them onto donkeys to carry them away. The message was that no Byzantine could possibly give their allegiance to such people.

Instead, they should recognise the pious rulers of Arta and Nicaea because before long both were claiming to be the rightful emperor. Theodore Laskaris was the first to do so but he was careful to do it in a way that looked legitimate. The Byzantine patriarch of Constantinople had fled the city in 1204 and died in Thrace two years later. The Byzantine clergy therefore asked Theodore Laskaris to provide a successor, in opposition to the Latin patriarch Morosini. Laskaris appointed Michael IV in 1208 and one of the new patriarch's first acts was to crown him as Emperor of the Romans. That gave him a distinct advantage over the ruler of Epirus, Michael Angelos, but Michael's half-brother and successor, Theodore Doukas, soon made up the lost ground. In 1223, he struck a major blow against the Latins by capturing Thessalonica. Military victory went a long way to conferring legitimacy and, shortly afterwards, Theodore Doukas was also crowned emperor, albeit by a mere archbishop. Thereafter, the courts of Nicaea and Arta were modelled on that of Constantinople before 1204, with the same titles and rituals, in preparation for the day when the emperor would be restored to his capital. But as long as there were two emperors in waiting rather than one, that day would remain far in the future.

14.2 John III and the expansion of Nicaea (1221–1259)

In 1230, Emperor Theodore Doukas of Epirus quarrelled with Tsar John II Asen and invaded Bulgaria, only to suffer a disastrous defeat at the battle of Klokotnitsa and be taken prisoner. Most of his lands in Epirus were overrun by the Bulgarians and although the statelet survived, its imperial pretensions were at an end. Thenceforth, it was left to Nicaea to lead the war against the Latin regime and by then it had acquired a new and very able emperor in Theodore Laskaris' son-in-law, John III Vatatzes. In 1225, John defeated the army of the Latin Emperor Robert of Courtenay at Poimanenon and was then able to occupy those few areas of western Asia Minor that were still in Latin hands. He expanded his army by recruiting Cuman mercenaries and bringing them across the

Dardanelles to settle in his lands. He also constructed a fleet to take on the main ally of the Latin Empire, Venice, and he used it to capture the Aegean islands of Lesbos, Chios, Samos and Rhodes. The next step was to expand Nicaean power beyond Asia Minor. By making an alliance with the Bulgarians in 1235, John was able to lead his forces across the Dardanelles to take part in a joint siege of Constantinople. The alliance soon broke down, but it left John in possession of the strategically vital town of Gallipoli, giving him a permanent entry point to Europe. He returned in 1246, to conquer Thessalonica and a large part of the southern Balkans, isolating Constantinople in land that he now controlled.

It seems likely that more than military ability lay behind John III's success. Luck doubtless played a part, for John did not have to face a threat from the Turks as Theodore Laskaris had. The sultanate of Ikonion had become increasingly divided by civil wars and then in the winter of 1242–1243 it was invaded by the Mongols and reduced to the status of a tributary state. So John III could campaign in Europe, safe in the knowledge that his lands in Asia Minor would not be attacked. The question remains as to how John managed to raise such a large army and fleet and how he paid for them. The strain of levying ever higher taxes to pay for defence was one of the factors that had weakened Byzantium before 1204, yet now John III had succeeded in providing a strong army and apparently without causing resentment from tax payers. Many historians have attributed that to a prudent economic policy described by the historian Nikephoros Gregoras (see Box 14.1).

Box 14.1 Nikephoros Gregoras on John III Vatatzes

Here the fourteenth-century Byzantine historian describes how Emperor John III harnessed the resources of his small successor state:

> The emperor himself marked out a piece of land, which was fruitful and suitable for wine growing and which he adjudged sufficiently able to supply the needs of the royal table, as well as the emperor's inclination for good works and generous actions: these were feeding the elderly and the poor and the care of those suffering from all kinds of injuries and diseases.
>
> He had these matters overseen by those who knew about agriculture and viticulture, and he had an abundant crop of fruit produced. But that was not the only thing for, in addition, he acquired herds of horses, cattle, sheep and pigs and all kinds of domesticated fowls. Their offspring brought him a rich annual income. He also called upon others to do likewise, both those who were related to him by birth and others who were of noble descent, in order that each one should have sufficient from his own estates to supply his needs, without laying greedy hands on commoners and the weak, and that the Roman state immediately and henceforth should be completely purged of injustice. Indeed, in a short while, all the barns were observed to be full of produce and all the roads, highways, the pens and stalls, were crowded with animals and there were at least as many fowls. By good fortune for the Romans, it happened at that time that the Turks were suffering from great scarcity

of necessities and a severe famine and because of this all the roads were full of the comings and goings of this race of people towards the Roman lands: women, men and children in want. The riches of the Turks poured in great abundance into the hands of the Romans: in the form of silver, gold, and woven vestments along with every pleasant and multi-coloured thing and each full of expensive luxury. It was seen then how many objects of value were given up so as to purchase a small amount of food; every fowl, cow and kid commanded a high price. In this way, the houses of the Romans quickly became full of the wealth of the barbarians and the royal treasury was replete with the great abundance of money. So, in order that I may sum up everything briefly: the people who looked after the flocks of hens which laid eggs, collected all these up every year and sold them. After a short period, in consequence of the large amount of money received, a crown, adorned with precious gems and pearls, could be commissioned for the empress. The emperor called this the 'Egg Crown', as it had been made from the selling of eggs. This is one example of his imperial and statesmanlike forethought. A second is the following: he noticed that Roman wealth was foolishly being poured away on garments from foreign nations, such as the multi-coloured silks which Babylonian and Assyrian weavers manufactured and the fine products of Italian hands. For this reason, he promulgated a decree that none of his subjects was to wear these clothes, and if anyone did, whoever he might be, both he and his family would be dishonoured. They should wear only those which Roman land had produced and Roman hands had made.

The passage should be read with some caution. Gregoras was writing about a hundred years later, by which time John III had been accepted as a saint of the Orthodox Church and the Byzantine empire was starting to enter its final decline. The historian may well have been looking back with rose-tinted spectacles, for neither George Akropolites nor George Pachymeres, who were writing nearer the time, mention these reforms. Remember too that Gregoras' aim in this passage is not to describe an 'economic policy' but to demonstrate John's morality and saintliness. On the other hand, he might just be providing the key to the emperor's success.

Source: Nikephoros Gregoras, *Byzantina Historia*, ed. Ludwig Schopen, 3 vols (Bonn: Weber, 1829–1830), vol. 1, pp. 41–3 (author's translation).

John was fortunate that he held some of the most productive and fertile land in the region, especially the valley of the River Meander, inland from Ephesus, and he took steps to improve agricultural production there, using his own estates as a model, with a view to making the empire of Nicaea self-sufficient in food. The agricultural surplus proved very useful when the Seljuk sultanate of Ikonion, whose lands on the Anatolian plateau were much less productive, was suffering from famine. Nicaea was able to sell food to the Turks at a huge profit, some of which was doubtless used to equip the army and the fleet.

John even seems to have attempted a kind of economic warfare, aimed at the main prop of the tottering Latin empire, Venice. Since 1214, for political reasons the Nicaean emperor had had a commercial treaty with the Venetians, allowing them to trade in its ports without paying the kommerkion. That did not preclude attempts by the Nicaeans to probe Venetian naval defences but the republic was a formidable opponent at sea. In 1241, 25 Nicaean warships sent to blockade Constantinople were driven off by a Venetian squadron of just 13. So John might have resorted to undermining Venetian trade instead. According to Gregoras, he forbade his subjects from purchasing luxury foreign goods, which would have been brought in on Venetian ships, which may well have been a way of hitting the profits of the Italian republic. On the other hand, the policy might simply have been ethical in origin, inspired by the poverty of Christ in the Bible, in line with the sumptuary laws introduced by other medieval monarchs. Whatever the exact motives behind John III's policy, there can be no doubt that by 1250 he had turned the empire of Nicaea into a major power that was poised to retake Constantinople (see Figure 14.2).

Figure 14.2 Seal of John III showing the image of Christ from the Brazen Gate of the Great Palace in Constantinople, an open statement of John's ambition to retake the city (© Dumbarton Oaks, Byzantine Collection, Washington, DC)

Figure 14.3 Michael VIII from a manuscript of the work of George Pachymeres in the State Library of Bavaria

Unfortunately the momentum was not sustained. John III died in 1254 and was succeeded by his son Theodore II Laskaris. Theodore was an able enough ruler and he began by campaigning in the west to defend the recent gains there against the Bulgarians. But his reign was cut short in August 1258, when he died of hereditary epilepsy at the age of 36, leaving as his heir John IV Laskaris, a child of seven. The boy's mother was already dead so George Mouzalon, Theodore II's chief minister, was appointed as regent. After less than two weeks in office, Mouzalon was murdered while attending a memorial service for the late emperor. The man behind the deed was probably one of John III's generals, Michael Palaiologos, who immediately replaced Mouzalon as regent and then in January 1259 had himself crowned as co-emperor Michael VIII (see Figure 14.3). The state was back in the uneasy situation of 1068 when Romanos IV had ruled alongside the young Michael VII and the future seemed very uncertain.

14.3 Michael VIII and the recovery of Constantinople (1259–1267)

John IV's co-emperor Michael was a member of the illustrious Palaiologos family which had already played a significant role in Byzantine history. Michael's ancestor George Palaiologos had been brother-in-law and close adviser to Alexios I Komnenos and he was related to John IV by marriage, as his wife Theodora was the great niece of the late John III. He had a good record as a soldier but he was not destined to be a great military leader like Basil II or Alexios I. During his reign the armies were led by others, often Michael's close relatives, while the emperor himself supplied the brains behind the brawn.

Almost as soon as he had been crowned, Michael faced a significant challenge. The enemies of the empire of Nicaea were quick to take advantage of its apparent weakness with the accession of a minor and formed a powerful coalition, consisting of the despot of Epirus, Michael II and the prince of Achaia, William II, along with an army sent by the king of Sicily, Manfred. In autumn 1259, a Nicaean army marched to meet the coalition at Pelagonia in Epirus. It was commanded by Michael's brother, John Palaiologos, but the emperor's hand can be detected in what happened before the fighting began. False information about the size of the Nicaean army was leaked to the coalition camp so that the despot Michael II took fright and withdrew with his troops. With the odds now tipped in his favour, John Palaiologos then gave battle. 'The sun', wrote George Akropolites, 'has seen few such victories': the coalition army was largely destroyed and William II was taken prisoner.

The triumph went a long way to legitimising Michael's seizure of power and what followed established him permanently. The Latin emperor of Constantinople, Baldwin II, had not joined William II's coalition in 1259 for he did not have a great deal to contribute. He controlled only Constantinople and a few miles of land round about and his army was no more than the city's garrison. In July 1261, an anonymous message was sent to the commander of a Nicaean force that was operating in Thrace with information that the Land Walls of Constantinople were virtually undefended because Baldwin had sent the bulk of his troops to capture an island on the Black Sea Coast. Moreover, one of the gates in the walls had been left open by a sympathiser on the inside. The chance was seized and Nicaean troops entered Constantinople that very night. By daybreak, they were in full control and Baldwin II quickly realised that all was lost. He fled by ship and the entire Venetian population, who feared reprisals, went with him. Typically, Michael VIII was not with the army. He only arrived a few weeks later, to make a ceremonial entry into the city and to give thanks for the victory at a service in Hagia Sophia.

As the euphoria died down and Michael VIII settled into his new capital, he must have decided that this miraculous deliverance, which had put right the disaster of 1204, entitled him to be sole emperor and his son to succeed him thereafter. At the end of 1261, he gave orders for his co-emperor John IV, who was still only 11, to be blinded and then had him immured in a castle in Asia Minor. The deed was not just brutal but politically risky. As soon as the news broke, the patriarch Arsenios excommunicated Michael and a revolt broke out in the area around Nicaea where there was still deep loyalty to the Laskaris family. Like Basil I, Michael VIII would have to justify his seizure of power if he did not want to end up like Andronikos I.

The excommunication he dealt with by simply sacking the patriarch and appointing someone more compliant, but he still needed to sell himself to the mass of the population. Even if he had employed the slickest of advertising agencies, the new emperor could hardly have come up with a better catchphrase than the one he chose to characterise himself: the New Constantine. After all, it had been Constantine I, a saint of the Orthodox Church, who had founded Constantinople in 324, filling it with relics of the Passion and making it the centre of the Christian world. In 1204, it had fallen to the schismatic Latins, but now

Michael had restored everything to the way it should be and hence he was the New Constantine. He used every means in his power to fix the phrase in the minds of his subjects. He put it on his seal and used it when signing official documents. He had a portrait of himself as the New Constantine embroidered into a huge silk awning, which was then strung between two of the columns in Hagia Sophia. Later in his reign, he commissioned new mosaics for a monastery church that included portraits of himself, his wife Theodora and one of his sons. The son chosen was not his eldest and heir, Andronikos, but a younger one who had been born after the recapture of Constantinople in 1261. The son's name, of course, was Constantine. Perhaps Michael did rather lay it on with a trowel, but in the end the sustained propaganda campaign worked and his family came to be accepted as the rightful ruling dynasty. When he died in 1282, his son Andronikos II succeeded without question and the Palaiologos dynasty ruled Byzantium for the rest of its existence, apart from a brief period between 1347 and 1354.

The state that Michael VIII presided over after his recapture of Constantinople was smaller than that ruled by Manuel I in 1180, although he held its wealthiest and most productive regions. It consisted of about a third of Asia Minor, a strip of territory across the Balkans from the Adriatic to Constantinople, and some of the Aegean islands. In 1262, a small part of the Peloponnese was added. The prince of Achaia, William II, had bought his freedom after his capture at Pelagonia by ceding Monemvasia and a number of other fortresses there. A new city grew up around one of them, Mistra, as settlers arrived from elsewhere in Greece who did not want to live under Latin rule (see Figure 14.4). It became the seat of the Byzantine

Figure 14.4 The castle at Mistra

governor of the area. Of the lands that had been lost since 1180, Bulgaria was now a large independent kingdom and Cyprus was under the rule of the French Lusignan dynasty. Trebizond was a rival mini-empire under a branch of the Komnenos dynasty and, although he had given up his imperial pretensions, the despot of Epirus had no intention of allowing his territory to be absorbed by the emperor in Constantinople. In Greece, the duchy of Athens under the de la Roche family and the principality of Achaia still occupied most of the land. Many former Byzantine ports and islands, including Crete, were under Venetian occupation (see Map 14.1).

In the early 1260s, the prospects for retrieving some of the lost lands looked promising. Trebizond, Achaia, Cyprus, Epirus and Athens were all small states which lacked the resources that Michael VIII now commanded. Of the two larger powers on its borders, the Seljuks of Ikonion had now declined into insignificance and Bulgaria was by no means as formidable as it had been under Kalojan. True, the seas were still dominated by the Venetians but even they were not having it all their own way. In the aftermath of the Fourth Crusade, they had laid claim to Corfu and the other Ionian Islands, to the long Aegean island of Euboea, which they called Negroponte, and numerous other ports and islands. The maritime republic needed these places as staging posts for its galleys on their way to and from Constantinople and Alexandria. They particularly wanted Corfu because it was a convenient first stop down the Adriatic from Venice. Laying claim was one thing; converting them into reality was quite another, as other powers also coveted these territories. They had bought Crete from Boniface of Montferrat in August 1204 but that agreement did not easily deliver it into their hands. Their arch-enemies the Genoese were determined to deny them the island and they had to fight a 14-year war to secure it. Even then their rule did not go unchallenged. In 1234, the Cretans revolted against Latin rule and Emperor John III sent them help from Nicaea. Although they had occupied Corfu in 1204, they were ejected from the island ten years later by the despot of Epirus. They were able to seize the ports of Methoni and Koroni at the southern tip of the Peloponnese (see Figure 14.5) in 1207, but in Euboea they were only able to gain a foothold by occupying the southern town of Karystos. They rest was occupied by assorted Latin lords who were usually at odds with Venice. It was a situation ripe for exploitation.

Michael VIII began planning further reconquests as soon as Constantinople was in his hands. He already had a valuable alliance in place to counter the Venetians at sea, for in 1260 he had concluded the treaty of Nymphaion with the Genoese, trading tax exemptions in the ports of the empire of Nicaea for naval support whenever it was needed. The treaty was to be extended in 1267, when Michael granted the Genoese a commercial colony at Pera (or Galata) opposite Constantinople. Given their long-standing rivalry with the Venetians, the Genoese were only too happy to take them on at sea on the emperor's behalf. In the spring of 1263, Michael launched a three-pronged attack into the lost lands of the Balkans and Greece. One of his brothers, John the victor of Pelagonia, was sent into the despotate of Epirus. Another, Constantine, was despatched to the Peloponnese with a force largely composed of Turkish mercenaries to take on the prince of Achaia, who had already signalled his intention of breaching the treaty made the previous year. Meanwhile a fleet was ordered to the Aegean to support Constantine's expedition and to attack the islands held by the

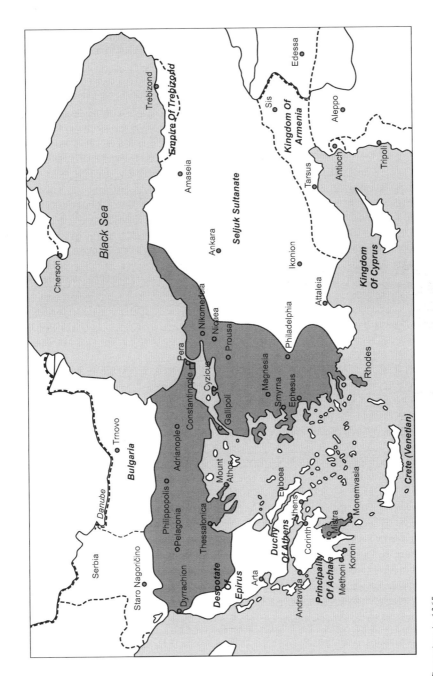

Map 14.1 Byzantium in 1265

Figure 14.5 Venetian fortification at Methoni

Venetians. At first the offensive went well. Despot Michael II was forced to capitulate and to accept Michael VIII's suzerainty over Epirus and Thessaly, though he was allowed to continue ruling them for the time being. In the Peloponnese, the Byzantines marched boldly out of their enclave and headed for William's capital at Andravida at the far side of the peninsula. For a moment it looked as if they were about to conquer the whole of the Peloponnese. In the Aegean, the fleet had some success too, plundering the Venetian enclave on Euboea and the islands of Paros and Naxos.

The initial momentum was not maintained. The Venetians soon demonstrated their supremacy at sea. In the early summer of 1263, an allied Genoese fleet that was sailing towards Monemvasia was intercepted by 32 Venetian galleys. Although outnumbered, the Venetians caused severe damage to the Genoese vessels, 14 of which fled even before the fighting began. The following autumn, the Byzantine campaign in the Peloponnese started to unravel. As Constantine Palaiologos approached Andravida, the garrison suddenly and unexpectedly sallied out and scattered the superior Byzantine force. Constantine renewed the campaign the following year but now he encountered much stiffer resistance. Then to make matters worse, his Turkish mercenaries changed sides because their pay was six months in arrears. They joined up with Prince William II and inflicted a severe reverse on Constantine's force in a ravine called Makryplagi. With further progress now unlikely, Michael VIII recalled his brother and the war in the Peloponnese petered out.

These were relatively minor setbacks and Michael was not deterred from making further attempts later in his reign. In 1277, he despatched a fleet and army to the Aegean where it seized a number of islands such as Skopelos and Lemnos, as well as landing a force on Euboea. Again, it looked for a moment as if the whole island was going to fall but the Byzantines proved unable to take the main town of Karystos. Michael even made an attempt to reassert Byzantine authority over Bulgaria. In 1272, he signalled his intent by announcing that the Churches of Bulgaria and Serbia would henceforth be under the jurisdiction of the archbishop of Ohrid, a town that was now back in Byzantine territory. A few years later, he took the opportunity to intervene in Bulgaria by sending a small expedition across the Balkan mountains to support the Bulgarian tsar John III Asen in his bid to overthrow the rebel Ivaylo. Unfortunately, although they captured Trnovo, the Byzantine troops were not numerous enough to win the war and John Asen ended up fleeing back to Constantinople.

Again these were relatively minor reverses. In theory, the prospects for regaining ground in Greece and the Balkans remained strong. The reason that these areas were not reincorporated was that from the 1260s, Michael VIII was faced with the enmity of a major power in the West so that he had to husband his resources for defence rather than attack (see Section 14.4). As a result, the despotate of Epirus was able to resist re-incorporation until 1338. The principality of Achaia did not collapse in the way that the Latin empire had and survived until 1430. The empire of Trebizond even outlived Byzantium by surviving until 1461. The biggest winners of all were the Venetians. In the decades that followed, they succeeded in consolidating their grip on Crete, taking over the whole of Euboea and eventually establishing themselves in Corfu and the Ionian islands. Their maritime empire was to last until the end of the eighteenth century.

14.4 The challenge of Charles of Anjou (1267–1282)

As soon as he heard the news of Michael VIII's capture of Constantinople in 1261, Pope Urban IV commanded the preaching of a crusade to recover the city. Justification was given partly on the grounds that the Greeks were schismatics who had fallen away from Rome, but also because the re-established Byzantine empire might bar the way for help to reach the beleaguered kingdom of Jerusalem. The ejected Latin emperor, Baldwin II, toured Western Europe to drum up support for the enterprise. In spite of all the publicity, the pope's appeal aroused little interest at first. Would-be crusaders preferred to go to the Holy Land rather than take up arms for a lost cause against fellow Christians. It was not until 1267 that the pope received an answer to his call and it came from the French ruler of Sicily and Southern Italy, Charles of Anjou. He had recently overthrown the previous ruler, Manfred, with papal blessing and had inherited the dream of the Norman rulers of southern Italy to conquer the lands beyond the Adriatic. On 27 May 1267, Charles and Baldwin II met and made a treaty at Viterbo, agreeing that Charles would send a fleet to take Constantinople, restore Baldwin to his throne and that he would receive half of the conquered lands.

Knowing that something like this was bound to happen sooner or later, Michael VIII had been seeking allies wherever he could. He reached out beyond the Christian world, to the Mamluk sultan of Egypt, Baibars, to the Mongol Ilkhan of Persia, Abaka, and to Nogai, khan of the Golden Horde. These agreements provided for Mongol troops to serve in the Byzantine army and other advantages, but they would not be enough to stop Charles. The emperor came to the realisation that, in spite of bitter memories of 1204 and their support for the Latin empire, he would have to come to terms with the Venetians. In 1265, he opened negotiations and a treaty was concluded three years later. The Venetians were allowed back to Constantinople, resuming possession of their old quarter alongside the Golden Horn. Their trading concessions were renewed and Venetian merchant galleys once again appeared in the Bosporus. Michael could not get the Venetians to commit to barring Charles' passage over the Adriatic but at least he could be sure that if the king of Sicily did launch an attack on Constantinople, it would not be in Venetian ships.

In the search for a way to stop Charles of Anjou, Michael resorted to another strategy. He learned that during 1274 Pope Gregory X was planning to call a general council of the Church in the French city of Lyon to discuss aid for the kingdom of Jerusalem. Michael despatched a Byzantine delegation led by George Akropolites who on arrival immediately agreed to end the schism between the Churches on the pope's terms. On Michael's behalf, Akropolites formally accepted the filioque, acknowledged the pope's authority over the whole Church and offered to assist with the forthcoming crusade. Pope Gregory was overjoyed and immediately told Charles of Anjou to call off the planned attack. Now that the Byzantine emperor was an obedient son of the Church, there could be no justification for it.

This clever stroke, which gained Michael time without a drop of blood being shed, soon backfired on him. His own propaganda had taken advantage of the deep hostility that had developed against the Latins for their sack and occupation of Constantinople. While his people had accepted the return of the Venetians to Constantinople, it was going too far to expect that they would now go along with a complete surrender to the Latin Church. Michael could depose the patriarch when he opposed the Union of Lyon and fling opponents into jail, but he could not stifle the opposition altogether. Rumours of the state of affairs in Constantinople drifted back to Rome and gave rise to accusations that Michael VIII had reneged on the agreement made at Lyon. In 1278, the pope sent legates to Constantinople to investigate and although Michael did his best to reassure them, they left with the impression that the union was a dead letter. In 1281, the pope excommunicated the Byzantine emperor and Charles of Anjou went back to building his fleet in the harbour of Palermo.

As it happened, the fleet never sailed. On the evening of 30 March 1282, a revolt broke out in the streets of Palermo against the French rulers of Sicily. Known to history as the 'Sicilian Vespers', it spread from town to town and before long the whole island was up in arms. Doubtless in due course, Charles would have put the revolt down but the following August, Sicily was invaded by King Peter III of Aragon. Within a year the French had been driven out of Sicily and although Charles managed to hold on in southern Italy, he died in 1285 with his dreams of conquest unfulfilled. Constantinople remained the capital of the restored Byzantine empire.

Box 14.2 Michael VIII and the Sicilian Vespers

The *Rebellamentu di Sichilia* is an account of the 1282 rebellion, written in vernacular Sicilian dialect. Its author, John of Procida, claims that he took a leading part in organising the rebellion by gaining the financial support of the Byzantine emperor Michael VIII. Here, speaking about himself in the third person, he describes his two visits to Constantinople and his conversations with the emperor:

I am here to offer you what you are hoping to find', responded Lord John [of Procida], 'I'll destroy King Charles [of Anjou] by bringing together your help and my advice. I'll explain what you have to do, and how to do it, with me and some other Sicilian rebels who have been injured by King Charles. You'll have what you seek. God willing, your worst enemy will be unable even to harm you, let alone defeat you.' 'How do you plan to do this?' the emperor asked. 'I will tell you if you promise me a hundred thousand gold ounces. Be assured that I can bring to bear the power of somebody who will seize the land of Sicily so quickly that King Charles will barely know what hit him.' 'Lord John', said the emperor, visibly pleased to hear this affirmation, 'take all the money from my treasury that you need and spend it as you must. Do whatever can be done.'

John of Procida returned to Constantinople after visiting Peter of Aragon in Barcelona.

'Be cheerful', John told the emperor, 'What you wished to see done has finally been done … We'll have the support of the Sicilian barons and our friends. Our most important ally, who will lead the battle, is King Peter of Aragon. He has sworn alliance to us in life and in death. His friends will be your friends and his enemies will be your enemies … Sire, give me thirty thousand gold ounces to raise an army and a fleet, and to recruit knights. I ask that you send with me to Catalonia your delegate and your best friend to consign the money personally to King Peter' … The emperor immediately had the gold weighed and placed in the Genoese galley on which Lord John was to sail to Barcelona.

The book reads like a spy thriller and if what John of Procida says is true, then this was one of the greatest triumphs of Byzantine diplomacy. Some historians, ever ready to attribute phenomenal skill to the Byzantines, have taken the story at face value and credited Michael VIII with paying the Sicilian rebels and Peter of Aragon to rise against Charles of Anjou. Others have dismissed the *Rebellamentu* as a work of fiction and argued that the Sicilians and Peter III had reasons of their own for hating Charles of Anjou, without any need for Michael's money. Certainly, none of this is recounted in George Pachymeres, the main Byzantine source for Michael's reign, but perhaps it is unreasonable to expect it to be, as the negotiations would have been carried out in great secrecy. Michael VIII himself certainly hinted that he had engineered the whole thing, but that means nothing. Astute politician that he was, he would have been quick to claim the credit for something that was going to happen anyway.

Source: Louis Mendola, *Sicily's Rebellion against King Charles* (New York: Trinacria editions, 2015), pp. 96–7, 107–8.

14.5 The Palaiologan Renaissance in art and education

The political revival of Byzantium in the later thirteenth century was matched by a cultural resurgence that is sometimes labelled the 'Palaeologan Renaissance'. The term is just as misleading as the 'Macedonian Renaissance' that has already been discussed (see Section 5.1). It suggests a parallel with the Italian Renaissance of the fourteenth and fifteenth centuries whereas the revival taking place here was very closely connected with the political and social changes in Byzantium over the previous hundred years, and especially the fall of Constantinople in 1204. Just as Michael VIII wished to be seen as re-establishing the proper form of government by retaking Constantinople, so he aimed to restore the city to its former glory after its neglect under the impoverished Latin regime. Some of his commissions were purely practical, such as raising the height of the Sea Walls along the Golden Horn to prevent a repetition of the tactics used by the Latins in April 1204. Others were designed to reinforce the political message. Hagia Sophia, in many ways the symbol of Constantinople, which had allegedly been neglected under the Latin regime, was provided with new communion vessels, altar cloths and mosaics. One of the latter can still be seen (see Figure 14.6).

Figure 14.6 Mosaic of Christ in Hagia Sophia, probably completed during the 1260s

Little of the spate of building and restoration that went on throughout the city after 1261 remains today, but there is one church that does survive almost completely intact, that of the Holy Saviour in Chora, near Constantinople's Land Walls (see Section 11.5). The monastery of which it was a part was largely in ruins at the time that Michael VIII reoccupied Constantinople, but in 1316 work began to restore it. The prime mover here was not the emperor, by then Michael VIII's successor Andronikos II, but Theodore Metochites who was chief minister during the latter part of Andronikos' long reign. The main church was given lavish new mosaic decoration depicting the lives of Christ and the Virgin Mary (see Figure 14.7). At first sight, these mosaics look much like those produced in earlier centuries but there are subtle differences. The scenes are not depicted against a solid gold background but are set in a landscape with buildings and trees. The decoration of the side-chapel alongside the church that houses Metochites' tomb is even more unusual. Here the decoration is not in mosaic but in fresco, painted onto the walls while the plaster was still wet. The frescoes show the Resurrection and Last Judgement and they look very different from earlier Byzantine art. The Resurrection in the apse of the chapel, which shows the risen Christ dragging Adam and Eve out of Hell while Satan lies bound at his feet, conveys a sense of movement and fluidity (see Figure 14.8).

Given the vibrancy of Byzantine art in this period, it was only to be expected it would remain influential in neighbouring countries, even if they no longer accepted

Figure 14.7 The enrolment for taxation in Bethlehem, mosaic in the Chora monastery church

Figure 14.8 The Resurrection, fresco in the side-chapel of the Chora church

Byzantine political domination. For example, Serbia had cast off its allegiance in the 1190s and its king, Stephen Milutin, was at war with Byzantium on and off between 1282 and 1299. But when he refounded the monastery of St George at Staro Nagoričino, Stephen called in two Byzantine artists, Michael Astrapas and Eutychios, to decorate it with frescoes (see Figure 14.9). Byzantine styles were also influential further afield, especially in Italy, where artists reproduced the dress and gestures of the figures (see Figure 14.10).

The period saw a revival in education as well. Soon after retaking Constantinople in 1261, Michael VIII refounded the university, entrusting its governance to George Akropolites, so that the traditional study of ancient Greek literature could once more be available to students. The revival continued under Andronikos II and Theodore Metochites. In his rare moments of leisure, Metochites was an avid reader, especially in history and philosophy, and he built up an impressive library at his Chora monastery. The Chora also provided a home for another influential classical scholar, Maximos Planoudes, even though he was the abbot of a monastery on Mount Auxentios near Chalcedon. Planoudes was responsible for two major advances in classical studies. The first was the rediscovery in around 1290 of the *Geography* of Ptolemy (fl.146–170 CE). Planoudes knew that a copy existed somewhere and when he finally got hold of it he was so delighted that he wrote a poem to celebrate and commissioned a series of maps to accompany the manuscript. His discovery ensured that Ptolemy was added to the list of authors studied

Figure 14.9 Fresco from the monastery of St George at Staro Nagoričino, now in the Republic of North
Macedonia

in Byzantium and that his work survived to the present day. Then, in around 1300,
Planoudes compiled a collection of 2,400 quotations and sayings from ancient Greek and
Byzantine authors which has since provided the basis for the *Greek Anthology*, a work that
preserves many fragments of ancient literature that would otherwise have been lost.

This Palaiologan revival had some differences from what had gone before. For example,
intellectual life was no longer exclusively based in Constantinople as it had been in the
past. Thessalonica became a centre of learning in its own right. The classical scholar
Demetrius Triklinios ran a well-regarded school there in the 1320s. Perhaps the
experience of exile in Nicaea and Arta had accustomed the Byzantine educated elite to
the idea that there was life beyond the capital. There were, however, political
considerations behind the shift as well. The quarrels among the Palaiologos family often
led one of its members to set up their own court in Thessalonica, starting with Irene, the
Italian second wife of Andronikos II, in 1303–1317. The same happened later at Mistra in
the Peloponnese, which after 1348 was always governed by a member of the royal family
and which later become of the home of the celebrated philosopher George Gemistos
Plethon, the teacher of Chalkokondyles.

Secondly, it has to be remembered that the renewed study of ancient Greek literature
was not just a matter of detached academic enquiry for its own sake: it was another way in
which thirteenth-century educated Byzantines were asserting themselves against the Latins.

Figure 14.10 Madonna and Child (c.1230), by the Italian artist Berlinghiero Berlinghieri, now in the Metropolitan Museum of Art, New York. The Virgin's gesture towards the infant Christ reflects Byzantine *Hodegetria* icons, i.e. 'she who shows the way'

The revival was linked to a change in the way they identified themselves. In the past, however much they had admired the literature, they had always drawn a clear distinction between themselves, as Christian Romans, and the ancient Greeks. They referred to the ancients as 'Hellenes', a word that was synonymous with 'pagans'. During the thirteenth century a certain shift is discernible as Byzantine writers started to refer to themselves as Hellenes. Why they did so is a matter for debate, but the change may reflect a growing feeling that the language that they shared with the ancient Greeks was what marked them out from their misguided co-religionists in the West. Thus the study of Greek was now no longer merely a training for government service or a pleasant academic distraction. It went to the heart of Byzantium's defiance of the supposedly barbarous and untutored Latins and their claims on Constantinople. As Niketas Choniates, writing in bitter exile in Nicaea, put it, 'the widest gulf' existed between Byzantines and Latins and it would therefore be wrong to accept the rule of those who spoke a different tongue.

Paradoxically, at the very time that the Byzantines were striving so hard to differentiate their culture from that of the Latins, Western influence can be discerned in Byzantine intellectual and artistic life. In the past, educated Byzantines had never bothered with Latin and it was certainly not on the curriculum in Constantinople's university. Yet now Maximos Planoudes had a good command of the language, perhaps learned when he took part in an embassy to Venice in 1296–1297. On his return, he translated a number of Latin classical texts into Greek, including works by Cicero, St Augustine and, an odd choice for a monk, the rather racy poems of Ovid. The need for translations shows that there must have been an interest, so perhaps this is a continuation of that curiosity about all things Latin that was first discerned at the court of Manuel I (see Section 11.4). Western influence on visual art is harder to trace but art historians have wondered whether the naturalistic style of the artists of the Chora church might have been influenced by developments taking place in Italy at the same time and especially by the work of the Florentine painter Giotto. In this way, cultural life reflected Byzantium's ambivalent political relations with Latins powers.

Points to remember

- The Latin empire of Constantinople proved to be feeble from the very start and this gave the Byzantines the opportunity to recover Constantinople.
- That it was Nicaea, rather than Epirus, that succeeded was partly due to the victory of the Bulgarians at Klokotnitsa in 1230 but also to the policies of John III Vatatzes.
- Michael VIII was a very effective ruler though his strength lay in his political and diplomatic skills rather than military leadership.
- After 1261, the restored Byzantine empire might have recovered more of its lost territory had it not been for the diversion caused by the threat of Charles of Anjou.
- The furore over the Union of Lyon is an indication of how keenly the Byzantine population remembered the events of 1204.
- Cultural developments in this period were strongly influenced by the political climate and especially by relations with the Latins.

Suggestions for further reading

Geanakoplos, Deno J. (1959), *Emperor Michael Palaeologus and the West, 1258–1282: A Study in Byzantine-Latin Relations* (Cambridge MA: Harvard University Press). Still the only book-length study of Michael VIII in English, though the emphasis is very much on his relations with the West.

Nicol, Donald M. (1993, 2nd revised edition), *The Last Centuries of Byzantium, 1261–1453* (Cambridge: Cambridge University Press). A detailed and helpful survey of the period, though some readers may find its narrative of unremitting decline rather depressing.

Ousterhout, Robert. (2002), *The Art of the Kariye Camii* (London and Istanbul: Scala). A discussion of Theodore Metochites' church of the Chora, now the Kariye Museum, one of the most important surviving examples of late Byzantine art.

Van Tricht, Filip. (2011), *The Latin Renovatio of Byzantium: The Empire of Constantinople (1204–1228)* (Leiden and Boston MA: Brill). Argues that the establishment of the Latin Empire of Constantinople was an attempt to reform and revive Byzantium, not to destroy it.

15   Decline and downfall (1282–1453)

The last chapter traced how after 1261 Byzantium was in a good position to recover much of the land and prestige that it had lost in 1204. The threat from Charles of Anjou prevented it from doing so, but in 1282 that menace was abruptly removed with the outbreak of the War of the Sicilian Vespers. Sadly, there was no glorious resurgence in the aftermath. Instead, rather than profiting from these circumstances, during the early fourteenth century Byzantium began to contract. Again, it is easy to blame personalities, and Michael's VIII's successor Andronikos II is often compared unfavourably with his father. That is not entirely fair. In his early years at least, Andronikos did a great deal to smooth over a difficult legacy and the seeds of the problems he wrestled with had been sown long before his accession. He just had the misfortune to be on the throne when the chickens came home to roost.

15.1 The calamitous reign of Andronikos II (1282–1328)

Michael died in December 1282, only a few months after the War of the Sicilian Vespers had removed the threat of Charles of Anjou. Andronikos' first concern was to heal some of the bitter internal divisions that his father had left behind. He immediately abandoned the Union of Lyon with the Western Church, which was now no longer needed anyway. The move was tremendously popular among the Byzantine populace. He also laboured to bring an end to the 'Arsenite' schism in the Byzantine Church which had begun in 1264 when Michael VIII had deposed Patriarch Arsenios, who had excommunicated him for blinding John IV. It took time, but in 1310 the breach between the two factions was finally healed. At the same time, Andronikos had to contend with the possibility of a renewed threat from the West. The abrogation of the Union of Lyon was hardly likely to go down well at the Papal Curia but at first the popes tried to negotiate. Nicholas IV wrote to the emperor urging him to return to the true faith and he encouraged plans for Andronikos' son Michael to marry Catherine of Courtenay, the granddaughter of the Latin Emperor Baldwin II, and thus legitimise the Palaiologos dynasty in Western eyes. When those negotiations came to nothing, in 1307 Pope Clement V finally excommunicated Andronikos and the way was open for some powerful Western prince to renew the ambitions of Charles of Anjou. Charles of Valois, brother of the king of France, at first looked to be a serious contender because he had married Catherine of Courtenay in 1301 and so inherited her claim. But although

Charles spent much of his life plotting ways to make himself master of Constantinople, these efforts had yielded no result by the time he died in 1325. In the meantime, Andronikos II had not been idle. In 1284, he married Irene, the daughter of Marquis William VII of Montferrat. For her dowry, she surrendered the old Montferrat claim to Thessalonica, thus defusing another potential pretext for Latin aggression. Relations with the papacy later improved too, with Andronikos sending envoys to the court of Pope John XXII during the 1320s, and by then the likelihood of a Latin attack on Constantinople had evaporated.

There was another piece of unfinished business from Michael VIII's reign. The recovery of Constantinople had been a great triumph, but it had meant that the emperor had become much less visible away from the capital while the cost of maintaining the vast showcase city and Michael's restoration work fell hard on the provinces. In the old heartlands of the empire of Nicaea in Asia Minor, there was still lingering support for the Laskaris dynasty and nostalgia for the days when the state had been smaller and its tax demands more modest. The alienation of the provinces that had been a feature of the later twelfth century had returned. To counteract it, Andronikos did his best to show himself as widely as possible outside the capital. In 1290 he proceeded to Nicaea and based himself there for three years. He made a point of visiting the castle where the unfortunate John IV Laskaris still lived, now aged around 40, and of asking John's forgiveness for Michael VIII's crime. Then the emperor moved west, spending time in Thessalonica and in Monemvasia (see Figure 15.1), in the isolated enclave of Byzantine territory in the southern Peloponnese.

The impression one gets of Andronikos so far is of a competent and dutiful ruler, doing his best in trying circumstances. Unfortunately, as his reign went on, those trying circumstances developed into a full-blown crisis. The danger came not from the west but from the east and it was another legacy from the reign of Michael VIII. On the face of it, in 1261, the eastern frontier looked like the most secure part of the empire. The Seljuk sultans of Ikonion were no longer the power they had once been and they had remained at peace with the Byzantine emperor for years. Yet the very weakness of the Seljuk regime was to have unfortunate results. In order to gain support from their more powerful subjects in their civil wars, the sultans made them grants of land in return for military service. Those lands tended to lie on the western edges of the sultanate, along the border with the Byzantine empire. The owners of these small lordships soon took to mounting raids into Byzantine territory in order to seize flocks of sheep and agricultural produce. To start with, their incursions, although damaging, were not too serious. The Turks soon discovered, however, that the defences of Asia Minor were very weak. To make matters worse the heavy burden of taxation that Michael VIII had laid on his subjects in Asia Minor apparently disinclined them to resist and some even joined the raiders. The Turks ceased to withdraw after their raids and began to occupy the land.

Michael VIII was not completely indifferent to the problem. In 1278, he put the young Andronikos in charge of an army and sent him down into southern Asia Minor. In 1281, Michael himself took a force into the northwest of the region, driving the Turks back over the border. In spite of these efforts, by 1282 a number of independent Turkish emirates had emerged, straddling the border between Byzantium and the Seljuk sultanate. As time went on, the holders of these territories became less and less like vassals of the sultan and more

Figure 15.1 The church of Hagia Sophia, Monemvasia, which may date from the time of Andronikos II's visit in around 1300

and more like local rulers in their own right. For example, Aydınoğlu Mehmed emerged as emir of a swathe of land opposite Philadelphia and his followers were known as the Aydın Turks. Further north, facing Nicaea, was the territory of a certain Osman. His followers were the Osmanlı or Ottoman Turks. To the south were the lands of the Karamanid Turks whose emir was to capture Ikonion in 1316 and finally put an end to the old sultanate.

On his accession, Andronikos II tried a number of measures to stem the encroachments of these emirates. During his three-year stay in Nicaea in 1293 he brought soldiers in from Venetian-ruled Crete and settled them in Asia Minor to provide a permanent defence. Unfortunately, they ended up staging a revolt and proclaiming their commander as emperor. By now the Aydın Turks were starting to occupy the fertile valley of the River Meander, so in 1302, Andronikos decided on a two-pronged offensive. One army, under his son Michael, would go down to southern Asia Minor and strike against the Turks there, while the other would stay in the north and take on the Ottomans. Both armies came to grief. Michael got as far as Magnesia, but there the mercenaries in his army deserted because they had not been paid, and he had to beat an ignominious retreat. The other army clashed with the Ottomans at Bapheus near Nikomedeia in July 1302 and was routed. Andronikos' last bid to retrieve the situation was to hire 6,500 Catalan mercenaries the following year and to unleash them on the invaders. They had some impact, recapturing the town of Cyzicus, but they soon became discontented with the debased coins with which they were being paid. They ended up crossing back to Europe and plundering Byzantine Thrace.

With the defection of the Catalans, the last hope of driving the Turks out of western Asia Minor faded, leaving the invaders free to occupy the countryside and to lay siege to the towns. One by one, those places were forced to surrender as there was no hope of relief from Constantinople. First to go was Ephesus in October 1304, followed by Smyrna in 1329, both of which were incorporated into the Aydın emirate. In the north the Ottomans gradually wore away resistance, taking Prousa in April 1326 and Nicaea in 1331 (see Figure 15.2). Even though the seeds of this disaster had been sown in the days of Michael VIII, Andronikos II and his chief minister Theodore Metochites inevitably got the blame. By 1328, discontent had reached fever-pitch and Andronikos II and Metochites were overthrown and imprisoned.

15.2 Civil war and controversy (1328–1354)

The new emperor was Andronikos' grandson, Andronikos III, and his chief minister was John Kantakouzenos, the future emperor and historian. For a time, it looked as if they might, to some extent, make good the disasters of the previous reign. There was not

Figure 15.2 The Ottoman Green Mosque at Nicaea, now Iznik, built between 1378 and 1392

much that could be done about Asia Minor at present so Andronikos III came to terms with the victorious emirs. In August 1333, he agreed to make an annual payment to the Ottoman emir Orhan who in return promised not to attack the remaining Byzantine footholds on that side of the Sea of Marmara. Two years later, the emperor and his chief minister made a similar treaty with emir Umur of the Aydın Turks who agreed to supply mercenary soldiers for the Byzantine army. Andronikos III then turned westwards and successfully restored Byzantine rule in territories that had seemed lost forever, notably the island of Chios, which was recovered from the Genoese in 1329, Thessaly and the old despotate of Epirus which were reincorporated in 1338.

Unfortunately, in the summer of 1341, Andronikos III died at the age of 45, leaving a nine-year-old son as his successor, John V. The usual council of regency was formed, headed by the boy's mother, Anna of Savoy, and the patriarch John XIV Kalekas, but in October John Kantakouzenos had himself proclaimed emperor by his troops in Thrace and a civil war began. These events were hardly unprecedented in Byzantium but this civil war was different: 'the worst the Romans had ever known', according to John Kantakouzenos. It was to have the effect of bringing the state to its knees and of making its eventual collapse inevitable (see Box 13.1).

What made this war so different was its duration. Usually these contests were over within weeks or months, with the reigning emperor either putting down the challenge or being dethroned. This time the fighting lasted for six years. The opposing armies manoeuvred and circled, towns and villages were captured and lost. Only by 1345 was it clear that Kantakouzenos was gaining the upper hand. Adrianople was taken, giving him a forward base for the march on Constantinople, and in February 1347 he took the city when some of his supporters on the inside managed to open up a hole in the Land Walls and allowed his troops to enter. To his credit, Kantakouzenos made a just settlement with his defeated enemies. Anna of Savoy and young John V Palaiologos did not suffer the fate of John IV Laskaris. Instead it was agreed that John V would marry Kantakouzenos' daughter Helena and would reign as junior emperor with his father-in-law, John VI, for ten years. Thereafter the two emperors would have equal status and John V would be the heir to the throne, succeeding on his father-in-law's death. In the meantime, young John V was to be kept out of the way by being sent to govern Thessalonica.

These generous provisions should have been the basis for a lasting peace, but they were not. Part of the problem was that John VI Kantakouzenos had two sons of his own whom he was cutting out of the succession by making John V Palaiologos his heir. The youngest, Manuel, was provided for by being sent off to be governor of the Byzantine Peloponnese. The elder son, Matthew, however, was left with nothing and he had many supporters who ardently believed that he, and not John V, should succeed his father. As John VI's reign went on, it became clear that the civil war was likely to begin again. In Thessalonica, young John V was growing impatient of his father-in-law's tutelage and was gathering a strong body of support. The emperor did his best to reconcile these competing camps but he only staved off the crisis and by the summer of 1352, John V and Matthew Kantakouzenos were fighting each other in Thrace.

The protracted nature of the civil war had had an unfortunate side effect. When both sides realised that they were not going to achieve a quick victory, they started to look for help from outside the empire's borders. In 1342, Anna of Savoy turned to the tsar of Bulgaria, John Alexander, who crossed into Thrace at her invitation. Around the same time, Kantakouzenos contacted the king of Serbia, Stephen Dushan, and Umur of Aydin, who both came to his aid. In the later stages of the war, Kantakouzenos also received help from the Ottoman emir Orhan who married Kantakouzenos' daughter and sent his son Suleyman with an army across the Dardanelles.

Unfortunately, these allies fought more for themselves than for the regency or for Kantakouzenos. John Alexander took over the town of Philippopolis as the price of his aid and Stephen Dushan helped himself to most of Epirus, Macedonia and Thessaly, the areas retaken in the optimistic years under Andronikos III. The Turks were generally more reliable, although Umur was forced to withdraw from Thrace in 1344 to defend his main port of Smyrna from a Western crusade. The Ottomans fought alongside Kantakouzenos until he captured Constantinople, but they did not then withdraw. During the summer of 1352, Suleyman quietly occupied the small harbour and fortress of Tzympe on the European side of the Sea of Marmara and ignored repeated requests by Kantakouzenos that he should evacuate the town. Even those who were supposedly unaligned in the conflict took advantage, the Genoese seizing back the island of Chios in 1346.

In view of the renewed civil war and loss of territory, it is not surprising that John VI's reign proved short. In late 1354, his son-in-law, John V, sailed to Constantinople with a force of adherents, landed and took possession of the city. After initial resistance, John VI gave up the struggle and abdicated. The Palaiologos dynasty was once more at the helm but of a state that was rapidly approaching shipwreck.

15.3 Urban and rural economy and society

Byzantium's steep decline in the fourteenth century was not just a matter of political weakness and instability: it had economic and social roots as well. There can be no doubt that by 1330 it was no longer the wealthy state that it had been in 1050. The emperor still enjoyed a tax income but his receipts were not on the scale that they once were. The territory he ruled was now much smaller, so inevitably the Land Tax and other levies would not have yielded the sums that they once did (Map 15.1). Customs duties such as the kommerkion were less lucrative as well, partly because an increasing volume of Constantinople's trade was now going through the Genoese colony of Pera. Andronikos II inevitably had to make economies, cutting back on Michael's rebuilding programme and reducing the precious metal content of the gold hyperpyron. More use was made of silver with the new basilikon coin being introduced in around 1300. Most controversially, to avoid the expense of maintaining a fleet, Andronikos decided henceforth to rely solely on the Genoese for naval defence. It is easy to criticise but the emperor probably had little other option.

The civil war of 1341–1347 was to have a disastrous impact on state finances. With Kantakouzenos controlling the provinces, Empress Anna and the regency had to find other sources of income to pay their troops. In 1343, they obtained a loan of 30,000 gold ducats from Venice, providing collateral in the form of the crown jewels. So when Kantakouzenos was crowned as John VI in May 1347, the diadem that was placed on his

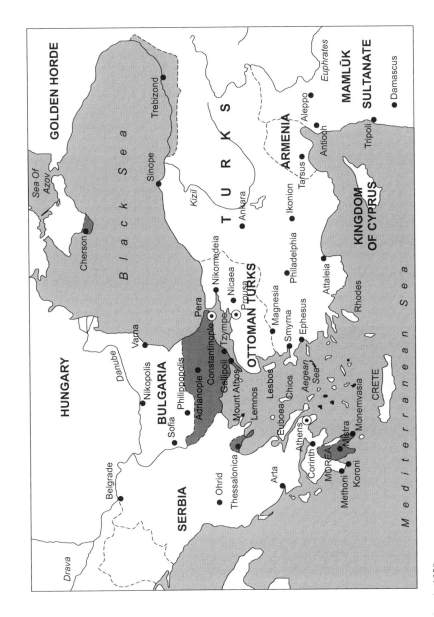

Map 15.1 Byzantium in 1350

head was a fake, adorned with imitation gems made of glass. At the banquet afterwards, the guests were served from pewter and earthenware, for the gold and silver dinner service had gone the way of the jewels. John VI also inherited an empty treasury and the possibilities for refilling it were limited. The Venetian loan was long since spent and was never repaid, while the loss of territory to the Serbs, Genoese and Bulgars meant that tax receipts dwindled still further. The emperor's poverty was now plain for all to see. After 1352, no more gold coins were minted, only increasingly debased silver ones. The churches and buildings of Constantinople, which Michael VIII had worked so hard to restore and maintain, began slowly to crumble.

All this had an impact on the wider population. The loss of territory meant that the only way to increase revenue was to tax the inhabitants of the remaining territories even more heavily, in order to pay for defence and the maintenance of the capital city. Unfortunately, the burden does not seem to have fallen equally across society. The great landowners of Thrace and Macedonia dominated huge tracts of land and in proportion to their wealth made only a tiny contribution to the treasury. The Kantakouzenos family, whose estates in Thrace boasted 5,000 head of cattle and 70,000 sheep, were a good example. Once he was emperor John VI tried to spread the burden by taxing luxuries like wine, but by then resentment had reached boiling point and it had already manifested itself dramatically during the civil war. When the news of John Kantakouzenos' proclamation as emperor was announced in the main square of Adrianople in 1341, the wealthier citizens were delighted. Not so their less affluent neighbours who that evening spilled out onto the streets and began rioting. They targeted the houses of known supporters of Kantakouzenos, ransacking their contents and forcing their owners to flee for their lives. The pattern was repeated all over Thrace and Macedonia. At Thessalonica, when Kantakouzenos arrived with his army to take it over, he found the city gates locked and barred against him. Inside a group of workers and farmers calling themselves the Zealots seized control and proclaimed that they were acting on behalf of Empress Anna and the regency for John V in Constantinople. In fact, they set up a kind of popular government that ruled the city completely independently for seven years. Only in 1350 did John VI finally crush them and restore his authority in Thessalonica.

When it comes to rural life, the fourteenth century is one of the best documented periods, thanks to the archives of Mount Athos, even if they only give us information about one area, Macedonia. One thing is abundantly clear from these surviving documents. The vast majority of peasants who farmed the land no longer owned it themselves, the outcome of a process that had been going on for centuries (see Section 12.2). Referred to as *paroikoi*, they were effectively serfs who tilled fields belonging to some great landowner, either an individual such as Kantakouzenos or a monastery, often one of those on Mount Athos. They had to remit rents, taxes and services to their lord and if the land was sold or transferred, they were transferred with it. They could not leave the service of their lord once they had entered it. There were exceptions, for some individuals still held their land in return for service in the imperial army even if their numbers were probably dwindling. We hear of a man called Michael, who had been a soldier but who was transferred to the monastery of Zographou as a paroikos in the early fourteenth century. Presumably he had fallen on hard times and could not fulfil his obligations anymore. Indeed, that is probably what accounts for the predominance of paroikoi: they were no longer able to carry the tax burden themselves and needed the protection of a lord or monastery to whom the overall tax obligation was transferred. This was a phenomenon that can be observed as early as the tenth century (see Section 7.6).

The move from free to dependent peasants was not necessarily oppressive or socially divisive. The paroikoi had certain rights and legal protections. They were not slaves, they could make wills and they were allowed to pass property to their children. There is no sign of rural unrest to match the upheavals that took place in Byzantine cities during the 1340s and there was certainly nothing like the Jacquerie uprising that convulsed France in 1358 or the English Peasants' Revolt of 1381. On the other hand, both the cities and the countryside suffered badly from the Black Death. The plague had originated in Central Asia and was brought to Constantinople on Genoese ships from the Crimea in the summer of 1347. The epidemic raged for a year, cut a swathe through the population and put all commercial and political activity on hold as people avoided each other for fear of contagion.

Box 15.1 Nikephoros Gregoras on the Black Death (1347)

Gregoras was living in Constantinople when the epidemic struck that summer:

> During that time, a serious and pestilential disease invaded humanity. Starting from Scythia and Maeotis [i.e. Russia] and the mouth of the Tanais [i.e. the River Don], just as spring began, it lasted for that whole year, passing through and destroying, to be exact, only the continental coast, towns as well as country areas, ours and those that are adjacent to ours, up to Gadera and the columns of Hercules [i.e. the Straits of Gibraltar]. During the second year it invaded the Aegean Islands. Then it affected the Rhodians, as well as the Cypriots and those colonising the other islands. The calamity attacked men as well as women, rich and poor, old and young. To put matters simply, it did not spare those of any age or fortune. Several homes were emptied of all their inhabitants in one day or sometimes in two. No one could help anyone else, not even the neighbours, or the family, or blood relations. The calamity did not destroy men only, but many animals living with and domesticated by men. I speak of dogs and horses and all the species of birds, even the rats that happened to live within the walls of the houses. The prominent signs of this disease, signs indicating early death, were tumorous outgrowths at the roots of thighs and arms and simultaneously bleeding ulcerations, which, sometimes the same day, carried the infected rapidly out of this present life, sitting or walking.

Even though Gregoras was an eyewitness, there is little in the way of personal experience recounted here. Many of the points he makes can be found in an account of the plague that raged in Athens in 430 BCE, written by the ancient Greek historian Thucydides: the origin of the epidemic, the inefficacy of treatment, the effect on animals and a description of symptoms are all there too. Even in the

most desperate circumstances, an educated Byzantine like Gregoras could not neglect his classical models.

Source: Christos S. Bartsocas, 'Two fourteenth-century Greek descriptions of the Black
Death', *Journal of the History of Medicine and Allied Sciences* 21 (1966), pp. 394–400, at 395
(reproduced by kind permission of Oxford University Press).

It perhaps goes without saying that life in fourteenth-century Byzantium was not
uniformly grim. There were always people and places that bucked the trend.
Constantinople and Thrace might have been impoverished and ravaged by civil war but
the Peloponnese had escaped largely unscathed. Although cut off from Constantinople by
Ottoman territory, the province was prosperous thanks to its natural fertility. It produced
grain, wax, honey, raisins, wine, raw silk and olive oil, and the surplus could be sold to
the Venetians through their enclaves of Methoni and Koroni, from where it was exported
to the West. Here the Byzantine empire was expanding rather than contracting as the
governors of Mistra slowly chipped away at the principality of Achaia. By 1430, most of
the peninsula was again under Byzantine rule (see Figure 15.3).

Even in crumbling Constantinople, some people were doing very well in the late
fourteenth and early fifteenth centuries. The city's international entrepôt trade
continued to flourish (see Section 7.1). Indeed, if anything it was probably busier than
ever before with the Black Sea trade having been developed by the Venetians and

Figure 15.3 The palace at Mistra, headquarters of the governor or despot

Genoese. As noted above, much of the traffic now went through Pera and the emperor's treasury drew little benefit, but individual Byzantine entrepreneurs were able to exploit it to great advantage. Anyone could buy a stake in a cargo, contributing to the cost of the goods and the provisioning of the Venetian or Genoese ship, and then taking a percentage of the profits when the voyage came to an end. Another route to wealth was through retail sales, buying imported goods such as cloth from Italian shippers and then selling it on at a considerable mark up. Advantage could also be taken of the Italian banking system by depositing funds with a commission agent who would then invest it and provide a return.

By these means some late Byzantine merchant houses acquired huge fortunes. One of them was the Notaras family, who moved from Monemvasia to Constantinople in the middle of the fourteenth century, probably to take advantage of the opportunities there. They made an immense fortune by buying and selling large quantities of grain through the Genoese colony of Pera and by 1420 the head of the family, Nicholas Notaras, was one of the richest men in Constantinople and he commanded far greater resources than the emperor did. To their credit, men like Notaras often used their money to step in where the impoverished emperor no longer could, raising loans on his behalf to pay the troops and funding vital repairs to the Land Walls.

At the end of the day though, neither the fertility of the Peloponnese nor the wealth of some Byzantine families could mitigate the inescapable fact that by the mid-fourteenth century, the Byzantine empire was finished. Its ruler had lost most of his land and was bankrupt. It was now merely a question of who was going to take over what was left of it. The Venetians were considering doing so, as was Stephen Dushan of Serbia. In the spring of 1346, Stephen had himself crowned as 'tsar of the Serbs and the Greeks', revealing his ambition to amalgamate Byzantium with his own realm to create a new Orthodox empire. As it turned out, it was neither Venice nor Serbia that filled the vacuum, but another power that had scarcely been noticed.

15.4 The descent into vassaldom (1354–1394)

In March 1354, there was a powerful earthquake in Byzantine Thrace which severely shook the towns in the region. At the port of Gallipoli on the Dardanelles, the tremors were so violent that they brought down the defensive walls and the damage must have been clearly visible from Ottoman territory on the opposite side of the strait. Emir Orhan was an ally and son-in-law of Emperor John VI but he could not resist such an opportunity. He instructed his son Suleyman to cross over and occupy the town. In this way, the Ottomans acquired a strategic bridgehead in Europe and in the years that followed they began to conquer the land round about. At some point during the 1360s they moved into Thrace and captured Adrianople. Lying at the confluence of the Maritsa and Tundzha rivers, Adrianople gave the Ottomans a commanding position in Thrace and effectively cut Constantinople off by land from Thessalonica.

One might well ask how the Ottomans were able to move into Byzantine Thrace almost unopposed. It was not just that Byzantium was weakened and exhausted by the long civil war. Neighbouring Bulgaria was going through its own period of internal turbulence and was in no position to intervene. So all that Emperor John V could do was watch events unfold from behind the Land Walls of Constantinople and take comfort in the thought that there was no direct threat to the city at this point. The Ottomans wisely did not even attempt to probe its formidable defences but concentrated on subduing the countryside. One of John V's courtiers believed that there was an alternative course of action to that of merely looking on helplessly. Demetrius Kydones had learned Latin back in the 1340s, in order to deal better with papal envoys, and in the process had become a fervent admirer of Western culture. Now as the Muslim Ottomans fanned out into Thrace, he made an impassioned speech before the emperor and the court in which he urged his audience to seek help from their fellow Christians in the West. Not everyone was impressed by his arguments. Bitter memories of 1204 had not been softened by the passage of time and the issues of the schism were as acute as they had ever been. Moreover, in recent years another fissure had opened up over the spiritual practices known as Hesychasm. By the fourteenth century many monks of Mount Athos were practising mystical prayer and claiming as a result to have experienced visions of the emanations of God. For intellectuals like Kydones and Nikephoros Gregoras such practices seemed irrational and dangerous, but after 1347 they were officially recognised by the Byzantine Church. Supporters of Hesychasm tended to be suspicious of any dialogue with the West, so that the schism between the Orthodox and Latin Churches was mirrored by a division within Byzantine society.

Luckily for Kydones, Emperor John V came to see the virtue of his arguments. After all, John's mother, Anna of Savoy, had been a Latin and it was a member of her family who was to give the Byzantines a demonstration of just how effective Western help might be. In August 1366, John V's cousin, Count Amedeo VI of Savoy, sailed into the Dardanelles, recaptured Gallipoli and handed the city back to the Byzantines. Once in Constantinople, Amedeo persuaded John that he should go in person to Rome to discuss the schism and the Ottoman threat with the pope. The visit took place in 1369, when John V knelt at the feet at the pope, declared himself willing to accept the faith as taught by Rome and then heard Mass. Mindful of the reaction to the Union of Lyon in 1274, John was careful to stress that his submission was a personal one only and he made no promises on behalf of his Church and people as a whole. Nevertheless, the pope accepted the submission and began urging Western princes to take up arms against the Turks (see Box 13.2). For a moment, it looked as if the policy advocated by Kydones had worked.

Unfortunately, the pope's pleas went largely unheeded. In the same year that John V visited Rome, the Hundred Years War between the kings of England and France had resumed, ruling out their participation in any anti-Ottoman crusade. In the years that followed, further conflicts distracted the powers of the West. In 1378, war broke out between Venice and Genoa and the papacy itself became divided by the Great Schism, with one pope in Rome and another in Avignon. So when John V arrived back in Constantinople on October 1371, he had nothing to show for his efforts and the situation in the Balkans had taken a turn for the worse in his absence. Serbia, which under Stephen Dushan had become a major power in the region, had initially done nothing to oppose Ottoman expansion into Thrace. That was largely because after Stephan Dushan had died in 1355, his successors had had increasing difficulty holding together the enlarged realm that he had created during the Byzantine civil war. Only in September 1371 did Tsar Vukashin march west against Emir Murad I, but when the Serbs clashed with the Ottomans at the battle of Maritsa in September 1371, Vukashin was killed and his army was almost completely wiped out. The military option had thus failed as comprehensively as Kydones' policy of appealing to the West.

It was the Ottoman emir Murad I who offered John V a way out of the apparently hopeless situation. He let the emperor know that if he became the emir's vassal, paid an annual tribute and provided a contingent of troops for the Ottoman army when required to do so, the emir would confirm the emperor in possession of those lands that remained to him and would make no attempt to seize Constantinople. In 1372, John accepted those terms and other Christian rulers in the region soon followed suit. Generally Murad remained true to his word and for the next 20 years, Constantinople was left in peace.

Nevertheless, there were strains in the Byzantine–Ottoman relationship caused by the behaviour of John V's sons, Andronikos and Manuel. Andronikos staged a revolt against his father in 1376, capturing Constantinople with the help of Ottoman troops provided by the opportunistic Murad. As a reward for this assistance, Andronikos handed back Gallipoli which the Ottomans had lost to Amedeo of Savoy in 1366. Three years later, John recaptured Constantinople with the help of Andronikos' younger sibling, Manuel, but Gallipoli remained in Ottoman hands. Then the emperor managed to fall out with Manuel as well. His younger son deeply disagreed with John's acceptance of Ottoman overlordship, so in 1382 he took himself off to Thessalonica to organise resistance. His bold gesture of defiance was unavailing as it merely provoked the emir into taking over Thessalonica in 1387. A chastened Manuel had to make amends by leading a contingent in the Ottoman army until the death of his father in 1391 brought him to the throne as Manuel II.

Box 15.2 A Byzantine prince appeals to Venice (1385)

Holed up in Thessalonica and short of resources with which to fight the Ottomans, John V's son Manuel sent an envoy to Venice to appeal for help. In this passage, the Venetian senate gives its response, referring to Manuel as emperor even though he had not yet succeeded his father.

An envoy of the Lord Emperor Manuel appeared in the presence of our government with his letters of accreditation. After conveying the greetings of the said emperor, he explained that it might be pleasing to our government to favour him in his urgent need with two horse-transporting galleys, two hundred suits of armour, 20,000 arrows and seventy crossbows to be paid for in three months' time. The envoy says that the cost of all these things will be paid to us on Negroponte [i.e. Euboea]. He also enquired whether we would be prepared to help him by way of a loan of 6,000 ducats, or whatever sum seemed appropriate to our government, for which the Lord Emperor would be happy to give us some of his territory and castles as collateral. He also asked whether there might be an alliance between our fleet at Negroponte and his fleet, so that our fleet could go to the assistance of his territories and in the same way his could come to help the island of Negroponte ... The emperor also desires that, because of the upheavals and the war that he has with the emir [Murad I], we might like to arbitrate between him and the emir so that peace can follow.

As regards the first request, the concession of two horse-transporting galleys, the two hundred suits of armour and the twenty thousand arrows, the answer is that we are always happy to accommodate the aforesaid Lord Emperor in so far as is possible. In reality, it could happen that if these galleys, arms and arrows were conveyed to Negroponte and then turned out not to be needed by the emperor, they would remain in our hands to our great loss. If, however, the Lord Emperor would be so good as to send the money for these articles to Venice, we will gladly and swiftly supply him. We are completely unable to supply him with crossbows because this year we are committed to equipping numerous galleys and to other demanding projects of ours, so that accordingly he must accept our apologies. As regards the second request, for a loan of 6,000 ducats or whatever sum seems right to our government, the response is that the envoy does not have authority to receive such a sum nor to pledge any of the emperor's territory as collateral. However, when the emperor sends full authorisation and when some of his lands are given over to us, as his envoy says, then we will do whatever we can ... On the [final] point that we should arbitrate between the said Lord Emperor and the emir, as God knows we greatly desire the Lord Emperor's complete peace and happy situation and on this account let us perhaps send our envoy to those parts and do every advantageous thing that we can.

The response makes an interesting contrast to Pope Urban II's reaction to Alexios I's appeal in 1095. The senate saw little reason to support this Christian prince against his Muslim enemy. They did not absolutely decline to provide weapons and a loan but only for cash and collateral up front. Their main concern was to bring to an end a conflict that was likely to be bad for trade.

Source: Julian Chrysostomides, *Monumenta Peloponnesiaca: Documents for the Study of the Peloponnese in the 14th and 15th Centuries* (Camberley: Porphyrogenitus, 1995), No. 28, pp. 60–1.

15.5 The last phase (1394–1453)

The uneasy period of vassalage came to an end in 1389 when Emir Murad I was killed while fighting the Serbs at Kosovo. His successor, Bayezid I, adopted the more exalted title of sultan and with it a more aggressive and expansionist policy. In 1393, he annexed Bulgaria and the following year he demanded the surrender of Constantinople. Manuel II refused, so Bayezid surrounded the city with a view to starving it into submission. This dramatic turn of events had the effect of finally galvanising Western opinion and in 1396 a Hungarian, French and Burgundian crusade crossed the Danube to relieve Constantinople. It only got as far as Nikopolis in Bulgaria where Bayezid, who had marched up from Constantinople in record time, routed it and sent those of its commanders who escaped fleeing to the Danube to be picked up by Venetian ships. The defeat was a bitter disappointment for Emperor Manuel but it did give cause to hope that further Western help might be forthcoming. He therefore decided to revive the pre-1372 policy of seeking Western help and in 1399, he left Constantinople by ship for Italy. He did not visit Rome, or make any promises about ending the schism, but instead toured the cities of northern Italy before moving on to Paris and then London. While he was sympathetically received everywhere, it soon became clear that sympathy was unlikely to translate into action. Then, while Manuel was still in Paris in late 1402, news arrived that the siege of Constantinople was over: Bayezid had been defeated and captured at Ankara by Timur, the ruler of Samarkand, and the Ottoman empire had descended into civil war.

Following this unexpected turn of events, Bayezid's eldest son, Suleyman, keen to fight for the throne against his brothers, made peace with the emperor in 1403, dropped the demands for troops and an annual tribute and returned Thessalonica to him. This treaty gave Byzantium several more decades of shadowy existence. During that time, Manuel II pursued a double-headed policy. On the one hand, well aware that the disunity among the Ottomans might not last, he continued to appeal to the West for help against the common Muslim enemy. At the same time, he manipulated the internal divisions among the Ottomans to keep them disunited for as long as possible. There was plenty of opportunity for the latter since the Ottomans had no rule that the eldest son was the legal successor to the throne. Any son of a reigning sultan, whether born of a wife or a concubine, could succeed and given that the sultans had large harems there were no shortage of candidates. So the Byzantines did well out of the civil war between Bayezid's sons, by backing one claimant against another. Even after it ended in 1413, they continued to harbour and encourage the reigning sultan's rivals. The risk with the strategy was that they might back the wrong candidate, as in 1422 when they supported Bayezid's nephew Mustafa against his grandson Sultan Murad II. When Murad had disposed of the challenge he laid siege to Constantinople, although once again the Land Walls held firm. Instead, the frustrated sultan concentrated his efforts on Thessalonica which he captured in 1430.

By then it was clear that the Ottomans had recovered from their defeat by Timur while Byzantium was now reduced to little more than the city of Constantinople and the Peloponnese. So on his accession in 1425, Manuel II's son John VIII took the decision to increase the likelihood of Western help by offering to end the schism between the Churches. In 1438, a large Byzantine delegation, headed by John himself, travelled to Italy to attend a Church council first at Ferrara and then at Florence. After protracted debate, the Union of the Churches was proclaimed on 6 July 1439 with the Byzantines agreeing to recognise papal authority and to accept the filioque in the Latin Creed. As in the case of the Union of Lyon in 1274, the agreement provoked bitter opposition in Constantinople but it did lead to the despatch of military assistance. In 1443, a combined Hungarian and Serbian force crossed the Danube into Ottoman territory and came close to capturing Adrianople. Had the crusade not been crushed by Murad II at Varna in November 1444, more Byzantines might have been prepared to accept the Union of Florence. As it was, the disaster seemed to suggest that it was not worth compromising on matters of faith.

What happened at Varna in 1444 might also explain why Murad II's son and successor, Sultan Mehmed II, made plans to attack Constantinople very soon after his accession in 1451. The initial success of the crusade had highlighted the vulnerability of the Ottomans. Not only were they a Muslim minority in the overwhelmingly Christian Balkans, but their dominions were split on either side of the Bosporus and Dardanelles straits. Murad II had been caught on the wrong side of the Bosporus in 1444 and had to fight his way across in the face of opposition from a Christian fleet. That was the reason given by Mehmed for his construction of a castle of the Bosporus, known as Rumeli Hisar, in the summer of 1452. The following spring, he mounted an attack on Constantinople itself, deploying two weapons that Bayezid had lacked in 1394: a large fleet to blockade the city by sea and a number of cannon that could hurl a stone large enough to have a significant impact on the Land Walls (see Figure 15.4). It was these advantages that enabled him to storm and capture the city after a siege of only six weeks when others had invested it for years without success. With his victory, Byzantium's wraith-like existence of the past hundred years came to an end.

Points to remember

- Andronikos II cannot take all the blame for Byzantium's weakness after 1282 as the situation in Asia Minor had already begun to deteriorate under Michael VIII.

Figure 15.4 Ottoman bronze cannon at Fort Nelson, near Portsmouth, England. It was cast in 1464 and is probably similar to types used in the siege of Constantinople

- Following the civil war of 1341–1347, Byzantium was effectively finished and it was merely a question of which of its neighbours would absorb what was left.
- Even though Byzantium declined politically in these years, Constantinople remained an important trading hub and some of its citizens were very wealthy.
- The Peloponnese also remained relatively prosperous and most of the area had been reconquered from the Latins by 1430.
- It was a number of unforeseen events, especially the Ottoman defeat at Ankara in 1402, that allowed Byzantium to linger on in a much-reduced form until 1453.

Suggestions for further reading

Barker, John W. (1969), *Manuel II Palaeologus (1391–1425): A Study in Late Byzantine Statesmanship* (New Brunswick NJ: Rutgers University Press). A detailed study of Manuel's career including his time in Thessalonica before he became emperor and his travels in the West.

Harris, Jonathan. (2010), *The End of Byzantium* (New Haven CT and London: Yale University Press). Concentrates on Byzantium's last years between 1402 and 1453 and the complicated factors that allowed it to linger on for so long.

Laiou, Angeliki E. (1972), *Constantinople and the Latins: The Foreign Policy of Andronicus II, 1282–1328* (Cambridge MA: Harvard University Press). As the title suggests, this book concentrates on Andronikos II's relations with the West, but it is the most detailed and scholarly account of his reign in English.

Laiou, Angeliki E. (1977), *Peasant Society in the Late Byzantine Empire: A Social and Demographic Study* (Princeton NJ: Princeton University Press). Needs to be read in conjunction with the more up-to-date Bartusis (see Section 11.1) but contains numerous detailed examples drawn from the archives of Mount Athos.

Necipoğlu, Nevra. (2009), *Byzantium between the Latins and the Ottomans: Politics and Society in the Late Empire* (Cambridge: Cambridge University Press). Analyses late Byzantine attitudes to both Ottomans and Latins and asks why the pro-Latin stance of the emperors ultimately failed to deliver any effective help.

16 Conclusion

Byzantium's legacy

The fall of Constantinople on 29 May 1453 is the obvious point at which to end the long history of Byzantium. Emperor Constantine XI, a younger son of Manuel II, who died in the fighting on the Land Walls was the last in the long line that stretched back to Maurice and from there to Augustus (see Figure 16.1). The Palaiologos family did not die out with him, for his two

Figure 16.1 Colossal statue of Constantine XI at Paleo Faliro, Athens, which reflects the emperor's current status as a Greek national hero

brothers, Demetrius and Thomas, still ruled in the Peloponnese but neither of them was ever recognised as emperor. That enclave was invaded by Mehmed II in 1460. Demetrius surrendered and handed over the castle at Mistra, while Thomas fled to Rome. The last outpost to fall to the Ottomans was Trebizond in August 1461, but that had been an independent state since 1204. All the lands that had once been Byzantine were now incorporated into the Ottoman empire with the exception of those which, like Crete, were still under Venetian or Latin rule.

Not everything was lost. There was some continuity in Byzantium's political tradition thanks to the marriage of Constantine XI's niece Zoe to Grand Duke Ivan III of Moscow in 1472. The match greatly enhanced Ivan's status, allowing him to adopt as his emblem the double-headed eagle of the Palaiologos family. His successors took the title of tsar and regarded their capital of Moscow as a third Rome, replacing fallen Constantinople as the centre of Orthodox Christianity. Ancient Greek literature, which had been so assiduously preserved, studied and imitated by generations of Byzantine intellectuals, survived too. In the sack of Constantinople in 1453, many priceless manuscripts were destroyed but many were saved. Some ended up in the library of Sultan Mehmed II and others were shipped to Italy where they were eagerly read, copied and translated by Renaissance humanists and provided the texts for the first printed editions in the early 1500s.

The Byzantine Church was another piece of salvage from the wreck. This was partly because the Ottomans knew that it was in their interest for the schism to continue as that would discourage any hope among the vanquished Byzantines for help from the West. In

Figure 16.2 St Bartholomew's Episcopal church, New York, built in 1914–1919 to the design of Bertram Good-
   hue (1869–1924)

1484, the patriarch of Constantinople officially abrogated the Union of Florence and so ensured that the Orthodox Churches of Serbia, Bulgaria, Romania and Russia remained distinct from the Catholic Church of Rome. Lastly, Byzantium has left a visible legacy too. Hagia Sophia still stands in modern Istanbul and other examples of Byzantine architecture can be found all over Turkey, Greece and the Balkans. Their distinct style still influences the design of Orthodox churches and cathedrals, but can also be discerned in churches of other denominations and in buildings that have no religious purpose at all (see Figure 16.2). It is a rather understated and hidden legacy for a society that once considered itself to be the centre of the Christian world.

Suggestions for further reading

Bullen, J.B. (2003), *Byzantium Rediscovered* (London and New York: Phaidon Press). Uses copious illustrations to show how elements of Byzantine art and architecture inspired European and American architects in the nineteenth and twentieth centuries.

Harris, Jonathan. (1995), *Greek Emigres in the West, 1400–1520* (Camberley: Porphyrogenitus). Traces the refugees who headed west after the fall of Constantinople.

Papademetriou, Tom. (2015), *Render Unto the Sultan: Power, Authority and the Greek Orthodox Church in the Early Ottoman Centuries* (Oxford: Oxford University Press). Covers the relationship of the Byzantine Church with its new Ottoman overlords.

Wilson, N.G. (1992), *From Byzantium to Italy: Greek Studies in the Italian Renaissance* (London: Duckworth). Shows how the surviving texts of ancient Greek literature reached Italy and how they were read and understood.

Glossary

allelengyon tax paid collectively by villages

Attic the form of Greek used by Athenian authors of the fifth and fourth centuries BCE

Basileus literally 'king' but the word used by the Byzantines for their emperor

Common Greek see Koine

defensores troops in close order who supported assault troops

Demotic Greek spoken today which was already developing in twelfth-century Byzantium

domestic of the Scholai army commander

dromon swift warship of the Byzantine fleet

filioque literally 'and from the Son', a word added to the Latin version of the Creed

follis (plural: folleis) copper coin

fresco wall painting where the paint is applied to wet plaster

hagiography biography of a saint

hyperpyron (plural: hyperpyra) gold coin issued after 1092

iconoclast opponent of the practice of venerating holy images

iconophile (or iconodule) supporter of icon veneration

kataphract heavily armoured cavalryman

Koine Greek language of the New Testament

kommerkion customs duty levied in Byzantine ports

Latins generic term used by the Byzantines for Western European Christians

magistros high-ranking official title

menavlatos (plural: menavlatoi) soldier armed with a menavlion, a short spear

Miaphysite see Monophysite

miliaresion (plural: miliaresia) silver coin

minuscule Greek script used after c.800 CE

Monophysite believer in the single, divine nature of Christ

mosaic wall decoration where the image is made up of hundreds of marble cubes

nomisma (plural: nomismata) gold coin issued before 1092

paroikos (plural: paroikoi) a dependent peasant who farmed the land of his lord

parrhesia literally 'access', the perceived close relationship between the holy man and God

patrikios high-ranking official title

pronoia grants of land which may have carried a requirement for military service

schism disagreement between two parts of the Christian Church

strategos the governor of a Theme and the commander of its army

tagma (plural: tagmata)   regiments under the direct command of the emperor

Theme   province of the Byzantine empire with its own army

topos   standard and unvarying literary description

typikon   foundation charter of a monastery

uncial   Greek script from c.800 CE composed of unconnected capital letters

List of Emperors

Emperors of Byzantium, 582–1453

582–602   Maurice
602–610   Phokas
610–641   Herakleios
641   Constantine III
641   Heraklonas
641–668   Constans II
668–685   Constantine IV
685–695   Justinian II
695–698   Leontios
698–705   Tiberios III Apsimar
705–711   Justinian II (again)
711–713   Philippikos
713–715   Anastasius II
715–717   Theodosius III
717–741   Leo III
741–775   Constantine V
775–780   Leo IV
780–797   Constantine VI
797–802   Irene
802–811   Nikephoros I
811   Staurakios
811–813   Michael I Rangabe
813–820   Leo V
820–829   Michael II
829–842   Theophilos
842–867   Michael III
867–886   Basil I
886–912   Leo VI
912–913   Alexander
913–920   Regency for Constantine VII
920–944   Romanos I Lekapenos
945–959   Constantine VII
959–963   Romanos II
963–969   Nikephoros II Phokas

969–976   John I Tzimiskes
976–1025   Basil II
1025–1028   Constantine VIII
1028–1034   Romanos IV Argyros
1034–1041   Michael IV
1041–1042   Michael V
1042   Zoe and Theodora
1042–1055   Constantine IX Monomachos
1055–1056   Theodora (again)
1056–1057   Michael VI
1057–1059   Isaac I Komnenos
1059–1067   Constantine X Doukas
1068–1071   Romanos IV Diogenes
1071–1078   Michael VII Doukas
1078–1081   Nikephoros III Botaneiates
1081–1118   Alexios I Komnenos
1118–1143   John II Komnenos
1143–1180   Manuel I Komnenos
1180–1183   Alexios II Komnenos
1183–1185   Andronikos I Komnenos
1185–1195   Isaac II Angelos
1195–1203   Alexios III Angelos
1203–1204   Isaac II (again) and Alexios IV Angelos
1204   Alexios V Mourtzouphlos

Latin Emperors

1204–1205   Baldwin I
1206–1216   Henry
1217   Peter of Courtenay
1221–1228   Robert of Courtenay
1228–1237   John of Brienne (regent for Baldwin II)
1228–1261   Baldwin II

Emperors of Nicaea

1208–1221   Theodore I Laskaris
1221–1254   John III Vatatzes
1254–1258   Theodore II Laskaris
1258–1261   John IV Laskaris

1259–1282   Michael VIII Palaiologos
1282–1328   Andronikos II Palaiologos
1328–1341   Andronikos III Palaiologos
1341–1347   Regency for John V
1347–1354   John VI Kantakouzenos
1354–1391   John V Palaiologos
1391–1425   Manuel II Palaiologos
1425–1448   John VIII Palaiologos
1449–1453   Constantine XI Palaiologos

Timeline

	Political events	Cultural and religious developments	Islamic world	Italy and the West
600	602: Overthrow of Maurice 610: Accession of Herakleios 626: Persian and Avar siege of Constantinople 627: Byzantine victory at Ninevah c.674: First Arab siege of Constantinople begins	638: Introduction of doctrine of Monotheletism 641: Pope John IV condemns Monotheletism 681: Sixth Ecumenical Council	632: Death of Muhammad 634: Beginning of Arab invasion of Byzantine eastern provinces 642: Arab capture of Alexandria 661: Beginning of Umayyad caliphate	624: End of Byzantine enclave in southern Spain 653: Abduction of Pope Martin I 663: Arrival of Constans II in Italy 698: Fall of Carthage to the Arabs
700	717: Second Arab siege of Constantinople begins 740: Battle of Akroinon 763: Defeat of the Bulgars at Anchialos 775: Death of Constantine V 797: Irene becomes sole empress	726: Probable initiation of policy of iconoclasm 731: Papal synod condemns iconoclasm 754: Council of Hieria 787: Seventh Ecumenical Council	750: Beginning of Abbasid caliphate 786: Accession of Caliph Harun al-Raschid	732: Arab invasion of France halted at Poitiers 751: Lombard conquest of Ravenna 755: Pepin's invasion of Italy 774: Charlemagne's annexation of the Lombard kingdom.
800	811: Defeat and death of Nikephoros I 865: Boris of Bulgaria adopts Christianity 863: Byzantine victory over the Arabs at Poson 867: Usurpation of Basil I, beginning of Macedonian dynasty	c.800: Introduction of minuscule script c.815: Completion of chronicle of Theophanes Confessor 867: Photian Schism	838: Abbasids capture Amorion 869: Beginning of decline of the Abbasid caliphate	800: Coronation of Charlemagne 878: Fall of Syracuse to Arabs 885: Nikephoros Phokas restores Byzantine rule in southern Italy
900	917: Symeon of Bulgaria's victory at Anchialos 919: Romanos Lekapenos seizes power 927: Treaty between Byzantium and Bulgaria 945: Constantine VII becomes sole emperor	920s: Construction of the Myrelaion monastery 989: Conversion of Vladimir of Kiev	944: Establishment of Hamdanids in Aleppo 969: Fatimids take over Egypt and Syria	962: Otto I crowned Emperor of the Romans 972: Marriage alliance between John I Tzimiskes and Otto I
1000	1025: Death of Basil II 1056: End of the Macedonian dynasty 1071: Battle of Manzikert 1081: Accession of Alexios I and the Komnenos dynasty 1091: Victory of Alexios I over Pechenegs	c.1050: Completion of St George in Mangana 1054: Papal legates excommunicate the patriarch of Constantinople c.1077: Completion of Psellos' *Chronographia*	1001: Truce between Byzantium and Fatimid caliphate 1055: Sultan Tughrul takes Baghdad 1099: Capture of Jerusalem by the First Crusade	1066: Beginning of Norman conquest of England 1071: Norman capture of Bari ends Byzantine rule in Italy 1095: Launch of the First Crusade

(Continued)

	Political events	Cultural and religious developments	Islamic world	Italy and the West
1100	1107: Bohemond lands in the Balkans 1180: Death of Manuel I Komnenos 1185: Accession of Isaac II and Angelos dynasty 1195: Alexios III Angelos seizes power	1136: Foundation of the Pantokrator monastery c.1145: Completion of Anna Komnene's *Alexiad* 1152: Foundation of the Kosmosoteira monastery	1144: Zengi captures Edessa 1174: Saladin becomes sultan of Egypt and Syria 1187: Saladin recaptures Jerusalem	1145: Launch of Second Crusade 1187: Launch of Third Crusade 1198: Launch of Fourth Crusade
1200	1204: Fourth Crusade captures Constantinople; establishment of Latin empire 1208: Theodore Laskaris crowned at Nicaea 1259: Usurpation of Michael VIII & beginning of Palaiologos dynasty 1261: Recapture of Constantinople by Michael VIII Palaiologos	c.1212: Completion of Choniates' *Chronological Narrative* 1274: Council of Lyon c.1275: Completion of George Akropolites' *History*	1243: Seljuks of Ikonion defeated by Mongols. 1268: Mamluk capture of Antioch. 1291: Mamluk capture of Acre, end of the kingdom of Jerusalem.	1265: Charles of Anjou proclaimed king of Sicily 1267: Treaty of Viterbo 1282: Sicilian Vespers and Aragonese invasion of Sicily.
1300	1341: Death of Andronikos III, beginning of civil war 1347: John VI Kantakouzenos captures Constantinople 1394: Ottoman Sultan Bayezid I lays siege to Constantinople	1310: End of the Arsenite Schism 1316: Work begins to restore the Chora monastery 1369: John V's submission to the Pope	1316: End of Seljuk sultanate at Ikonion 1354: Ottoman Conquest of Gallipoli 1387: Ottoman conquest of Thessalonica	1337: Beginning of Hundred Years War between England and France. 1378: Beginning of papal schism between Rome and Avignon 1396: Launch of the Crusade of Nikopolis
1400	1403: Byzantine treaty with Suleyman 1453: Fall of Constantinople to the Ottoman Turks 1460: Fall of Mistra 1461: Ottoman conquest of Trebizond	1439: Union of Florence between the Byzantine and Western Churches c.1478· Completion of George Sphrantzes' *Chronicon Minus*	1402: Ottoman defeat at Ankara 1444: Defeat of the crusade of Varna 1451: Accession of Ottoman Sultan Mehmed II	1400: Emperor Manuel II visits Italy, Paris and London 1453: Pope Nicholas V calls for a crusade to recover Constantinople

Weblinks

Byzantium 1200, a site that recreates Constantinople as it was in the year 1200: www.byzantium1200.com

Byzantium and the First Crusade: Three Avenues of Approach: www.publicacions.ub.edu/revistes/estudiosBizantinos02/default.asp?articulo= 1024&modo=resumen

Dumbarton Oaks Byzantine Manuscript Collection: www.doaks.org/resources/manuscripts-in-the-byzantine-collection

Dumbarton Oaks Online Catalogue of Byzantine Seals: www.doaks.org/resources/seals

Internet History Sourcebook for Byzantium: https://sourcebooks.fordham.edu/byzantium/index.asp

Machines Time Forgot: Greek Fire (Windfall Films) www.youtube.com/watch?v=u8fWxc_m8P4

Prosopography of the Byzantine World, a site that allows you to access biographical information on Byzantines living between 1025 and 1180: http://pbw2016.kdl.kcl.ac.uk

Bibliography of secondary literature

Introduction: reference works

Harris, Jonathan. (2005), *Palgrave Advances: Byzantine History* (Basingstoke and New York: Palgrave Macmillan).
James, Liz. (2010), *A Companion to Byzantium* (Chichester: Wiley-Blackwell).
Jeffreys, Elizabeth, Haldon, John F. and Cormack, Robin. (2010), *The Oxford Handbook of Byzantine Studies* (Oxford: Oxford University Press).
Kazhdan, Alexander P. and Talbot, Alice-Mary. (1991), *Oxford Dictionary of Byzantium*, 3 vols (Oxford: Oxford University Press).
Stephenson, Paul. (2010), *The Byzantine World* (London: Routledge).

Introduction: background on the period 300–602 (Late Antiquity)

Cameron, Averil. (1993), *The Mediterranean World in Late Antiquity, AD 395–600* (London and New York: Routledge).
Mitchell, Stephen. (2006), *A History of the Later Roman Empire* (Oxford: Blackwell).

Introduction: general histories of the period 602–1453

Cameron, Averil. (2006), *The Byzantines* (Oxford: Blackwell).
Gregory, Timothy E. (2010, 2nd revised edition), *A History of Byzantium* (Oxford and Malden MA: Blackwell).
Harris, Jonathan. (2015), *The Lost World of Byzantium* (New Haven CT and London: Yale University Press).
Herrin, Judith. (2007), *Byzantium: The Surprising Life of a Medieval Empire* (London: Penguin).
Mango, Cyril. (2002), *The Oxford History of Byzantium* (Oxford: Oxford University Press).
Shepard, Jonathan. (2008), *The Cambridge History of the Byzantine Empire c.500–1492* (Cambridge: Cambridge University Press).
Stathakopoulos, Dionysios. (2014), *A Short History of the Byzantine Empire* (London: I.B. Tauris).
Treadgold, Warren. (1997), *A History of the Byzantine State and Society* (Stanford CA: Stanford University Press).
Treadgold, Warren. (2001), *A Concise History of Byzantium* (Basingstoke and New York: Palgrave Macmillan).

The development of Byzantine studies

Savvides, Alexios G.C. (2018), *The Beginnings and Foundation of Byzantine Studies: A Survey. With a Bibliographical Appendix* (Athens: Herodotos).

1 Major literary sources for the period 602–820

Alexander, Paul J. (1958), *The Patriarch Nicephorus of Constantinople: Ecclesiastical Policy and Image Worship in the Byzantine Empire* (Oxford: Oxford University Press).
Chatzelis, Georgios. (2019), *Byzantine Military Manuals as Literary Works and Practical Handbooks: The Case of the Tenth-Century Sylloge Tacticorum* (London and New York: Routledge).

Efthymiadis, Stephanos. (2014), *Ashgate Research Companion to Byzantine Hagiography* (Farnham and Burlington VT: Ashgate).

Kaldellis, Anthony and Siniossoglou, Niketas. (2017), *The Cambridge Intellectual History of Byzantium* (Cambridge: Cambridge University Press).

Treadgold, Warren. (2007), *The Early Byzantine Historians* (Basingstoke and New York: Palgrave Macmillan).

Watts, Edward J. (2007), *City and School in Late Antique Athens and Alexandria* (Berkeley CA: University of California Press).

Whitby, Michael. (1988), *The Emperor Maurice and His Historian: Theophylact Simocatta on Persian and Balkan Warfare* (Oxford: Oxford University Press).

2 Herakleios and the wars of survival (602–642)

Butler, Alfred J. (1978, 2nd revised edition), *The Arab Conquest of Egypt and the Last Thirty Years of the Roman Dominion* (Oxford: Oxford University Press).

Reinink, Gerrit J. and Stolte, Bernard H. (2002), *The Reign of Heraclius (610–641): Crisis and Confrontation* (Leuven: Peeters).

Whittow, Mark. (1996), *The Making of Orthodox Byzantium 600–1025* (Basingstoke: Macmillan).

3 The dark age (642–718)

Kaegi, Walter E. (2010), *Muslim Expansion and Byzantine Collapse in North Africa* (Cambridge: Cambridge University Press).

Lightfoot, Chris S. and Lightfoot, Mucahide. (2007), *A Byzantine City in Anatolia: Amorium. An Archaeological Guide* (Istanbul: Homer).

Stratos, Andreas N. (1968–80), *Byzantium in the Seventh Century*, trans. Marc Ogilvie-Grant and Harry Hionides, 5 vols (Amsterdam: Hakkert).

4 The beginnings of the revival (718–820)

Becher, Matthias. (2003), *Charlemagne* (New Haven CT and London: Yale University Press).

Brubaker, Leslie and Haldon, John F. (2011), *Byzantium in the Iconoclast Era, c.680–850: A History* (Cambridge: Cambridge University Press).

Collins, Roger. (1998), *Charlemagne* (London: Macmillan).

Noble, Thomas F.X. (1984), *The Republic of St. Peter: The Birth of the Papal State, 680–825* (Philadelphia PA: University of Pennsylvania Press).

Partner, Peter. (1972), *The Lands of St Peter: The Papal State in the Middle Ages and Early Renaissance* (London: Methuen).

5 Major literary sources for the period 820–1045

Jeffreys, Michael and Lauxtermann, Marc D. (2017), *The Letters of Psellos: Cultural Networks and Historical Realities* (Oxford: Oxford University Press).

Kazhdan, Alexander P., Sherry, Lee F. and Angelidi, Christine. (1999–2006), *A History of Byzantine Literature, 650–1000*, 2 vols (Athens: National Hellenic Research Foundation).

Papaioannou, Stratis. (2013), *Michael Psellos: Rhetoric and Authorship in Byzantium* (Cambridge: Cambridge University Press).

Toynbee, Arnold. (1973), *Constantine Porphyrogenitus and His World* (London: Oxford University Press).

6 Amorians, Macedonians and Lekapenids (820–959)

Dagron, Gilbert. (2003), *Emperor and Priest: The Imperial Office in Byzantium*, trans. Jean Birell (Cambridge: Cambridge University Press).

Runciman, Steven. (1924), *The Emperor Romanus Lecapenus and His Reign* (Cambridge: Cambridge University Press).

Signes-Codoñer, Juan. (2014), *The Emperor Theophilos and the East, 829–842: Court and Frontier in Byzantium during the Last Phase of Iconoclasm* (Farnham and Burlington VT: Ashgate).

Tobias, Norman. (2007), *Basil I, Founder of the Macedonian Dynasty: A Study of the Political and Military History of the Byzantine Empire in the Ninth Century* (Lewiston NY, Queenston and Lampeter: Edgar Mellon Press).

7 Economy and culture

Cormack, Robin. (1985), *Writing in Gold: Byzantine Society and Its Icons* (London: George Philip).

Cormack, Robin. (2000), *Byzantine Art* (Oxford: Oxford University Press).

Foss, Clive. (1979), *Ephesus after Antiquity: A Late Antique, Byzantine and Turkish City* (Cambridge: Cambridge University Press).

Haldon, John F. (2009), *A Social History of Byzantium* (Chichester and Malden MA: Wiley-Blackwell).

Laiou, Angeliki E. (2002), *The Economic History of Byzantium: From the Seventh through the Fifteenth Century*, 3 vols (Washington, DC: Dumbarton Oaks).

Patricios, Nicholas N. (2014), *The Sacred Architecture of Byzantium: Art, Liturgy and Symbolism in Early Christian Churches* (London and New York: I.B. Tauris).

8 Expansion and social change (959–1045)

Decker, Michael J. (2013), *The Byzantine Art of War* (Yardley PA: Westholme).

Stephenson, Paul. (2003), *The Legend of Basil the Bulgar Slayer* (Cambridge: Cambridge University Press).

Treadgold, Warren. (1995), *Byzantium and Its Army, 284–1081* (Stanford CA: Stanford University Press).

9 Major literary sources for the period 1045–1204

Buckley, Penelope. (2014), *The Alexiad of Anna Komnene: Artistic Strategy in the Making of a Myth* (Cambridge: Cambridge University Press).

Krallis, Dimitris. (2019), *Serving Byzantium's Emperors: The Courtly Life and Career of Michael Attaleiates* (London and New York: Palgrave Macmillan).

Neville, Leonora. (2012), *Heroes and Romans in Twelfth-Century Byzantium: The Material for History of Nikephoros Bryennios* (Cambridge: Cambridge University Press).

Simpson, Alicia J. and Efthymiadis, Stephanos. (2009), *Niketas Choniates as Historian and Writer* (Geneva: Pomme d'Or).

10 The eleventh-century crisis (1045–1091)

Cahen, Claude. (2001), *The Formation of Turkey. The Seljukid Sultanate of Rūm: Eleventh to Fourteenth Centuries*, trans. P.M. Holt (Harlow: Pearson).

Ellenblum, Ronnie. (2012), *The Collapse of the Eastern Mediterranean: Climate Change and the Decline of the East, 950–1072* (Cambridge: Cambridge University Press).

Lauxtermann, Marc D. and Whittow, Mark. (2017), *Byzantium in the Eleventh Century: Being in Between* (London and New York: Routledge).

Vryonis, Speros. (1971), *The Decline of Medieval Hellenism in Asia Minor and the Process of Islamization from the Eleventh through the Fifteenth Century* (Los Angeles CA: University of California Press).

11 Stability under the Komnenos dynasty (1091–1180)

Angold, Michael. (1995), *Church and Society under the Comneni, 1081–1204* (Cambridge: Cambridge University Press).

Birkenmeier, John W. (2002), *The Development of the Komnenian Army: 1081–1180* (Leiden and Boston MA: Brill).

Chadwick, Henry. (2003), *East and West: The Making of a Rift in the Church* (Oxford: Oxford University Press).

Hill, Barbara. (1999), *Imperial Women of Byzantium 1025–1204: Power, Patronage and Ideology* (Harlow and New York: Pearson).

Lilie, Ralph-Johannes. (1993), *Byzantium and the Crusader States, 1095–1204*, trans. J.C. Morris and J.C. Ridings (Oxford: Oxford University Press).

Neocleous, Savvas. (2019), *Heretics, Schismatics or Catholics? Latin Attitudes to the Greeks in the Long Twelfth Century, Studies and Texts 216* (Toronto: Pontifical Institute of Mediaeval Studies).

12 The road to catastrophe (1180–1204)

Angold, Michael. (2003), *The Fourth Crusade: Event and Context* (London and New York: Pearson).

Perry, David M. (2015), *Sacred Plunder: Venice and the Aftermath of the Fourth Crusade* (University Park PA: Pennsylvania State University Press).

Phillips, Jonathan. (2004), *The Fourth Crusade and the Sack of Constantinople* (London: Jonathan Cape).

Queller, Donald E. and Madden, Thomas F. (1997, 2nd revised edition), *The Fourth Crusade: The Conquest of Constantinople* (Philadelphia PA: University of Pennsylvania Press).

13 Major literary sources for the period 1204–1453

Kaldellis, Anthony. (2014), *A New Herodotus: Laonikos Chalkokondyles on the Ottoman Empire, the Fall of Byzantium, and the Emergence of the West* (Cambridge MA and London: Harvard University Press).

Nicol, Donald M. (1996), *The Reluctant Emperor: A Biography of John Cantacuzene, Byzantine Emperor and Monk, c.1293–1383* (Cambridge: Cambridge University Press).

Shawcross, Teresa. (2009), *The Chronicle of Morea: Historiography in Crusader Greece* (Oxford: Oxford University Press).

14 Exile and restoration (1204–1282)

Angelov, Dimiter. (2007), *Imperial Ideology and Political Thought in Byzantium, 1204–1330* (Cambridge: Cambridge University Press).

Angold, Michael. (1974), *A Byzantine Government in Exile: Government and Society under the Laskarids of Nicaea, 1204–1261* (Oxford: Oxford University Press).

Bartusis, Mark C. (1992), *The Late Byzantine Army: Arms and Society (1204–1453)* (Philadelphia PA: University of Pennsylvania Press).

Chrissis, Nikolaos G. (2013), *Crusading in Romania: A Study of Byzantine–Western Relations and Attitudes, 1204–1282* (Turnhout: Brepols).

Dunbabin, Jean. (1998), *Charles of Anjou* (Cambridge: Cambridge University Press).

Lock, Peter. (1995), *The Franks in the Aegean 1204–1500* (London and New York: Longman).

Nicol, Donald M. (1957), *The Despotate of Epiros* (Oxford: Oxford University Press).

Runciman, Steven. (1958), *The Sicilian Vespers: A History of the Mediterranean World in the Later Thirteenth Century* (Cambridge: Cambridge University Press).

Russell, Eugenia. (2013), *Literature and Culture in Late Byzantine Thessalonica* (London and New York: Bloomsbury).

15 Decline and downfall (1282–1453)

Angold, Michael. (2012), *The Fall of Constantinople to the Ottomans* (London and New York: Pearson).

Crowley, Roger. (2005), *Constantinople: The Last Great Siege, 1453* (London: Faber and Faber).

Kiousopoulou, Tonia. (2011), *Emperor or Manager: Power and Political Ideology in Byzantium before 1453*, trans. Paul Magdalino (Geneva: La Pomme d'Or).

Nicol, Donald M. (1992), *The Immortal Emperor: The Life and Legend of Constantine Palaiologos, Last Emperor of the Romans* (Cambridge: Cambridge University Press).

Philippides, Marios. (2019), *Constantine XI Dragaš Palaeologus (1404–1453): The Last Emperor of Byzantium* (London and New York: Routledge).

Runciman, Steven. (1965), *The Fall of Constantinople, 1453* (Cambridge: Cambridge University Press).

Ryder, Judith R. (2010), *The Career and Writings of Demetrius Kydones: A Study of Fourteenth Century Byzantine Politics, Religion and Society* (Leiden and Boston MA: Brill).

Index